FOLKLORE: THE PULSE OF THE PEOPLE

RANCHI ANTHROPOLOGY SERIES-7

RANCHI ANTHROPOLOGY SERIES

1. Process, Performance, and Pilgrimage: A Study in Comparative Symbology/ Victor Witter Turner
2. Development of Researches in Anthropology in India: Bihar–A Case Study/ L.P. Vidyarthi and V.S. Upadhyay
3. Nature-Man-Spirit Complex in Tribal India/ R.S. Mann and Vijay S. Sahay
4. Microevolution/ B.M. Das
5. Tribal Festivals of Bihar: A Functional Analysis/ Ajit K. Singh
6. The Spectrum of the Sacred: Essays on the Religious Traditions of India/ Baidyanath Saraswati
7. Folklore: The Pulse of the People/ Mazharul Islam
8. Museums, the Public and Anthropology/ Michael M. Ames

About the Author

Mazharul Islam, born at Charmabipur, Pabna, Bangladesh on 10 September, 1928, he was a first class first in M. A. at Dacca University in 1951 and holds two doctorates, one in Bengali Literature from Rajshahi University in 1958 and a second in Folklore from Indiana University, USA in 1963. He was also awarded the highest literary prizes of the Bangla Academy in 1967 and the Daud Prize in 1970. Starting his career from Dacca Govt. College, Dr. Islam joined Dacca University and went later to Rajshahi University as Reader, Professor, departmental Chairman and Dean. After the birth of Bangladesh, he became Director-General, Bangla Academy and then Vice-Chancellor, Rajshahi University. A freedom fighter, a true lover of democracy and socialism, a close associate of Sheikh Mujib, he was imprisoned soon after Mujib's assassination in 1975. After his release in 1978, he was invited to become a Visiting Professor (UGC) at Calcutta University from 1979 to 1981 and at Visva-Bharati, Santiniketan from 1981 to 1983. Invited by the Indian Council of Social Science Research, New Delhi, joined it as a Senior Fellow. A widely travelled person, he has taught at Chicago and Harvard as a Visiting Professor and participated at various international congresses all over the world. He was elected Executive Member of the International Union of Anthropological and Ethnological Sciences at the XIth ICES held at Vancouver, 1983 for the current five-year term.

RANCHI ANTHROPOLOGY SERIES-7

Gen. Editor: **L.P. VIDYARTHI**

FOLKLORE
THE PULSE OF THE PEOPLE
In the Context of Indic Folklore

MAZHARUL ISLAM

CONCEPT PUBLISHING COMPANY PVT. LTD.
NEW DELHI-110059

ISBN: 978-81-7022-109-8

Edition 2023

Published and Printed by

Concept
Since 1974

Concept Publishing Company Pvt. Ltd.
A/15-16, Commercial Block, Mohan Garden
New Delhi-110059 (India)
T: +91-11-4110 1460
E: publishing@conceptpub.com, W: www.conceptpub.com

In the memory of my daughter

URMI

who left us before she blossomed

GENERAL EDITOR'S INTRODUCTION

THE Department of Anthropology of Ranchi University celebrated its Silver Jubilee in 1978. Again, it received the recognition of being the only U.G.C. Centre of Special Assistance in Anthropology in the country almost in the same year. During the tenure of my Presidentship of the International Union of Anthropological and Ethnological Sciences (1973-78) as well as the Xth ICAES (1978), the Department was also called upon to perform several academic and professional roles involving it at the international level.

With this background, we ventured to launch a new series of publications entitled "Ranchi Anthropology Series" in the year 1980. This series is designed to provide a short but scholarly treatment of key problem areas in anthropology. Under this series, in addition to lectures delivered at Ranchi by visiting scholars of national and international repute, we have also been publishing the theoretically oriented research work of local scholars as well as proceedings of national and international level seminars and symposia. This volume on folklore is seventh in the series and has been shaped out of the lectures delivered by Dr. Mazharul Islam as Visiting Professor at the University. Dr. Islam with his background of Bengali literature and training in the study of folklore has made an outstanding contribution to the subject on this subcontinent.

In this book he deals with the definition, dynamism and scope of folklore and critically elaborates the function of folklore as the pulse of the people. Dr. Islam further analyses how social change is reflected in folklore and how folklore in its turn plays a role as an instrument of social change. A wide range of social strata is covered: urban, rural, industrial, and agricultural. In indicating the interrelationship of anthropology, folklore and sociology, Dr. Islam also emphasizes the need for their closer interdisciplinary study in a scientific manner. The treatment of the theoretical study of folklore is elaborate here and in contradistinction to the west, Dr. Islam applies structuralism to Baul songs, rhymes and proverbs where the story element is negligible. Taken together the essays in this volume cover all the important aspects of folklore as well as the manner in which this fascinating subject should be studied. It gives me great pleasure to include Dr. Islam's book in the Ranchi University Series and I recommend it strongly to all those, researchers and laymen alike, who are interested in folklore and the oral tradition that is so much a part of the culture of a people.

L.P. VIDYARTHI

Director, U.G.C. Centre of Special
Assistance in Anthropology and
University Professor and Head,
Department of Anthropology
Ranchi University, Ranchi.

PREFACE

I WAS invited by Professor L.P. Vidyarthi, Head of the Department of Anthropology, Ranchi University, to deliver some lectures in his department as a Visiting Professor for the month of February 1983, and I decided to speak on Folklore and its relation mainly with Anthropology and Sociology. After two or three lectures, Professor Vidyarthi told me that he would very much like to have my lectures published as a book and would be happy if I would submit the manuscript to him within two or three months. I readily accepted his proposal and was greatly encouraged to shape those lectures in the form of a book. All the topics have been selected from my lectures except 'Folklore: Definition, Dynamism and Scope', which has been included as an introduction. This has helped me in reducing my preface both in size and content, as the points that I would have liked to introduce and clarify in short as the preliminary remarks, have been raised there and analysed at length.

As a discipline folklore deserves to be treated anthropologically, ethnologically and sociologically and its relation with these disciplines demands a thorough assessment. Folklore as a discipline in the Indian subcontinent is still passing through a preparatory phase. It is not that there is a dearth of material or the methodology of treatment, for, this subcontinent has the richest treasure of folklore and through the endeavours of western scholars for the last one century, the theoretical orientation in the field of folkloristics has been more than adequate to make this subject a discipline. But the seriousness, sincerity and dedication, as are expected from the folklorists of the Indian subcontinent, are lacking. The elder scholars, who pioneered the study of folklore in all the languages of this subcontinent, have more or less performed the job of collectors, having practically no theoretical orientation whatsoever. It is up to the present and future generations of scholars to take up the responsibility and enhance the dignity of our folklore study to give it a place that it rightly deserves as a discipline in the academic field.

I have, in this book, in my humble way, tried to remove precisely those deficiencies and to highlight folklore from the points of view of anthropologists, enthnologists, sociologists, psychoanalysts, aesthetic-literature critics, historians, nationalists, comparative folklorists and structuralists. In all my assessments and analyses, folklore has been my main concern. How far I have been able to succeed, is a matter to be decided by others. This much I can say that my attempts are sincere, though my drawbacks are many.

Part I of this book receives emphasis on the theoretical aspects, while Parts II and III contain stress upon the analyses of the sociological perspective of folklore.

I am indeed grateful to Professor Vidyarthi for kindly inviting me to deliver these lectures and more so for his magnanimity in having them published in the form of a book. I am also grateful to him for kindly writing the foreword to this book, which has given it a special significance and prestige. I must express my gratitude to the authorities of both UGC and Visva-Bharati for kindly allowing me to work in Ranchi University for a month during the time when I was still a Visiting Professor in Visva-Bharati, Santiniketan.

The manuscript of the book was completed while I was at Visva-Bharati, but it has seen the light of publication when I became a Senior Fellow, Indian Council of Social Science Research, New Delhi and affiliated to the Council for Social Development. I am deeply grateful to Mrs. S. Ramaswamy, and Mr. Naurang Rai of Concept Publishing Company for their very sincere endeavour to bring out the book within such a short time.

Mazharul Islam

Council for Social Development
53, Lodi Estate
New Delhi-110 003
28 November 1984

CONTENTS

GENERAL EDITOR'S INTRODUCTION vii
PREFACE ix

PART I

1. Folklore: Definition, Dynamism and Scope 1
2. Studies in Indian Folklore and Modern Theories 35
3. A Morphological Analysis of a Bengali Folk Song 181
4. Structural Analysis of Two Santal Myths of the Baha Festival 210

PART II

5. Social Change and Folklore (In the Context of the Indian Subcontinent) 227

PART III

6. Folklore as the Vehicle of Ethnological Studies in Bangladesh 361
7. Folklore: The Pulse of the People A Socio-cultural Analysis 384

INDEX 423

PART I

1

FOLKLORE
Definition, Dynamism and Scope

THERE EXISTS amongst the folklorists of India, including those of Bangladesh and Pakistan, a misconception as to what folklore is, how it should be defined and what would be its scope and jurisdiction. I conclude this from my experience, after attending a good number of conferences and seminars on folklore in India. Some believe that folklore is nothing but the literature of the folk that is handed down to us from generations through oral tradition. Others hold that the elements of folklore, either in the form of literature, beliefs and customs, drama and dance, art and craft, painting and sculpture, belong to the past; and with the development of modern societies, these elements are gradually dropping out. According to them, folklore depends on tradition, mainly oral, and there is no scope for its creation or re-creation and change in the developed societies. Still, there are many who maintain that the elements of folk literature can never be created through writing and as soon as they enter the written tradition, they cease to be what is called folk literature. The upholders of this view tend to maintain a clear-cut line between folk literature, which is oral and belongs to the past, and the literature of art as well as modern literature, which is written. Many folklorists have vague ideas about what is folk and what is lore. Most of the folklorists of West Bengal and Bangladesh, including the senior ones, who worked more as collectors than as scholars and scientists, all through their lives, did understand the distinction between folklore and folk culture and thus use the Bengali term *Loksanskriti* to mean folklore without any reservation or hesitation whatsoever. Not to speak of others, there are even some folklorists amongst us who have hardly any notion of the dynamism of folklore in the context of society. Then again, the process of constant change within a society is a powerful phenomenon and folklore has a close link with that process, which many folklorists do not try to understand. All this happened and is still occurring in the field of folkloristics* because of a lack of seriousness on the part of the folklorists of the Indian subcontinent. Most of them belong to other disciplines who take folklore as the secondary base for their study and their attempt to focus folklore is concentrated on enriching their own discipline with the help of folklore than to raise the status of folkloristies itself. The speed of progress towards the rational approach and scientific methodology uptil now has been lamentably poor and it is hardly possible to term the achievements and performances of these folklorists as a real part of folkloristics, which has assumed the status of a discipline. The condition as it prevails today cannot be bettered unless folklorists imbued with theoretical orientation, scientific knowledge, profound scholarship and experience of methodical fieldwork come forward and dispossess the amateurs.

Taking all these things into consideration, I am attempting to remove the vague ideas about folklore and the misconception regarding its scope and dynamism.

William Thoms was the first scholar who coined the term folklore in English in 1846 to replace 'popular antiquities' and 'popular literature'. Using the name Ambrose Merton, Thoms wrote a letter to *The Athenaeum* and proposed the "good Saxon Compound, Folklore—the Lore of the people", with the hope that "the connection between the folklore of England (rembember I claim the honour of introducing the epithet folklore, as Disraeli does of introducing Fatherland, into the literature of this country) and that of Germany is so intimate that such communication will probably serve to enrich some future edition of Grimm's Mythology" (*The Athenaeum*, August 22, 1846, 862-63). In the footnote to the letter Thoms expressed, "It is only honest that I should tell you I have long been contemplating a work upon our folklore and I am personally interested in the success of the experiment, which, I have

**Editor's note*: This term is explained by the author on page 11.

in this letter, albeit imperfectly, urged you to undertake" (1846, 863). The word is a hyphenated one, folk-lore, but later on the hyphen was omitted. This short but significant nature of the word helps us to understand what is folk and what is lore. "The manners, customs, observances, superstitions, ballads, proverbs, and so on of the olden time", is the view of Thoms as reflected in his letter and he believed that these were dying out. Besides, his influence on the study of folklore was partly responsible to the increasing awareness of a nationalistic spirit and romantic idea hidden in the elements of folklore which received the attention of scholars of the later half of the nineteenth century.

But I will focus mainly on the understanding of folklore from various points of view. Since the introduction of the word folklore, there arose a controversy about its definition, which prolonged for a long time, leaving a turbulent history behind it. Twenty-one definitions given by different scholars as quoted in the *Standard Dictionary of Folklore* edited by Maria Leach (New York, 1949, 398-408) prove the gravity of this disagreement. This controversy was complex because of the characteristics of the oral tradition of folklore (as generally accepted). In the non-literate society where the cultural base requires an oral tradition for propagation (the written tradition being absolutely unknown), it so happens that some of the folklorists or the anthropologists tend to use folklore to determine their language, the system of their hunting, the laws guiding their marriage, the sense of right and wrong as it prevailed amongst them, all of these being traditional and transmitted orally. On the other hand, in the literate society, there exist many learnings which are basically oral as, for example, how to drive the tractor, how to plough and plant, in what manner one has to brush his teeth, and so on. If we imitate the above scholars, we would have to accept these learnings, both of literate and non-literate societies, as folklore, since they are traditionally oral. But, I feel, it would be misleading to do this as these learnings, as mentioned above, are part of culture, not of folklore. Thus, it is wrong to argue that all the elements of learning that are passed through an oral tradition from generation to generation in a society belong to the domain of folklore. Here then arises the question of distinguishing between culture, specially folk culture and folklore. The canvas of culture is far wider than that of folklore which forms part of the culture of any society. Although there is a tendency of refinement in the performances and activities of a society which we include in the fold of its culture, the area of culture embraces almost the total way of life, while folklore restricts its jurisdiction to the creativity of a society taking shape both in material and non-material or spiritual form of things. This distinguishing folklore from non-folklore on the basis of oral and written traditions alone does not seem sound. Alan Dundes rightly observes, "Since materials other than folklore are also orally transmitted, the criterion of oral transmission by itself is not sufficient to distinguish folklore from non-folklore." (1965 :I).

The second problem is, there are parts of folklore which evolve through the written method, as in the case of the Baul songs (a very significant part of Bengali folk songs as many songs of Lalan, Pagla Kanai, Hassan Raza, and poets of later generations originated from their pens), also the short poems written on the hand-fans made of cloth or palm-leaf, proverbs and riddles by medieval Bengali poets like Mukunda Ram Chakravorty, Daulat Kazi, Alaol, Bharatchandra (examples may be cited from all Indian languages), many elements found in the great Indic epics like *Ramayana*, *Mahabharata* and *Cilapatticaram*, tales in *Kathasarit Sagara*, *Panchatantra*, *Betal*, and so on. Should we drive them out from the pasture of folklore only because that they were born written? No, no folklorist will ever do that. I would like to remember my friend Dundes (we were class-mates in Indiana University under Prof. Dorson) again to strengthen my argument, "there are some forms of folklore which are manifested and communicated almost exclusively in the written as opposed to oral form, such as autograph-book verse, book marginalia, epitaphs, and traditional letters (for example, chain letters). In actual practice, a professional folklorist does not go so far as to say that a folktale or a ballad is not folklore simply because it has at some time in its life history been transmitted by script or print. But he would argue that if a folktale or ballad had never been in the oral tradition, it is not folklore. It might be a literary production based upon a folk model". (1965: I).

The folktales and ballads all over the world, specially in India, had to pass through the written as well as oral traditions, most of them originated by word of mouth, but there are many which were written. In the Indian tradition, oral literature seeped into written literature in a massive way and then in course of time the elements from written literature was again transmitted into the field of oral literature, thus making it impossible to separate the oral from the written and the written from the oral elements. Our folk literature and literature of art were almost inseparable during the medieval period and even today there are at least a few examples where only one difference exists between the two—one is written, the other is oral. Many folk songs presented through radio and television are composed and written by modern artists, but characteristically they differ little from those preserved by oral tradition. Should we not accept them as folk song? My view is that these songs, like the Bengali songs composed and sung by Abbasuddin and Nirmalendu Chaudhury, would be accepted by the folk and passed on to oral tradition in future, when, in spite of their famous authors, they could become folk song—a real part of folklore. And in this perspective, I am not ready to accept the validity of the term "fakelore" coined by my great teacher Professor R. M. Dorson. In any way, it is thus obviously true that many elements of folklore have been delivered through the pen.

Thirdly, what about folk dances, folk arts and crafts, folk paintings, sculptures, which are neither oral nor the products of written tradition. One has to learn and acquire the know-how of these elements of folklore through imitation, observation and in some cases rigorous training. These cannot be categorised as the products of only visual tradition either. As a matter of fact, oral, written, visual, imitational, a process of learning through training, all these have a combined effect on the creation and transmission of these elements of folklore.

From what has been stated so far, we may view folklore as the product of oral as well as written traditions handed down from generation to generation. Some elements of folklore depend on visual tradition, imitation, observation and a process of learning through training and performances. But can we define folklore simply on the basis of these characteristics?

I am afraid we have still a long way to go.

'Folk' generally means the ordinary and non-literate people like the village farmers, the labourers, the tribals, the backward and so on. There was a time when the idea of folk was related to the primitive. Those who try to define folklore by this limited notion shut the door of city-life or the town-dwellers to folklore and thus refuse its entry into the society which is literate. From this attitude, folklore could be regarded as the product of the past—the scope for its creation in the present-day society being completely denied and blocked. This being so, naturally, with the development of society, folklore would not be so designated.

On the other hand, there are some who feel that folklore is the creation of a group of people who share the contiguity of dwelling place and culture; no matter where they live in a city, town or village. Their customs and beliefs, the way of life, the language, the tradition, the livelihood are patterned in the same manner. Their creative ideas and some common aspects of their life are reflected in their folklore. It is basically the product of the community, though the individual genius also sometimes works.

Despite these observations, the question what folklore is remains unanswered. A sentence would not suffice to answer this question. But the points raised in the foregoing pages certainly help us to understand folklore as the creation of human civilization, the creation of people who live in a particular geographical area, share the same language, culture, mechanism of livelihood, and living conditions; whose way of life and traditional heritage are bound by a common identity. Folklore is the outcome of the creative ideas of people expressed through verbal art as well as material forms—it may originate from a community or an individual, it is transmitted orally or through one written process from one generation to another and from one country to the other—it exchanges its position between written and oral traditions. Without any touch of bookish knowledge, a person may create folklore, both material and non-material, which may, in course of time, be accepted by the people. Folklore may belong to a non-literate or the literate society, to a tribal or non-tribal community, to villagers or town-dwellers. Folklore constitutes a major part of culture specially of folk culture. Should we consider folk culture as something unsophisticated and uncouth? Culture cannot be divided on the basis of sophistication and unsophistication, as folklore cannot be treated as unpolished.

Compared to folklore, it is easy to define a lion, sodium chloride, an electron or the beauty of a woman, as their shape or nature can be seen and perceived. We can certainly define what poetry is, but this would simply give an idea of a particular type of literature, not the total realization. A poem can be understood, not defined. Those who signify folklore as folk literature can easily term it as 'verbal art' (Bascom, 1953, 283-90). Folk dance is art, but it is not verbal, so is folk painting or sculpture. On the contrary, folk beliefs, the folk-etymology, chants and charms, are verbal, but not art. Customs are neither completely verbal, nor art, though they are very much the elements of folklore. What about folk games and folk medicines? They are neither verbal, nor art, but folklore.

> Dundes clarifies some of the points very clearly. Definitions of folklore based upon the folk rather than the lore are more rare but no more satisfactory. There are still some folklorists who mistakenly identify the folk with peasant society or rural groups. If one were to accept this narrow conception of folk, then by definition one would have to conclude that city dwellers were not folk and hence city dwellers could have no folklore. An equally fallacious view is that folklore was produced by a folk in hoary past and the folklore still extant today consists solely of fragmentary survivals. According to this incorrect view, the folk of today produce no new folklore; rather, contemporary folk are forgetting more and more folklore, and soon folklore would have died out completely. (1965, 2).

It will be easy to understand folklore through the elements of folklore. Of course, each item of folklore such as folktales, myths, which are part of folktales, proverbs, ballads, folk songs, if it is to be defined and analysed individually, would require a book-length discussion for every item. Before that let us see what the items* could be:

1. Folk literature

Folktales, which include myths, legends, fairy tales, fables, animal tales, household tales, numskull tales, humorous tales, ghost stories, witch tales, anecdotes, short stories, and so on; proverbs, riddles, ballads, songs, lullabies, rhymes, etymology (hospital becomes *'haspatal'*, ananas becomes *'anarash'* in Bengali), dramas (mime, the *jatras* in Bengali) blessings (like, "you grow hundred heads", as in Bengali, *tomar sato matha gozak baba*, "may you have many children"), curses (like, "let the faeces of cat fall on your mouth", as in Bengali *tor mukhe jeno bilaier gu pore*, or *tor jeno kur baray*, "let your body embrace leprosy"), similies (blind like a rat, as in Bengali, *badurer lahal kana*), folk titles (giving a title to a person resembling the name of a bird or an animal as his behaviour resembles that bird or animal), chants, charms (there are some literary elements in some of the chants and charms), education (there are some educative elements in the advice rendered to youngsters by their elders, besides proverbs and sayings), speeches (language as well as the pattern of public lectures of the folk differ from that of professors or political leaders), metaphors (for example, "to paint the town red"), chain letters, graffiti (poems or short prose written on the walls of public latrines or trains and so on), names (for example, nicknames, place names), limericks, instrumental music (for example, fiddle tunes), oaths, taunts, tongue-twisters, greetings and leave-taking (for example, "see you later, alligator"), traditional comments made after body emissions (for example, after burps or sneezes, the symbolic language (as in Bengali, *Chi+a, Chi+mi, Chi+Kha, Chi+i,=ami khai*=I eat, 11,9,19[2] =kiss), poetry ranging from oral epics to autograph book verses (some of the verses like two short lines embroidered on the hand-fans made of cloth by a newly married bride, for example in Bengali, *Jao pakhi bolo tare se jeno bholena more* ="O the bird, go and tell him that he cannot forget me"), the vendor's cries, the traditional conventional sounds used to

*These items or elements pertain to the folk.

summon or command animals, folksong, parody, and so on.

Most of these elements have been created and passed on by word of mouth, some of them have been preserved in script, but, as explained before, some have been of traditional written origin.

2. Folk-practices (They are neither literature, nor arts):

(*i*) *Day-to-day practices* (some are occasional):
Folk beliefs, customs, superstitions, rites and rituals, folk festivals, some of the religious practices of the folk, traditional procedures (for example, knocking on wood, throwing salt over one's shoulder). Some of these elements are oral.

(*ii*) *Occasional:*
Folk games, folk sports, fighting competitions of animals and birds. In some society, games, sports and gladiatorial performances are related to rituals, customs or festivals.

3. Folk arts or artistic folklore:

(*i*) *Performing*:
Folk dances, folk dramas (they are also literature), rhyming and rope-jumping, folk-caricature, folk gestures (in all these three elements, there are arts, sometimes pro-minent, sometimes very minor).

(*ii*) *Non-performing*:
Folk paintings, sculpture, arts and crafts, embroidered quilt, doll-making, images of gods and godesses, alpana (drawings on the ground or door-steps drawn using rice-powder mixed in water) designs on cakes, on furniture; body paintings, ornaments, archery, costumes (colourful), traditional swastika emblems.

4. Folk science and technology

(*i*) *Folk science*:
Folk treatment, medicine, arithmetic, churning milk for

preparation of butter, butteroil, curd, food recipes, preparation of drinks from rice, palm juice, chemicals used for colouring cloth, dye, use of fertilizer, preservation of plants, crops and trees by the folk in a manner different from botanists or agricultural scientists.

Some of the items of this group like treatment by chants and charms, folk arithmetic belong to the non-material group of folklore, they are basically oral.

(ii) *Folk technology*

Folk architecture (tools made of iron, wood and bamboo are used in day-to-day life), houses, fences, barns, nets for fishing, carts, palanquin, *duli* barks, knots, armaments, smoking pipes, pottery, bags, cooking (preparation of cakes and other foods, with designs, from rice and other materials. These items may even belong to folk science), hot cross buns (cited by Taylor), mode of stacking hay or straw, weaving and so on.

Though this is a long list, it gives only a few samples and does not include all the elements and forms of folklore.

Many scholars have divided folklore broadly into two categories, non-material and material. According to this division, all elements of item 1, for example, folk literature, and item 2, for example, folk practices, all items from 3 (i) and some from 4 (i) would come under the non-material category; the rest would form the material group. But then, the performing arts are not absolutely non-material as some of the non-performing items are not completely material. Hence, division on the basis of material and non-material things seems somewhat arbitrary. Folklore, as we have seen, could be scriptural or verbal, oral or speech-centric, could be gestural and expressed through body-movements, could be custom and belief oriented, game-centric, artistic, and last of all there are folk science and technology. We may assume that from the points of view of its structure and characteristics, folklore has been broadly divided under two heads, non-material or spiritual and material. But this division, as pointed out, does not appear to me to be very realistic and sound. Material folklore means or includes those lores which have physical existence. On the contrary, folk literature includes those lores which do not have a physical existence, but find expression through language, oral or written. Folk beliefs, superstitions and all non-literary elements, some of which are verbal, also belong to the non-material group. But folk dance, a visual art, belongs to neither the material nor non-material group, for it is not oral, neither is it material. It finds expression through the movements of the body, but the body and art are two different things, one is physical, the other non-physical and are not verbal. Some difficulty also lies in the customs and folk festivals, which are practised and observed as they are neither oral, nor material or physical, nor can they be taken as an art form. Keeping these facts in view, it is desirable to divide folklore in four broad categories: 1. folk literature, 2. folk practices (day-to-day and occasional), 3. folk arts or artistic folklore (performing and non-performing), 4. folk science and technology. I have listed the elements of folklore and arranged them according to this division, which, I consider, are more methodical than the non-material and material divisions.

I have marked that many scholars, specially of India, Bangladesh and Pakistan, consider the materials composing folklore and the study of the subject as folklore. To eliminate ambiguity and confusion, I would like to make clear, and (following Dundes) suggest that the term folklore should be used to denote only the vast materials, the samples of most of which have been mentioned above. For the study of these materials the term folkloristics,* like linguistics, would be the best choice. I have used these two terms with great confidence in all my writings. Through a long and unbiased discussion based on facts and reasons, I have shown that the Bengali synonyms of folklore as used and advocated by some scholars, including the senior ones, like *lokjan*, *lokvidya*, *loksanskriti*, *lokayan*, *loksruti*, *lokbritta*, *lokkriti*, *lokcharona*, *loktatta*, *lokbigyan*, cannot be considered as appropriate synonyms of folklore. No word in Bengali really bears the sense of lore; while *lok* in Bengali exactly expresses the meaning and even the sound of folk. Hence, I have successfully used and recommended the use of the term folklore in Bengali, as we have adopted hundreds

*The sense of the term "folkloristics" as explained here is used throughout the book.

of foreign words in Bengali like chair, bench, pant, registry, Congress Party (English); *kolom, boi, jahaj, kolop, tufan* (Arabic); *khushi, poshak, chanda, bosta, gorom* (Persian); *pera, thokor* (Hindi), *peyara, perek* (Portugal) and so on. Since Bengali is a powerful, progressive and lively language, it has an extraordinary assimilative quality. In a similar manner, I have accepted and also suitably used in Bengali either of the two words, 'folklore *bigyan*' or 'folklore *tatto*' as synonyms of folkloristics.

I have no doubt that to define folklore in a traditional manner or stereotyped way is a difficult task. But A. Taylor, an eminent American folklorist, has done this with some success. His definition is the only one which seems more rational than all others, though this also does not cover all points and lacks in many respects. He defines :

> Folklore is the material that is handed on by tradition, either by word of mouth or by custom and practice. It may be folk songs, folktales, riddles, proverbs or other materials preserved in words. It may be traditional tools and physical objects like fences or knots, hot cross buns, or easter eggs; traditional ornamentation like the Walls of Troy; or traditional symbols like the swastika. It may be traditional procedures like throwing salt over one's shoulder or knocking on wood. It may be traditional beliefs like the notion that elder is good for the ailments of the eye. All of these are folklore (1948, 216).

Of the twenty-one definitions of folklore found in *Funk and Wagnal's Standard Dictionary of Folklore, Mythology and Legend* edited by M. Leach (Vol. I. 1949, New York), as mentioned before, there are some common words like 'survival', 'communal', 'oral', 'transmission', thirteen of them used 'tradition'. Synonyms of oral, such as 'spoken', 'verbal', 'not written' appear clearly in thirteen, and in one, it is rather vague. Six scholars have mentioned 'transmission', which also seems a synonym for 'tradition', as the process of transmission is a vital point in the definition of folklore. The controversial words used by some of these scholars are two— 'survival' and 'communal'. In six, 'survival' appears almost as a concept, which, in view of further development of folklore study since 1949, can be discarded forthwith. Similarly, the words 'superstition', 'preserved', 'fossil' are also to be rejected. Preservation is, of course, partially true, because some of the things have been preserved in words, written form, in rituals and customs. The word 'superstition' has today been replaced by 'folk beliefs'. The term 'communal' has still some significance, because the denounced theory of communal origin apparently holds a few similar points with group origin. From these key-words if we turn to the analysis of content, we find that at least fourteen of the definers consider folklore as primitive, tribal as well as from the subculture groups of a literate society. Eighteen of these scholars indicate folklore as folk literature, twelve include beliefs, but four are not ready to accept them. Scholars like Espinosa, Herzog, Kurath and Loumala consider folklore to be mainly rural.

The reason I entered this discussion is that many of our scholars very often quote from this very dictionary to substantiate their own view about folklore. They may be cautioned against attributing any special significance to these twenty-one definitions, all of which have become obsolete and antiquated. Later many of these scholars have changed their views and discarded their own definitions which they found to be out-dated. I have, thus, before going into a rigid definition, presented the elements of folklore to help understand how folklore is constituted and what are the particles that make the whole structure and body of this discipline. Besides, I have provided a new method of categorizing the samples of folklore elements which I consider as more pragmatic and reasonable.

Before passing on to other points, I should clarify slightly the relation of folklore with culture. Folklore is the outcome of the human mind imbued with creative feelings, Since ancient time, two faculties of the human mind have been responsible for the creation, preservation and transmission of folklore: (1) the creative idea and urge; (2) aesthetic and artistic impulse. The lore or traditional learning was inspired by these two to help creation of folklore. The field of folklore expanded as the experience of man became broader and deeper. On the other hand, culture requires the training and refinement of the human mind, tastes and manners—the condition of thus being trained and refined. "Culture is the intellectual side of civilization (Oxford University Dictionary 1955, 437). If culture is the product of the intellectual faculty of man, folklore is the result of his urge for creativity and impulsive love for beauty—in one ne finds his intellect and sense of refinement released, in the other his creative ideas are expressed and shaped, his aesthetic impulse speaks. By doing so, man also nourishes his culture through folklore. Folklore is thus the product of culture, a component part of culture. A Bengali loves to eat rice with fish, the Punjabi would prefer meat. These are parts of their two cultures, not of their folklore. But when we get two Bengali proverbs on the basis of fish and meat-eating, such as "a Bengali is known by rice and fish" and "meat increases meat, while ghee (butteroil) brings the strength", we land on the solid ground of folklore. Thus, folklore finds its expression through culture, it is born in culture's womb. And, because of this, the study of a culture cannot be fruitful and perfect without the study of its folklore.

To an anthropologist, the content of culture can be best analyzed through the study of its component parts like customs, traditions, peoples, institutions, along with their productions and techniques of productions, their science and technology, literature and art, economy and amusement, social and political organizations and religion. Folklore thus comes into the picture as a part of culture, as it basically is the product of man's learned traditions and customs based on social heritage. From primitive, pre-literate sub-cultures or dominant cultures to civilized, literate, urban, elite or sophisticated cultures, folklore, as a component of culture, played a vital role, as in all these stages of culture of any society, some very determinant aspects of culture have been mirrored through folklore.

The term culture is little over nineteen years younger to folklore, for it was introduced in English by Edward Taylor in 1865 (1865, 3, 4, 150-91), who defined it as "that complex whole which includes knowledge, belief, art, morals, law, custom and any other capabilities and habits acquired by man as member of society" (1871, I). Taylor, of course, had drawn largely from Gustav Klemm of Dresden, whose works used the word culture, the first appearing in ten volumes published between 1843-1852 (E.B. Taylor 1965, 13). Klemm refers to culture as including "customs, information, and skill; domestic and public life in peace and war; religion, science and art," and says, "it is manifest in the branch of a tree if deliberately shaped; in the rubbing of sticks to make fire; the cremation of a diseased father's corpse; the decorative paintings of one's body; the transmission of past experience to new generation" (1854-1855, Vol. I, 217; Vol. 2, 37; translation from R.H. Lowic, 1937, 12). I have quoted two European fathers of "culture," not to go into the history of culture or to enter into its elaborate discussion, but to highlight the point that some component parts of culture are reflected through folklore in all the societies more or less in the same way.

Folklore can be analyzed in the same way as other systems, practices or traditions in terms of forms and functions or interrelations with other aspects of culture. "It presents the same problems of growth and change and is subject to the same processes of diffusion, invention, acceptance or rejection, and integration. It can be used, like other aspects of culture, for studies of these processes or those of acculturation, patterning, the relation between culture and environment, or between culture and personality" (Bascom, 1953, 286-87). Besides, folklore not only functions as the mirror of a culture, it also works as a bridge between two cultures through its transmission from one culture to another. Even within a culture, it sets a close tie between the groups, links one section with another and relates sub-culture with the elitist one or substructure with the super-structure of the society. The performance of folklore in a society, thus, deserves to be considered as dynamic in the context of its culture.

When we view the performances and achievements of folklore, its three characteristics draw our attention—the body of knowledge, mode of thought and kind of art, drawn as reflection from culture. Folklore is, in many respects, moulded by the geographical conditions, linguistic position and social interest based on conformity of livelihood. Thus, any element of folklore deserves to be analyzed from the points as to how it is related with the society, when it started functioning as a component of culture and the medium through which it is transmitted. Besides, the kind of knowledge, the type of thought and the pattern of art, as reflected in them, must be taken into consideration. Let us put them in a rough sketch to understand them a little better:

The root inspiration	*The social perspective*	*The test of time*	*The medium of transmission*
Knowledge	The wealth of the society	Ancient	Oral or imitational
Thought	Collective representation	Traditional	Oral
The art	Created or transformed through combined efforts of the society	Belongs to the past (but was passed through heritage)	Oral or imitational

Firstly, the knowledge in folklore is the result of experience of not a person, but of the community or the society at large. We may call it the wisdom of the people or the learning of the community. The individual earns knowledge through experience and when experience and knowledge are combined together, they voice the same feeling which becomes the feeling of the society. This feeling gets its expression in the elements of folklore. American scholar Francis Cummeri, thus, overenthusiastically viewed that folklore, specially folksongs and ballads, are the creations of the community. But this view has been discarded by scholars of later generation. A community or group no doubt plays an important role in the creation and transmission of some of the elements of folklore, but not all. Almost all the elements of folklore are the creation of individual genius, but that individual, with his uniformity of experience with others sharing the same social conditions, is inseparable from the community or society. When he speaks, the community or the society speaks, when he expresses, it becomes the expression of a community or a society. Thus, the creation of an individual when accepted by the sceiety as its own wealth, becomes folklore. Hence, the test of time is required for an element which is the creation of an individual, to be what is called folklore. It has to pass through tradition, oral, written, visual or practice-oriented. Of course, it cannot be denied that some items are dependent on group for creation as well as for performance. The Santal women cannot dance unless they are grouped together. Many arts and handicrafts are manufactured by groups.

Secondly, like knowledge, the thought of the community, not of any individual, gets preference in folklore. The practices including customs, rites and rituals, beliefs, festivals, are not only religious, but social as well. We may say the conventional modes of human thought are reflected through these elements of folklore. Not only these, all materials of folklore contain, in the langunge of French scholar Levi-Bruhl, "the collective representation of thought." (1949, preface). The English proverb "Necessity knows no law" or a Bengali proverb "To oil a oily head" represents the collective thought of the society.

There is no bank, no shore of the river
From what bank to what shore shall I go?
I know not whom I shall ask.

is a famous Bengali folk song, that holds the inner mental agony of the people of riverine Bangladesh. Thc song symbolizes in it the endless endeavour of the people of this area to overcome the struggle for existence.

Thirdly, the test of time lays an essential embargo on all elements of folklore before they are regarded as a part of folklore. "Cowards die a hundred times before their death" was not popularly accepted as an English proverb as soon as it was published in a drama of Shakespeare, a reasonable test of time was required for that. Bharat Chandra's (eighteenth century Bengali poet) famous proverb "Do or die"* had to wait nearly half a century, or even more, before it became current as a proverb. There are no two opinions about the essentiality of the test of time. But there is no guardian of folklore to declare the right moment to accept a particular

* Translated from Bengali.

material as folklore. None can determine the length of the test of time. It is for the society to decide whether or not a proverb, a riddle, a rhyme, a painting, a sculpture, a drama, a dance can be adrorned as a component of folklore, no matter when it was created and who was the creator. By saying so, I do not mean that a popular cinema song should be regarded as folk song because it is widely accepted in the society. The charisma of a cinema song, however popular it might be, does not last long. On the other hand, a real folk song or a proverb or a riddle, despite the fact that it has got its circulation even through the media of radio or the modern press, will gradually impinge upon the mind of the society and find its permanent position as a piece of folklore. As I have mentioned, a folk song may be written and sung by an artist over a radio or a long-playing record (L.P.), a proverb may be written by a modern writer and used in his novel, but through a test of time and oral media, both these two would become part of folklore. Many examples can be cited from Bengali folklore. "O the cart-driver your cart to the town *chilmari*" was composed in Bengali and sung by Abbasuddin and this *vaoayia* song is still available on records. On the other hand, "My heart cries in agony, today, O, the rider of the buffalo, my friend"* has been collected by Dr. N. Bhowmick (1977: 473, 2nd pt. collection) from North Bengal and published along with hundreds of such songs of that area. We tend to accept the latter as real folk song because it is anonymous and is in vogue amongst the people, while discarding the former, as it has a creator and is available in L.P. In contrast to some scholars who know that the song was composed by Abbasuddin, there are others who unknowingly quote this song as the best example of *vaoayia song* of North Bengal. The people of both West Bengal and Bangladesh consider this rendition dear to them. Under no consideration have we the right to expel this song of Abbasuddin from the arena of folk song. This is a vital question that poses a serious problem before us: My answer is plain and simple. We have to depend on the test of time and on the acceptability of the people and transmission through the oral tradition. The prejudice that folklore materials cannot be composed, practis-

*Translation of the Bengali version

ed, painted, patterned, constructed, made, manufactured, designed, prepared, invented, shaped, or sculpted by modern man has to be shunned from the study of folklore.

Besides a body of knowledge, a mode of thought and a kind of art, the media of transmission, which is vastly oral or verbal, bears a considerable significance to the students of folklore. Unrecorded mentifacts and oral transmission are the two criteria that hold true for folklore to distinguish this discipline from the allied ones. Apart from these, two other factors are also important to determine its characteristics —(a) folklore requires to be collected through field work, and (b) its study has to be fundamentally based on traditional heritage. It has been discussed whether folklore is created or transmitted only through word of mouth or through other means as well. Folklore is not based totally on tradition and it also creates a new tradition—the point has been raised and sorted out before. So far as collection is concerned, it is for the scholars to go to the folk and collect their lore, the folk have no concern about preserving it outside the functions it performs in society. Whether collection is made or not, folklore remains where it is and plays its vital role in the society and culture—the role played since ancient time to the present day. An element of folklore is not created on the consideration that it will once be collected, but from the urge and impulse of the people to fulfil some of the needs attained through the functions of folklore in the society. When a story-teller relates a tale the others listen to it for entertainment and amusement. Here the teller and the listener are bound by a strong thread of communication. A professional teller or singer knows what style he would adopt in his presentation and his listeners are prepared for it. They react with applause and other sounds or gestures as and when occasion demands. Thus a teller or a singer and his listeners cannot be isolated from the tale or the song presented. This brings us close to a problem—the study of folklore without the context of the folk or the society. Malinowski's observation, in this connection, may be fruitfully remembered:

> The limitation of the study of myth to the mere examination of text has been fatal to a proper understanding of its

nature. The forms of myth which come to us from classical antiquity and from the ancient sacred books of the East and other similar sources have come down to us without the context of living faith, without the possibility of obtaining comments from true believers, without the concomitant knowledge of their social organization, their practical morals, and their popular customs—at least without the full information which the modern field worker can easily obtain (1926, 18).

The anthropologist is not bound to the scanty remnants of culture, broken tablets, tarnished texts or fragmentary inscriptions. He need not fill out immense gaps with voluminous, but conjectural comments. The anthropologist has the myth maker at his elbow. Not only can he take down as full a text as exists, with all its variations and control it over and over, he has also a host of authentic commentators to draw upon: still more he has the fullness of life itself from which the myth has been born. And as we shall see, in this live context there is as much to be learned about the myth as in the narrative itself (1926, 17-18).

Malinowski goes on to argue:

The text, of course, is extremely important, but without the context it remains lifeless. As we have seen, the interest of the story is vastly enhanced and it is given its proper character by the manner in which it is told. The whole nature of the performance, the voice and the mimicry, the stimulus and the response of the audience mean as much to the natives as the text; and the sociologist should take his cue from the natives. The performance, again, has to be placed in its proper time-setting—the hour of the day, and the season, with the background of the sprouting gardens awaiting future work, and slightly influenced by the magic of the fairy tales. We must also bear in mind the sociological context of private ownership, the sociable function and the cultural role of amusing fiction. All these elements are equally relevant; all must be studied as well as the text. The stories live in native life and not on paper, and when a scholar jots them down without being able to evoke the atmosphere in which they flourish he has given us but a mutilated bit of reality (1926, 24).

What Malinowski says about the importance of text and context in the study of folklore appears to me almost indisputable and, this is applicable equally to folklorist, anthropologist, sociologist or a linguist. So far as thousands of texts which have been handed down to us through written sources are concerned, we are helpless, because there is hardly any scope to collect them from the people, like the tales of *Kathasarit Sagara* or *Panchatantra*, or the Biblical riddles, or the *Jatakas*. Some might be available from the mouths of the folk, but not all. Here, the question of collection of text along with context arises. Unfortunately, in Bengali folklore, or this may be true about folklore of the languages of the whole subcontinent, both major and minor, almost all who made the collections so far are not even aware of this fact. If we go through the volumes of collections of Bengali folklore made and published by Dr. Ashutosh Bhattacharya, which include tales (myths, legends, and other types), songs of all types, ballads, proverbs, dances, and so on, we find that most of his collections were made by his students and the texts have no reference whatsoever in the context except the names and addresses of a very few informants. Despite the important contributions made to the study of folklore from literary or literary-historical points of view by such scholars like Ashutosh Bhattacharya, K.D. Upadhaya and many others in the subcontinent, in addition to their collections without context, the fact remains that only a limited range of problems can be envisaged within this framework. Among other things, it seems pertinent to ask whether the study of folklore has by any means contributed its full share to our understanding of culture and its functioning in human societies or whether the study of myths or legends or customs and beliefs has nothing whatsoever to do with investigation of human world? Collections without contexts and literary or historical approach in the study of folklore as have been done so far by the so-called scholars would bear no significant result to enhance the prestige of folkloristics as a discipline, unless we understand that such studies need to be put upon a much more comprehensive basis. In my view, we must give sufficient emphasis to the collection of text with context and broaden the footings of the study of folklore to other frames such as functional, psychological, social and structural to supplement each other.

Folklore elements have a place in the society who use them or tell them. The texts which are already in our hands from ancient literature or from oral form entering in the written tradition may not have left enough scope to us to verify them from the context of the people, but while making collections, we must record the series of related facts along with the texts. This will help us to analyse the relation between folklore and culture, social change and folklore and folklore as the pulse of the people. To attain these objectives we have to emphasize the following aspects : (1) Time and place of telling, singing, performing, sculpturing, painting, playing, designing, framing, making; (2) informant or teller, performer, group or an individual who are the audience, all particulars in detail of these people belonging to two sides; (3) the gestures and postures of the narrator, the whole nature of his performance, facial expression, mimicry, his dance and acting, impersonation, pantomime; (4) the total reaction of the audience, his occasional comments and laughter, his response in the form of dancing or singing or acting out parts in a tale; (5) people's attitudes in general towards these elements of folklore, and (6) the materials and the categories recognized by the people themselves.

While we are concerned about the text and context, we cannot escape another important aspect related to these two which is texture. The factors, as explained, as to how a tale is told or a song is sung, for example, the context, are the components of the tale or the song. In similar manner, the morphological elements or the structure and the thematic base of the tale or the song of any item of folklore are as important as the item itself. The way in which threads are put together to make a cloth must be taken into consideration with equal importance along with our attempt to know the type and other characteristics of the cloth. Here comes the question of texture along with text and context. This approach, I feel, should not be exactly in the line of the literary formalists who are more concerned with physical form than with the spirit. Levi-Strauss puts it rightly:

> The supporters of structural analysis in linguistics and anthropology are often accused of formalism. This is to forget that formalism exists as an independent doctrine from which structuralism—without denying its debt to it—separated because of the very different attitudes the two schools adopt toward the concrete. Contrary to formalism, structuralism refuses to set the concrete against the abstract and to recognize a privileged value in the latter. Form is defined by opposition to material other than itself. But structure has no distinct content; it is content itself, apprehended in the logical organization conceived as property of the real (1973, 115).

Texture-oriented study in folklore is lamentably poor specially in the Indian subcontinent. This was partially true so far as the European or American achievement in the study of folklore is concerned even twenty years back. Dundes repents:

> It is true that while the structural or pattern approach was sweeping through linguistics, psychology, ethnomusicology, and anthropology proper in the 1920's and 30's, folklore as a discipline remained oriented to a narrowly historical approach and dedicated to atomistic studies (*South-Western Journal of Anthropology*, Vol. 19, 1953, 122).

Importance of performance study in folklore has of late received almost a theoretical significance. The systems that order people's lives should, in the opinion of many scholars, form the basis of the study of culture. Since the publication of the Griaule team's studies of Dogon thought and analyses propounded by Levi-Strauss, it has without doubt been established that the non-western cultures have also complex characteristics. It is also recognized that such cognitive systems for ordering the chaotic mass of perceived reality exists cross-culturally and in diverse formations. Besides, the organization of reality is structured not only in cognitive categories, but in behavioural patterns as well. Accordingly, performance in any traditional culture is really interpretable drawn on both performance theory and model analysis. Over the past decade the formulation of a performance approach to the study of folklore has been mainly done by some folklorists (Abrahams, 1961; Ben-Amos, 1972) and secondarily in the allied field of socio-linguistics (Hymes, 1974, 1975). Of course, while making application, diverse emphases have been laid, in spite of the consensus that the fundamental premise of the performance approach puts stress on event over text or on process over product. Some scholars view performance as a dynamic event, while the others consider this as a process which is artistic. Bauman, one of the original upholders of performance analysis, in his recent and elaborate work, has emphasized language with context in relation with the ethnography of the speaking school (1977). Thus, the signal to return to formal analysis could be found; a de-emphasis of the original behavioural slant of performance theory has become effective (we may mention the work of Lomax, 1968, in this connection).

The notion of performance is not absolutely unknown in the cultural context of the Indian subcontinent. In Dhaka or Calcutta we used the term, 'cultural performance'. While I was in Calcutta for two years (1979-81), my friends, Brahmins and non-Brahmins, used to invite me to witness some feature of Hinduism through some rites or life-cycle ceremony in some temple, or on the occasion of some festivals, and they would arrange a variety show along with that religious ceremony and call the whole affair a cultural performance. Of course, I was interested in the cultural performance as well as the religious rites and rituals, because they provide the links in the levels of civilization and culture and I believe that they do serve to organize meaning for the people living in the city of Calcutta; and to generalize, the same meaning holds true for many cities and towns of the Indian subcontinent. It is a paradox that we very often speak of cultural performances, but have never tried to use this concept in the study of our folklore and develop it as a theory. Even the experimentations made by scholars like Bauman, Ben Amos, Abrahams, Hymes and some others received hardly any attention of the folklorists of this subcontinent till now.

Context study along with the text and texture, if pursued with all seriousness, will ultimately lead us to the concept of performance and application of this methodology to Indic folkloristics with fruitful results.

Folklore is handicapped in communicating the wide relation between man and man in exchanging their thoughts in a massive way, as it is mostly limited to two persons or the group. A man can utter a proverb or a riddle to another man in the course of their conversation, or sing a song or tell a tale in front of a group of people who compose his audience. Thus, a direct communication capability of folklore is limited to a group of two or of several persons varying from three to four thousand (in case of folk drama, a dance, a musical performance). This is the context of folklore. This group concept has already been utilized for their analysis by many sociologists in their own discipline. But folklorists in this subcontinent speaking of folklore tend to feel that all the people of our dear motherland are in their presence. But to a real scientist, a group means a group of people who can communicate through the same language, and they do it face to face. This group may be a family, a small number of people who sit and gossip at a roadside shop, a village community consisting of several families, a tribe. Two conditions are essential for the effectiveness of folklore—one, the social status of the teller, singer or presenter and that of the listeners, audience or observers must be on an equal footing; two, those who belong to a group must have an equal sense of participation. Thus, they can come closer to each other and express themselves directly. It is true that the materials of folklore are the valuable treasures of the nation, folklore bears the cultural heritage of the people, it is the mirror of culture; but it is also equally true that folklore does not function all over the country at a fixed moment, rather its utility and function is limited to a group. This being so, we have to accept this group concept in the definition folklore. Who then are the folk of folklore? I would say this group. The peoples of a culture or a country are folk and their lore is folklore, in similar manner, a group is also folk in a limited way and their lore is folklore Thus, along with the text of folklore comes the context—without studying and defining the folk, there cannot be a study and a definition of folklore. Dundes realized this truth nearly twenty years ago and truly remarked;

> It is possible to define both folk and lore in such a way that even the beginner can understand what folklore is. The term folk can refer to any group of people whatsoever who share at least one common factor. It does not matter what the linking factor is—it could be a common occupation, language, or religion—but what is important is that a group formed for whatever reason will have some traditions which it calls its own. In theory a group must consist of at least two persons, but generally most groups consist of many individuals. A member of the group may not know all other members, but he will probably know the common lore of traditions belonging to the group; traditions which help the group have a sense of group identity. Thus if the group we composed of lumberjacks or railroadmen, then the folklore would be lumberjack or railroadmen folklore. If the group were composed of Jews and Negroes, then the folklorist could seek Jewish or Negro folklore. Even a military unit or a college community is a folk. In the latter instance there are many customs (for example, fraternity pranks and initiation rituals), stories (for example, about dumb athletes, absent-minded professors and difficult deans) and songs about college life. Probably the smallest group would be an individual family, whose traditions of ten include sayings and such items as a family whistle (to call or locate a family member lost in a crowd). Often competent investigation can show that these individual family traditions (which a family may insist are its very own, unknown to anyone outside the family) are found among many families and sometimes even among many people of the world. The family tradition for disposing of a child's baby teeth (by means of a good fairy, tooth fairy, or fairy mouse) is an example of an international family custom (1965: 2-3).

Wm. Hugh Jansen has made a study of the esoteric-exoteric factor of the groups and revealed that the thinking of one group about another also helps create a new tradition of folklore (1959 : 205-211). With a possible exception in the case of primitive peoples, as Jansen feels, folklore is that portion of a group's culture and belief that does not derive from formal, institutionalized educational forces, indeed it frequently exists despite such forces. It is within this context that the exoteric and esoteric are to be understood. There are some points concerning the group folklore, specially of esoteric and exoteric elements:

1. Within reason, the smaller the group, stronger the element of folklore, specially the esoteric one.
2. The more distinctive or distinguishable a group, the more likely the occurrence of exoteric folklore about that group.
3. The larger and more self-confident the group, the weaker the esoteric element in its folklore; but
4. There are no indications that great size and self-confidence in a group offer any deterrent to the formulation of exoteric folklore about the group.

But apart from the esoteric-exoteric elements, group folklore has certainly some characteristics which may be summed up in a paragraph here. There is a general assumption that the folklore of a group has certain inherent qualities, perhaps virtues, because it belongs to or has been shaped by the group. Some qualities of a given group's folklore reflect the group's approach towards life and the current trend of the society the members of the group live in. Anyone may tell tales within such a group about an evil stepmother, a fairy, a salior, tales that rely upon beliefs of various kinds. A new proverb, a riddle or a humorous story may evolve through the discourse of the members of the group. Even, certain types of folklore material are likely to be rich in the reflection of esoteric-exoteric concepts. Group conflicts or the sense of rivalry may cause the birth of a new element or the regeneration of the old one and it can be said that folklore not only acts as a unifying force in terms of one group's identity, but also as a devisive force in terms of moulding or confirming one group's attitudes towards another group. Besides, isolation or lack of communication with others (which is considered peculiar knowledge) and the fact of being held in peculiar respect may also influence the group and provide the members some subjects for their folklore.

When we speak of the group-folklore, it reminds us of a similar type in our traditional folklore, like *pala*, the *jatra* and some group dances. *Pala* is different from the rest of group-folklore in the sense that the leader of the group, who is a poet, composes the songs or the tale from his own imagination on the stage impromptu. This is popularly known as *kabigan* (poet's songs) or *kabir palla* (the competitive songs of two poets). The group led by one poet consists of five or six persons. The *bayak* or the drummer plays on the *mridanga*. Others play on the cymbals and dance and accompany the chief singer and explain the meaning of the song to the audience. The chief singer's dress sometimes differs from the others. He may decorate his hands with silver armlets and bangles, his waist with silver chain, his forehead with vermilion (in case of a Muslim, he will not have this) and his eye with collyrium. His dress is traditional having no tinge of affinity with modern fashions. He puts on a blue or a red shirt, silk *chaddar*, a cap with silver embroidery. This traditional dress, of course, has, in many places, specially in Bangladesh, changed its tradition and one would not be surprised to see the chief singer having the same dress as the members of his group. During the course of his singing he plays on a pair of small cymbals held in between his right fingers and thumbs. A melodious voice, a smiling face, sweet, humble and courteous behaviour, and a capacity to create humour are great assets to the poet, the chief singer. The drummer sometimes displays the skill of his fingers, tells humorous stories to please the audience for the sake of diversion in between the long speeches of the chief singer. The *kabi's* or *gayak's* helpers form a group called *pali dohar* (*sira-palia* in Oriya) who assist him in singing and remind him of forgotten lines.

This group connotation is, of course, different from the ones found in industrial units or the farm belts of the highly developed countries. But nevertheless, groups like *pala* or the *kabi gan* (or *jari gan* in Bangladesh) conform to the idea of group who create folklore and may be identified as the folk of folklore.

Sometimes the group consciousness works not only for the creation of folklore for the present or future, it also helps preserve the traditional aspects of folklore from the past. In such situations, the group even resists the present temptation and reacts adversely to accept the total situation it is placed in and instead follows the old tradition. As, for example, the Pennsylvania Dutch are quite unique in the U.S.A., in that they have tenaciously clung to a great many of the peasant traditions which their ancestors had brought with them from the old country. Again and again they migrated in larger and smaller groups from the same parts; mostly the Upper Rhine, the Rhenish Palatinate (*Rheinpfalz*) and Switzerland, but also from other West and South German states. They are further unique in that they maintained their communal form of life in the New World, both to their own benefit and that of William Penn and his Quaker associates. The greater number of these so-called Palatines landed mostly in the harbour of Philadelphia, between 1710 and 1775 (Strassburger : 1934 : 3 Vols.). This adherence of the Pennsylvanian Dutch, for more than two centuries, to the native peasant customs of their German forefathers can only be explained by the fact that they did not lose their original group consciousness after they had settled in America.

While defining a group of people as the folk of folklore, we come very close to the question of tradition, which is deeply linked with lore. I have repeatedly mentioned that folklore is basically the product of tradition. Tradition, of course, bears a greater impact in the non-literate society or tribal community or in the subculture of an elite culture, for in these areas of culture, tradition helps in the creation of a new tradition, one belief leads to the birth of another, one custom generates many. But in the society which has completely come out of the fold of such an old tradition, the appeal of traditional folklore works in a different way. We may say, in such highly developed societies, people do not care much or have enough time to assemble and listen to tale telling. The labourers of big industrial units in USA or the farmers of huge agricultural farms of the USSR, on the contrary, would sit in the small groups at dusk after their day's work and exchange their gossip in a light manner. Such a group, through their banter and persiflag, creates a new folklore, a tale, mostly humorous, proverbs, riddles, songs, and so on. This is a new trend in folklore in the developed countries, a new base, a new tradition. Folklorists have, without any hesitation whatsover, accepted these elements as folklore.

Folklore is traditional, but too much dependence on tradition in the search for and research on folklore, arrests folklore within a small compound of traditional heritage. When the answer to a riddle is revealed, its appeal becomes lost to those to whom it is revealed and then arises the need for creating a new one. Thus, a new riddle on the basis of a new or modern tradition takes the place of the old, keeping only the structure of riddling almost intact. The text, texture and context of this riddle is different from the traditional one. Context plays a vital role for shaping the text and texture of folklore. Hence, instead of maintaining that all folklore are the crops of tradition and all traditions are not folklore, we may hold firmly that some traditions are folklore, but all folklore is not traditional.

Thus, an element of folklore deserves to be considered as folklore not only on the basis that is traditional or is handed down to us from generations, but also on the basis that it fulfils the conditions of being a component of folklore by its characteristics, form, structure, mode of expression, to some extent, by its language. The question, how old is the element, has to be done away with to readily accept the assertion that it belongs to the folk. A small group or a family having not less than two members would be considered as folk and their creations as folklore subject to the fulfilment of certain minimum conditions. A folklorist, with experience of fieldwork, or of research on folklore would be able to, without any difficulty, fix an element as a part of folklore, which will frankly tell him, what those conditions are.

In the primary stage of folklore study, attempts were made to utilize folklore for philological interpretations and since then a notion was somehow developed that folklore belonged to the primitive society, the materials of folklore were roaming on the oral traditions and they had to be collected and preserved before they were extinct. The notion received theoretical orientation in the hands of T. Beney, Max Muller, Andrew Lang, Frazer and many others. Folklore was later tagged alongwith historical science by the scholars like Kaarl Krohn, Alexander Crappe, Stith Thompson and others, and this concept received wide recognition all over the world. Folklore received a great impetus from the contributions made to its study by anthropologists, sociologists, psychoanalysts and linguists. But all these explorations have inclined to focus folklore as a thing of the past, a thing which is purely traditional and oral. Folklore received dignity as the mirror of culture, but its dynamism hardly received the attention it deserved. This dynamism of folklore, though accepted since long in the western world, is still a neglected phenomenon in Indian subcontinent. Our definition of folklore in all the languages of this subcontinent suffers from this serious lack and it is high time that we liquidate that deficiency and accept the reality. Society is the organization of human rela-tionships, built, sustained and constantly being changed by human beings. Change in society brings change in culture or vice-versa. Folklore belongs to the society as an important part of its culture. When we accept social change and the change in culture, we cannot remain blind to the changing pattern inherent in folklore as a component of society. Let me cite an example from my own collection, which would substantiate the dynamism and the wide scope of folklore. There is a proverb in Bengali meaning 'A little learning is a dangerous thing'. This is a traditional proverb which can be found almost in the major languages of the world. Another modern proverb in Bengali created on the basis of the earlier one is, 'A little learning is dangerous, for it makes one dependent on the dictionary for every word'. The English dictionary has been successfully rhymed at the end with a Bengali word (*Vayankari*).

This is an excellent example the like of which are avail-able in abundance in our culture, examples as to how folklore attunes itself to the changed situation of the society. Thus, folklore can embrace the constant changing order of the society and culture because of its dynamism, which must not escape inclusion in its definition.

Do I really need to provide a definition of folklore after all that I have said? I feel that it is no longer required. But in the interest of academic discipline, I venture to define folklore, as I have defined it in Bengali (Udichi, 1983; Paush, 1389, Bengali Era 18-19), in several sentences, supplementary to each other, since, as I have indicated, it is not possible to define folklore in one or two sentences.

Folklore encompasses the customs, games, beliefs, festivals, and some practices, which human societies have owned through tradition from generation to generation; the literature, performing and non-performing arts, paintings, sculptures, arts and crafts, embroidered quilts, *alpanas*, and their related mechanism and designs, which have been handed on by tradition to the societies from previous generations through word of mouth or traditionally by non-oral means; the patterns of houses, fences, tools, and many other material being used by the societies, as well as those materials, their traditional manufacturing techniques and architectural designs, which the human societies have inherited from their forefathers; the medicines and other objects invented through experimentations and traditional scientific method, which passed on as heritage to the societies through generations. The process of creation, making, designing and construction of these elements, as well as their sustenance in the societies, has been in operation since ancient times and in a similar manner their transmission, diffusion, creation of variants, reshaping and renewal have also been a continuous phenomena since long past. Some of these elements were handed down through the oral tradition, some through the written method, practice and imitation, some were born either oral or written or through practice, imitation and observation, but all have been the products of tradition. The process of their transmission is still in vogue in the present-day societies and this will remain so in the future days to come. While passing from one generation to another, one culture to another culture, some of these elements create their variants and are diffused, although their morphological structure remains almost intact. Folklore is dynamic in the sense that with the social and cultural change, as an important part of culture, it also accepts some changes to suit the new situation. Any material of folklore may originate even today, but would be regarded as folklore if it survives the test of time and is accepted by the folk, composed of a family of minimum two persons, a village community, a tribe or a nation, who may be non-literate or literate, no matter where they live, in a village, a town or modern city. Though basically traditional, a folklore may create its own tradition.

The study of folklore, specially in the western countries, has come out of the lattice of amateurism through the various researches of the scholars, which has placed folkloristics as an academic discipline. In the countries of the Indian subcontinent, though the study of folklore suffers from many deficiencies, an interest has been aroused amongst the scholars and this is encouraging.

REFERENCES

Abrahams, Roger 1968 "Introductory Remarks to a Rhetorical Theory of Folklore", *Journal of American Folklore*, Vol. 8:143-58.

Bascom, William R 1953 "Folklore and Anthropology", *Journal of American Folklore* (*JAF*), Vol. 66.283-290.

Bauman, Richard 1977 *Verbal Art as Performance*, Newbury House Publishers, Rowley.

Ben-Amos, Dan 1972 Toward a definition of Folklore in Context. In America Paredes and Richard Bauman (eds.) *Toward New Perspectives in Folklore*, 3-15, University of Texas Press, Austin.

Bhowmick, Nirmalendu 1977 *Pranta Uttar Banger Loksangit* (written in Bengali), Calcutta University, Calcutta.

Dunnes, Alan (ed.) 1965 *The Study of Folklore*, Prentice-Hall, Inc., Engle-Wood-Cliffs, N.J.

———— 1963 "Structural Typology in North American Indian Folk Tales", *South Western Journal of Anthropology*, (*SWJA*) Vol. 19, 121-130.

Hymes, Dell 1974 "The Contribution of Folklore to Socio-Linguistic Research" *In* Hymes, *The Foundations of Socio-Linguistics*, pp. 125-42, University of Pennsylvania Press, Philadelphia.

———— 1975 "Breakthrough into Performance", *In* Dan Ben-Amos and Kenneth Goldstein (eds.), *Folklore: Performance and Communication*, pp. 11-74, Mouton, The Hague.

Islam, Mazharul 1982 *Samogrik Parichiti O Sanger Sandhane* (Bengali), Udichi, Paush, 1389 (Bengali era), Santiniketan.

Jansen, William Hugh 1959 The Esoteric-Exoteric Factors in Folklore, *Fabula: Journal of Folklore Studies*, Vol. 2:205-11.

Leach, Maria 1949 Funk and Wagnal's Standard Dictionary of Folklore, *Mythology and Legend*, Vol. I. New York.

Leenhardt, Maurice (Preface by Leenhardt) 1949 *Les Carnets de Levi-Bruh*, Paris.

Levi-Strauss, Claude 1973 *Structural Anthropology*, Vol. 2. England, Penguin Book Ltd. Trans from the French by Monique Layton. This trans was first published in U.S.A. in 1976, in Great Britain again in 1977.

Malinowski, B 1926 *Myth in Primitive Psychology*, New York, 1955 (edition), Oxford University Dictionary.

Strassburger, RB 1934 *Pennsylvania German Pioneers*, 3 vols, Norristown, Penn.

Taylor, Edward B 1865 *Researches into the Early History of Mankind and the Development of Civilization*. Boston, 1878, first published in 1865.

Taylor, Archer 1948 *Folklore and the Student of Literature*, The Pacific Spectator, Vol. 2. 216-223.

Thoms, William 1846 *The Athenaeum*, No. 982 (August 22, 1846) 862-63.

2

STUDIES IN INDIAN FOLKLORE AND MODERN THEORIES

A SCIENTIFIC study of a particular subject is based on a methodical approach to and a disciplined arrangement of the subject undertaken for the study. Methodologies are thus the results of constant endeavours of the scholars through the ages. They have been evolved in all the modern disciplines through the ceaseless efforts to emphasize on the well-organized thoughts, the expression pregnant with reasons and on the presentation based on facts. This is true about the study of folklore. The study of folklore known as folkloristics has been accepted as a discipline since it requires as much effort and hardship to master it as the study of other disciplines like the humanities and social sciences. In folklore the modern scholars have embraced methodologies such as aesthetic and literary, comparative, nationalistic, anthropological, psycho-analytical and structural. These methodologies have received so much importance in different parts of the world that they seem to have assumed the stature and dignity of theories. Study on the performance aspect of folklore, in recent times, assumed sufficient importance and there are scholars who tend to define this methodology as a theory.

Since the methodologies or the theories have been invented by western scholars and have been applied in the study of European or American folklore, the question arises, should we accept them and impose them upon the study of Indian folk-lore? It is true that we must not follow the west with blind-folded eyes. But so far as the methodologies of the study of folklore are concerned, I find in them a true scientific approach and an outlook loaded with reasoning and facts. The types of analyses they incorporated in their own areas are thoroughly scientific and full of profound wisdom. They have opened before us a new horizon of knowledge. I also find that all the methodologies can be profitably applied to the study of Indian folklore. In this chapter I have introduced these methodologies or theories in short and made some applications of them on our myths, folk songs, rhymes and proverbs. It is a reality that a lot of time has been lost in publishing the materials of folklore mostly without much analysis or interpretation. A few attempts in this direction are also not based on the search for deeper knowledge. Our folklore study is dominated mostly by the lack of a methodical and scientific approach. If our scholars can evolve some methods of folklore study different from those so far invented, highlighting the scientific interpretations and emphasizing deeper analysis rather than a mere statement of facts, they would certainly be received with great admiration. In a similar manner the achievements in this field both by western and eastern scholars are to be judged on their own merits and adopted to suit our own situation. One can certainly discard any one or all of them, but in doing so one needs a scholarship not easy to acquire. If we turn our face away from them only because they are western, we will probably do great disservice to the study of our own folklore.

Let us see what those methodologies are or we may call them theories, and how far they are applicable to our folklore.

Aesthetic and literary methods of folklore study

Compared to the state of affairs that existed in the field of folklore study during the nineteenth century, the condition was by far the better in the first half of the present century. Even those who were engaged in the search for beauty and literary value of folklore received a new impetus during the thirties of the present century. A human approach with a sense of reality of life with its joys and sorrows, with its struggle for existence became more pronounced day by day in the present century. There are elements in folklore which attracted the man of literature and those who are dedicated to aestheticism from time to time. As time passed on the process of assessment of literary value as well as of aesthetic quality of folklore underwent many changes. No more the passions and exuberance, but rationalism. a sense of historicity, social background and economic conditions gradually prevailed upon the process of judgement.. The treatment of folklore from an aesthetic and a literary point of view is accepted everywhere in the study of folklore as one of the main methodologies. In the Indian subcontinent, as a matter of fact, this process of treatment occupies a prominent position so far as methodologies are concerned. There was a time when, in the Bengali language, the term folklore was known more as folk literature than as anything else and the literateurs or folklorists of Bengal during the last decades of the nineteenth century and the first half of the present century studied folklore purely as folk literature. This is more or less true about the folklore of all the Indian languages. Even today, when folkloristics has advanced as a discipline, the scholars of all the three countries of the Indian subcontinent, India, Bangladesh and Pakistan seem to be quite content with a literary assessment of folklore and aesthetic values hidden in its spirit and form. Of course, their efforts are not condemnable, but their contentment can surely be questioned. Besides, they must keep pace with the progress and advancement made in the literary and aesthetic treatment of folklore in the developed countries of the East and the West. Most of those who uphold this view in our countries do not appear to be serious about the deeper study of aestheticism and literary fervour of folklore. In spite of these drawbacks, this is the only area where the performances of the scholars of our subcontinent may claim to have some mentionable value. I have examined several Ph.D. and D.Lit. dissertations of West Bengal universities for the last few years dealing with the aesthetic and literary values of folklore as well as with the glamour of folklore within the vast sphere of Bengali literature and I am happy to observe the trend of approach of some of the scholars as pragmatic and modern compared to the achievements of the elder ones. Still this area demands more elaborate and deeper concentration, hard labour and scientific treatment.

Since the primary materials of folklore must be certain categories of creative ideas which have become traditional among the people of any society and which may be recognized as their common property, the search for beauty in them or the determination of their literary value seems quite natural. The elements of folklore may also be the subject of theology, philosophy, aesthetics and ethics because of their closer relation with the heart of the people and mind of society. Being moved with the artistry in folklore, W. Bascom termed it as 'Verbal Art' (*Journal of American Folklore*, 1953, Vol. 66; 283-90). When a folklorist seeks the aesthetic quality and literary value of folklore, he must understand the relationship of oral and written literature. Since the creative idea is a common factor behind the two, both folklorists and students of literature must deal with the equally wide range of materials and include in their studies much more than the uttered or written words that convey an emotion and are moved by imgination. The typical folkloristic items like 'evil eye', 'sign of the horns', 'animal helper', 'mourning black', 'milk-white' and many others deserve consideration from both literary and aesthetic points of view. Some folktales relate to the beauty of the heroine or the charm of natural environment with such a vivid description, the style of which is even hard for a modern writer to achieve. Consideration of style, artistry and aesthetics in folklore is obviously a vital question which is closely linked up with the study of folklore.

While considering the theoretical orientation of the literary and aesthetic approach, to me it appears quite clear that there is no fundamental difference in both matter and style between folk literature and the literature of art or what we now call modern literature. Some very striking generalizations might come through the similarities found between the two. The theme and manner of treatment of a folktale, if viewed from the literary point of view, seem identical with the vast medieval Bengali literature or even some of the themes and treatment of modern Bengali literature. This is true about the literature of all languages of the Indian subcontinent, both medieval and modern. The tale of a prince, who loved a poor village girl, beautiful and charming, and who was opposed by the king, led to the appearance of themes of conflicts and suffering. The ultimate happy or rarely tragic ending is a common episode in the literature of all the Indian languages, specially in the medieval period. Quite a few examples of themes like this one in medieval Bengali literature can be cited. A number of examples of this fame could be found in our modern novels and fictions. Thus, it is obvious that the aims and objects of those working in the field of literature of art are basically the same as those of folklore. The stories about fools and detectives may be compared as another example. If we set up definitions of each genre and try to trace each back to its origins, we may discover stylistic variations and differences in subject matter which may be interpreted historically and evaluated critically. Graham Greene's ingenious manner of telling the story from the point of view of the culprit and not the detective, brings before us an example of stylistic variation. On the other hand, the restriction of the theme to a murder with the consequent desperate search for a new and surprising way of committing it, which is a popular theme for modern writers, exemplifies a variation in subject matter. Thus, when we compare the two fields of study, for example, folklore and literature, in general terms, their similarities call for a literary and aesthetic analysis of folklore in the line of literary criticism developed since the days of Aristotle. The formalistic study of folklore compared with literature has always proved fruitful.

I feel tempted here to quote from Archer Taylor:

> Perhaps the most interesting and attractive problems in folklore arise when one regards folklore as literature and asks the questions that a literary historian might ask. Take riddles as an example. We are all familiar enough with a vague definition of a riddle as a puzzle. We may take it for granted that the puzzle is stated in words and solved by a word. But, does such a definition include all the puzzles that have been printed in collections of riddles? It does not. There are puzzles expressed in terms of acts. An example of the latter variety is the game requiring some one to put a light where everyone but himself can see it. He must put it on his head. And we can go still further with the analysis of definitions. Not all pictorial

puzzles are of the same kind. Some involve a special interpretation of the pictures: an eye and a tin can represent 'I can' and some contain pictures of the actual objects intended in place of the words. The latter variety is most often found in Sunday School readers and the so-called hieroglyphic Bibles. Each of these varieties has its own history. If we turn to riddles expressed in words, we find many varieties that have been recognized and many that have not. We have the simple descriptive riddle like Humpty Dumpty, in which an egg is personified as a man and the personification is then contradicted by saying that the man falls and cannot be put together again. This is something entirely different from Samson's riddle in Judges 14, and both are entirely different from such a question as the Dennish "Which would you rather have; seven holes in your head or drink a cup of blood?" There are already seven holes in your head. Like the choice of caskets in *The Merchant of Venice*, the proper choice in such alternatives is the one that is apparently the least attractive. These are by no means all the kinds of puzzles that men have used to confuse and entrap one another. There are arithmetical problems, Biblical questions, genaeological puzzles, and still other questions that can be answered by straining one's wits and all of them are paralleled by such whimsies and parodies as "Is it right for a man to marry his widow's sister?" If we proceed still further with description of one of these varieties, we find curious subvarieties that have not been previously identified. There is a widely known riddle of the bed, the door and the window: "One waits for the day, one waits for the night, and the third says, 'It is always the same for me." We can safely say that this presents a special category of the descriptive riddle, for it concerns three objects and not one as in an ordinary riddle, it employs the characteristic device of contrasting the three objects, and in the three-score and more examples that I have noted it deals with limited range of themes. In this tripartite riddle we have noted that one of the objects is described by the words that it speaks. There are riddles consisting solely of dialogue :

> "Zigzag where are you going?"
> "Bold is your head, what is it to you?"
> "Hair will grow on my head before the straightening of your crooked steps."
>
> (A hayfield that has been moved speaks to a winding brook that flows through it)
>
> This, too, is a special variety of a riddle with a history of its own.
>
> I need go no further with this illustration of a stylistic analysis of riddles. The procedure is the same as that of the literary historian who recognizes and discusses the distinction between the Petrarchan and Wordsworthian sonnet, the differences between Shakespeare's use of five acts and Ibsen's use of four. The study of folklore can be an elementary exercise in literary history." (1948, 219-21).

The problems before the students of literature and folklorists seem identical on many points. The students of literature are frequently faced with the task of publishing history of an author's work through different editions. However, in folklore, the problem is much more complicated in that the oral tradition goes on to exist side by side with those variants which have entered written tradition. A man who published some ballads like the Mymensingh Ballads and some later collections in Bengali, for example, might have copied them down from some earlier booklets or he might have set down some versions he heard in oral tradition. But their variants are still available in oral tradition as well as in written tradition in the form of a small booklet. As I have mentioned earlier, the two traditions, the literary and the oral, specially in Indic folklore tradition, has mutually reciprocal influence. To trace the publishing life-history of an item of folklore, one must be both a folklorist and a bibliographical sleuth.

Creative urge

There have always existed human beings who not only felt the impulse to create works of art, but who possessed the ability to do so, and those men and women for whom artistic creation and the communication of their experiences is one of the chief means of finding satisfaction. This creative impulse, which seems somewhat mysterious in the human personality, found expression on word of mouth or in written form, in colour or sound, in works which either admit some function or of no purely utilitarian explanation. His architectural achievements, it is true, have arisen in the first place from the need to create dwellings and public buildings. But the same cannot be said of tales, ballads, songs, proverbs, rhymes, riddles, poetry, painting, sculpture, drama, and dance and so on. Although it is believed that some of these had their origin in magic or religion, that in itself is an inadequate explanation of the urge to create works of art; this urge continues where magical and religious motives have been long forgotten, and where they have not existed. Even when it is granted that magic or religion provided the original inspiration for certain artistic manifestations, such as drama, the paintings of cave-dwellers and primitive sculpture, that admission does not in any way diminish the mysteriousness of the impulse and of the ability to create.

To understand the nature of the creative urge as well as the characteristics of the creations in the fullest way, it is necessary to discover certain methods and modes of analysis which we call literary criticism and aestheticism. Thus, the approach of a literary and art critic may be different from that of a folklorist, but the aims and objects of both are the same.

The first step towards an understanding of the creative mind is an analysis of the deep-lying desires which the creative man attempts to satisfy by his creativity. The creative man is a person who wants to say something, sometimes it appears urgent to him. His nature leads him constantly to explore constantly to seek new aspects of truth. This truth may be the result of his experience, as in myths or proverbs or in poetry or drama. Every work of art, be it written or oral or sculpture, be it folk or non-folk, is started with great hope. The desire of a creative man for expression contains two elements: (1) the wish to express what is true, and (2) the wish to give this truth as far as possible a full and perfect expression. Hence truth is a quality every creative man is trying to reveal, and the expression of this constitutes his craft, his technique. Besides, the creative man in his endeavour towards perfect expression, with certain ideal conceptions in his mind, as in fairy tales or fiction and poetry, reorganises life and nature with the help of his experience and imagination. Thus, the world of a creative man is somewhat different from the world around us. Here we come to the question of imagination which goes along with creativity.

Imagination

The causes that stir the emotions of ordinary men and women have always spurred the creative man—the poet to write poetry, the mythmaker to make myth, the singer to sing and the painter to paint. This is the simplest effect of excitement on the creative man and concerns only the style of his utterance—the speech or the technique, not the substance. The image of the world's dark edge, which Mathew Arnold uses in 'Dover Beach', may be cited as an example of the mode of speech, imagery, personification and exaggeration:

The sea of faith
Was once, too, at the full, and round earth's shore
Lay like the folds of a bright girdle furld
But now I only hear
Its melancholy, long, withdrawing roar,
Retreating to the breath
Of the night-wind, down the vast edges drear
And naked shingles of the world.

In Bengali folk song we get the expression of imagination almost close to this:

Wherever I turn my eyes, I find the terrible darkness
As if it is fathomless,
The world-river is infuriated with violent storm
O God! how shall I cross over to the other bank.*

Imagination is one of the guiding factors behind the creation of folklore, literature of art and art of other forms. The imagination is the supremely creative faculty, a faculty which all men possess in some degree and use every moment.

*Author's translation of a Bengali folk song

Without it men would be incapable of creating or enjoying art, unable to conjure up the past and anticipate the future; no speculation about the absent, no day-dreaming or ambition would be possible for him. Since this faculty is inherent in man, there is no other means by which the reader, the listener or the observer be so directly or so poignantly affected by the truth reflected in the imaginative form in any artistic creation. A creative man is the man with a high degree of imagination under the control of reason by which he can rely on the imaginative response of others. This power of entering into another personality is a gift of the imagination without which tale, fiction, and drama would be impossible.

Experience of life no doubt plays a vital role in moulding the faculty of imagination, specially if he is a man with creativity. The subject springing up before the mind's eye of a creative man may arise from everyday experience or it may be concerned with some mythological, legendary or fantastic subject. The men, whose creative work is done through the hands, depend, to a considerable extent, on their imaginative power obtained through the visualization of the process of creation. They have the feel of their medium in their imagination.

Sensitiveness

(1) A creative man is sensitive in more ways than the ordinary man and it can be said that he feels certain things more quickly and more deeply.

(2) Because of his sensitivity, the imaginative powers of a creative man are both more vigorous and more easily set in motion.

(3) He is more conscious of his inner life and more analytical of it. He is subject more than other men to expound on feelings the transports of happiness or the depths of misery.

(4) He is quicker to attach permanent significance to transient circumstances, and to see around him evidence of those unchanging laws which govern man's existence. He endeavours to understand life, frequently expressing his conception of the meaning by images. Thus the drawing of a boat is a symbol of death, the blooming of a flower is the laughter of a baby.

There is distinction between the sensitive nature of poet, a song-composer, a story-maker and the painter or a sculptor. Though there are experiences to which both a poet and a painter respond, they are sometimes, by reason of the nature of their creation, stimulated and moved in quite different ways. While the views of life of the former is primarily literary and descriptive, the view of the latter is essentially visual. All of them see, but what the writers, song-composers or story-makers see, it appeals to them by ideas and associations or by sequence of events, on the contrary what the painter or a sculptor sees, it appeals to him by form or colour. Moreover, to the former group of creative men the excitement of handling materials begins only when the words start to assume intelligible patterns in their head. In that they miss the joy of a painter or a sculptor in handling the medium for its own sake, for they cannot enjoy words apart from their meaning to the same extent that the painter can enjoy paint or a sculptor his sculpture.

Medium

The question of medium is linked up with sensitiveness. All men and women are accustomed to the use of words, and because the medium is not strange to them, they can appreciate the fine handling of language, rich vocabulary and resonant sentences. That is why rhetoric has so ready an appeal : The medium it uses is universally familiar.

The most interesting thing that proves to be central is the meaning of the much-used word creation—a creative man creates a work of art. He does not create oil pigments, or the structure of tonal vibrations, or words of language, or in the case of dancer, his body and its mobility. What then is created? This involves the key concepts for a philosophy of art, such as apparition of the image, expressiveness, feeling, motif, transformation and some other interrelated aspects. A dance does not present only the movement of body, muscular strength, forces of gravity, muscular control, objects, dress, and secondary assets such as light and sound but something else as well, which is not physically before us. What a dancer creates is a dance; and a dance is an apparition of active powers, a dynamic image. Secondly, the dynamic image created in dancing has a different character. It is more than a perceivable entity; this apparition given to the eye, or the ear and eye, and through them to our whole responsive sensibility, strikes us as something charged with feeling. It belongs to the dance itself. A dance, like any other work of art, is a perceptible form that expresses the nature of human feeling—the rhythms and connections, crises and breaks, the complexity and richness of what is sometimes called man's inner life, the stream of direct experience, life as it feels to the living. What is expressed in a dance then, besides dynamic image, is an idea; an idea of the way feelings, emotions and all other subjective experiences come and go—their rise and growth, their intricate synthesis that gives our inner life unity and personal identity. What we call a person's inner life is the inside story of his own history, the way living in the world feels to him.

Yet subjective existence has a structure; it is not only met from moment to moment, but can be conceptually known, reflected on, imagined and symbolically expressed in detail and to a great depth. Only it is not our usual medium, discourse—communication by language—that serves to express what we know of the life of feeling. There are reasons why language alone cannot meet this purpose. What language does not readily do—present the nature and patterns of sensitive and emotional life—is done by works of art. Such works are expressive forms, and what they express is the nature of human feelings. Thus, like language, art is also a vital medium of expression.

Most men and women are far less sensitive to the language of painting; the actual quality of the paint and of the drawing, the colour and the organization of the picture. These are things which appeal to the senses, but only when the senses are trained to respond as the brain is trained to respond to words and the sound of words. Yet if we were as familiar with the language of the literary arts, the plastic arts would be found to be a more direct means of communicating feelings from one person to another, for, whereas in the interpretation of words the mind intervenes, painting and sculpture can speak directly through the senses. A folk art to a folk is something more than a language.

Intellect

In art, beauty and truth are invisible and one. We may, for beauty substitute form, and for truth, content. Narrowing them even more, we may speak of technique and subject matter. When we speak of technique, then, we speak of nearly everything. For technique is the means by which the writer's experience, which is his subject matter, compels him to attend to it, technique is the only means he has of discovering, exploring, developing his subject, of conveying its meaning, and, finally, of evaluating it. Here comes the question of intellect which helps develop experience and experiment technique.

Man's experiences are interpreted in all forms of art. Art is thus a criticism of life. The reaction of man to his environment is revealed through art. If a creative man fails to think and so arrives at no personal standpoint, his lack of conviction and decision will be reflected in his creation. If he does think, he may become persuaded that human existence has a meaning or that it has none; he may adopt an attitude of confidence towards death and fate, or one of stoicism or defiance. Though the non-logical, instinctive, subconscious part of the mind must play its part in his work, he also has a conscious mind which is not inactive. The creative man works with a concentration of his whole personality, as in painting and sculpture, or even even in poetry and riddle, myth and proverb, and the conscious part of it resolves conflicts, organizes memories and prevents him from trying to work in two directions at the same time.

A work of art presents feeling for our contemplation, making it visible or audible or in some way perceivable through a symbol, not inferable from a symptom. Artistic form is congruent with the dynamic forms of our direct sensuous, mental and emotional life; works of art are projections of felt life. Henry James classified it into spatial, temporal and poetic structures, there are images of feeling that formulate it for our cognition. What is artistically good is whatever articulates and presents feelings to our understanding. All creative men must ask themselves the question, "What form of art am I most suited and most inclined to undertake?" This question brings him face to face with his own nature, and he must understand its complexity clearly to know whether he is choosing a form of art for which he is fitted. A humourist, if he is a folk, would tend to create a humorous tale rather than a proverb, if a novelist, he would create humour novels. Thus, it is by thought that a sequence and consistency can be maintained within the work of art. He must understand the nature of his own power and ability, or we may call it his genius; and the nature of the work, both traditional and modern, he is about to produce. This understanding can only be achieved by an intellectual effort.

Artistic forms are more complex than any other symbolic forms we know. They are, indeed, not abstractable from the works that exhibit them. We may abstract a shape from an object that has this shape, by disregarding colour, weight and texture, even size; but to the total effect that is an artistic form, the colour matters, the thickness of lines matters, and the appeerance of texture and weight. A given triangle is the same in any position, but to an artistic form its location, balance and surroundings are not indifferent. Form, in the sense, in which artists speak of 'significant form' or 'expressive form' is not an abstracted structure, but an apparition; and the vital process of sense and emotion that a good work of art expresses seem to the beholder to be directly contained in it, not symbolized but really presented. The congruence is so striking that symbol and meaning appear as one reality. In fact, in good painting, sculpture, building, as in music or poetry, in fiction or ballad, balanced shapes and colours, lines and masses convey emotions, vital tensions and make their resolutions felt.

There has been a constant and sometimes embittered argument about the precise place of the creative man, the artist, and it is difficult adequately to define his role and function in the society. His activity is in part that of a teacher, philosopher and entertainer. Knowingly or unknowingly the mythmakers or the coiners of proverbs or the poets of the past have rendered great services to mankind, his culture and civilization. His aim was and still is unselfish, it is fundamentally to delight other men. Through this, he achieves some greater objectives, the search for truth, love and beauty. This itself is a result of an intellectual power. Intellect is certainly an essential quality of the creative man, for none of the questions related to artistry can be answered, nor can a conscious creativity be acquired without thought.

Concentration

An artist expresses feeling but not in the way a politician blows off steam or a baby laughs and cries. What he expresses is not his own actual feelings alone, but with them his knowledge of human feeling also. Once he is in possession of a rich symbolism, that knowledge may actually exceed his entire personal experience. A work of art expresses a conception of life, emotion, inward reality. But it is neither a confessional statement, or expression nor a frozen angry outburst—it is a developed metaphor, a non-discursive symbol that articulates what is verbally ineffable—the logic of consciousness itself. This demands a mental concentration of the creative man.

Rilke said in a letter from Sweden that he had often asked himself whether those days on which they were forced to be indolent were not just the ones they passed in profoundest activity. This indicates the concentration of a creative man—and his mental absorption in the thought of creation. If he is a poet, a singer, a tale-maker, he must be continually using words, and, if not actually writing or composing, constructing, works in his mind. If he is a painter or a sculptor, not only must he be thinking in terms of paint and sculpture, but also increasing the dexterity of his hand and the penetration of his eye by incessant practice. The conception of the artist, a creative man, besides suggeting that he does not need to think, in laying too much emphasis on inspiration, has tended to overlook the necessity for sheer hard work and to create the impression that creative man has only to listen to his genius. It is, of course, indisputable that the creative men have periods of inspired creation, when the power by which they are possessed drives them to write, or compose, or sing, or paint as though it were some outside force beyond their control. These are the rare and precious moments of exaltation for which he waits, it is true, but not, if he is wise, in idleness.

Every order of art has its own primary illusion; that is what sets the great orders apart. The unity of orders in art is asserted as an article of faith, instead of reasonable proposition. But the principle of creation is the same in all the arts even if that which is created differs from one to another. Every work of art is wholly a creation; it does not have illusory and actual elements mingled with it. Once the work is seen purely as a form, its symbolic character, its logical resemblance to the dynamic forms of life, is self-evident. We perceive them when we see or hear or read the work, and they seem to be directly contained in it, not symbolized by it. The work itself takes on the semblance of life: When artists speak of 'living form' they mean something in art, not in biology, as the art is the expression of human consciousness, according to some, in a single metaphorical image, that image must somehow achieve the semblance of living form. It cannot be denied that every aspect of nature, the form of things, animate and inanimate, the anatomy and characteristic attitudes of men and animals and some great stores of other information have been at the command of creative man, the painter, the poet, the talemaker. Leonardo provides the most striking example of inquisitiveness about the nature of visible things. His notebooks contain drawings of plants, roots, muscles, veins, limbs, hair, the folds of materials, rocks, floods, clouds, storms, machines and inventions. Such drawings by painters are objects of great interest in themselves, but they were never intended to be more than studies towards some greater work, pieces of observation noted down, things seen and loved and learnt. In the same way a writer, a poet, a ballad writer, a coiner of proverbs, a myth-maker adds to his experience of life and to his knowledge of men and women through ceaseless effort and initiative. Just as a painter or sculptor cannot invent a rock or a tree or a bird without the knowledge of their structure, so a writer, a poet, a tale maker, a ballad writer cannot make up men and women, or the aspects of nature without an understanding of human nature and the characteristics of natural phenomena. All these clearly establish that a great part of a creative man is intense living. His mental concentration forms a firm basis for his creation.

Artistic form is a projection, not a copy. Consequently, there is no direct correlation between the constituents of an organism and the elements in a work of art. Art has its own laws, which are laws of expressiveness. There are countless devices in the arts for the creation or enhancement of the living form. A creative man, thus, has a responsibility to acquire those devices and incorporate them in his creation. He is required to absorb, to comprehend the meaning of art and its scope. The passion for work and the craving to produce something that shall express the fire within the creative man, demand his efforts to know things around him, animate and inanimate, and the concentration of his thought. No man will be found more responsible or devoted than the creative man once it is realised that the authority to which he bears allegiance is not only the society or group he lives in, or the person he loves, but to his creative genius as well. The more deeply he goes into the artistic composition of an art, the more lucidly he sees its likeness to the composition of life itself, from the elementary biological patterns to the great structures of human feeling and personality that are the import of our crowning works of art; and it is by virtue of this likeness that a picture, a song, a riddle, a poem, is more than a thing. It becomes a living form, created, not mechanically contrived, for the expression of a meaning that seems inherent in the work itself: our own sentient being reality. In his service to this power, none can judge him but himself; he is his own taskmaster.

The treatment

The treatment of art by an artist is the root of his style. One can specify and discuss the characteristics of a dancer's dancing or a bard's writing in general terms, in so far as it has a characteristic style. Style, then, one may say, from the performance point of view, is precisely that aspect of activity which admits criticism. There is as well a formal or structural criticism that deals with actions, a textual criticism that deals with (not activities themselves, but) person's performance of his activities. It is to such textural properties that one is referring when one speaks of the quality of the writing, singing, or of the paint, in a particular piece; and one can speak thus with no less propriety of an artist's achievement as a whole in a particular creation, or of any extended section of it, so long as those properties remain constant. And, as in art so in life, a man may have a moral style, a way of comporting himself, either in some one of his moral activities, or in large area of his life, or in all.

The creative man gathers experiences, which before being expressed, pass through his mind. Naturally, when he expresses his experiences, his mind works and his creativity functions. Here comes the question of individuality and personality. Every creative man has an individual approach towards life and an individual method of dealing with it. The greater the individuality, the more clearly he shows a style of his own.

The term style, as I have mentioned, if introduced to indicate the criticizable aspects of the performance of activities, will appear ambiguous. Sometimes it is used simply to refer to whatever describable properties such a performance may have, sometimes to refer to only the desirable ones. A stylish dancer may be one who has a characteristic way of dancing, but is more likely to be one who dances in the approved fashion. When 'stylish' is thus used as a term of praise, one who performs the activities in question in a recognizable but unorthodox manner will be called, precisely, 'mannered', and the recognizable features of his style will be called not his style but his mannerism. Sometimes style may, through facilities earned, bring in an artist what we call gracefulness as a synonym of 'stylish'. But even then the difference between style and mannerism remains ever distinct, which creative man is expected to understand.

An object a creative man sees has many aspects and qualities. Here comes the question of selection—he selects the ones which seem to him vital. This selection is not a question of leaving out that he cannot understand, but of leaving out what he fully understands and does not want. To a writer of proverbs empty vessel appears vital when he says empty vessels sound much, to another a bird becomes vital when he says a bird in hand is worth two in the bush. So far as form of expression is concerned, a creative man, if he is one who depends on word of mouth, interprets form in terms of thought, he transforms it into an idea. If he is a painter or sculptor, he is compelled to substitute personal symbols for visible objects. When he comes to the question of technique, it also depends on individual ability. An English bard uses dramatic techniques in his expression of themes and becomes precise, whereas his Bengali counterpart uses the technique which is more lyrical and tale-oriented. H. Caudwell, whom I have followed in some of my observations, rightly observed :

> There can be only one criterion for technique: does it honestly subserve the artist's aim? If it helps him, then it is good technique for him. It may be intensely individual, like the verbal technique of Gerand Manley Hopkins or the paintillisme of Seurat, or it may be much less easily distinguishable. If what he wishes to say is banal, if his eye and his mind are uninteresting, then no brilliance of technique will save him from mediocrity. It is important always to consider with care and content of a work that appears particularly brilliant (1951, 121).

The creative impulse, imagination, sensitivity, intellect, concentration and treatment, as I have referred to in connection with aesthetic-literary theory of folklore, are not irrelevant in the sense that these are essential virtues of a creative man, a folk or a non-folk writer, a singer, a painter, a sculptor. Most of the elements of folklore are the products of this creative man and hence the qualities and virtues which we ascribe to the written literature, classic or modern, or we may call as literature of art, and to the sophisticated painting and sculpture, are very much common in all the elements of folk literature, artistic folklore, and in some items of folk technology, folk practices or even of folk sciences. Besides in the creation of folk literature and artistic folklore, a sense of creativity, imagination, intellect, concentration and treatment are also required for the creation and invention of some practices taking shape as customs, of some beliefs, for the making of tools, houses, fences, knots, and of scientific elements like folk medicine, churn-milk and so on. At least, so far as folk literature and artistic folklore are concerned, they deserve to be treated as an expression of art, and the methodology to be followed for their analysis on the basis of aestheticism and literary criticism should not be very different, if not exactly the same. This view of folklore analysis constitutes the basis of the aesthetic-literary theory.

Literary criticism

Theories of literary criticism seek for both literary work of art and artistic work of literature. Besides, the literary theorist tends to be interested in people who are willing and able to use the concept of literary work to distinguish a class of utterances —more appropriately referred to as texts—as having aesthetic properties, an aesthetic dimension or as constituting aesthetic objects. Readers of literature are not theorists or literary critics, but they appreciate and enjoy and in a sense they are the best critics also. I do not consider it wise to single out any special sub-group of people among those who use the concept of a literary work of art as having superior insight into the aesthetic nature of literary works and, therefore, having a monopoly of correct opinions about what features of a literary work are aesthetically significant. The ability to apply the criteria of a 'literary work' is a matter of knowing how; it is a skill which is a part of practice. Recognizing and dealing with a text as a literary work does not imply that the reader has a theory about what a literary work is; his practice in dealing with the work may even contradict any explicit theory has about the nature of literature, a not unknown phenomenon.

On the other hand, a literary work, folk or non-folk, as I have enumerated, is a work art. It has aesthetic properties and values which distinguish it from other types of utterance, written or spoken. It is by virtue of these aesthetic properties that the literary work, produced by a creative man, folk or non-folk, has a special claim to a reader's attention as one of the great cultural goods and it is the aesthetic properties which yield the value that makes the reader's attention to the text worthwhile. Besides, literary work has a dimension of being a linguistic fact. The literariness of the literary work is a given fact, provided one knows the language in which work is written or expressed through word of mouth. Aesthetic features are a type of linguistic feature and they are not at most due to an extension of the conventions of language.

Theories

A considerable number of theories of literary criticism have been developed since the time of Plato and Aristotle as well as from the time of Bharata in Sanskrit literature. Some old theories have become obsolete and some new ones have gained acceptence from scholars, but it is not my purpose to focus on them all here, because I feel no work of criticism is final. Criticism is never done once and for all. It is always contingent on the historical process and the state of social evolution.

Two types of theories

The question what is literature links itself with another, what is literature for. The earliest human enquiry into literature since the time of Plato is precisely an enquiry into its place in the totality of human experience (*Republic*, III, 386-402; X, 595-608; Ion; *Laws*, II, 653-6; VII, 810-12). Little is said about the nature of literature in itself, or its internal constitution. Immediately after Plato we have another enquiry, from Aristotle, into what literature is and how it works. (*Poetics*; "Rhetoric," 1, 1, 2.). While Plato's emphasis is on the effects of literature on the character and emotions of those who experience it, the weight of Aristotle's enquiry falls on the internal structure of literature. These two theories or types of theory appear as soon as literature attains self-consciousness; and they have remained fundamental ever since. Those who are concerned primarily with what literature is for tend to have only a feeble and unanalysed notion of what it is; those who are concerned primarily with what it is tend to be vague about what it is for. The former see literature as a part of human activity in general, but care little about how it works in itself. The others see literature as a self-contained activity, with its own methods and its own ends.

The semantic theory

Each art has its own medium; that of literature is language, which represents things, persons, actions, emotions and the structural relations between them. Emphasizing on the language, the semantic theory of literature builds on a distinction between what a word or a sentence means and what it suggests. There is a complex relationship between meaning and suggestion. When Beardsley defines literature as "discourse with important implicit meaning", (1967, 127) he puts his definition on semantic line which locates the aesthetic features of the work in the quality of its language. He observes:

> The essential structure of a poem resembles that of architecture or painting: it is a pattern of resolved stresses. Or, to move closes still to poetry by considering the temporal arts, the structure of a poem resembles that of a ballet or musical composition. It is a pattern of resolutions and balances and harmonizations, developed through a temperal scheme (1967, 166).

This theory has its limitation to cover uses of language which are not semantically dense. To this question, Beardsley has suggested that a literary work creates a world where events, characters and objects display a multiple relatedness to each other (1967, 128), and Cleanth Brooks insists that "the relation of each item to the whole context is crucial" (1968, 169). Nevertheless the semantic theory has remained a theory of texture rather than structure. Semantic density has a function only in a context.

The view of the literary work as a piece of discourse which is semantically dense goes together with the metaphor of the literary work as an object, a "porcelain vase", "verbal icon", (Wimsatt, 1970, 231), a "well wrought urn". At the same time, the supporters of this view insist on the objective nature of the literary work. Those who oppose, on the contrary, hold that it cannot by itself turn a passage into a literary work or guarantee that it is part of one. To them, it concentrates too heavily on the texture of the work to the exclusion of its structure.

Formalist theory

This theory has been expressed in diverse and partial states. The Aristotelian formula for the tragic plot; neo-classic demands for decorum and the three unities. Schlegel's and Coleridge's preference for organic over mechanic form; Henry

James' structural exigences for the novel; various notions of poetic diction that poetry should never be written in the language of the age, or that it should always be written in the language of the age, even certain material systems; each of these is a demand for a certain kind of formal perfection. The upholders of this theory plead for three principles, which are integrity, consonance and radiance. Everything that formal theory has to say about literature can be brought under one of these three heads. But there are cases where this can be done only with some straining. To look at the work of literature in the way of formalist theory is to regard it as a finished artefact. And so it is; and thus these principles can be regarded as universal. But there are kinds of literature where the reader's attention is most forcibly called not to the finished product but to the continous experience, as in many elements of folk litetraure. There are yet occasions where attention is called to certain focal points, moments of illumination, epiphanies. Other varietes of formal criticism may, therefore, be developed, some already we have, which will consider works of literature from different points of view.

Flaws in the formalist theory lie in several factors. Literature could be viewed as continous experience, it may function by continually arousing interest rather than by the expectation of a completed from, there may be examples of inorganic additions to works that were wholes already like the second part of *Pamela*, or the further exploits of Robinson Crusoe and so on; there may be moments of illumination as the imagists would stress upon. Of course, it also holds true that the literary experience is by its nature extended in time, as held by Aristotle. To try to reduce it to something like instantaneous apprehension is to contradict its mode of being.

Structuralism

As the form and structure in literature are not the same thing, so the formalist's approach and structuralist's view, though structuralism owes much to formalism, is not the same. To understand what structuralism is, I would quote from Levi-Strauss, who says:

His goal is to grasp, beyond the conscious and always

> shifting images which men hold, the complete range of unconscious possibilities. These are not unlimited, and the relationships of compatibility or incompatibility which each maintains with all the others provide a logical framework for historical developments, which, while perhaps unpredictable, are never arbitrary (1972, 23).

This theory suggests that since the literary work is a type of discourse, its structure can be explored with the same kind of method as is applicable to other types of discourse. It is closer to the linguistic approach. For the upholders of this view, the paradigm case of such a method is the linguistic analysis of sentences into words and morphemes and the suggestion is that just as the sentence is one type of linguistic unit, so the literary work is another, only much larger and vastly more complex. Structuralism, as I realize, is something that goes deeper to understand the real meaning, the meaning of meanings. Literature is the product of mind, but the mind is not open to our inspection. We know it only through the projects it undertakes, which means the text. Structuralism intends to go deep into the texture. It cannot be denied that literature presents us with certain formal structures and these structures are linguistic and stylistic; they are composed of language as paintings are composed of paint. But language also signifies things, persons, actions, events, emotions, and the relations between them; it also reflects ideas. This is social and moral material; and we cannot, therefore, give even a formal analysis of a work without considering the nature of this material. We may consider it in a merely conventional and abstract way (as Dryden does in discussing the drama); but to give a complete account of a work, even a complete formal account, we must consider this material in its concrete actuality; for it has had its reciprocal effect on the form.

On the other hand, literature presents us with moral and social material. But this material is presented in a certain structure of its own beyond the form. If we consider the moral-social material without considering the structure, as we consider a sentence in its totality, in which it is realized, we are not really considering literature at all; we are considering history, sociology, ethics and so on. To give a complete account of work, even complete moral account, we must consider its structural organization by arranging the main components in a paradigmatic order and see that the structure has had its reciprocal effect on the moral, formal and the social tenor of the whole. From whichever side we start, the interaction between semantics, form, socio-cultural element in a *literary work, folk or non-folk, is a dialectical process* embodied in the structure, like a sentence with all its components and interaction of those components, and the structure alone allows us to see the deeper inside and the work as a totality.

There are arguments both in favour and against this theory. (More details of discussion and analysis are given in structuralism as a theory of folklore which form the last part of this article).

Moral and social theories

Moralists demand that the law of perfection of literature should be the same as the law of perfection for life. Literature is to be guided by the same sets of principles which govern the rest of man's experience, and it is rightly judged by the degree to which it contributes to the fullness of human activity. Literature provides us with notable examples of virtues to be emulated and vices to be discarded. This is the way moral theory has been commonly felt and overtly expressed in most periods.

Social theory, on the other hand, considers literature as a social phenomenon. The creation of literature is a social act. By writing or composing verbally, we intend to communicate by means of written tradition or oral transmission. Even the most esoteric literature postulates an audience of a few kindred spirits. Here comes the question of a group, a group conception of literature as that of folklore, which I discussed earlier. All literature, we may say, as all folklore, is addressed to a group. This conception again goes in favour of social theorists. The group may be a class in the Marxist sense, may cut across class barriers, it may be a group that is only struggling into self-awareness. The literature of alienation from society, which comes into its strength with Baudelaire and his successors in France seems at first to be addressed to a handful of exceptional and isolated individuals, But with the passage of time, this literature became world literature.

Thus, moral theory sees literature as a contributory part of the activity of the social group and values and explains it by reference to this group. But the social group is a part of the social totality. A moral theory, if it pushes its analysis far enough, must value and explain literature by reference to this social totality. Tolstoy sees literature as an instrument for bringing all men together in brotherhood, that is, literature addresses itself to all men without distinction, to a classless society. This critical attempt to achieve concreteness and universality at the same time, as some believe, narrows the concept of art.

The expression theory

> The works of art, I.A. Richards says, "spring from the perpetuate hours in the lives of exceptional people, when their control and command of experience is at its highest hours when the varying possibilities of existence are mostly clearly seen and the different activities which may arise are mostly exquisitely reconciled hours when habitual narrowness of interest or confused bewilderment are replaced by an intricately wrought composure" (1926, 32).

According to Richards, language can work on a reader's emotions in two ways. It can evoke ideas in him which in their turn evoke emotions or it can work directly on his emotions without the mediation of ideas. According to this theory, the fact that literature can arouse and balance emotions gives it its particular value. A man's life is one long attempt to order conflicting impulses. "Always some impulse, or set of impulses, can be found which in one way or another interferes or conflicts with others" (Richards, 1926, 46).

Richards's observation, though modern, has supporters. Sussanne Langer strongly upholds this view and argues that "art is the creation of forms symbolic of human feelings" (1953, 40). In her later work she elaborates her views and says, "Sheer self-expression requires no artistic form. A lynching-party howling round the gallows-tree, a woman wringing her hands over a sick child, a lover who has just rescued his sweet-heart in an accident and stands trembling, sweating and perhaps laughing or crying with emotion, is giving vent to intense feelings; but such scenes are not occasions for music, least of all for composing." (1957 a, 216). The work of art is not to be understood by analogy or causal manifestations of powerful emotions. It is conceived by Langer and Ernst Cassier as a symbol, not of objects or of a set of facts, but of emotion. Besides, according to Langer, this theory of art must be based on language, as language consists of words which name things or relations.

The operation of the symbolizing power, a fundamental power of the human mind, has been most fully analysed by Cassirer. He sees it as the central, typical, universal human faculty, at work impartially in myth, religion, language, art and science, creating the human reality by giving it a symbolic form. Instead of reproducing the outer world, art reproduces the inner life, the life of the affections and emotions, in his view (1956, 177-81). Cassirer's massive and elaborately documented presentation of art as a symbolic form amounts virtually to a new insight (for further study, see his works, *The Philosophy of Symbolic Form*, Berlin, 1933, English trans, New Haven, 1953—his thought is more easily accessible in his shorter works, *An Essay on Man*, New Haven, 1944, 2nd edn. New York, 1956; *Language and Myth*, New York, 1949. For replacement of mimetic by expressive theory, see also Abrams, *The Man and the Lamp*, New York, 1956.

A poem can do more than say, and also can say more than it does. It is only through its meaning that a poem can be at all a poem. Thus, in art, there is something beyond what the symbolists or the expression theorists ever seek for.

The theory of cognitive emotion

This theory puts stress on the object or target of emotion, also on the reason for it :

> Poetry is characteristically a discourse about both emotions and objects, or about the emotive quality of objects. (Wimsatt and Beardsley, 1949, 38).

John Casey gives a concrete example :

> The murder of Duncan by Macbeth, whether as history of the eleventh century or chronicle of the sixteenth, has not tended to become the subject of a Christmas Carol. In Shakespeare's play it is an act difficult to duplicate in all its immediate adjuncts of treachery, deliberation and horror of conscience. Set in its galaxy of symbols—the hoarse raven, the thickening light, and the crow making wing, the babe plucked from the breast, the dagger in the air, the ghost, the bloody hands—this ancient murder has become an object of strongly fixed emotive value (1966, 106).

Thus, a link between emotion, objects and the work is made conceptual, which forms the basis of this theory. The interpretation provided by the upholders of this theory yields proposition unacceptable to many, since the emotion resulting from the contemplation of a work cannot really be identified as an emotion at all. But in spite of that, the two theories combined the expression theory and the theory of cognitive emotion, contributed to a great extent to the reorientation of our thought in understanding the works of art. The later generation of critics have emphasized again on analytical method and they try to display the structure of the revelation, the means by which the unique essence is realized. That the literary work is an object of a unique aesthetic emotion has also been regarded as an alternative view by some modern critics. But most of them assume that the only behaviour and symptoms are reader-symptoms and that the object is the work, and the nature of the satisfaction attending the activity can only be analysed through an analysis of the activity of reading a text as a literary work.

In the foregoing pages I have named and discussed in short some of the theories of literary criticism. To me they appear to be the prominent ones. Besides, there are other theories current in the field of literary criticism such as act-theory, nemesis, theory of kinds, myth theory, organic theory, and so on. There are also alternative approaches to the literary works. It is not my purpose to go into details of all these theories, concepts and approaches. But this much can be repeated that major portion of folklore belongs to the works of art and hence the theories, concepts and approaches applicable to the study of literature and works of art are applicable to the study of a major area of folklore.

Aesthetics

Before I pass on to another theory of folklore, I will deal in short with aesthetics as a component of the aesthetic-literary theory of folklore.

All art and literary works have aesthetic properties, an aesthetic dimension, or have aesthetic objects as constituents. Philosophers as well as literary and art critics in all ages have sought to explain what aesthetics is and what it tries to do. The findings, as we see them today, have created a cluster of problems, which keep expanding and changing. To decide which of these problems is the most important, is, moreover, itself a strategic philosophical problem and one on which the philosophers disagree. Hence, I might offer something like a definition here, but that would be, I am afraid, either arbitrary or else so general that it would be worthless. Besides, aesthetics is a branch of philosophy and criticism, a branch of the study of all art. Like philosophy and a study of art or literary criticism generally, it is a competitive exchange of ideas. It is ideas thursting against each other, making their claims upon the loyalty of the mind, changing each other. Conclusions are arrived at, but aesthetics cannot be set out as a body of conclusions. Like all philosophy, aesthetics is a process, not an end-product, an inquiry, not an almanac. Probably the best way to put it is as old Scorates thought—it is a conversation among earnest.

A poem may be very pretty and elegant, but is soulless. A folk narrative has precision and method, but is soulless. What do we, then, mean by soul here? Soul in an aesthetic sense, as it appears to me, signifies the animating principle in the mind. My proposition is that this principle is nothing but the faculty of presenting aesthetic ideas. By an aesthetic idea I mean that representation of the imagination which induces much thought. The imagination, as a productive faculty of cognition, is a powerful agent, as I have explained before, for creating a second nature out of the material supplied to it by actual nature. Such representation of the imagination may be termed ideas. In a word, the aesthetic idea is a representation of the imagination, annexed to a given concept, with which, in the free employment of imagination, such a multiplicity of partial representations bound up. No expression indicating a definite concept can be found for it—one which on that account allows a concept to be supplemented in thought by much that is indefinable in words, and the feeling of which quickens the congnitive faculties, and with language, as a mere thing of the latter, binds up the spirit (soul) also. If we wish to discern whether anything is beautiful or not, we do not refer to representation of it to the object by means of understanding with a view to cognition, but by means of the imagination we refer the representation to the subject and its feeling of pleasure or displeasure. The judgement of taste, therefore, is not a cognitive judgement, and so not logical, but is aesthetic—which means that it is one whose determining ground cannot be other than subjective. Every reference of representations is capable of being objective, even that of senstations, in which case it signifies the real in an empirical representation. The one exception to this is the feeling of pleasure or displeasure.

The aesthetic attributes do not not like logical attributes, represent what lies in our concepts of the sublimity of creation; but rather, something else—something that gives the imagination an incentive to spread its flight over a whole host of kindred representations that provoke more thought than admit of expression in a concept determined by words. They furnish an aesthetic idea, which serves the rational idea as a substitute for logical representation. But it is not alone in the arts of painting or sculpture, where the name of the attribute is customarily employed, that fine art acts in this way; poetry, ballads, folk songs, myths and tales, proverbs, also derive the soul that animates their works wholly from the aesthetic attributes of the objects—attributes which go hand in hand with the logical, and give the imagination an impetus to bring more thought into play.

For roughly a century the conception that art is an emotional language, a personal utterance addressed to the reader or beholder by means of which he grasps the emotion the artist has felt and makes it his own, has probably been the dominant one. Then again, according to some, neither artist, nor the spectator seeks beauty in art. Art begins with a man feeling some emotion, and it fulfils itself when another man shares this emotion. Some views are that story-telling and description on canvas are not, as has been generally thought, art at all, only its organization of the elements of line, mass and colour, which may be called significant form, entitles a painting or sculpture to be termed a work of art. So, if we go on considering the views on art, specially the aesthetic aspect of it, there will practically be no end. Modern aesthetics say since the eighteenth century, it has found a rationale for the artist and his audience in the uniqueness and autonomy of art. The work of art is not a scientific document, a vehicle of knowledge, it is not a religious icon, important only because of what it represents; it is not a moral tract. The nature and value of art is peculiar to itself. It is more to be understood than to be defined.

Most of the elements of folklore contain the aesthetic qualities—the aesthetic sense of creative man found its expression in those elements. Thus, there is hardly any scope to eliminate folklore from the aesthetic study of art, the study which forms the basis of aesthetic-literary theory of folklore. This position of folklore has been, in the past, quite distinctly understood by literary folklorists who devoted their whole study to this direction. The trend to assess folklore from an aesthetic point of view, has, during the last few decades, been more intensified, specially in the Indic languages. What the imagination seizes in beauty of art must be truth. Art, manifest in folklore, painting, sculpture and literature or in any form is doing the right thing in the right way and beauty is the evidence of it. What we find beautiful in a work of art is not found beautiful by the eye, but our imagination through the eye. The study of art in all forms has usually centred on the consideration of work, achievement of the author in a historical period. But, increasingly, there is a demand for a more analytical approach for investigation and exploration of literary concepts of crucial ideas and issues both in literature and folk literature—topics which are of great importance to the critical consideration of particular works of art—poetry, fiction, myth, ballad, painting and sculpture.

Comparative theory of folklore

The Finnish method, known as historic-geographic method, is the basis of comparative methodology or theory. This theory puts the folklorists under some rigid obligations. To achieve results under this theory a comparative folklorist must have hundreds of variants of a particular myth, tale, or ballad or any item of folklore. Then he goes for analysing the basic plot into essential components, makes percentage of frequencies of occurrences of each trait, finds out the regional distributions through map, judges the early literary or oral version and fixes the oldest form of the tale known as archetype. Kaarle Krohn invented this method in 1926 which was elaborately indicated in his book *Die Folkloristiche Arbeits Methode* (1926, Oslo). Since its inception there were arguments both in favour of and against this method. Scholars like Albert Wesseleski, C.W. Von Sydow, Raider Christiansen, Laurits Bodker, Walter Anderson mentioned many drawbacks of this method and criticised it from different points of view. On the contrary, scholars like Stith Thompson, W.E. Roberts, Archer Taylore, Holger Olof Nygard defended the Finnish method with examples cited from tales and ballads where it could be successfully applied. Instead of going into this controversy I would like to say that with the development of the synchronic study of folklore, the Finnish method, which stands on diachronism, has lost its solid ground. But even then I feel that the process of comparison as introduced and covered by this method will continue to have a permanent appeal. We may not perspire copiously to locate the archetype of a tale, ballad or proverb, but certainly we may make a comparison between the tale, or any item of folklore under our study with the variants of the same found in other parts of the country or of the world or in other languages and cultures. Besides the historic-geographic distributions, which may be somewhat erroneous, the objective of our findings could be anthropological, cultural, social or literary. With this objective in our mind if we enter the area of folklore of the Indian subcontinent, we will find that the historic-geographic method, if in its entirety does not appear to be suitable to the Indian context, the sense of comparison focused in it is perfectly applicable. Let us take an example from a Bengali proverb. "*Pola na kandie mae dud dei na*" which means that the mother does not give milk to the baby unless he cries for it. The same proverb is found in the Tamil language but its shape is different—"*Aluta pillai paal kutikkum*" meaning that a baby that cries will get its milk. While the structure of the Bengali proverb is based on a negative form, that of Tamil is on the affirmative. The Tamil proverb is used completely in a different social context. The Bengali proverb indicates that a man who has the resources to help the needy one will do so only when the needy one prays or demands it. The Tamil proverb on the other hand points that a needy one who can rightly pray or make a demand for his needs will succeed. In the Bengali proverb the giver is more prominent than him who takes. In Tamil there is no giver, the receiver is a single person, but even then he receives if he cries from a source not definitely mentioned. The historic-geographic method, irrespective of its shortcoming, establishes this spirit of comparison which is essentially the basic principle of this methodology and if we can adopt it in the study of Indian folklore to enunciate a thorough comparative approach, our folkloristics will receive a new impetus. The books mentioned* appear to me to be very helpful in the task of such a comparison of the folktales of the Indian subcontinent.

*Stith Thompson *Motif Index of Folk-Literature*, 6 vols. 1957, Bloomington, Indiana. *The Folktale*, 1951, New York.

Stith Thompson and Jonas Balys *The Oral Tales of India*, 1958, Bloomington, Indiana.

Stith Thompson and WF Roberts *Types of Indian Oral Tales FF Com.* No. 180. Vol. XXIII, 1960, Helsinki.

Antti Aarne and Stith Thompson *The Types of the Folktale*, 2nd (ed.) FFC 184, 1961 Helsinki.

Richard M. Dorson (ed.) *Folklore Research Around the World*, 1961, Bloomington, Indiana.

Allen Dandes, (ed.) *The Study of Folklore*, 1965, Berkeley.

Mazharul Islam, *A History of Folktale Collections in India and Pakistan*, 1970. Dacca (first ed.) Second enlarged ed., 1982, Panchali Prakason, Calcutta (Bangladesh and Pakistan are two separate states since 1971).

Since the Grimm Brothers started to speculate about the characteristics of the tales they collected in 1820, the European scholars began to take interest in the study of folktales. It appeared to them that there existed a chain of association between the variants. If version A was written in a text of the fifth century in one language, B was written down in another language in the eighth century. So the scholars set themselves to find out the link specially asking them which of the variants would be the earlier version. This search led the study of folklore to embrace the historical approach.

Stith Thompson, one of the world's greatest folklorists, in his study of "The Star Husband Tale" enumerates the development of the historic-geographic method in the following lines:

> We find ourselves confronted with five hundred versions of a well-knit story coming from all parts of Europe and much of Asia and showing significant or insignificant resemblances to other tales, not only in this region but in the remote parts of the world. At first view these hundreds of variants may seem to be filled with chance divergences—a mere kaleidoscopic shifting about of motifs and episodes. But as we look at them more closely we become aware that men and women have been telling the tale through the centuries and in many lands and that the life of the tale is a part of their lives and can be understood only when we know these tellers and hearers. We are not surprised therefore that the seeming lawlessness is only apparent and comes only because so many men and so many places have left their marks on the tale. The study of such a story, the attempt to find order in the seeming confusion, involves the use of elaborate analysis which will show that all these variations are obeying laws or combination of laws, however complicated or baffling. If one is to determine the direction the tradition has travelled, he must try to reconstruct a theoretical original and at least attempt to trace the historical and geographical conditions under which the tradition has been kept alive in the interests of the intervening generations. For such an investigation of an oral tale, the ordinary techniques of literary history are useless.

> But the scholars of the nineteenth century did not immediately approach the problem just stated. They had but few versions of folktales before them and did not realize the difficulties of the study of a single tale. Instead, they at once and prematurely tried to solve the leading questions: (1) Where do folktales come from? and (2) What does folktale mean? By the end of the nineteenth century it was becoming increasingly clear that the only way to arrive at any valid statements about folktales in general is to study folktales in particular. After many of these come to be known then we shall be ready for larger synthesis and statement of tentative laws. The leading spirit in the promotion of these monographic investigations was Kaarle Krohn of Finland, so that the historic-geographic method evolved by him and his disciples for these studies is sometimes called the Finnish method (1953, 93-94).

If I am to trace the entire history of the historical consideration as well as geographical importance accepted in the study of folktale which this method has embraced, I need to go into details of the contributions made to the development of this processs by Grimms, Theodor Benfey, Max Muller, Frazer, Andrew Lang, and their contemporaries. In the precise but pointed enumeration of Thompson, we get the gist of this development. The successful use of this method depends on the thorough analysis of a large number of versions—enough to give the findings some statistical validity. The analysis attempts to establish an archetype and subtypes and to arrive at a probable life history of the tale.

Origins of folklore

I would like to throw some light on the much controversial views on the origin of folklore, for I consider this quite a relevant occasion to raise it along with historic-geographic method, which also, in a way, searches for origin. It is said that,

> "even if there were some agreement as to what folklore is, it is unlikely that there would be much accord as to how

folklore began. The history of the discipline of folklore is riddled with the remains of elaborate theories explaining how folklore arose. Some of these theories are still championed; others are revived only to serve as straw men to be ritually killed in modern surveys of folklore. An example of the latter is solar mythology, which few, if any, folklorists seriously entertain at the present time (Dundes, 1965, 50).

Multiple existence and irrationality: the theory of polygenesis

To have an actual being in manifold order is one of the characteristics of folklore, which received the attention of many folklorists. They mostly dealt with the repeated appearance of some folklore in different cultures. And there are another group of scholars who emphasized on the irrationality of folklore. Thus, two major opinions on the origins of folklore became distinct in the not-far-away past: (1) the multiple existence of folklore, and (ii) irrationality of folklore. The multiple existence of many tales, proverbs, riddles can be cited from the different cultures and languages of the same country or from different countries. As, for example, the tale of magic flight, or the swan maiden has vaiiants almost in all parts of the world. This is also true about some myths, like "Oedipus" or "the sun and the moon", or some proverbs like "Child shows the man as morning shows the day" or "Empty vessels sound much". The study of these striking similarities led to the development of the theory of the naturalistic origin of folklore. In his study of Oedipus, Michel Breal took a naturalistic position and explained Oedipus as the personification of light, and his blinding as the disappearance of the sun at the end of the day. The chief event in the legend is the struggle with the Sphinx, the storm cloud, which is the prototype of mythical monsters. Breal separates these events in the story from certain others, namely, patricide and incest, which he maintains as later additions. This accords with his hypothesis that the elements of legends are not created simultaneously (1877, 163-185). Thus, the observation of Breal establishes the naturalistic origin of folklore, which si opposed to the theory of polygenesis, according to which the same element of folklore could have originated any time and anywhere under the same circumstances and same favourable environment. But sometimes, the naturalistic origin theory may come closer to polygenesis in the sense that the same natural conditions may have provoked the folks of different countries to create almost the same type of folklore, specially the proverbs and riddles or even customs and beliefs. But that is a different topic to be studied which I will not elaborate here. The theory of polygenesis is often quoted in support of the concept of the psychic unity of man by those who believe that because of the psychological uniformity of man, folklore created in different culture can be the same. Many English scholars, specially the anthropologists, accepted and advocated the theory of polygenesis in the study of folklore as far as it is related to anthropology on the ground that all men have passed through a uniform and identical evolutionary process from savagery to barbarism and then to civilization.

Psychic unity and polygenesis provided to some of them the right answer to the seemingly resembling cultural traits and phenomena existing in different countries. But their efforts led the study of folklore to a dangerous proposition that folklore was the creation of men when they were in savagery stage. As they advanced, folklore ceased to exist, their creations have been stopped and whatever we have received today as the elements of folklore are from the survivals. This necessitates the collection of folklore from those who are considered still as living savages or half-savagevillage-dwellers to help reconstruct the history of cultural development. This theory has been discarded by the folklorists on the ground that folklore is a dynamic organ of culture, with the change of society and culture it adapts itself to the new situation, and it originates from peoples of any class of society, irrespective of where they dwell or what they do. Of course, the theory of polygenesis as such holds good in some cases of folklore origin.

The theory of diffusionism

The twentieth-century anthropologists accepted the explanation of multiple existence of folklore combined with diffusionism. They hold that the cultural traits move from person to person and from culture to culture. They discarded the polygenesis theory, the view that the elements of folklore arose independently and advocated that they were born in one place or probably in a very few places and they were transmitted to other places by diffusion. Thus, a combination of monogenesis and diffusion was the salient point of their argument. They maintain that "if an item is complex rather than simple (though the question remains how simple is simple) and if there is continuous distribution of the item in the area intervening between points A and B, the occurrence of the item at A and B is to be attributed to diffusion rather than to independent origin." (Dundes, 1955, 54). The upholders of this view have termed some nations of the world as borrowers of folklore, and some suppliers, some are manufacturers and some consumers. Is it possible to decide and pinpoint who are in what position? Folklore travels, but does not travel up to the extent as to destroy the independent birth of folklore in other areas where they travel. The elements are transmitted and diffused, they also exert influence over the other, one variant is mixed up in a peculiar way with the other variant of another country, near or far away, which has given folklore an international character; but in spite of these factors which are true, every culture gives birth to its folklore according to its own requirement and characteristics.

The irrationality of folklore, as held by some scholars, also poses an equally vexed problem. There are motifs like magic wands (Motif D 1254.1) or vagina dentatas (F 547.1.1.), which do not have any relation with reality of life, nor can they be found in nature. The only explanation of their appearance in folklore could be to relate them with human fantasies. Thus the question of psychological as well as historical origin of folklore opened a new chapter. The former deals with why the item came into being, and the latter emphasized when and where the item was born and probably how it was spread. The psychological origin of an item ignored the how and when of the diffusion of the item. This explantation is based on the behaviour of the people of modern time. It is hardly possible to prove that the ancestors of modern man also had the same mental make-up as that of modern man and created folklore with that mental make-up where fantasies of the human mind were reflected in a crude way. Besides, since the upholders of the psychological origin consider folklore-fantasies as products of the human mind, they indirectly accept the psychic unity concept which holds that human psychology is constant and the question of its variability does not stand. The historical origin concept, on the other hand, seeks to find out the origin of folklore through some historical method. As a method, this is no doubt commendable, but without the available as well as dependable data, its applicablity on the study of folklore seems to be absurd. So far as the evolution of man is concerned, historical records may go back, but folklore does not supply such records of its evolution, and it is hardly possible to trace out the origin of folklore item as such, though the historic-geographic method, and to some extent the comparative theory of folklore, endeavours to put its search towards the same direction.

> 'Another way of viewing the historical versus the psychological approach to origins is through recourse to a literal-symbolic dichotomy. Those who interpret folklore literally feel that there is historical truth underlying folklore. What appears to be irrationality is simply rationality distorted or history misremembered. According to the literal interpretation, folklore is more fact than fiction. The English folklorists of the late nineteenth century held this position, and thus in their aim of historical reconstruction they sought to find the factual truth underlying the folklore fragments of civilization. What appeared to be irrational to the civilized man was no doubt rational to a savage (and by philosophical extension to the child and the poet). Thus folkloristics in the late nineteenth century was regarded as a historical science.' (Dundes, 1965, 55).

All elements of folklore cannot provide the authentic data for the reconstruction of history, but some certainly can. There are legends, some proverbs, even some riddles, some customs and beliefs, the very careful and minute study of which may lead us to reach a historical basis closer to truth.

But mostly such findings would be hypothetical rather than authentic in the historical point of view. Amongst all elements, legends have, of course, some solid basis for historical findings, but that also is secondary source material, not like a document or rock-inscription.

In the search for the origins of folklore, symbolism also played a distinct role. The symbolic approach considers folklore something like a mental phenomenon meaning that it has to be studied like a dream being translated in the symbolic code. Every symbolic school has a means to interpret the underlying thought and message of folklore and reveal the truth. The upholders of symbolism prefer to analyse folklore psychologically rather than historically.

Conclusion

The theories relating to the origin of folklore as described along with their drawbacks in the foregoing paragraphs may be avoided as theories. The modern folklorists feel that the search for ultimate origins, whether by means of the cultural evolutionist approach or the age area concept, is a fruitless one where the historical documents and archaeological evidence are lacking. In folklore, where archaeology can be of almost no help, and where documentation does not yield the answers directly, attempts to reconstruct the history of society as well as of a particular element of folklore even on a restricted scale can yield results only in terms of probability rather than proven fact, and there lies the constant danger of being enticed into the realm of pure speculation for which one can never hope to discover supporting evidence. This conclusion has been reached after many serious attempts to reconstruct history using a wide variety of data and although anthropologists and folklorists have not completely abandoned the subject of distribution of specific tales or ballads, the question of diffusion and possible origins is receiving less and less attention and is approached with increasing caution. I would like to formulate my own opinion about the origin theories in such a way that I may accommodate all of them by accepting none. Some elements of folklore may be treated as of polygenetic origin, which means, they have their independent birth; some have travelled from their places of origin, diffused themselves as well as diffused others in space and time; there are some which provide us with historical data and help reconstruct history; and yet there are some where we find the true reflection of human fantasies and psychological reality; some of them are symbolic and deserve to be translated with symbolic code. But, above all, I would like to examine every item of folklore with a pragmatic view and critically evaluate it from the point of view it is aimed to be studied, rather than to fit it in a particular set of theoretical frame like the ones searching for the origin of folklore. In fact, the western folklorists do not any longer subscribe to these views and instead they tend to be concerned with text, texture and context, with structure and form, with performance and functions, with aesthetics and linguistic value, and with socio-cultural importance. Folklore is the mirror of culture, it is the pulse of the people.

I hope, in the background of the foregoing discussion on the theories of origin of folklore, it will be convenient for us to understand the Finnish method and the comparative theory of folklore in a clear way. The grasp of origin theories, in fact, helps us to develop a dispassionate attitude for the comprehension of all the six theories under discussion. The Finnish method, as stated earlier, demands a series of specific steps. Firstly, all the available versions, both from the oral and the written sources must be collected, located, assembled and arranged methodically in some convenient form of organization. "The next step is one of the most critical. By empirical inspection of the corpus of text, the folklorist breaks tales into principal traits that demonstrate some variation. The variation of a trait's content is a potential means of distinguishing smaller groups of versions that share a particular sub-type. For example, if one of the traits, say, Trait A, is the number of women in the tale, then verisons may be distinguished on the basis of whether they have one woman, two women or some other number of women. Eventually, if one finds that a whole group of versions share a number of identical sub-traits, one may have isolated a sub-type of the basic tale type. A way of facilitating the identification of similar tales is to write each version of the tale in using the abbreviations for the sub-traits. If, for example, the first trait, Trait A, has such trait as Al (one woman) A2 (two women), and so on then the abstract of a tale having two women will begin with A2. In similar fashion, one would write a tale in symbol shorthand such that the formula might look like A2, B1, Cl, D2, and so on. The formula could be easily compared with formulas of other versions. For example, of the following three versions, it is obvious which two are more similar to one another:

A2, Cl, Bl, D2, E3, F5, F10, K3a, I1, Li, M3c, M3b, N2.
A1, C2a, B3b, F2, E2, G1, H1a, I2, J2, K3b, L3, N1.
A2, Cl, B1, D2, E3, I3, J2, K2, L1, N2.

Of the tales, the first and third have more in common than do either with the second. This method may appear to be unnecessarily complicated, but one must remember that if a folklorist is trying to compare as many as a thousand versions of a tale, it is almost impossible to do so by reading the full narrative accounts and keeping them all in mind. By comparing the trait sequences, one can much more readily note similarities and differences. No doubt some enterprising folklorist will one day use an electronic computer to help him separate groups of similar tales from an unwieldy corpus of texts." (Duudes, 1965, 414-415).

Dundes goes on to say, "The hypothetical archetype is established by looking at each trait individually to determine what was the probable archetypal form of the trait. Such factors as early recordings or literary versions (in the case of Indo-European materials) and widespread or peripheral distribution are taken into account. [It is the combination of chronological criteria (historic) and of geographical spread (geographic) that has led to the historic-geographic method.] After the archetype for each individual trait is hypothesized, the projected list of archetypal traits is put together as a possible basic type or archetype of the whole tale. (In case of complex tale, archetypes for the traits of each subtype may be postulated in order to arrive at subtype archetypes. Then from these, the folklorist may reconstruct a projected archetype of the parent form of the tale from which the subtypes might have evolved). The hypothetical archetype is in part a statistical abstraction that may or may not correspond to even one actual recorded version of the tale in the initial corpus." (1965, 415).

I have partially applied this method on Aarne-Thompson type 313 "The Girl as Helper in the Hero's Flight" or "Magic Flight" and on type.9 and 1030, "Unjust Partner and the Deceptive Crop Division" or "Greed and Punishment", which may be found in my Bengali book *Folklore Parichiti Ebong Loksahityer Pothon Pathon* (first edn. 1967, Rajshahi University publications; revised and enlarged 2nd ed., 1974, Bangla Academy, Dacca). I have expressed my feelings about this method at the beginning of the discussion. The same views have also been expressed by Dundes, "one of the chief criticisms of the historic-geographic method is that it is the study of folklore for its own sake that the study of variation and stability is not meaningfully related to human factors. Tales spread and traits drop off with super organic case, and it is for this reason that some anthropological folklorists eschew this type of study, on the other hand, there is in theory no reason why the comparative method could not and should not be the preliminary basis for other kinds of analyses of folklore. The folklorist who collects one version of the "Star Husband" from an American informant may be interested in knowing if and how his particular informant has varied the tale. For the determination of such facts, the historic geographic method is of great value. However, the conclusions of most historic-geographic studies leave some significant questions unanswered. Why did the archetype, assuming the reconstruction is valid, arise in the first place? Why did the subtypes evolve and why did they evolve precisely where they did? Why does the tale in its multiple forms continue to be told (or not to be told)? For such questions, a synthesis of approaches is needed. The study of historical origins and of paths of diffusion are a part, an important part, of the whole. But the study of psychological origins and of function is also a part of the whole. The combination of these approaches can lead to a fuller undertanding of the nature of folklore (1965, 415-416).

The spread of an element of folklore from one society to another and the question of acceptance or rejection of a religious ritual or concept, tool or a technique, and if accepted the subsequent modification to fit the new item into the other cultural patterns, attracted the attention of anthropologists in the form of social integration. "There are again the same problems in interpreting the present distribution of a given cultural trait or a folktale or a proverb. Does one explain this in terms of migration as the Grimm brothers believed; in terms of borrowing as the diffusionists insisted; or in terms of independent invention as the Nature Allegorical school assumed?" (Bascom, 1953, 289). These same problems have been faced a great many times by anthropologists, and a considerable body of materials bearing on this problem has been assembled. Folklorists could profit considerably from the numerous anthropological discussion on this point and from the various principles such as limited possibilities, contiguous distribution, parallelism, convergence, form, and quantity, which have been developed as a basis for choosing between these alternative explanations; they could also profit from an examination of studies such as Spier's analysis of "Plains Indians' Sun Dance" or the discussions of the age-area concept and its limitations. (Leslie Spier, 1921 "The Sun Dance of the Plains' Indians: Its Development and Diffusion", *Anthropological Papers of the American Museum of Natural History*, Vol. 16, No. 7. N.Y.) "These have implications of fundamental importance for those who employ the methods of Finnish Folklore Fellows" (Bascom, 1953, 282). The age-area concept is closer to the historic-geographic method, as it in simple terms indicates the notion that the wider the distribution of a culture trait, the older the trait may be.

One advance in folklore study whose importance the Finnish school has particularly recognized is the conception of the variant. The Finnish folklorists codified and systematized procedures that any thorough scholar would at least initiate the gathering of all available evidence, and the organizing of this evidence in meaningful units. The nearest available texts were employed by many folklorists to establish their proposition, but they probably failed to grasp that all texts in folktale are variants, as they underwent changes at every point of their transmission from one age to another, one culture to another culture. A. Taylor, however, expresses his faith in the common sense of the Finnish method and holds that it is fit to be applied in the comparative study of any genre of folklore.

Dorson has rightly observed, "The comparative folklorist of the Finnish school has diverted attention from philosophical and metaphysical questions of meaning to empirical questions of fact. If his question of urformen has been challenged, he has succeeded in establishing the normal formen. No one can question that this species of folklorist is unscholarly." (*Current Anthropology*, Vol. IV, 1963, p. 95). The Finnish method may of course be described as "a protracted exhaustive and tiresome procedure", its body is thorny with annotations. "It ignores some of the important questions that most interest the scholars. Consideration of style and artistry, of the mysterious processes of creation and alteration, of the influences of national cultures, the social contexts, the individual genius, are out of order among the percentage tables and the plot summaries. Such questions have been left by the Finnish method for the speculation of other groups of folklorists" (Dorson, 1963, 95). It may also be said that it is humanly impossible to gather all the texts and variants of a particular material of folklore, be it a tale, a proverb, a riddle or a ballad or any item, from both oral and written sources. Hence, there always remains a scope for questioning even the hypothetical conclusion arrived at about the archetype or urform or oicotype. Even the procedure of its application can also be questioned. Thus the Finnish method which forms the basis of comparative theory as such has been discarded by many scholars. The Finnish method, I must say, has lost its ground entirely leaving before us only the spirit of comparison.

In conclusion I would like to emphasize that even if we forget about the achievements through the Finnish method, the importance of comparative theory does not diminish. My personal feeling, which derived from some successful experimentations, is that this method is a living force like Comparative Literature. We can accept it in that spirit and compare the materials of one language and culture with another or others to arrive at a reasonable conclusion. Comparison is the main and underlying spirit of this theory and its scope is wide as to enfold the materials of the whole world. The comparative analysis in any discipline or branch of knowledge is regarded as the fundamental necessity. Folkloristics, thus, can make a very satisfactory progress by accepting this truth. This was hardly realised by any scholar belonging to the nineteenth century as well as even by a handful of those who devoted their study on the basis of Finnish method during the current century. The more we try to stress upon the truly comparative study of folklore emphasizing the combination of the other approaches of folklore origins (as enumerated in the foregoing pages) with the Finnish method, the more the results will appear to be immensely beneficial.

The following portion entitled "In Search of Indian Archetypes" (only the important ones) is written with an aim to provide a sample of an approach which combines some of the methods enumerated in the foregoing pages in connection with comparative theory and the Finnish method and origin theories. The search for frame study and oicotype of tales, as embodied in the following pages, I hope, will open a new dimension of research in Indian folklore. This part of the chapter has been prepared on the basis of the paper entitled "Frames, Tale-Types And Motifs: Steps Towards the Discovery of Several Important Indian Oicotypes" presented by Dr. Brenda E.F. Beck, Department of Anthropology, The University of British Columbia, Canada, at the Indo-American Seminar on Folklore held at Central Institute of Indian Languages, Mysore, on July 31, 1980. I do not know if the paper has been published in some of her books or not, but I gratefully acknowledge my indebtedness to her. The argument that with the development of synchronic study in folklore, diachronic approach, the historical search and the atomistic classification like type and motif indexes, have become obsolete does not hold good. For, the findings below to sort out the frames of South Indian tales have been established entirely on the basis of Aarne-Thompson's Type and Thomson's Motif Indexes.

IN SEARCH OF INDIAN ARCHETYPES (ONLY THE IMPORTANT ONES)

The term oicotype signifies the pattern of folktale specially popular with a group of people or in a limited geographic region. An Indian oicotype when defined would be almost similar to that of South Asian folk form. But I believe that particularly Indian story-telling patterns actually exist.

Work on oicotypes is still in the primary stages the world over. A few useful findings have recently been made about the specialized North American folktale patterns. Mention of these in brief could help in evolving parallel generalizations about India.

Baughman (1966, introduction) made a comparative outline of traditional Anglo-Saxon and New World story types and concluded that the tall tale form is predominantly American. He expresses that the American "lying tale" built on an exaggerative style is traditionally European but this tendency has been deepened by the physical, intellectual and emotional climate of America. Richard Dorson has further outlined certain traits of a national character which enjoy a vivid expression in American mainstream folklore. Without specifically using the term oicotype, Dorson stresses the importance of optimism in America. He also links this idea to a popular public vision in the US of this country as an earthly paradise. He then links America's western frontier, and the central role of advertising in the national economy, with an important US folk theme which he calls "boosterism". American folklore has the double quality, he argues, of gross exaggeration and of entrepreneurial self-aggrandizement. The boosterism he speaks of, one must note, appears in older stories about self-made frontier heroes as well as in the modern-day salesmanship typical of small town tourism (1980 86-87).

Both Dorson and Baughman stress on the importance of historical experience in deciding the major features of the folktale pattern of a nation. Similarly, in India we should look for themes of folklore that link to prior social experiences of this region. For instance, there are plenty of examples of social, religious and political rivalries in India, and dacoit and robber stories where the frontier spirit may be found. The courageous farmer-warriors who in course of time settled in India's dry, upland areas may also be called frontiersmen. The frontier spirit in the Indian context could be best understood in an ancient tradition of great forests, where kings have searched for magical power and ascetics try to escape from earthly attractions. Rather than boosterism in the American sense, Indian culture has a preference for linking local heroes to great epic figures. Reincarnations of personages as in the *Mahabharata* and *Ramayana* are specially common in local story-telling. There are tale motifs which connect Indian folklore with myths found in standard religious and mythical works (the *Puranas*). Indian oicotype may have retained a mythologizing tendency rather than boosterism. If America's folk patterns are clearly future-oriented (Dundes, 1975, 227), Indian folklore characteristics show a constant faith in linking the past.

These peculiarities in Indian folklore habits presents some significant ideas for study. By establishing oicotypes and thereby comparing similar tale forms across varied social boundaries we may hope to gradually determine what aspects of story-telling are universal and what aspects are specifically expressive of more localized attitudes and values. Once we can identify specific cultural and national oicotypes in folklore, furthermore, we may then hope to study processes. For example, we can try to assess in what ways, and how fast, a tale borrowed from one culture has become transformed to suit its host environment (Dundes, 1975c, p. 33). Similarly, it will then be possible to ask how different social groups each adjust a given story to suit their own special perspective on the human condition (Blackburn, 1978). An identification of oicotypes, then, can make a major contribution to understanding the interplay between local cultures and more universal features of the human mind.

Dundes has recently introduced while discussing oicotypes, a "frame" concept into which many similar stories from a given group or area can be accommodated. A frame is a kind of background of very general cultural attitudes against which the events of an individual story must be viewed if the account is to be properly understood. For example, in discussing East African folk tales, Dundes points out that many of them fall within a "friendship" frame (1975b). That is, two characters in the story form a friendship bond but later that newly-formed trust is somehow misused or betrayed. This frame is larger than a given tale plot, and friendships can be formed between various types of characters in a variety of ways. A friendship can also be broken in many ways. Dundes argues that a concern with the formation of friendship bonds and the display of their ultimate fragility "frame" the many variations and unite them under a single, broad, East African theme.

Thompson's tale type has four similar frames which describe that part of the index catalogued as uniquely Indian. These four Indian frames have been called: (1) the sibling bond, (2) the patron/client bond, (3) the threat of an adversary, and (4) the strength of individual desires. The four perspectives can be defined if one seeks to combine Indian social attitudes with a repeated sorting of specific tale types of Thompson index.

An important aspect like respect and support between siblings is inherent in Indian culture. Their mutual obligations towards one another exist from birth. These bonds of morality can either be retained in the story context, or shattered by undesirable behaviour. Similarly, the hierarchical bond of patron and client is respected in India. Here the senior partner is expected to be protective and giving, while the junior is enjoined to be devoted, helpful and submissive. These relationships, too, can either be upheld by a story or shown as wrongfully broken. In Indian stories, even friendly ties tend to have this hierarchical and complementary quality. But they differ from the sibling ties described by frame one, however, by being basically voluntary in nature.

The third and fourth frames differ from the first two in that neither of the latter takes a particular moral bond as its primary base. The third frame, instead, deals with the idea of an unprovoked attack from some unexpected source. Like the repeated attack of the asuras in Hindu mythology, in frame three a protagonist is forced to protect himself against thieves, demons or from poverty and illnes which are of general nature. Frame three, as in the previous two cases, encompasses both stories that show the protagonist as successful, and those who do not succeed in meeting such a challenge. The fourth frame does not ultimately depend on a protagonist's link with any particular counterpart at all. In the fourth frame, rather, the story's perspective becomes centered on the desires of one person, who sets out to fulfil a wish or obtain a goal, whatever the social context or the practical odds might be. A more general Hindu moral imperative meaning that selfish desires be carefully controlled is revealed through this theme.

Primary social values are upheld by some Indic tales, while others emphasize the fragility of human bonds and the difficulty of attaining an ideal outcome. Indian folk tales can thus be said to balance pessimism with optimism regarding man's ability to live up to his basic social responsibilities. The depiction of East African stories by Dundes sugggests, by contrast, that they favour a bleak view. Most friendships are ultimately broken by deception in Native American Indian tales—another kind of frame. The individual actions in these tales are self-centered and relate more directly to the demands of a spirit-dominated world (1971). The superstructures of friendship are not apparently found in these American Indian tales. This latter culture, unlike India, also tends to show a bleak view. Men consistently violate contracts made with supernatural forces or beings in those tales, whereas in India the protagonist most often works with these spirit beings.

The Aarne-Thompson index of contents, if broken into four large categories, would stand like this: (1) animal tales, (2) oridinary folktales, (3) jokes and anecdotes, and (4) formula tales. This preliminary work on frames choses to study only parts two and three (types numbering 300 to 1999) form the bulk of the material outlined, which contain the richest descriptions. All the stories where the main protagonist is human are fitted in this section where a repetitive sequence of events befall in turn to a number of characters in Indian cumulative tales, which tend to focus on animals and, which except for their special genre form, might well have been included in category one. Once a convincing set of frames for the human stories is established, these remaining animal ones can be quickly understood. This is because stories about animals usually revolve around human ethical issues that become projected into a non-human realm.

Very few of the anthropologists, historians, philosophers and psychologists, who attempted to isolate specific Indian patterns or themes, have approached Indian folklore with this important question in mind. To begain with, the Aarne-Thompson *Tale-Types Index* can be of much help. Its data base consists of roughly 266 published books and papers. Each source re-tells some selected Indian folk tales in English. The translations are of varying quality. Most of the publications referred to in this index, furthermore, rely on older, preindependence ethnographic work. Some volumes date as far back as the nineteenth century. Though several of the collections used are of a high standard, others are poorly done (Islam: 1982). This opens to argument a criticism of the Aarne-Thompson selection of source materials. It is also easy to criticise the tale typologies. Thompson's works have been used here to begin a careful search for the themes which are unique in nature.

In chart one given below, all of the tale types in the Aarne-Thompson index from categories two and three have been isolated (all those that are reported to rest solely on South Asian sources). These selected folk tales, jokes and ancedotes should provide us with a useful first step towards defining a set of India-specific oicotypes. A full listing of these specific tale types, by number and by name, can be found in the appendix. Furthermore, all the optimistic, socially-valued outcomes have been listed on the left, while the relatively pessimistic ones appear to the right. Now each of the four frames outlined before would be taken up in detail (Beck, 1980, 4).

CHART ONE : FOUR STORY FRAMES

(Showing all Aarne-Thompson tale-type numbers lying between 300 and 1999 that have a strictly South-Asian set of sources listed)

The frames	*Tale-type numbers having:* *A successful outcome for the protagonist(s)*	*An unsuccessful outcome for the protagonist(s)*
(1) Sibling bond	450A, 576A, 897	315A, 780A, 923B, 976A, 1633
(2) Patron-client bond	302B, 465D, 516A, 53 A, 535, 546, 622, 670A, 674, 709A, 910H, 939, 949, 978, 11640	875E, 875B$_2$, 875B$_3$, 1532, 1534A, 1692, 1693, 1707
(3) Threat of an adversary	655A, 926A, 934D, 951C, 1152, 1646, 1653E	910J. 1168B, 1525N, 1962A
(4) Action motivated by the strength of individual desire	411, 413, 433C, 459, 467, 516B, 653B, 855, 856, 881A, 888A, 977, 1409C, 1525Q	369, 462, 612A, 896, 926B, 1250B, 1295B*, 1331B*, 1511, 1685A

Frame 1

Two or more brothers' patterns or half-brothers' types, where the brothers go for a series of adventures together appear to be very important and general theme in Indian story-telling. The pattern is apparent as early as the earliest recorded versions of the great *Mahabharata* and *Ramayana* stories, which themselves, as I believe firmly, derived from folk sources. This group of the brothers theme again appears to be particularly linked to Indian epic and adventure stories where male siblings repeatedly face outside challenges together. Two features of common pattern are characteristically Indian, which stand out in contrast to other cultures. For one, Indian brothers regularly appear as a co-operative set. Their aggression, when apparent, seems to be mainly directed against outsiders or relatively more distant kin (agantic cousins and in-laws in particular). Brothers are, in other epic traditions, more commonly placed in situations of direct and aggressive competition (Beck, 1980, p. 1). Besides, according to Thompson's motif index, number A 515.1.2, Sworn Brothers as Culture Heroes, is widely reported from India. So is p 311, Sworn Brethren. The second feature of this folktale frame is that elder/younger interaction patterns are commonly highlighted even when the two are twins (as is fairly common). Then again, in Indian stories a younger brother often becomes king at the end of the tale, while an elder sibling choses to retreat into religious activities.

All of these sibling patterns play a role in the strong Indian tradition of joint inheritance and the accompanying joint management by brothers of family property. They also depict a hierarchical Hindu value framework where religious duty is respectfully associated with the stage of old life. Finally, the same older/younger norms which govern most brotherly interaction merge with a general cultural stress on the hierachical ordering of relationships in general. Tale type 567A, the Magic Bird-Heart and the Separated Brothers, have all of the above features (except the twin element) and also the interesting fact of a lengthy sibling separating is added occasionally to them. In this tale type each brother goes through a specific chain of adventures independently, but the two are eventually reunited after the elder is somehow chosen king. This framework allows for a dramatic sense of brotherly unity in adversity, without giving scope for direct competition. The elder brother eventually yields his political position to the younger, an opportunity that does not exist where the junior sibling wins a kingdom for himself (frame four and the discussion of the Arecanut Princess oicotype may be seen).

In Indian tales the other key dimension of sibling unity involves the rights and obligations that bind brother to sister. Old Hindu tradition usually decrees that women should inherit their share of the wealth as dowry, movable objects, and not as land, which is immovable. Even the brothers are not freed of their sisters by the dowry. They are again expected to support their sisters from common holdings if such a woman should encounter grave hardships during the early years of her marriage or in case she becomes a widow. Sisters, in turn, are seen to offer their services to the family of brothers. It seems likely that this brother/sister support pattern is, compared to North India, particularly a prominent feature of South Indian folk traditions. The comparative role of sisters in folklore, both North and South, may form a very useful subject for research in this light.

Tale-type 450, Little Brother and Little Sister, has no specific entries from South Asia in the Aarne-Thompson index, but several important examples appear in the folklore collections of Dr. Beck (1974, 1980). Most of them describe a cruel sister-in-law who mistreats her husband's younger sister. This type is recorded in the Aarne-Thompson index as number 897, The Orphan Girl and Her Cruel Sisters-in-law. It is supported by thirteen examples from India and none from elsewhere. From the wife's perspective, a sister-in-law provides obvious competition for his affections.

Brenda E.F. Beck's collected stories also describe the key bond between an unmarried sister and her elder brother. Brothers' swords may be blessed by sisters, or they may inspire the brother's heroic endeavours in a general way. In such cases, the sister appears as a magical source of the brother's prosperity, and in return such men are seen to protect their sister in comfort. Tale type 450A, The Brother Transformed To a Snake, presents this idea more clearly. A brother and sister in such a tale are first driven forth together (by a step-mother). The brother then protects his sister by killing a snake. Next the sister finds a flowering tree growing from the snake's body and tries to bless her brother by touching him with its blossoms. But at this moment the brother becomes a snake, though later he is transformed to his normal self. This tale type illustrates well both the principles of reciprocal care and of blessing expected of opposite-sexed siblings. That some special magical bonds exist between them is also revealed in these types.

There seem to be very few stories that significantly stress the third logical sibling bond, that between sisters. Though several sisters may be compared in a story, particularly in regard to their marriage prospects, Indian folktales do not usually focus on mutual obligations between women. This absence is reasonable, of course, in a patrilineal and patrilocal society where sisters go their own way at marriage. It would be interesting to pursue this correlation further by looking at the folklore of matrilineal, or matrilineally influenced areas in India.

The contents of the other half of frame one are folktale types that describe transgressions against these important sibling relations. In one mild tale type, 976A, The Thief Exposed By a Story, one brother steals from a jointly-held hoard of jewels. This dishonest sibling is then later exposed by self-implicating answers to a wise man's questions. The tale types that break social convention by depicting acts of sibling cannibalism give more vivid examples. The Cannibalistic Brothers, or 780A is represented by twelve Indian examples. Here a group of brothers kill and eat their sister after noticing how tasty is the food she has prepared because it contains a drop of blood from her cut finger. Type 315A simply reverses the direction of this sibling-to-silbing aggression by describing The Cannibal Sister. There are five such examples reported, all depicting a princess who became a cannibalistic ogress. After consuming animals, kings, and the inhabitants of a city, she finally turns to her own brother. He is captured but later escapes from her by some clever ruse. The sister finally kills herself.

A strong frame of such sibling obligations was found

countered by an equally strong set of reversals, which appear significant. What could be more horrifying than eating one's own brother or sister? A sex difference is quite noticeable in these several tale types. The brothers actually commit the terrible act of murder. The sisters die in their attempts. This, too, fits a broad Indian pattern: men tend to commit sacrifice by outward aggression in war, in hunting, or even by scarificing animals at temples. Women, on the other hand, most frequently turn violent against themselves, in suicide or other forms of self-torture (Beck, 1980). While the former theme is certainly found in many cultures, female suicide is a noticeably popular Indian motif. All of these reversals, furthermore, play upon two main sibling bond types. Brother/brother cannibalism is reported in stories from Central India (motif G73.2) and brother/sister cannibalism from U.P. (motif G73.1). There is only one example of girls eating a sister, however, and it comes from Mirzapur (motif G73). It would be interesting to ask if this story can be linked to localized matrilineal customs.

The sibling bond framework includes the type in which reversal concerns the aggressive behaviour of a younger child against its elder competitors. In tale type 1633, Joint Ownership of a Cow, an older brother claims the back half of the shared animal and gives his younger mate the front. Thus the elder gets to milk the cow while the younger has to feed it. Here is an obvious exploitation of an age difference and the breaking of contract about equal sharing. It is later countered by a trick that the younger sibling uses to gain a fair portion of the goods. In another example, 923B, The Princess Who Was Responsible for Her Own Fortune, a king asks his several daughters their opinion on who has been responsible for their good fortune. All the elder girls flatter him by saying that he himself is responsible, but the youngest refuses to fall in line and instead claims that she should take credit. Her father punishes her severely for this. However, eventually this daughter gets her revenge through a combination of wit and skill. In the end her husband becomes wealthy and inherits a kingdom. Meanwhile, her father loses his own domain. This could be seen as an example of a parent-child struggle. But the story, viewed overall, clearly singles out only the youngest female as a deviant and a challenger. Hence it seems to be, at least equally, a story about the potential oppression of the weak, by stronger and older family members. The father, for example, marries all his other daughters well, while he gives his youngest to a pauper or a cripple. It is only through the girl's special efforts that this undesirable husband later succeeds. Thus is the rule of sibling equity seen to be transgressed and the youngest member unfairly exploited. This tale type ends with the protagonist's sweet revenge.

Generally, the triumph of the weak and the small is a very important Indian theme. Though it is not uniquely South Asian, this motif does have an important expressive quality in a society where hierarchy is strong and the inferior very often is at a disadvantage. The result is a wide range of stories where a junior partner is seen to succeed against great odds. Three parallel examples from animal motifs are L315.10, Mice Overcomes Camel; L315,11, Lizard Defeats Leopard; and L315.12, Rabbit Slays Rhinoceros. It would be interesting to ask whether the incidence of such themes is greater in areas where social hierarchies are especially rigid or elaborate, and if their incidence decreases in areas where rank ordering is moderate or weak.

Frame 2

The relationships in frame two are more voluntary than kin based. Other aspects of this frame is similar to frame one. Here the key bond lies between two persons having different social positions. The involved characters are thus patron and client, advisor and pupil, or simply two acquaintances of unequal rank. More prevalent are the first two types. As in the interaction of elder with younger siblings, each senior partner is here expected to support and protect, while the junior is asked to aid and to serve loyally.

Three archetypical examples of such mutual bonds of loyalty can be located. A king and his minister, or a prince and a youth of lower rank may be cited as first example. Together the two set out on a series of adventures. During this the junior partner helps and serves his senior all the time. In 516A, The Sign Language of the Princess, for example, a youthful friend helps a prince to win a lovely high-status woman. The Aarne-Thompson index reports twenty stories of this kind which have been indexed in this Aarne-Thompson index. A second sub-type regards a similar relationship between a king or a hero and his friend. The main figure is someone here who is threatened by an outside adversary. This idea is best illustrated by 302B, Hero With Life Dependent on His Sword. In that tale type the rival converts the protagonist's wife. In order to destroy the king's defensive sword, he sends an emissary to steal her. But the friend recovers and restores the heros' weapon. He also rescues the stolen wife and loyally returns her to his patron. A third variant enlists a demand from a god, or the imposition of a curse, either demanding that a hero make the great sacrifice. This theme is illustrated by 949, The Faithful Servitor, where a poor man befriends the protagonist and steps in to offer himself or his children in the king's place. Being pleased by these actions, the gods restore the willing sacrificer to life later on.

The faithful servant theme shows the protagonist as a servant of a god himself; this gives an important variant. The particular god or goddess then "tests" that follower's loyalty directly. A devotee, for example, may be required to wander in poverty, labour at menial tasks, or to sacrifice in other ways for an extended period. At the end of these trials, however, the god or goddess is pleased and the devotee is restored to his former status. This is tale type 939, known as The Offended Deity.

A man is helped by an amoral but rather sociable demon, this is another subtype which seems less common. The two enjoy a covenant similar to that which commonly exists between a devotee and a god, or a king and his loyal minister. That is, the demon serves the man and helps him to obtain personal ends (rescue a tormented wife, seek a fortune, and so on) in exchange for various material rewards or social recognition. The senior member after his ends are accomplished quickly terminates the partnership, unlike ones cited previously. Nonetheless, the parting is amicable and the demon appears satisfied by the fair deal. This is tale type 1164D, The Demon and The Man Join Forces. Nine such examples are found in the collected tales of India.

A partnership between a protagonist and an animal is a final variation in the use of frame two. In 910H, Never Travel Without a Companion or Stay Alert, a man decides to take a crab on a journey. Later, when the man unexpectedly becomes a king, this crab helps him in many ways, including killing several attackers. In another tale type, 465D, or Animal Brothers Help the Hero, the protagonist's special bull helps him fight adversaries. In 535, The Boy Adopted by Tigers, wild animals of various types help a hero survive in the forest, and/or arrange his marriage with a lovely woman. In 534, The Youth Who Tends the Buffalo Herd, buffaloes or cows help the protagonist. In 546, The Clever Parrot, a talking bird wins a princess for the king. Animals also help women under similar conditions. Now, however, the helpful tend to be child-like or small (a calf instead of a bull). Birds are common assistants for women (although they also help men), as in tale types 670A, 674 and 709A. Women are commonly said to understand animals speak, an ability not mentioned about males. In tale type 622, of course, a man listens to an inanimate object (his bedlegs talking). Supports such as squeaking and so on warn him of impending danger or in other ways help him.

Less fortunate outcomes are also covered by the second frame. A relationship is simply exploited in most of them. Here the senior member breaks his contract of protection and nurture. In tale type 1532, The Voice from the Grave, two men connive to get hold of the wealth of a recently buried man. In this crime the lesser partner hides near the grave, while the more effective one goes to the relatives. He tells them of the dead man's major debt. Being convinced, the relatives come to the grave to verify this from the dead man's spirit, and the confederate declares from hiding that the debt must be paid. The partner who calls the relatives absconds with the payment and his hidden confederate loses out. Themes like this also occur in many animal stories. Subordination of the weak, and a relative advantage enjoyed by the strong also comes out in a number of Indian examples catalogued as J420 through J429 in Thompson's motif index. For example, in motif J426.2 the friendship of a snake and a frog ceases when the snake wants to eat the frog. Such stories no doubt reflect the darker realities of any hierarchically structured milieu.

The themes of exploitation are carried to a still more extreme point in many tale-types. The weaker member of the confederation is made a fool in many of them. In tale type 1692, The Stupid Thief, one of a band of robbers is sent into a house while the others wait outside. But there, he is unable to grasp directions accurately (his confederates know he was slow-witted), and is caught. In this and similar tale types such as 1693, The Literal Fool, and 978, Youth in the Land of Cheaters, the person who takes advantage of failure to see behind someone's superficial words or actions, plays a major role. Confederates or patrons as a result either take advantage of this innocence, or make fun of it, or both. Sometimes, as in 1534A, The Innocent Man Chosen to Fit the Stake, a person even of high status, such as a king, is made to appear a fool.

Specifically in tale types 875E, $875B_2$ and $875B_3$, a person giving an order or making a claim is simply embarrassed by someone who makes the claimant see the absurdity of his demand. Some element of initial trust in the words of a respected person is found in all of these reversals. The particular trust then becomes misplaced when those words are either (a) purposely spoken in a way they can easily be misunderstood, or (b) purposely calculated to embarrass and undermine their unsuspecting receiver. Tale type 1707, The Noseless Man, gives excellent example. A man in such a story frame who has lost his nose, persuades others that they too can see God if they chop off their own noses in a similar manner. With trust, the listeners soon perform the painful act, where upon the shrewd advisor laughs at their foolishness. The great importance given to seeing through the superficial is significant in Indian origins." As Hinduism lays great stress on the illusory life of the senses, so Indian folklore makes much of the fool who takes the pretended wise man too literally" (Beck 1980:9).

A t ist of another kind often given to frame two is supplied by situations where a patron comes to unjustly doubt the faithfulness his loyal subordinate. In tale type 178B, The Faithful Dog as Security for a Debt, a master lends his dog to a wealthy creditor to help drive away thieves. The dog serves the creditor well and is finally returned with a letter of thanks. But the master, upon seeing the delegated dog at his door, thinks it has run away from its assignment. Impetuously, the master kills it in anger. Later the man reads the letter of thanks attached to the dog's neck, but it is too late to reverse his actions. Emeneau (Islam 1982:204-7) has linked this to a second well-known story called The Brahman and the Mongoose. There a mongoose is killed for having blood on its mouth when the baby of the house is found missing. In reality the mongoose has killed a snake in a loyal attempt to protect the child (J 05, LXI, 1941:1-17). Several South Indian stories, notably the epic story of *Shilappadikaram*, carry the same idea further by having the person misjudge his subordinate and then die in grief over a similar error by himself.

Frame two finally contains tale type 243, The Parrot Pretends to be God. A contract is broken here by a pet bird demanding respectful service and either (a) decides a lawsuit against its master, or (b) reports an infidelity in the household. Then the owner tries to kill the faithless pet who escapes and has the last joke. The parrot now leads the former master to believe it is a god. When its orders are followed in front of an assembled crowd the parrot uses this opportunity to ridicule its patron. The theme here is again of the literal fool but it is in reversed order where a superior is ridiculed by a subordinate.

Frame 3

Frame three may be found as a contrast with the previous two in that now all normal responsibilities of social actors are suspended. In situations covered by this frame an adversary appears on the scene and a challenge is thrown. No prior social relationships are recognized that might influence the contest. The most noticeable Indian motif or theme in this category is disguise. In a large proportion of the available examples, either the protagonist or the assailant appears in a visible, unexpected form. The protagonist, of course, sometimes uses various deceptive props to trick the adversary instead of dressing in an unexpected fashion himself. Type 951C, The Disguised King Joins the Thieves, may be considered here as a first example. A king, threatened by a group wishing to steal from him, joins with these enemies after putting on a disguise.

Since this king has no formal understanding with that gang, the social contract is not broken by him when he secretly listens to their plans and boasts. He then encourages them to rob his palace and meanwhile skilfully arranges their capture.

It is the enemy who wears the disguise in similar examples. In tale type 926A, for example, a demon challenges the protagonist as to who is the true husband of the victim's wife. A judge cleverly suggests that whoever succeeds in entering a particular pot must be the real spouse. As soon as the demon takes up this challenge, of course, his true nature is revealed and he is caught. A man finds himself challenged by an ogre in a third variant, tale type 1152. To overawe his assailant the clever hero claims that an even bigger ogre resides inside his own house. To prove this, the protagonist pokes objects through his doors and windows. He claims a displaying rope to be a hair from the hidden ogre. A winnowing fan is claimed to be an ear, curds are said to be its spittle, and a beaten drum is said to be sound emanating from the great monster when he beats his chest. The challenger, of course, becomes intimidated when the hero continues in this manner. In one further example, type 655A, four clever men successfully allay suspicions that they have stolen a camel. Here features of cleverness and superficial appearance are again combined. All of the above stories combine what seem to be two key characteristics of a special Indian value pattern: (a) great respect for intelligent or clever solutions to difficult dilemmas, and (b) a great respect given to those who can differentiate appearance from reality.

A reference to the concept of fate is prominently visible in the sub-theme which appears in association with frame three. Fate itself is seen in tale type 934D[1] as an adversary. There the protagonist finds a clever solution to a decree that, though poor, he will always have one bullock. The man goes to sell his bullock each day so that the gods must replace it. Similarly, when the same man learns that his sister is fated to be a prostitute, he advises her to demand a handful of pearls per customer. The god must come in disguise to make the latter decree come true and visits the girl himself, since no ordinary human can afford her price. This fate-wielding god soon tires of these regular duties and agrees to lift the pronouncement of fate.

The concept of sheer luck is also an important theme in Indian folk literature. In type 1646, The Lucky Blow, a man unwittingly knocks off a king's crown. When he finds a poison snake concealed within his headgear, the king believes that the man has saved his life. In this and similar ways, the opposite of clever scheming, luck, is also illustrated in many Indian stories. In 1653E, for example, a fool acquires a fortune by accidentally dropping animal entrails onto a prince seated under the tree he has climbed. The prince is frightened and flees with his followers, leaving behind all his goods. Thus to distinguish the Indian concept of luck from the wider ideas about fate is a difficult proposition.

Inverted outcomes of various nature for stories classified under frame three are also quite common. In 1525N, for example, two thieves attempt to deceive each other. They exchange various things, but repeatedly discover that false claims have been made by both parties. It is a stand off and neither party gains. In a second sub-variant of the same idea, only one party to the contest tries deceit. In tale type 1168B a demon and a man come to an agreement that the latter will pay the former an annual sum. But the demon becomes tired of this arrangement and tries to devour the man without delay. The latter responds by striking the demon with a mallet which severely frightens the adversary. The tale comes to an end with a stand off. Both above endings remind one of the great mythological contests between demons and gods in Hindu tradition. After the churning of the ocean, for example, neither the devas nor the asuras can be declared winners. When it comes to the struggle of evil forces against good ones, therefore, the Hindu perspective would seem to favour balanced outcomes. A series of recurring contests are allowed to extend into the indefinite future.

One more variant of the theme of an unresolved contest is tale type 19622A. A major confrontation is carried on through an infinite regression, so that it becomes inconsequential in the wider view of things. For example, when the great wrestler in this story brags and challenges a skilled opponent, the two find themselves: (a) wrestling on a woman's arm, (b) contesting on a handkerchief, and (c) finally battling in the eye of a princess. Ultimately, she perceives the struggle as a simple speck of dust which momentarily affects her vision. Tale type 910J, Never Plant a Thorn Tree presents picture from another perspective, which is something like the old English proverb "Do not throw stones if you live in a glass house." Probably hoping to keep others off his property, the man who plants the thorn tree ends up catching his own turban on the barbs. Hence, if braggartry and aggression tend to end in stalemate, a reasonable counterstrategy is to avoid inflicting difficulties on others. This philosophy is also reminiscent of a major aspect of Hindu values, the emphasis on pacificism and self-restraint.

Frame 4

The fourth frame differs from frame three by taking the egocentric interests of one protagonist as its main reference point. No matter what outside norms may dictate,'personal interests are to be pursued. All four distinct tale types in the Aarne-Thompson index (413, 467, 516B, and 856), use this frame. The key focus for this frame is a man who seeks after one (or several) exotic women. All together 51 stories are listed under these four tale types. In about half of the cases the protagonist first obtains some sort of a magical object. In the other half he is himself magically transformed, and, using some sort of disguise he gains access to the woman he courts.

In tale type 411, however, there are varied patterns. A king marries a girl who is a snake woman. When the king discovers her true form he becomes frightened and has her burnt to death. But in the ashes is found a magic pebble that can turn anything to gold, indicating that the chosen lady must have been very valuable. This female-snake transformation theme seems to be specially popular in India. The larger concept of an inexorable male quest for magical and beautiful women, however, is something this culture shares with many other areas of the world.

The quest theme has a common variant about several suitors, often four, wooing a woman by different individualised means. Now the question arises, who shall be chosen as groom. The tale type listed as specific to India in this is 653B, The Suitors Restore the Maiden to Life. Its structure resembles a dilemma tale, and is similar to a form Dundes describes as popular in Africa (1971 : 182). The question as to who should marry the girl demands resolution and seems specially suited to societies where local legal cases are debated by village elders, as is the case in rural India. Another variant is 855. The Substitute Bridegroom, in which a bride is whisked away by a man wishing to serve only as a stand-in for the groom at her wedding. She falls in love with the real groom, however, and later manages to identify him from a large group who each tell her a story. In 1525Q a woman who promises to become the wife of the cleverest one is courted by two thieves—they outdo themselves demonstrating their wit. A man is the chooser in tale type, 306A. This time the girl is preselected but insists upon hiding herself amongst others who are similarly clad. These are all variations of the quest theme. They introduce a note of disguise, of cleverness, and of formal or legalistic marital reasoning. If the general story type is not limited to India then, these motifs do point towards specially valued local ways of telling a popular romantic tale.

Since there are so many quest stories involving men who seek after women, then what about the reverse situation where a woman pursues a man? There are fewer Indian tales that can be described this way. But those limited situations where a female seeker is depicted are clearly worth discussion. In one exemplary parallel, 433C, The Serpent Husband and The Jealous Girl, a woman marries a snake who later becomes transformed into a handsome man. This clearly inverts tale type 411 where a man marries a woman who becomes a snake. Both serpent spouses are magical. But the male is frightened of his bride, while the woman is happy with her groom. In the latter tale type, furthermore, another girl is jealous of the first one's good luck. Thus, she tries to marry a snake herself. But it is sad that the woman is bitten and killed for her presumption. Two of the three women in this tangle of motifs, therefore, are killed at the hands of males for their affinities with or attraction to a reptile form. None of the males suffer a similar fate. Women are thus almost as a rule very often depicted as the victims of aggression rather than as aggressors themselves, which has been mentioned before. The snake-human disguise motif appears to be particularly popular in this frame. It can be linked, of course, to a whole channel of motifs in classical Hindu mythology.

The focus on a wife who is faithful to her husband through many adversities is a more common pattern in Indian folk stories. Three tale type classified in this category are 881A, 888A and 977. It could be argued that these perhaps provide elements for a separate frame concerning the social bond between spouses. But the difficulties in adopting this latter perspective are two-fold. For one, there are no male stories existing to illustrate a man's obligations in this partnership. A single tale type, supported by one example only, (1409C) speaks of an obedient husband who followed his wife's instructions and walked home slowly. But, unfortunately, he was thereby too late to find her lover visiting. Here, then, a trusting husband is made to be a fool. More important his wife is clearly acting in her own self-interest, ignoring her side of the marital contract. My argument concerning these faithful wife stories, therefore, is that they are (like the male stories) quite self-centered. If the male quest is described as seeking after beautiful women, then the female one can be labelled "holding onto one's husband." Without a husband there is a great "lack" for Indian women, to use Propp's terminology. A woman's husband is somehow threatened in all the relevant tale types, her secure social position becomes endangered consequently. All the magical techniques women use to revive their husbands from death, free them from the hands of enemies, or re-identify them after a long separation, then, seem to be directed at overcoming this basic problem. If the males in these stories are motivated by desire in the simple sense, then their female counterparts are driven by fear of a social lack of a more formal kind.

In Indian tales women have great anxiety for their husbands which again is extended by a similar concern for their children. The common thread here is the fear of being childless, and of the consequences of being disowned if barrenness continues. The classic example is tale type 459, where a woman goes to the extent of using a doll's image of a child after being turned out of her husband's home for not bearing one naturally. She eventually informs the husband that she has a son whom he must not see. When the time for the child's wedding comes the woman then puts the doll's image in a sedan chair. Seeing this wretched condition of the woman a god pities her and gives the doll life. Afterwards the husband agrees to take his wife back.

A special cultural concern is also linked up with persecuted wives which is specially Indian, such motifs include: S411.2, Wife Banished for Some Small Fault; S411.3, Barren Wife Sent Away; and S416, Queen Banished When She Defeats King in Argument. The fate of the rejected female partner is also vividly portrayed in many stories. Examples of a few motifs are S436, Cast-Off Wife's Head Shaven; S437, Cast-Off Wife Sent to Herd Cows; and S438, Abandoned Queen Blinded. Such typical motif patterns reinforce the conclusion that many tales document female fears about losing a husband.

Brief mention may also be made about tale type 369, The Youth On a Quest for His Lost Father. The search here features a juvenile male who seeks to retrieve a lost parent. This is a "lack" syndrome similar to that described above for females. Ramanujan has pointed out (1971) that South Asian Hindu stories seem to favour inverted Oedipal themes. In tale type 369, for example, a young boy seeks to restore his father to life. This lack theme provides a contrast with the focus on a son killing the father that is found in many Greek and European tales.

Frame four also includes tales which typically show situations where a protagonist is unsuccessful in his or her quest. Tale type 896, The Lecherous Holy Man and the Maiden in a Box provides a good example for males. A beautiful girl spurns the man who loves her. He continues to try in every manner to capture or seduce her, but the girl is finally rescued and the suitor is killed in the process. The major point of difference here, in addition to a negative result for the male seeker, is the totally inappropriate affection that was highlighted in the beginning. Unlike the stories about an unwed prince who sets off to find a queen, a holy man is first and foremost enjoined to be sexually abstinent and devoid of desire. Indian folklore, of course, has much to say about the burning sexual desires of holy men, a contradiction that is prominent as a particularly Indian theme. This idea, too, is one that is widely documented in classical Hindu mythology (O'Flaherty, 1973).

Frame four emphasizes the theme of the fool, another type of male-oriented tales. For example, a dumb man may seek something unattainable (1250B, A Visit to the Sky), and fail through some silly error, or an incompetent son-in-law (1685A) may search for sustenance, even for sexual satisfaction from his mother-in-law. Both of these are highly inappropriate desires so that when the character is unsuccessful, it becomes clear that he was involved in a quest not sanctioned by society. Type 1295B, where a man orders his doorway to be broken down so that he need not dismount from his camel to enter the door belongs to the same category. Though successful in attaining a limited goal, this protagonist makes a public fool of himself in a wider context. Two other minor tale types, 926B also seem to belong to this group.

Tale types as mentioned in frame four are somewhat similar where women are concerned. In 612A an ungrateful wife becomes a prostitute, receives a boon from a king who is happy with her, and then asks that her husband be killed. He cleverly asks her to return what he has given her and ultimately she ends up being murdered. This female variant also contains several of the motifs mentioned above, including inappropriate desires that backfire or remain unfulfilled. A high value is also placed by it on a clever escape from a tight fix. Two other tale types complete the category. They are 1511, The Faithless Queen, who murders her husband but is then spurned by her lover, and 462 where an ogress pursues married men but is finally slain. This last is the sole tale type where a woman pursues a man openly. Such women are ogresses and also operate in the forest. Furthermore, they end up being unsuccessful. This tale type is vital in the sense that there are 24 Indian examples reported. The fact that such ogresses commonly assume the disguise of young girls is not worthy. Men, as opposed to this, do not flaunt their sexual identity when wooing women, but rather try to conceal it.

This completes the findings on the basis of the Aarne-

Thompson folk tale, joke and anecdote types reported uniquely from South Asian sources and their link to the proposed four frames. To make it helpful as a next step one popular folktale has been selected, which is given below, as an example of how the materials in an individual folktale collection can also be usefully studied following this scheme. The story chosen for this illustration is a popular one in southern Karnataka called The Arecanut Princess (Handoo, 1978). This is a fanciful tale which falls easily into frame four, that is, action motivated by the strength of individual desire. The story goes like this :

THE ARECANUT PRINCESS

Once a king had five sons. The elder four were married but the youngest prince did not marry the bride shown to him. Hence he had to search for a wife himself. He departed, hoping to marry the daughter of an arecanut king. On his way, however, he met a saint who blessed him with a magical lemon, a stick, coal and some bits of turmeric. The saint also advised the prince to meet his brother. This the prince did and that second saint also gave him magical agents. He then asked the prince to meet a third brother. This also the prince did. That saint gave the prince some more magical agents and told him to use each one in turn if he got into trouble. This man also advised the prince not to place the arecanut (in which he would find the princess) on the ground, once he had obtained it.

The prince left, crossed seven seas and finally reached the arecaunt king's tree. There the princess lay inside an arecanut. When the prince was about to pluck the nut, a Rakshasa appeared. The prince threw his magical lemon at it. The Rakshasa disappeared. At this point lions, tigers and other monstrous beings also appeared. The prince, out of fear, threw all his magical things at them. But these animals and monsters killed the prince. The third saint then happened to see this dead, half-eaten prince. He brought him back to life, and gave him back his magical things. This time the prince plucked the arecanut and returned. The animals and monsters pursued him, but the prince escaped to a town with the help of his magical objects. Feeling tired, he then put the arecanut on the ground and retired into a fast sleep beside a well. While the prince was asleep, the princess came out of her arecanut. Soon a Kumbara girl came to fetch water and felt jealous of the prince and princess; she then managed to change dress and jewellery with the princess and to push the latter into the well. Then the Kumbara girl assumed the position of the princess and entered the nut. The prince, unaware of this, took her and walked home. Sometime later, however, the prince happened to pass by the same well again. There he saw a beautiful flower. He plucked the flower and gave it to his wife. She recognized it as the real arecanut princess and ordered it thrown into a ditch. A sandalwood tree grew from that blossom. Next she ordered the cutting and burning of that plant. However, the woodcutter hid a piece of the cut tree inside a huge pot at home.

After sometime the woodcutter and his wife saw that the piece of wood had changed into a beautiful maiden whom they adopted as a daughter. Later, the prince went on a hunting expedition and overheard some girls narrating the arecanut princess' story. In this manner the prince finally came to know the truth a bout what had happened. He then buried the Kumbara girl alive, married the real princess, and ascended the throne.

(Adapted from Handoo, 1978, pp. 82-5).

There is a short reference in the first part of this tale to a sibling group, but the action never returns to a comparison between the hero and his siblings. The attempt to connect the saints who is helpful is also a passing one. These examples are suggestive that several frames can be combined in one story. All four are present in this arecanut tale: siblings, adversaries and a quest motivated by individual desire, but then one will be clearly dominant. In this case the prince's quest for a marriageable princess is the central theme, and hence a frame that binds the protagonist's many adventures together.

To be more clear about the unifying effect of the quest theme in this South Indian tale, attention should be given to the second phase of the action. The prince faces and meets challenges of his forest adversaries and finally finds the arecanut he was looking for. He plucks it, but then fails to follow one saint's instructions and allows the nut to lie on the ground while he sleeps. Next a jealous low-caste girl comes along, finds the princess emerging from her nut. The conniving woman arranges to change clothes with the arecanut lady and then pushes the princess into a well. The false impostor crawls into the nut to replace her. The prince wakes up, and unaware of this exchange of identities, takes the false spouse home.

Some suggestive similarities could be encountered here with all four Aarne-Thompson tale types previously discussed that revolve around the lover-seeks-exotic-bird principle. Type 467, The Quest for the Wonderful Flower, may be cited as the closest similar tale since this type is also connected with a male's love quest. The only difference is between flower and arecanut. There is also a hint of tale type 413, Marriage by Stealing Clothing, since this is the way the low-caste impostor manages to make herself the bride. There are overtones in the same way of type 516B, The Abducted Princess, as the arecanut woman is temporarily done away with. We can not also ignore type 856, either, where a youth is driven forth by his father when he expresses that he must marry four wives. Here the hero is driven out when he claims that he would marry only the daughter of an arecanut king. Besides, in the original tale type, the prince with an aim to elope becomes an impostor. The arecanut story provides a simple inversion of this when a female decides to act as an impostor. It seems, in this particular tale, it would be reasonable to speak of a pattern called "Man seeks/wooes one or more beautiful women." Specially the sociological variations on this theme which could be found in the arecanut story include the fact that the seeker gets saints as his patron(s) and his desired spouse has an exotic family heritage (she is daughter of an arecanut). Such a set of circumstances speak for the social setting in which the actions occur. Added to the general frame which interprets the actions of the protagonist in terms of individual determination and desire, these aspects bring us close to have a special Oicotype formulated.

After the exchange of the false and true princess some time the prince passes by the side of the well where the true spouse was thrown in by the false one. The prince is won over by this woman who sees a flower growing from the well. She recognizes this as an embodiment of the real princess. When the prince plucks it, therefore, she orders the prince to throw the flower in a ditch. Then a sandalwood tree grows from the flower. She orders that tree cut down. The woodcutter does not obey and saves a piece of the tree to hide it inside a pot at home. That very wood chip at last becomes transformed into a beautiful young maiden soon adopted by the woodcutter's family. Still later, on a hunting expedition, the prince overhears some girls describing the story of the arecanut princess and mentioning her current whereabouts. The prince understands the truth about what has happened at this point. He then buries his present wife alive, marries the real princess, and ascends a throne.

Thus we get at the end of the tale a happy outcome for the male bride-seeker. His heart's desire is won and his early rebellion against his father becomes justified. It would be an important task at this point to mention some of the vital motifs which are by their character Indic. For example, although saints who give the hero magical tools are not specific to India, it seems quite likely that at least two of the tools they offer him are true Indic cultural markers: the lemon and a piece of turmeric. Similarly, the fact that the maiden is hidden in a series of magical containers: first, an arecanut, then a well, a flower, a sandalwood tree and, finally, a woodcutter's pot, stand out as a possible cultural marker of the Indian subcontinent as well. A series of other important motifs contained in this story are also listed in chart two in the following page (Beck, 1980, 17):

CHART TWO

Frame	*Tale pattern*	*Associated motifs*
Action motivated by the strength of individual desire	Man seeks/wooes one or more beautiful women	Youngest brother becomes king, Saint provides magical tools (lemon, turmeric, etc.)
	(Variations observed in this oicotype)	Maiden is hidden in magical containers (arecanut, well, flower, sandalwood tree, pot)
	(1) Seeker has patron(s)	Saint revives protagonist after his death
	(2) Woman sought has an exotic ancestry	Exchange of indentities: False and true spouse; Burial alive, Discovery of truth through listening to a story

It is unfortunate that the concept of motif markers in relation to the social context has not yet been adequately defined. Thompson suggests that a motif is the smallest element in a tale having the power to persist in tradition (Dundes 1975a, 63). Baughman has further called the motif "a phenomenon, a characteristic, a power, a happening, a creature, or an object" (1976: introduction). In my opinion, motif is a vital element of the tale that gives the theme a complete shape as the flowers joined together makes a garland, the motifs likewise, joined to each other in an orderly manner, make the whole story. According to Beck, "a motif is a relatively simple and concrete story element. In this sense motifs are culture-markers since they indicate specific habits, customs and settings. When motifs are described in a detailed fashion (a donor saint gives a piece of turmeric to a protagonist and calls it a magical object) they may be identifiable as culture specific. For many purposes, however, it seems more useful to speak about the cultural popularity of a motif rather than about its local uniqueness" (1980, 18). An appendix to this paper provides a list of the most extensively indexed South Asian motifs, to date. This list ranges from motif N 451 (secrets overheard from animal conversation), which has been noticed in roughly thirty different sources, to T 511.1 (conception from eating fruit) which appears in about fifteen indexed accounts. None of the 142 motifs included in this list could be called unique to India. But their special popularity in South Asia does add an important dimension to the oicotype concept.

A frame is a general value context upon which a large number of folk tales, jokes and anecdotes draw for significance. A frame adds meaning to a story and enables it to have some bearing upon our understanding of the human condition in general and in relation to his culture in particular. Frames vary significantly from culture-area to culture-area—as shown in the foregoing pages. Indian materials vary in so many respects with those provided by Dundes, Dorson, and Baughman from other areas of the world. Yet without a reference to specific tale patterns and motifs, a given frame remains too abstract to constitute an oicotype by itself. In order to build up culture and group-specific themes, we have to flesh out a set of general frames by connecting them to more specific descriptors. The table patterns for this purpose are important as indicators of particular social settings and social interaction structures.

"Tale types serve as sub-units within more general tale patterns by focussing on typical action sequences. And motifs provide the concrete and culture-rich details that add local colour to a given account. In order to define specific oicotypes successfully, we must search for an association of specific frames with specific tale patterns, tale types and motif clusters" (Beck 1980, 18). Chart two, which describes the tale of the arecanut princess, approaches an oicotype. It could be fleshed out further by discussing other variants.

Chart number three attempts to provide a rough outline of a number of other South Asian oicotypes. This table summarizes the discussion of four basic frames presented in the foregoing pages. In that table each tale pattern can be considered a separate, nascent oicotype, but only in relation to a more general frame (on the left) and a cluster of specific motifs (on the right). Each of these patterns needs to be explored individually, and in depth. The arecanut story, for example, helped fill out our understanding of one of the tale patterns contained by frame four./ The motifs culled from that example, however, greatly expand upon the list provided in this summary chart. Only the first four motifs in this cluster seem to bear a relation to the so-called arecanut oicotype. After having this work done, I feel that there remain many things to be done in this line and further research needs to be directed in linking motifs with specific tale patterns and frames. The appendix at the end of this chapter on popular motifs in the Thompson-Balys index should be helpful in this task.

CHART THREE

A summary of Aarne-Thompson folktale, joke and anecdote reported solely from South Asia (Beck, 1980, 19)

Frames	*Tale patterns*	*Motifs*
1) Sibling bond	A set of brothers A special devotion expressed between brother and sister A weak or disadvantaged junior sibllng tries harder	Younger brother becomes king, elder chooses retreat Mistreatment of husband's sister by his wife A sister blesses her brother or there are other magical interchanges Siblings steal from each other Sibling cannibalism Women kill themselves, men succeed in killing others Triumph of the weak or small elders
2) Patron-client bond	A loyalty between king and minister or prince and his friend who : a) set out on adventures	Deity tries a person's loyalty and eventually rewards him Woman helped by birds or youthful small animals
	b) are challenged by an adversary	Women understand animal speech

	c) must meet demands from a god or deal with a course	A person is made a fool because he cannot see truth behind superficial signs or a literal wording
	A loyalty between a person and some supernatural being or animal	A senior unjustly castigates or murders a loyal subordinate
	A partnership is exploited by its senior member	
	Roles of a junior and senior partner get reversed	
3) Threat of an adversary	A king contests	Great value placed on intelligent or resourceful solution
	a) with thieves	Great value placed on seeing through superficial appearances
	b) with a demon	A contest is unresolved and ends in a balance
	c) with fate	A confrontation ends in an infinite regression to inconsequentiality
	A man gains benefits by sheer luck	
4) Action motivated by strength of individual desire	A man seeks/wooes one or more beautiful women	Attempted seduction by stealing a woman's clothing
	Several suitors woo one woman and she must choose	Use of disguise, clevernees, and formalistic reasoning in matters pertaining to weddings
	A wife is faithful to and attempts to preserve her husband despite adversity	Description of the cast-off, persecuted or barren wife
	A woman goes to great lengths to obtain a child	A female-snake (or male snake) transformation occurs
	Child seeks a parent, especially the son seeks a father	An ogress pursues a man in a forest
	A person seeks something inappropriate and fails to obtain it	A holy man is full of sexual desire

> Some of the more interesting questions that can be asked using this chart concern the variable popularity of various frames, tale patterns and motifs by South Asian region and social group. Might the sibling bond frame, for example, be particularly prominent in Dravidian (and perhaps tribal) areas ? Might the patron-client frame be particularly popular with peasant groups? And will variations by social class relate to differing degrees of emphasis placed on intelligent or resourceful dilemma solutions? Linking popular patterns to particular areas and groups will also help us to see much further into the social norms, mores and ideals of the varied types of people who make up the South Asian culture area (Beck, 1980, 20).

And finally, there is the question of genres. I have dealt only with ordinary folk tales, jokes and anecdotes. Now animal stories need to be studied for parallels and for differences with tales told about human actors. And what about myths? Can mythical material be fitted into these same frames? It is difficult to answer these questions on myth.

> Myths tend to blend into each other more than stories do, so that discrete beginning and end points are hard to recognize. Weaker action sequences and stronger motif patterns, furthermore, seem to characterize the myth genre. Furthermore, myths tend to focus heavily on nuclear family bonds, and particularly on parent-child or husband-wife interaction patterns (Beck, 1980, 20).

National folklore theory

Folklore has been used to focus the national spirit in many countries since the last half of the nineteenth century. But in Nazi Germany this approach assumed such an aggressive role that Professor Dorson called it an 'evil theory'. He remarked, "With powerful aggressive nations folklore has proved to be a formidable and diabolic weapon of propaganda and hence in our consideration of theory, we must recognize the existence and pursuasiveness of evil theory". ("Current Folklore Theories," *Current Anthropology*, 1963, Vol, IV, p. 96). This is of course true. But in most of the countries of the world, this methodology of judging folklore on national perspective has produced good results. In Latin American countries the Indian culture, specially the dance, music, tales and customs form a living part of national folk traditions even today. Japan's Shintoism and Sweden's rural-based culture are still glorified as their national assets by the folklorists of the two countries. After the October Revolution in the Soviet Union, gradually folklore became an important subject for consideration by the scholars and much light has been thrown since then to evaluate folklore as the main weapon of protest by the have-nots. Folklore is not only an echo of the past—it is also a forceful voice of the present and a feeling of class-conflict is always reflected in folklore. Thus in Socialist Russia the national theory drew most of its strength from sociological thought. Contrary to this, the U.S. scholars eulogize the folk-heroes of their own like Paul Banian, Peks Bill, Stormolang and others, as the products of their national vigour reflecting their show of strengh. Unlike their European colleagues, they consider oral tradition as most trustworthy, failing to recognize its value as a record of social thought. Their theory, as Dorson puts it, focuses on the role played by traditional lore within the development of U.S. civilization and is a nationalist theory only in this sense. American folklore has mostly migrated from Europe and Africa. Folklore of the land belongs to American Indians. The search for U.S. national identity in folklore is thus mainly spear headed in these three directions involving the comparative method in the tracing of new world tradition to the old. The nationalist folklorists in the US, of course, greatly value the folklore originated in the US during the last two centuries and the concept of acculturation and function dominates their findings. In Hungary it is commonly believed that the preservation of national identity lay in an extensive evaluation of folklore. A new channel in the Hungarian folklore study was opened up in the later part of the nineteenth century when more and more traditional materials were discovered. This is true about Egypt. The rise of Nasser buried the kingship in Egypt and a new nationalistic fervour was aroused everywhere. Egyptian folklore provided a flood of inspiration to the folklorists as well as scholars of other disciplines to establish the glorious traditions of Egpyt in the Arab world. Their proud assertion that they are Arabs first and then Muslims, was mainly taken from the teachings enshrined in the spirit of their folklore.

Germany

Hitler's National Socialist Government pioneered in Europe in capitalizing the elements of folklore politically. Under the direction of his government the scholars were engaged in collections, documentations and publications. All that the scholars were obliged to do was to focus the national glory through folklore, the cultural superiority of the German nation over others, so that the cultural domination may call for the political domination of fascists. The folks, who were since long considered as having a sub-culture tradition, became the real nation overnight. Hans Naumann's peculiar concept that folklore found its origin in the intellegentsia and passed to the folks (*Grundzuge der Deutchen Volkshunde*, 1922, Berlin), provided a new impetus, and a modified edition of his book had to be published in 1929. The outstanding German scholars like Grimm, Mannhardt, Kohler and Bolte were not remembered, while Riechl, who professed folklore as a science and pleaded for the concentration of social science on things German (1858, 23-37), received wide appreciation. During the later part of the 1920s folklore was introduced in the universities as an important subject under social science. Hitler regarded the folk philosophy as the central point of his political thought (Shirer, 1962 : 130). When an *Arbeitsgemeinschiaft fur Deutsche Volkskunde* was organized in 1937, its founders included Alfred Rosenberg, a philosopher of the Nazi revolution, Walter Darre, Hitler's Minister of Agriculture, Baldur von Schirach, leader of Hitler's Youth Movement and even Heinrich Himmler, Hitler's Propaganda Minister (W. Hand, 1946). Folklore was not only patronized by the establishment, but was endowed with political meaning.

Russia

The Communists, because of their ideological orientation, became increasingly interested in the collection, preservation and study of folklore. During the later-half of the nineteenth century, A.F. Hilferding, made some valuable collections from North Russia. He was one of the pioneer scholars to emphasize on the detailed information of the informants. Besides, the Russian byliny was first detected by him from his own collections. Gradually after the October Revolution, the scholars began concentrating their attention to develop an independent, mode of thought in the study of folklore and come out of the conceptual fold so long moulded by the western scholars. Thus V. Propp replaced the western formalism by structural study of folklore (1926), Andreyev denounced the Finnish method, and Sokolov and Zhurminsky condemned Naumann's view as vulgar sociology. Sokolov emphatically declared that the Soviet folklore provides a meaningful contrast between folklore of the prerevolution era and of the period following 1917. Amongst many of his findings, two certainly deserve appreciation from the folklorists: one, folklore is an echo of the past, but at he same time it is also the vigorous voice of the present; two, folklore has been, and continues to be, a reflection and weapon of class conflict.

Scholars like Azadovski, Baranov, Gusev, Afanasiev and many others enthusiastically maintained that their folklore was their proud heritage and a national consciousness was always vividly reflected in them. Some modern Russian historians, such as M.D. Priselkov, tried to discover, by a violent interpretation of sources, the traces of the mighty anti-Greek current within the Kievan church and folklore clinging to it. These constructions, reflecting modern trends of mind, have some social and historical facts in the form of protest. After the October Revolution, proverbs such as:

> By birth a landlord, by deeds a Jew
>
> or
>
> Trust not the landlord until he is in the coffin
>
> (*National Proverbs*, Russia, 1913, 6, 7)

occupied the foremost position in the discussion of the balladists. Even pure folk rhymes were composed and dedicated to Lenin's memory:

Sleep little babe, sleep my pretty one
Sleep pretty babe of mine.
The moon looks sweetly, down on there;
Sleep my little babe, sleep
The moon shines softly down
Into thy mausoleum.

(Published from anonymous collection,
Pravda of Youth, January, 1929)

The Soviet methods of government since the October Revolution are fully in keeping with the people's life and living conditions. The post-revolution folklorists and historians feel that this was not the case with the pre-revolutionary rulers. An art critic thus argues: "The development of the capitalist relations in the Russian countryside during the second half of the 19th century struck most cruelly at folk art. Folk handicraft masters could not compete with factory industry and their art rapidly waned. Realizing the artistic value of the rich folk traditions that had been built up through the centuries, progressive Russian intellectuals and members of the public at large made attempts to revive these arts, attempts that proved fruitless prior to the Revolution." (J. Katzer. 1959:6-7)

Most of the scholars since 1917 are nationalists and their approach is eminently historical. Thev echo the same voice that it was only with the advent of Soviet power and the general advance of socialist culture that new conditions arose for the development of folklore. The flourishing of folklore as well as its study is inseparably connected with the October Revolution and since then with nationalism.

Japan

Japan, as an industrially and technologically advanced nation, turned to folklore with careful attention to both collection and study. In the beginning of the present century, Professor Kumio Yanagita's effort to study folklore gradually received wide appreciations. Later on he established the Institute of Folklore to train young scholars in his own way. Since then Japan's folklore has been taken by scholars as the treasure of heritage and culture. As a result, folkloristics developed in this country without much of paternistic approach and theoretical orientation. During the last few decades, of course, folklorists have shown their profound interest in developing the study of folklore on scientific lines. Massive collections of mountain folklore as well as folklore of the plains, towns, cities and villages have been done. Influenced greatly by Yanagita (1954-58), the Japanese folklorists still tend to pursue their findings on the consideration of folklore as historical science professed by English scholar Gomme, who maintained that past periods of history could be reconstructed from the surviving fragments of folk beliefs and customs. Although Japan's progress in the study of folklore on anthropological, linguistic, sociological, and psychological approaches cannot in any way be undermined, her contributions to historical and nationalistic evaluation of folklore is greater. Japanese folklorists seemed to have shown little adherence to the Finnish method, though their historical consciousness is strong, because of the fact that their folklore did not have much occasion to travel world-wide like Indian and European folklore. Dorson observes,

> Wanderings and migrations play no part in the reconstruction, for the evolution of Japan's folk and cultural institutions has taken place within the island confines of a stationary and insular people. Instead of accumulating and analysing a great many variants, the Japanese folklorist employs the single example which will point back to an earlier usage. (1963, 78).

Thus the old tradition of double-grave system was comfortably chosen by some to prove their faith in past identity. Ishida, who calls himself a comparative ethnologist, analysed the Kappa tradition of Japan and its parallel appearance from Asiatic and European Cultures (1950). *Minkon shinko,* which means a folk religion, is still prevalent in the remote villages and this became an interesting topic of research to many. Most of the monographs on folklore prepared by Japanese scholars include the deities of the rice fields, the fishing grounds and the household hearth, the taboos of various kinds, purification rites, functions of the priests of village-shrines, relationship of the spirit which inhabits everybody to Kami and many other rituals and their functions. Even the narrative tradition reflect *minkon shinko,* for the local legends so abundant in Japan revolve around the village shrine (Hori, 1959).

Dorson rightly assesses Japan's nationalistic spirit in folklore study :

> The development of interest in Japanese folklore has run parallel with rising curve of aggressive nationalism. When the flag of the Rising Sun was born into South East Asia by bombers and carriers, the folklore scholars of Japan has solidly established their field inquiry into the household supernaturalism of the Japanese villagers. The nationalistic and unilitaristic policies which produced the kamikaze pilots of the second world war, capitalized on an ancient folk tradition. Not only will the spirit of the dead enjoy happiness from the offerings at his shrine, but the anger of the deceased warrior will reck vengeance on his enemies.

India and the subcontinent

At the time of her independence in 1947, India was partitioned into two sovereign countries, India and Pakistan. Then again in 1971 the then eastern part of Pakistan declared independence and came into being as a sovereign country named Bangladesh. Although the three countries are now different, all of them inherit the great cultural heritage of India which may be called as Indic. The study of folklore, which is an important part of culture, reveals this truth more vividly than anything else. There is a close bond of tie between the folklore of India and the other two countries; it is the product of purely Indic culture—the creation of one people and his civilization.

The state of affairs in the field of folkloristics on the Indian subcontinent does not present a satisfactory picture. During British rule, some of the European scholars like Mary Frere, Maive Stokes, George Grierson, R.C. Temple, Charls Swynnerton, William Crooke, P.O. Bodding, Hinton Knowles, William McCullock, Verrier Elwin, Thomas Hodson, J.H.

Hutton, J.P. Mills, H. Risley, Charls Kinkaid, John Shakespeare, William Rivers, Edward Dalton made a commendable study of Indic folklore (Details are given, Islam, 1982). Some Indian scholars like Lal Bihari Dey, Shovona Devi, Upreti Ganga Datta collected and published some materials in English. Most of these scholars concentrated on understanding India through her vast materials of folklore. Mostly, they played the role of collectors and whatever scholarship they had under their command was directed towards a purposeful approach of enlightening themselves as well as the western world about their richest harvest. Thus, in a sense, their endeavour partially served the purpose of Indian nationalism.

After independencc the condition in all the three countries did not improve qualitatively, though quantitatively a change could be felt. Some individual works published in Indian languages by authoritative field workers, some of these scholars, like Ashutosh Bhattacharya, Nirmalendu Bhowmik, Subhash Banerjee, Dulal Chaudhury, Barun Chakravorty, Shankar Sengupta (Bengali); Durga Bhagavat, R.C. Dhere, Pravakar Mande (Marathi); Ramnaresh Tripathi, Devendra Satyarthi (Hindi); Krishnadeva Upadhyaya, Udainarayan Tiwari (Bhojpuri); Ramikbal Singh Rakesh (Maithili); Induprakash Pandey (Awadhi); Satyendra (Brajbhasha); Motilal Menaria, Narottomdas Swami (Rajasthani); Shyam Parmar (Malvi); Jhavarchand Mcghani, Madhukar Randaria (Gujrati); Amrita Pritam (Punjabi): Sivaram Karanth, G. Ramaswami Iyengar (Kannada); Mallikarjun Rao, Rama Rajan (Telugu); Kunjabehari Das (Oriya); Agasthialingam Pillai (Tamil); Prafulladutta Goswami (Assamese); Irom Babu Singh (Manipuri), J. Handoo (Kashmiri), may be mentioned as valuable contributors to the study of folklore, more in respect of collection than scientific and theoretical orientation. Almost all are imbued with the feeling of national pride and cultural brilliance, as one openly says, "The study of folkliterature of Bengal is a movement which requires to be carefully studied for it may exert a healthy influence on the national character." (Sankar Sen Gupta 1967, 91). The same author, almost in the same breath, remarks, "No doubt many things began to change with the dawn of independence. A sense of national pride in our ancient history, literature and culture gradually arose. An irresistible desire was felt for an Indian renaissance and for a revival of the past glories" (1967, 91). This author echoes the voice of folklorists not only of India, but of present Bangladesh and Pakistan as well. This is more specially true in cases of the latter two for the administrations in both these countries are occasionally and mostly taken over and handled by the military dictators, sometimes stabilizing themselves over a decade, who consider folklore as the best means and media to divert people's attention from democracy to religious nationalism and fanatic idealism. Besides being dynamic, folklore, in the hands of military dictators could be diabolical, a dangerous weapon for fascism and militarism.

Expectations from the folklorists of the Indian subcontinent are reasonably greater because of India's almost unique position in respect of the richness as well as complicated characteristics of her folklore. India's long and steady historical past, great diversity of ethnic and linguistic groups, inherent unity in cultural diversity, consistently coherent nature of her vast folklore, attracted the West in various ways. "Western scholars have long realized that India is very rich in myths and folktales. During the second half of the nineteenth century, they were continuously involved in arguments and counter-arguments over the richness of Indian culture, specially of Indian folklore. European scholars focusing their attention on India propounded such conflicting views as Indianist theory of folktale origins (Stith Thompson, 1951 : 375-388), the solar theory of myth origin (Dorson, 1955 : 393-416) and the linguistic theory postulating an Indo-European parent speech as the origin of most Western, Asian and European languages. These theories, once espoused so enthusiastically, have subsided, lost their followers, and left as their solid contribution only the widely accepted fact that although India is not the only source of international folktales and myths, her contribution in originating folktales and myths is undoubtedly considerable" (Islam : 1982 : I).

Dundes voiced this expectation from purely modern folkloristic point of view and hoped that the Indian scholars in the world would rise to the occasion and take the leadership: "India is such a rich storehouse of living folklore that its folklorists should be the best of the world so as to take advantage of such extraordinary traditional treasures. The opportunities of folklore research in India are unequailed anywhere in the world." (Sankar Sen Gupta, 1967 : 17). How best they could be and in what manner? "Traditional treasures", as most of them feel, "must be utilized for national integration and uplift of society" and "the study of folklore developed on national line." (Sankar Sen Gupta, 1967, 17, 23).

At least to the scholars of the Indian subcontinent, I hope I do not need to elaborate further what a national folklore theory is.

United States of America

Most of the American scholars dealing with folklore seem to have a more rational approach towards national theory. They have demonstrated diversified attitudes to their own folklore. This encouraged some American scholars to determine a separate theory under the heading "A Theory of American Folklore" (Dorson 1959, 1960, Jack Phillip 1960). While American historians are mostly found to be distrustful of folk materials, the conservative folklore-collectors and folklorists do not seriously depend on the history and institution of American civilization. This gap of understanding forms a basic drawback of American nationalistic study of folklore. Gradually, of course, a team of folklorists grew who have turned their attention to the interpretation of folklore on the basis of American civilization and culture and to locate the national identity through folklore. The scholars like Stith Thompson and Warren E. Roberts made historic-geographic studies of tales focussing on the tradition of the new world, Dorson viewed American folklore through the scientific approach befitting a true historian, the anthropologists like Boas, Malinowski, Benedicts, Herskovits, Bascom and many others highlighted the functional aspects of American folklore and the folklorists like Dundes, Mahr, Strassburger and many others concerned themselves in the analysis of American culture in the true sense of the term. The American culture has two clear directions, sometimes opposed to each other—the culture of the soil and the culture transplanted from Europe and Africa. The American folklore combines in it the three distinctive features which form the basis of the nationalistic study of folklore. Technologically and scientifically advanced U.S.A. cannot deny the existence of American Indian as well as the Negro folklore on the one hand, and the migrant folklore from all parts of Europe on the other. Their national approach is thus different from that of an Indian or a German or a French scholar—their responsibility to the complex problem is far greater, their task is far more difficult. Those who began to take interest in the study of folklore during the twenties and thirties of the present century, like poet Sandburg (1927), Alan Lomax (1944), B. A. Botkins (1944), did not realize this basic truth and endeavoured to glorify the American heritage borrowed from Europe. These scholars, basically known as collectors, and many of their contemporary folklorists were enthusiastically engaged in depicting the folk heroes like Paul Banian, Pecks Bill, Stormalang, Joe Magares and others to prove that these heroes are the proud products of the USA and they can be set against the European heroes like Titan, Samson, Hercules and others. It is only after the second world war that the scholars became conscious of the plurality of their culture and a solid basis of their search for truly American identity through the study of three distinct sources of folklore was identified. Norman Brown, M. Bloomfield, Child, Kittrege, Taylor and a few others dedicated themselves to the rational and pragmatic study of folklore. The national theory thus gradually developed in the USA is not based on a blind and narrow emotional attachment to nationalism—most of the scholars studying folklore on this perspective, founded their arguments with a broad outlook and a comparative spirit of realization. Their theory, according to Dorson, focuses on the role played by traditional lore within the development of US civilization and is a nationalist theory only in this sense. It involves the comparative method in the tracing of new world tradition to the old and the anthropological theory in using the concepts of acculturation and function. Unlike the deep-rooted folkculture of the old world, a major portion of folklore in the US is transplanted or newly sown. Hence, such major forces in American history as immigration, the westward movement, Negro slavery and industrialization determine the framework within which folklore in the US functions and changes. A comparative folklorist gathers his tale, tests whenever he finds them, in Europe, Occanic, North America and seeks to reconstruct their wanderings. The US folklorists considering, say, the Italian belief in the evil eye, fastens his attention on the adoption of the Italian belief to its new world environment as a facet of the larger problem of immigrant acculturation (Williams, 1938).

Hungary

In Hungary folklore provided the source of inspiration to all the poets since the middle of the nineteenth century. Pitofi himself collected the songs and searched in them the glory of the past, Jokai arranged to collect folkstories and jokes to highlight the traditional brilliance of Hungary, Tompa used folk legends for his subjects, Arany engaged his children to collect fairy tales to focus the bright Hungarian heritage of story-telling. The fashion of interest in the nineteenth century was mainly restricted to collections and emotional interpretations. After the end of the first world war a genuine impulse to establish the Hungarian national culture, the culture of the people, began to grow stronger. The Folklore Fellows of the Ethnographical Society, since 1920, published a series of booklets to develop the interest in the study of folklore in a methodical and scientific order. The scholar of an international reputation like Gyula Ortutay and his followers took an active interest in the theoretical orientation which formed a solid ground for folklore study in Hungary. At the time when the nation observed the hundredth anniversary of the Hungarian war of liberation in 1949, a drive for folklore collection was made and about fifty-thousand items were collected. Between the two world wars and during the period subsequent to the liberation of the people of Hungary (1955), apart from scientific development of folklore study, many Hungarian scholars turned towards nationalism in the line of Marxist-Leninist ideology. They feel that the study of folklore must be benefitted from the guidance of the party. "It goes without saying that in the course of the building up of the socialism, the cultural evolution of our people and the bringing about of a culture, national in appearance and socialist in essence, ethnography and folklore will have important tasks to perform" (Ortutay, 1955, 76-77).

Examples could be cited from more countries. In the countries of the Indian subcontinent folklorists have been since the twenties of the current century evaluating folklore from the nationalistic point of view and still now this method of eulogizing the national heritage through the mirror of folklore occupies a prominent position in the folklore study of the subcontinent. What is lacking here is not the spirit or the emotion, but the fact-based analysis and a rational approach. Judgement of folklore, even from nationalistic point of view, requires the necessary notes and annotations, comparative evaluation and a scientific interpretation. Without having these aspects established, emotional outbursts or raising a hollow uproar will simply continue to prove our chauvinism, not scholarship.

Anthropological theory

Through the contributions of anthropologists like Boas, Malinowski, Ruth Benedict, Parsons, Jacobs, Herskovits, Bascom Katherine Luomala, Levi-Strauss, Messenger and many others the study of folklore has been enriched with a new approach and a trend which has been accepted by folklorists as a theory. Boas's concept of transmission of tale incidents by diffusion from tribe to contiguous tribe at points of culture contact, Benedict's concept of the release of the suppressed tension of the society as manifest in the oral literature, Malinowski's concept of psychological reflection of the primitive man in their myths, Bascom's concept of functionalism in folklore, are, in spite of having some scope for disagreement, the proud possessions of folkloristics. The anthropologists seek for the content, context, function and the style of folklore in their studies and their interpretations of these aspects have revealed some home-truths hitherto unknown to many folklorists. Besides, some of them have arrived at a technique resembling that of the comparative folklorists. The theory of structural analysis is another domain of folklore study where the contributions of antropologists are no less important than the folklorists.

Anthropological theory of folklore is greatly indebted to Boas. Tales are always helpful to formulate the ethnographic study of the tribal community and Boas was one of the pioneers who established this truth through the study of tribal tales. He found in them the missing link of tribal history. The concept of transmission of tale and tale incidents by diffusion from tribe to contiguous tribe at points of culture contact, a theory Boas was able to establish with very impressive evidences (Boas, 1981). He avoided the attempt to find out the archetype or urform of a tale, as was developed later by the Finnish method, as he felt that the lack of evidence in dating the tales is one of the main hindrances in the research of historic-geographic location of a tale. His main focus was thus concentrated on the dissemination process. Melville Jacobs' main objection to Boas was that his findings were never concerned with the analysis of style, social values, humour, ethics and the world view of the tribe he worked with. His Tsimshian mythology failed to tabulate the frequencies of occurrences of traits in tales and hence his major work hardly provides any information of the stress given on these traits of the tales and the lack of emphasis on such traits. The contextual study of the tales collected by Boas is thus virtually impossible because of this deficiency. Besides, Jacobs feels that Boas followed mostly the conventional folklore categories of characters, themes and incidents which permitted no search into the latent meanings of the narratives. He and many of his followers collected tales possibly directing no questions at informants or the tellers which would illuminate features of content and concealed values of the tales (Jacobs, 1959 b, 1959 c).

Benedict (1935), a close follower of Boas, established the concept that the suppressed tension in the society is released and expressed in the tales. She recognized that "tales tally with and yet do not tally with the culture". The motif like abandonment of babies is very common in the tales of the Zuni tribe, though it has no relevance to Zuni culture. According to Benedict, the children's resentment against their parents is the convert theme. The tales constitute a fantasy world constructed from the cultural realities. If the taboo against one's mother-in-law did not exist in Plains Indians' culture, its violation by Coyote would not create laughter. Benedict holds style as well as content as equally important, calling attention to the creative artistry of individual narrators —the co-existence of multiple variants of which some are far more elaborate than others. The style of an individual differs from the tribal. Hence, as a prerequisite to the development of any theory, Benedict suggests, the folklorist or anthropologist must possess an intimate knowledge of a given culture and a full record of its tradition.

The cultural anthropologists consider folklore as the component of culture only upto the extent of literature in the oral form. The materials such as folk beliefs, magic, demonology, which are considered by the folklorists as the important parts of folklore, are regarded by the anthropologists as parts of the vital belief and system of the culture. To avoid ambiguity, Bascom suggested the word verbal art to replace folklore. According to Bascom, folklore is studied in anthropology because it is a part of culture. It is a part of man's learned traditions and customs, a part of his social heritage. While Benedict explains some of the discrepancies between Zuni folklore and custom in terms of cultural lag, Bascom calls attention to the functional role of folklore. Legal decisions are taken with the help of proverbs, riddles sharpen wits, myths validate conduct, satirical songs release part of hostilities. These aspects demand the search for context along with the text. The anthropologists have come to the conclusion that the search for the ultimate origins, whether by means of the cultural evolutionist approach or the age-area concept is a hopeless one where historical documents and archaeological evidence are lacking (the age-area concept in very simple terms is the notion that the wider the distribution of a culture trait, the older the trait may be. The principle is employed by practitioners of the so-called Finnish method of studying folklore although the principle is not specifically termed the age-area hypothesis (Dundes, 1965: 30). In folklore, where archaeology can be of almost no help at all, and where documentation does not yield the answers directly, attempts to reconstruct history using even a wide variety of folklore data, can yield results only in terms of probability rather than proven fact. Thus, the anthropologists have not though completely abandoned the subject of distribution of specific tales, but they have been receiving the questions of diffusion and possible origins with less and less attention and are approaching it with increasing caution. On the other hand, anthropologists are turning to other problems which are now felt to be of equal or greater importance, and more susceptible to study. In line with this, Bascom draws our attention to the creative role of the narrator and cites an example from Cushing, who told the Italian tale The Cock and the Mouse to a Zuni informant and collected the same from the same informant a year later. The comparison of the Italian and Zuni variants spotlights many Zuni stylistic features and serves not only to show what transformation the original underwent in such a brief period, and how well it has been adapted to Zuni environment and mode of thought, but also to give a glimpse of the Indian method of folktale-making. Here one can approach the dynamics of folklore on the solid basis of known and recorded fact rather than inference, probability or speculation. (Cushing, 1931, 411-22).

Anthropologists are also interested in finding the place of folklore in the daily round of life, in its social settings and in the attitudes of native peoples toward their own folklore. One cannot determine these facts from the texts of tales alone, nor whether a tale is regarded as historical fact or as fiction, yet without them one can only speculate as to the nature of folklore and its full meaning.

The functions of folklore are important aspects which drew the serious attention of the anthropologists more than that of folklorists. Luomala's "Voices on the Wind" (1955) reveals the ways in which mythical narratives, chants, prayers and heroic songs function in Polynesian societies. She weaves her texts into descriptions of ceremonial observances among cult groups, the forms of hospitality and courtesy and instruction in Geography and history (1955). Bascom, in his article "Four Functions of Folklore" (*JAF*, Vol. 67, 1954, 333-49) enumerated the social context of folklore, the relation of folklore to culture and the various functions of folklore. Bascom suggests that the comparative folklorists can develop fresh and rewarding theory by relating folklore to culture. The concept of culture which has greatly enriched the twentieth century American anthropology can furnish a meaningful framework for the study of folklore (1954, 346).

Jacobs' contribution to the development of anthropological theory of folklore seems to be very significant (1959a). He made an elaborate study of Clackamas Chinuk narratives and enlarged upon the literal texts to supply details of cultural reference and seeks an imaginative advance in the line of Boas. Both Jacobs and Herskovits, who worked with the Dahomean narratives (1958a), recognize the need for furnishing considerable additional information about the 'givens' of the culture, whose cosmogony, social arrangements, economic habits, linguistic structure and value system so alien to the reader form reference points within the tales.

Jacobs not only elaborated the text, he also drew some lines of interpretation so that the deeper meaning of oral literature could be clearly understood. The tribal narratives appear to be more like drama than a piece of literature, as according to Jacobs they are mostly acted out before a critical and enthusiastic audience, with mimicry, gesture, song, and dance. The characters in the plots are properly understood as actors in a play. Moreover, even if they have animal names, these actors represent people and they stand for aggression, hostility and fantasy wishes projected into the tale. According to Jacobs, an oral literature does not mirror the external life but projects the stresses and anxieties of the culture. Serene and stable institutions and relationships may have been barely mentioned. He thinks that Boas and his fellow folklorists mistakably considered animals to represent animals, whereas they are human beings, they are people—sadistic youths and wealthy headmen—given animal guise through the customary Indian association of individuals with spirit-powers (1959a : 73). To arrive at a verifiable conclusion about psychological traits and stylistic elements in tales, Jacobs has recourse to 'minimal units'. These units which could be tabulated for frequency of recurrence will include situational elements, emotional attitudes, stylistic ways of indicating time and place and movement. By this method he analysed humour and discovered, for example, the high frequency of humorous stimuli concerning bodily injury, specially the injuries of the anus, mouth and glottis in the clackamas tales, but there are too few instances of burning or death which could provide a meaningful alternative. Such specific data illuminate values of the culture reflected in the oral literature and prepare the way for theoretical interpretation (1960, 185).

While highlighting the anthropological theory of folklore, it may be noted that the anthropological folklorists have now arrived at a technique resembling that of the comparative folklorists. Both anthropologists and folklorists, such as Jacobs, Thompson, Dundes, slice the texts into the component elements to reveal frequency percentages. But the only difference is this that while the Finnish method aims at locating the oldest narrative traits of an international tale, the anthropologists seek to find out the dominant psychological attitudes projectcd into a tale, specially into a tale belonging to a tribe.

Beyond the functional approach of folklore, the anthropologists also emphasized on the psychological frame mostly directing their attention towards the attitudes of the people about their own folklore. Hallowell thus viewed :

> Over a long period of time, at least, the major contributions to the study of oral narratives, both inside and outside of anthropology, seem to have remained within the literary-historical orbit. Consequently, anthropologists uninterested in the problem defined by this frame of reference have not bothered much with oral narratives, and those concerncd with such problems have not made use of the material in any other way (1947, 544-45).
>
> "Despite the important contributions that have been made to the study of oral narratives from a literary-historical point of view and the further work that undoubtedly needs to be done, the fact remains that only a limited range of problems can be envisaged within this framework. Among other things, it seems pertinent to ask, for example, whether the study of oral narratives has by any means contributed its full share to our understanding of culture and its functioning in human societies, or whether the study of myth and tale has nothing whatsoever to do with investigation of human psychology and the adjustment of the individual to his culturally constituted word ? If the

> use of oral narratives is relevant to such questions, then they should be one of the primary concerns of the anthropologists rather than an isolated subject-matter that occupies marginal position. In my opinion, such studies need to be put upon a much more comprehensive basis than that represented by the literary-historical approach alone. For this, two other frames of reference, which nicely supplement each other, are needed—the "functional" and the "psychological" (1947, 546).

Among the students of anthropology there is difference of opinion about their roles as to what they should do to solve the human problems. According to some, the anthropologists should divorce themselves from practical human problems which they cannot effectively influence. Others say that anthropologists should concern themselves with practical problems but only as fact-finders (Piddington, 1970 : 129). A few expect the anthropologists to be social doctors and would like them to take the responsibility of bringing about health and happiness in the society in which they conduct research (Vidyarthi, 1978 : 177). Roy thinks that social and cultural anthropology, besides being an intellectual discipline by itself, has the quality of a good guide for social action and social change (Ray, 1969 : 17-26) : But so far as folklore is concerned, the anthropologists have evolved a pattern of study which highlights the textual, contextual, functional and stylistic aspects of every folklore.

The application of anthropological theory on the folklore of the Indian subcontinent is very much desirable. Some anthropologists as well as folklorists have already achieved wonderful results by successfully applying this method to the study of Indian folklore. If we look back to British rule in India we find that some of the British administrators who tried to understand the Indian people at large in order to run the administration in a more effective way started taking deep interests in anthropology in India. Some of them became interested in the study of tribes and tribal culture. European missionaries also followed the same approach to penetrate deep into the tribal belts of India with almost the same motives. Some of the European trained anthropologists carried out studies on tribal ethnography, social structure, family and kinship systems, which are still considered valuable pioneering work in this field. After India and Pakistan became independent, new trends in anthropological studies in the pattern set by American scholars were such. The village studies, urban and industrial studies, study of power structure, applied and action anthropology, textual, contextual, functional and stylistic aspects of oral literature received a new momentum. Anthropologists of the subcontinent are doing their job in their own way. It is the responsibility of the folklorists of the three countries, India, Bangladesh and Pakisthan, to carry them ahead and apply the anthropological methodology to the vast field of folklore for better yield of crops and a good harvest. Unfortunately, Bangladesh has no department of anthropology in any university and no anthropologcial survey department under the administrative set up of the Government. While the folklorists of Bangladesh have been trying in their own way to enhance the prestige of folkloristics and fill up the big gap caused by the thoughtless absence of anthropolgy in the disciplines of humanities and social sciences, where the right of anthropology is not even voiced by proxy, we look forward to the anthropologists of India to provide the befitting leadership.

Psychoanalytical theory of folklore

The current folklore study is greatly enforced with the advent of psychoanalytical theory propounded and developed by Freud, Abraham, Jones, Jung, Campbell, Dollard, Roheim and many others. This is the school not acceptable to the orthodox folklorists even today. The scholars belonging to this school established that in the major area of folklore like myths, legends, folktales, ballads, proverbs and songs there are elements the interpretation of which proves the hidden sexual impulse of men and women since ancient time.

Dorson links the psychoanalytical readings of myths and folktales that reflect sexual symbolism with the nineteenth century symbolism of heavenly phenomena. A direct historical connection can be seen between the German celestial mythologists and the Austrian psychoanalytical folklorists who seemed to have borrowed the method of their predecessors and changed the symbols. There are some who tend to equate psychoanalytic interpretations with those offered by solar mythologists and consider both sets of analyses as absurd. But this cannot be accepted, as the difference between the two is distinctly prominent. The solar mythologists, specially Max Muller and his followers, seek to project the folk narratives relating to human beings, upon the position and movements of celestial bodies such as the sun. According to this view, an act of cannibalism in a folktale is to be interpreted as the heavens devouring the cloud, the sun, the moon. This explains away the allusion to cannibalism. Contrary to this, the psychoanalysts consider folklore as the projection of the movements of human, not celestial, bodies. The "psychoanalysts have argued that just as the folk have to project their emotional life into a safe, externalized, socially sanctioned form (e.g. folklore) to provide a needed outlet for dealing with it, so the solar mythologists were similarly unable to face the nature of folklore and had to protect themselves against the sometimes ugly elements by projecting these disturbing features onto a safe, distant, externalized, academically sanctioned form, namely, the sun, moon and stars. The point is that although both psychoanalytical and solar mythological interpretations may well be wrong in any given instance; they are, from a theoretical perspective, not at all identical and should therefore not be equated." (Dundes, 1965, 88).

The very extensive and original contributions made by the psychoanalysts to the study of folklore in the past seventy years deserve to be treated as a theory. Folklore is the product of the human mind. The dynamic mental process, the response of the folk soul to either outer or inner needs, the expression of various longings, fears, aversions or desires are mainly responsible for the creation of folklore. Freud provided the special technique of psychoanalysis for the exploration of the unconscious to make it possible to trace any mental process to its ultimate source (1900, *Interpretations of Dreams*). Freud's discoveries of the unconscious and subconscious stages of human mind, as is well known, proved to be startlingly revolutionary and have led to a fundamentally new concept of the working of the mind. This in its turn was bound to have repercussions in all the sciences, including folklore, that are concerned with the products of mental activity.

In an early work to employ the Freudian method, *Dreams and Myths* by Abraham (1913), the author hails Adalbert Kuhn as the founder of comparative mythology, and build upon Kuhn his own interpretation of the Prometheus myth. According to the prediction, Kuhn saw Prometheus the fire-bringer as lightning supporting his view with the usual Sanskrit etymology of the nature mythologists. Abraham agreeably concedes that the astronomical considerations may influence outer form of myths, but asserts that several symbols often cloak the same persons; Prometheus is both lightning and again a Sanskrit key 'borer' or 'generator'. Lightning brings fire to primitive man but early man also learns to make fire by twisting a straight hard stick—the borer, into a soft round wooden disc. These are obvious genital symbols, and Abraham interprets the myth of Prometheus to proclaim the masculine power of procreation as a principle of all life (Abraham, 1913 : 70).

> Perhaps the most important conclusion reached by psychoanalytic work is that what we call our mind, that is, the mental processes known to consciousness, is only a transformed selection of the whole mind, derived from its deeper and absolutely unconscious layers and modified by contact with the stimuli of the outer world. The deeper unconscious layer, originating in our organic instincts, is mainly composed of wishes which are actively striving for expression. They come into conflict with opposing forces, especially those relating to fear and guilt, the nucleus of what later will become the moral conscience. What is allowed to seek expression by entering consciousness represents a compromise between the two groups; the wishes achieve fulfilment only in a modified and disguised form. In our judgements and beliefs about the outer world far more contributions from the obscure inner world of the mind are to be found than is commonly supposed, and it is particularly subjective and less rational contributions to thought and conduct that folklore is concerned. (Ernest Jones, 1930, 222).

"Psychoanalysis has produced much evidence to show that all our conscious ideas, feelings, interests and beliefs originate in the unconscious; the conscious mind originates nothing, its functions being confined to criticism, selection and control. Unconscious impulses may be called primitive both as being earlier in development, thus being synonymous with the infantile stage and as representing a lower stage in mental evolution, one out of which more highly differentiated forms of mental activity develop. Now these primitive impulses may come to expression in consciousness in, broadly speaking, one of two ways. Normally they undergo a process of transformation and adaptation in accordance with external reality; in this process they become adjusted both to the claims of reality and to the demands of inner conscience (what is today called the super-ego). The other way in which they may come to expression is through the formation of complicated forms of compromise which act in effect as disguises, the impulses themselves remaining in their unaltered form and undergoing none of the transformation characteristics of the first mode. The former thus gives rise to what may be called the normal interests, ideas and occupations of mankind. It is the second class that is of special interest in the present connection. They represent relics of the primitive mental state, fragments left over in the process of evolution. In the language of folklore they would be termed survivals. The value of them to the psychologist is the direct light they throw on the primitive mind before it has undergone evolution." (Jones, 1930, 222-23). To Jones the practical value of this finding is that the study of survivals in folklore can be usefully supplemented by the study of survivals in living individuals, where they are far more accessible to direct investigation. In his most extensive treatise of folk beliefs on the nightmare, Jones (1959) deals with medieval demons such as the vampire, werewolf, incubus, witch and the devil. In the terrors of the nightmare and the dreaded bogeys of goblindom, Jones perceives direct associations between the infantile fantasies projected in dreams and in points to nocturnal emissions and a repressed oral sadism, the devil whose phallic symbolism is evident in his frequent identification with the snake is a father figure incarnating two repressed wishes, the desire of the son to imitate and to defy his father; the witch is an exteriorization of a women's unconscious thought about herself, her mother and her ritual, fornications with the devil spells an unconcious incestuous fantasy. Repressed incestuous wishes are latent in all these beliefs, and can be attributed to the Oedipal emotions fostered by a patriarchal ascetic church.

According to Frued the Oedipus-type is the best example of man's suppressed impulse. Thus the psychoanalists have made intensive use of the Oedipus story, for to them it provides an excellant example of their significant assumption that folklore embodies the substitutive gratifications of desires in men which in the distant past were given free rein but in the course of time were surrendered. These desires have never become lost, merely repressed. In the instance of the Oedipus story, the suppressed desires are basically two: to possess the mother and to slay the father. The theoretical position of Sigmud Freud so far as the Oedipus tale is concerned forms one of the bases of psychoanalytical school. In the ancient time there existed a primal horde, in which an old man retained himself all the females of the group and drove his sons away from their mothers and sisters. Eventually the sons banded together and killed and ate the old man, after which they committed incest with their mothers and sisters. Later, in remorse for their act of violence towards their father, they tried to atone through a ritual act of commemoration around his image or totem. The feeling of guilt that they felt at that time has been perpetuated through the ages and exists today in the form of a complex affecting every person in the earlier states of his life-time. This complex involves a normal incestuous striving toward the mother and an ambivalent feeling toward the father, but if these attitudes become fixated, a neurosis develops. For Freud, it would not be surprising to find Oedipus-type stories anywhere in the world. In fact, he would expect them to be present in the folklore of all peoples, because they are symbolic expressions of the most fundamental of all human relationships and conflicts. Freud accepted the hypothesized primal horde events with caution (1918).

While the folklorists consider the great many variants of folktale as the results of transmission through oral tradition, Jung speaks of ever present elements in the unconscious psyche, which keep reproducing similar tales, myths and their elements. He calls these mythological components 'motifs', primordial image or preferably 'archetypes.' Primitive man does not invent myths, he experiences them as revelations of the preconscious psyche and modern man re-experiences them in 'autochthonous revivals'. The archetypes are lodged in a collective unconscious. They usually take the form of mythical fragments rather than whole myths (Jung and Kerenyi, 1949). Jung's reference to an old man who figures in the tale repeatedly through dreams, is interesting. The spirituality of this old man is shown by Jung in his qualities of helplessness and goodwill and his intellectual nature in his wisdom and cleverness. Jung may even connect this man with god. In primitive fairy tales, the old man is identified with the sun. He further conjectures that the old man appears as his own opposite by being both life-bringer and a death-dealer. This interpretation is still more plainly presented in his analysis of the winnebago trickster, whom he sees as an amalgam of god and beast, hero and clown, superconsciousness and unconsciousness (Jung, 1956).

Besides, Carl Jung adds some innovations of his own to the Freudian scheme by desexualizing the libido to a great extent. The love of a male child for his mother is mainly due to the fact that she provides protection and nourishment. In time this kind of love may tend to be sexual which may be termed as Oedipus-complex. Then, Jung argues, when it involves a girl's love for her father, we ought to call it the 'electra complex.' The first feelings of jealousy are concerned with food and only later with eroticism. Besides, he feels that as for similarities in forms and themes exhibited by myths in various unrelated parts of the world, they are to be explained as expressions of a collective unconscious. As part of his psyche each individual has a component which is, as it were, the repository of the history of mankind's experiences. Within the collection unconscious are 'engrams' or 'imprints' of the past. They are expressed in the form of mythical motifis and primordial images or archetypes. When the 'mother' and 'father' as well as such other facts ingrained in racial memory, as 'male', 'female', 'generation', 'growth' and 'decay' appear symbolically in our present thinking, it is because of the basic impression they have made on the human race. If we wish to understand the collective unconscious we must enlist the aid of myths. According to Jung, these are valuable for us because in the unconscious we find greater wisdom and guidance than in the conscious. Thus incest merely signifies an adult's desire to return to childhood, when he enjoyed protection and freedom under his parents. This line of reasoning provided by Jung to explain the incest theme in the Oedipus myth forms the basis of a new school of psycho-anlysis of folklore somewhat different from the Freudian one.

Otto Rank's interpretation gives his theory of birth trauma (1929). Broadly speaking, his theory is that man finds the womb to be free, protective, secure and altogether pleasurable, and that he spends the rest of his life trying to undo the trauma of birth, which has ushered him into a world of pain and insecurity. Rank accepts Freud's idea of a primeval horde but gives it new meaning. Here the father opposed his son's wishes to return to the mother by penetrating her through the act of coition.

Erich Fromm considers the conflict in the Oedipus motif as the struggle between father and son over parental authority (1949). The theme that runs throughout is not one of sexual rivalry, but one of child's reaction to parental authority. Fromm has analysed the function as well as the destiny of this theme by depending more on rationalism than merely on the sex libido. The son's inclination towards his mother Does not spring from falling in love with the mother, which is more or less guided by sex, as in the case af Oedipus, and as such it deserves to be treated from an other angle rather than from the purely sexual.

The psychoanalysts believe that the unconscious ideas are not only more concrete but also cruder than the ideas represented in metaphorical processes, and the crudity and simplicity of unconscious ideas is a matter on which they would find it is necessary to insist. As, for example, in the custom of throwing an old slipper or shoe after the departing couple, a custom which has more than one meaning in different layers of the mind, one regards the object thrown as the symbol for the female organ itself, an interpretation that may be supported by quoting the saying that used to accompany it—"May you fit her as my foot fits this old shoe." Symbols with the same meaning that play a very considerable part in folklore are the cowry shell, the crescent moon, innumerable cups, goblets, cauldrons and caskets and almost any object with an opening, from door portals and snake-stones to hollow trees or even the opening under a leaning ladder. Perhaps the most familiar example of all, as cited by Jones (1930, 228), is the inverted horseshoe still to be seen over most stable doors. Jones considers it as the descendant of the actual gential organ of the mare or cow displayed in eastern countries to ward off the evil eye, just as the *Shela-na-gig* did that used to be found outside the door of Irish churches. To him, it is fair to say that the phenomena studied in folklore relate for the most part to simple or even lowly themes. The same is true *a fortiori* of the unconscious mind. Jones suggests that in folklore we have to do with the simple wishes and fears of the people and very little with elaborate philosophical, spiritual or artistic preoccupations. We find the people concerned with such matters as the preservation of health, the warding off of danger and death, the hopes of fortune and the desire for happy marriage and the blessing of children. The unconscious is similarly engrossed with such topics and in even more primitive terms. The first, Jones illustrates, is that it is mainly concerned with the themes of birth, love and death. These are the springs of life and psychoanalysis would go so far as to maintain that all our manifold imaginative interetss originate there and consist only in ramifications of these themes modified by the influence of two other factors, the defensive reactions against certain dangers inherent in them (the moral super-ego) and contact with outer reality. Jones thus concludes that these two influences exercise a constantly moulding effect on the primitive impulses that are striving for expression in their naked form. They control them, thwart them, select from them and modify them to such an extent that in the final forms in which they emerge they are mostly transformed or distorted out of recognition. From time to time, of course, they emerge in ruder forms in various contexts. Jones proceeds to argue that if, for instance, myths and nursery tales were taken seriously and not as a form of entertainment, we should doubtless be horrified at the recurring evidences they present of barbarous and loutish impulses. The unconscious, viewed by Jones, primarily recognizes no human beings except the immediate blood relatives, such as parents, siblings and children. The part played by animals in fantasy, in children's games, in nursery tales, in legends, and last but not least, in dreams. They display the human characteristics which provides a hint for real meaning. They peculiarly represent most often the parents, specially the father. The brothers may be seen in tales mostly where the father has cast the spell form jealousy of his daughter's fondness for the brothers, as in Aarne-Thompson tale type 451, The Maiden who Seeks Her Brothers. The other figures of fantasy are giants, dwarfs, fairies, and ghosts. According to Jones, the conception of giants with their clumsy stupidity and their alternation of kindliness and ogerish devouring of children is a projection of various infantile thoughts about grown-ups, particularly the parents and perhaps one might say the same as regards the sexual significance of jesters, and dwarfs. Jones considers the punishment for sin as always the same in the unconscious. It appropriately takes the talion form of deprivation of sexual capacity, this being typically expressed in men as impotence—which is a conscious equivalent of castration in the unconscious—and in woman of sterility. (1930, 232).

Geza Roheim offers an interpretation of the Oedipus tale by saying that the primeval horde posited by Freud did really exist as an archaic form of human social organization, but myths of the primal horde type may be based not on the unconscious memory of primeval tragedies but may be actual narratives of events of human times (1942, 454). In short the primeval horde is still with us in the ethnological present and in support of this Roheim offers some seeming instances from central Australia. Roheim also criticises some of the neo-Freudian interpretations offered by Lessa in his book, *The Gates of the Dream* (1952, 529-44). Sendor Feldmen follows Roheim in accepting both the phylogenetic and the ontogenetic viewpoints, but emphasizes that "it is not necessary to refer to former or different cultures of mankind in order to understand the rituals practised at the present time and in our present culture because as far as instinctional needs are concerned there is no difference between the human being in primeval and present times" (1947, 173). Roheim's authority lies in his further analysis of a good many myths and tales in the light of psychoparallel theory. He finds the dream as a precursor to rather than parallel with myth and tale, or combining with unconscious fantasies to form myths. Demon Grendel's chocking sleepers and drinking their blood is a nightmare episode. Odysseus rams a spit into the eye of Polyphemus while the giant sleeps, and so, the sleeper's castration anxiety (blindness) is projected into the father image. The widely distributed fairy tale incident of the magic flight, in which the little hero fleeing from the giant throws objects in the path which swell to enormous size, Roheim interprets as a urethral awakening dream. Roheim postulates a basic dream that forms the substance of mythical tales. The dreamer falls into a lake or a hole, and this symbolized the penis entering the vagina. Out of his body he then forms a womb symbolized by an ocean or a lotus and here is the origin of creation myth such as the earth diver. The deeper the dive, the greater the penis, for diving in a dream signifies an erection. Roheim believes that one person once had such a dream and repeated it to others, who had experienced similar dreams, and from the repetitions a myth developed (1952, 423-28).

Keri demonstrates the children's game of hide-and-seek as the infantile trauma of the clingling child separated from its mother and by the reenactment softens the blow (1958). A strange pastime of ritual insults exchanged by Negro youths, known as 'the dozens', provides the taunter with an opportunity to voice repressed wishes for incest, homosexuality and exhibitionism (Dollard, 1939). Sterta mentions the Dutch folk festival of the innocents, coming soon after Christmas, who lead into the Christ figure and explains it through psychoanalytical process (1941). In it the children play at being father and mother and this make-believe reveals their repressed wishes to kill their parents. The proximity of this festival to Christmas further reveals that Christ died sacrificially to expiate the same sin of rebellion against parental authority. Now his Oedipal nature comes clearer. The father figure of king Lains in Oedipus Rex is divided in the New Testment between God, the father and king Herod. Thus, all manner of folk materials, not simply myths and tales, yield their latent content to the psychoanalysing folklorists.

From Munden's findings (1958), Dorson tries to establish that even the contemporary myth of the cowboy has been subjected to psychoanalysis. A cowboy's strongest attachment to guns and horses has something to do with sex. In the myth the cowboy hero appears as a celibate nomad, challenged by his father and siblings whom he defeats and kills (removes from the scene). Always in evidence is the hero's gun (phallus), accurate, deadly, potent and ever loaded. In the death ritual hand and gun are prominently displayed, a round dark office is thurst at the spectator in the close-up, there is the ominous silence, the sudden explosion, the slumping body—all painting to an originastic climax. The mother figure emerges as the well-to-do leader of the opposition who hires the gunman but himself lacks the gun. When the hero rejects this as paltry, he gratifies both Oedipal emotions simultaneously. Notching the gun is a symbolic act of self castration as atonement for killing the father. In its manifest denial of the female and mother figure, the cowboy myth represents the intense desires and persistent fears of the child for its mother.

Joseph Campbell uses the Jungian approach to religious-magical-mythological tradition with an eye of a new-world scholar. In the Hero with a Thousand Faces, Campbell explored universally recurrent themes of the separation, travail, and return of the mythological hero to illustrate their archetypical patterns (1949). Then in the Masks of God, he sets out to present a systematic treatise on mythology for the twentieth century (1959, 1961). To the concerns of the folklorists these studies of Campbell, which recall Frazer in their literary splendour and their extraction of examples from their cultural environment, are peripheral. He sees in myth the playful reflection of the profound themes which engage and find their serious utterance in the visions of seers and the sacred scriptures.

It is interesting that while objection to psychoanalytical method came from a host of folklorists, the anthropologists have displayed more respectively ranging from cautious and qualified to enthusiastic acceptance of this most striking method. They have, for instance, the Oedipus complex in the light of the familial structure and tribal narratives of non-western cultures. Herskovits extends the classic theorem by pointing to factors unconsidered by Freud, such as sibling jealousy for the favour of the mother and the father's fear of displacement by the son. Dahomean family relationships, in which the child is always dependent on mother and little aware of his polygamous father, explain the dominance of these themes (1958b). Malinowski had earlier shown that among the Trobriand Islanders the father's brother who brought up the son becomes the object of childhood resentment (1927). In the ingenious examination of Oedipus type tales collected in Oceania, Lessa points out that the plots appear within a kin group society of Ulthi Atoll and are not similar to the Euro-American nuclear family.

In Ulthi, though there is an Oedipal tale, the design for living, with particular reference to the way in which the family is defined by members of the culture, is not the same as Euro-American design. Oedipus tales thus appear in cultures lacking Oedipal complex situations and fail to appear in Africa, China, much of Asia, Americas and Australia. They are, therefore, not a universal development from a universal complex, nor does the plot seem related to its social environment. Presumably the tale has travelled from Europe to Oceania by diffusion (Lessa, 1956).

The anthropologists like LaBerre (1948), Abram Kardiner (1945) Linton, DuBois, Oplar, Jacobs, Hallawell and some others of the later generation, who are thoroughly conversant with folklore, devoted some of their studies to the psychoanalytical theory and their contributions to this line are no less great than many of the psychoanalysts.

One notes with approval the growing efforts of psychoanalysts, anthropologists and folklorists to amend some of the more glaring errors of the past, which at a time, were accepted as approaches to right directions.

To conclude, I would emphasize that the psychoanalytical theory has opened a new and broader vista in the field of folkloristics. Some of us may not agree with these interpretations as I have shortly enumerated, but it cannot be denied that the psychoanalysts have gone deeper in the structure of folklore and revealed the feelings of the unconscious and subconscious mind of the characters reflected in the elements of folklore. The articles used, the actions and interactions and the functions of the tales have also received a new significance through the interpretations of the psychoanalysts. Thus the application of this theory on the Indian folklore seems to be immensely useful. Some scholars have already experimented it in Indian myths and tales and achieved wonderful results. Since this theory has a strong scientific basis, the folklorists of the countries of the Indian subcontinent, I feel, should adopt in it their search for knowledge and analysis.

Structural theory

While discussing the literary theory of folklore, I have described in short what structuralism means in literature. Folklorists dealing with structuralism in folklore do not principally differ much with the literary critics, though methodically their approach is not exactly the same as held by the latter. The semantic theory of literature concentrates too heavily on the texture of the work to the exclusion of its structure. The structural theory puts the emphasis the other way round. It suggests that since the literary work, including folk literature, is a type of discourse, its structure can be explored with the same kind of methods as are applicable to other types of discourse. As R. Barthes puts it, "the structure of the sentence, the object of linguistics, is found again, homologically, in the structure of works. Discourse is not simply an adding together of sentences: it is, itself, one great sentence" (1972, 136). Long before Barthes, V. Propp, a Russian scholar, invented this method and considered folktale for the purpose of his interpretation, as a sentence (1928).

The sentence is a linguistic unit which is made up of an ordered set of minimal linguistic units which for the present purposes may be taken to be words. Minimal units can be combined according to certain rules to form sentences. Each minimal linguistic unit has a meaning or a semantic value which it carries over from one context to another and which contributes to the meaning of the sentence into which it enters. The meaning of a sentence is a function of all the words of which it is constituted, and of the interrelation between them. According to the stucturalists, language is a system of finite number of such minimal units and set of rules imposing combinatorial restraint on these units. The meaning of a minimal is determined by the totality of relationships it can have to the other units of the system. This means that the unit of meaning is identified as a member of the system only by its meaning in that system being understood. The signifier and the signified are two aspects of the sign which can be abstracted for theoretical purposes but which in practice belong together like the recto and verso of a sheet of paper. The signifier "is purely a relatum, whose definition cannot be separated from that of the signified" (Barthes, 1967, 47).

If folk literature, specially the tales, myths, legends, and ballads can be seen analogous to a sentence, it is possible to see them as a hierarchy of semantic units, the meaning of which is a function of lower-level semantic units and their interrelation, the work itself then being the highest-level semantic unit. Since the combination of semantic units in a literary work or folk literature would have to be in accordance with certain rules, the task of literary theory would be to observe literary practice and to formulate these rules. It should be possible in this way to learn the second-order language which a piece of literature or folk literature employs. Of course, there is a strong point in favour of the argument which recognizes certain repeatable structures in literature and specially in the elements of folk literature and this is an important aspect of this theory that the structuralist approach means to draw attention to. This is an insight as old as Aristotle's *Poetics*. It cannot be denied that there exists a critical vocabulary which identifies certain set categories dealing with both the language and the world of the work. For some purposes one can certainly talk about the meaning of a work and trace elements from work to work, tale to tale, myth to myth, or proverb to proverb to discover how different authors or the creators of folk literature use the same device and pattern. There are, furthermore, undoubted regularities in literary or folk literary practice in the patterns which can be inquired into and formulated in rules and method called structuralism.

To consider a literary piece or a piece of folk literature a sentence for the interpretation of its structure may lead to some vagueness. Though Propp propounded this methodology, he stressed more on the functions than on the outer form. Thus, Propp's approach may not be subjected to that much of criticism as the others, specially the literary critics, who view that the literary work can be seen as analogous to a sentence. Structuralism allows the theorist to call it most normal, literary criticism, while at the same time giving a theoretical account of the structuralist position, he uses precise linguistic concepts and definitions. He thus arrives at a precise model, which, if taken as a model of literary or folk literary practice, is too strict, and in application it yields nothing that would be considered interesting criticism. Any challenge to the structuralist position can always be answered by pointing to the fact that there are structures in literature or folk literature, and an appearance of theoretical interest may be kept up by hinting that the precise theoretical model somehow underlies these structures. The analogy between the sentence and the literary work including folk literature is inadequate as a basis for a theory of literature. If it is pleaded that this is not really what structuralism says, the point must be made that a weaker version of this theory is unlikely to be structuralism in a significant sense, that is, in the sense of being a branch of the much heralded science of semiology.

Another objection to the view of the literary work or folk literature as a semantic structural unit is that this is simply not the way the reader or a listener sees it or understands it. A member of a language community has clear and reliable institutions as to what sentences are meaningful and what the units are of which the sentence is constituted. He recognizes immediately that the sentence "he likes to read books" is composed of five words. He understands its meaning and also knows very well that it means something different from "he likes to eat rice", and "book likes to read him," which is meaningless. Linguistics is concerned with systematizing these intuitions with the help of a set of minimal units and combination rules and thus makes explicit and regular the intuitive linguistic knowledge possesed by the native speaker. The *bona fide* member of a community where the institution of literature is alive, that is, the trained reader, has no idea about how the sentences in a literary work combine to term larger articulation. He cannot recognize the heirarchy of semantic units which enters into a literary work to make it a great sentence. Nor does it make sense to him to say that a literary work is meaningful or meaningless; nor can he be expected to know what change in the meaning of a work, a change in the relationship between the presumed semantic units, of which it is constituted, would occasion. There are no recognizable larger articulations in a literary work which are parallel to the phrases in a sentence. Moreover, the structuralist using semiological system must believe that the practices he observes will yield to analysis in structural terms. Whether the object of study is fashion, literature, or motor cars, the difference between the system studied by the semiologist is that while language is essentially bound up with meaning, all the other systems have different purposes. While it cannot be denied that social phenomena can be interpreted and that a model for interpretation will rely on a notion of structure, there is no reason to believe that the structure of these phenomena will also fit the sentence mould, or that the meaning one can assign to such phenomena will in any way be similar to sentence-meaning.

The underlying assumption that the structuralist theory has a similarity with the semantic theory is mainly based on the point that institutional practices like literature are objectively given phenomena which can be studied from outside. If we go through and acquaint ourselves with sufficient number of literary work and folk literature, certain structural units might start to appear before us. But a literary element in folklore or literature of art will only reveal their features to those who know literary practice. Literary works or folk literature themselves will reveal nothing to the neutral observer. An institution can only be analyzed from within. A linguist must learn a language to be able to make semantically significant discoveries about its structure. As long as he stays outside and watches for regularities he will get nowhere. A last-ditch defence of the structuralist method might concede this, but still maintain that there is a distinctive structuralist method, that is, a method inspired by, or taking its methodological orientation from linguistics. As Janathan Culler puts it, "If the meanings assigned to objects or actions are not purely random phenomena, then there must be a system of distinctions, categories and operations to be described. The other linguistic terms and concepts, which help to identify structuralist prose, are inessential compared to this basic methodological orientation" (1973, 25). If one accepts this view of structuralism, the distinction between the structuralist approach and the semantic approach may even collapse.

As regards the fairly typical article by Roman Jackobson and Levi-Strauss, Charles Baudelaire's *Les Chafs* (1962, trans., 1970), one may not be quite sure what to do with this information. In any text one can always describe an indefinite number of structures, both concerning language and content. The problem for the critic is to decide which structures are important to the aesthetic dimension of the work or element of folk literature, and the task of literary theory is to provide him with a principle for justifying his choice. By listing stylistic features, motifs, and so on which form or do not form some sort of pattern, without giving reasons why this information is relevent, structuralism tends to support the conclusion that the structuralist models do deal with systems where there are no firm intuitions as to the relevance and meaning of structures.

An answer to these criticisms may stress the fact that what structuralism does is to seek out those structures of our unconscious mind which underlie different social phenomena. Whether one deals with literature, art, language, kinship-systems, myths or fairy-tales, they will all display certain invariable structures, which, though they are not immediately apparent can still be stressed by observing that the surface of the phenomena manifest certain regularities. Here, about the task of the anthropologists and folklorists, we may again remember what Levi-Strauss emphasizes:

> His goal is to grasp, beyond the conscious and always shifting images which men hold, the complete range of unconscious possibilities. These are not unlimited, and the relationships of compatibility or incompatibility which each maintains with all the others, provide a logical framework for historical developments, which, while perhaps unpredictable, are never arbitrary. (1972 23).

If the structuralist's task is seen in this light, the objection that there is no community of readers who are intuitively aware of the structures of literary works, becomes obvious. At the same time, however, structuralism becomes irrelevant to literary theory in the sense that it tries to trace "the underlying reality" of social phenomena, which may be useful as a science of the mind or applicable to the study of the society, but it may not tell anything about the institution of literature, as the literature is dependent for its existence upon a framework of assumptions, concepts and practices, which, though not known in a systematized form by the reader, are nevertheless consciously and deliberately applied by him to literary texts. Literary theory may seem to be less concerned with the reality hidden beneath. Discoveries concerning the unconscious mental structures underlying literature or folk-literature may not be of much help to critics as well as the readers in their evaluative and interpretive task, though a similar discovery about language can no doubt help the speaker of that language to decide whether a sentence is correct, incorrect, clumsy or unsuitable. Those who oppose structuralism as a theory in the study of literature or folk literature, hold that literary theory must be directed towards the foundation of a rational basis for literary judgements, and not towards something beyond, which is indifferent to literary practice. On the other hand, since literature as well as folk literature is the product of the human mind and the society is reflected in them, their underlying meaning and the something beyond what they say and look like, which is one of the main objects of the structural theory to trace out, as propounded by Propp and Levi-Strauss, may not seem at all irrelevant to folklorists, anthropologists and sociologists.

With these critical observations, I would now pass on to the theory of structuralism, describe it in detail and finally apply this theory on some of the elements of folk literature, specially of this subcontinent.

In my discourse on the structuralist theory of folklore, I have started with some doubts and critical notes. But the fact remains that this theory has changed many old concepts of folklore study, which I have analysed in detail in my book *Folklore Charchaye Roptattik Bisslation Paddhati* (The Morphological Analysis of Folklore, 1982), and saved folkloristics from the streak of almost streamlined approach of search for origin or atomistic manoeuvre. Structuralists have worked out with considerable seriousness and revealed some truth like binarism or binary opposites, deep-structure, motifeme, mytheme, cause and results, sequences, and so on. It is through their ceaseless efforts that folklore study has changed its course from diachronism to synchronism and accepted more rationalism than ever before. Dundes has rightly observed :

"It is true that while the structural or pattern approach was sweeping through linguistics, psychology, ethnomusicology and anthropology proper in the 1920's and 30's, folklore as a discipline remained oriented to a narrowly historical approach and dedicated to atomistic studies. In 1934, there appeared Benedict's *Patterns of Culture*; in 1933 Helen Roberts published *Pattern Phenomenon in Primitive Music* as well as her *Form in Primitive Music*. In linguistics, Sapir's *Language* (1921) and *Sound Pattern in Language* (1925) were followed by Bloomfield's *Language* (1933) and Swadesh's *The Phonemic Principle* (1934). Kohler's *Gestalt Psychology* (1929) and Koffa's *Principles of Gestalt Psychology* (1935) reflected the same theoretical movement in psychology. In the Thirties, the search for patterns was itself a pattern of culture. However, in the field of folklore, there was apparently no interest in a holistic synchronic approach. The major piece of folklore scholarship of the middle Thirties was Stith Thompson's mammoth *Motif-Index of Folk Literature*, lexicon par excellence, epitome of the atomistic emphasis on folklore. The culture lag in folklore theory has unfortunately increased since the Thirties and this is one reason why there have been so few notable theoretical advance in folklore" (1963, 121).

Thus structuralist theory has set folkloristics in the right footings. Its onward march has been directed to some deeper understandings and progress towards realistic acme. The whole approach has placed folkloristics in a dignified position amongst the academic disciplines. "The study of form *per se* is not an end in itself. The delineation of form is only a step that should be taken before investigating origin and function. It is through studies of form that one sees what folklore is.

Once folklore can be accurately defined in terms of formal criteria, it will be much easier to search for origins, to comprehend the process of oral transmission and to analyse the diverse functions." (Dundes, 1965, 206).

I hope I have been able to explain what structural theory in literary criticism and folkloristics is and what it stands for. I agree with Todorov when he says, "While in speech the integration of units does not go beyond the level of the sentence, in literature sentences are integrated again as part of larger articulation, and the latter in their turn into units of greater dimension, and so on until we have the entire work (1972, 130).

The structural analysis of folklore becomes somewhat irrelevent without the context of a particular culture in which folklore is sustained. Structural analysis of folklore does give us a clue to understand the culture in a better way, because of the organic relationship of the two. Elliot's definition of culture in this respect is appealing :

> By culture, I mean first of all what the anthropologists mean : the way of life of a particular people living together in one place. That culture is made visible in their arts, in their social system, in their habits and customs, in their religion. But these things added together do not constitute the culture, though we often speak for convenience as if they did. These things are simply the parts into which a culture can be anatomised, as a human body can. But just as a man is something more than an assemblage of the various constituent parts of his body, so a culture is more than the assemblage of its arts, customs and religious beliefs. These things all act upon each other, and fully to understand one, you have to understand all (1948, 120).

Thus, when we analyse a myth or a song or a proverb structurally, we get this "something more than what is assembled" through adjoining the words or sentences and receive the proper directive to reach its organic and mental relation with the culture. When a Bengali proverb says *Nachte Na Janley Utthan Banka* meaning a man who does not know dancing, the courtyard appears to him as curved, we clearly get two opposite forces who are in conflict with each other, the courtyard and the unskilled dancer, through structural analysis :

Proverb : *Nachte Na Janley Utthan Banka*

Parties

(a) The unskilled or ignorant dancer
(b) The courtyard

functions (f) :

(x) The ignorant dancer wants to overcome the courtyard
(y) The courtyard overcomes the ignorant dancer by posing to him its curve.

Thus, according to Levi-Strauss's formula, it follows:

$$FX(a) : Fy(b) :: FX(b) : F_a^{-I}(y).$$

This means, one has to deserve, then desire. Unless one knows a thing perfectly, he will only receive a rebuff and an unsuccessful return. The two opposing forces have come here in a binary process, one has a closer link with the other. They stay in the deep structure of this proverb and signify through their functions something great which is true about the culture of the Bengali-speaking peoples. These opposing forces are inherent in the nature and culture, ignorance and knowledge. Here, obviously, the courtyard represents the nature and the ignorant dancer, by exposing his failure, cannot represent culture, which, a true dancer does, who has the knowhow to overcome the curve of the courtyard through his skilled knowledge. So, in the deep structure of this particular proverb lies some truth such as, impossibility is a word which can be found in the dictionary of fools, a bad workman quarrels with his tools, and so on. Only the people with a strong sense of perseverance, as the British and Bengalis are, can create proverbs like these. So far as nature-culture relationship is concerned, even this particular Bengali proverb also provides us the binary elements which can be framed in the following sketch :

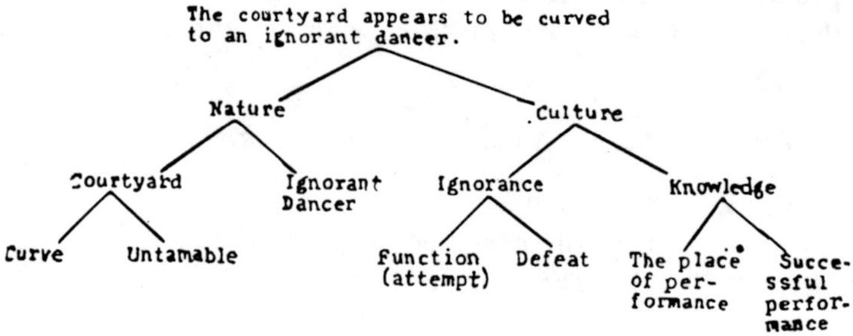

Thus, the structuralist approach is different from the one pursued by the formalists. The formalists are more concerned with the body and physical construction of a piece of literature or folk literature, but the structuralists would go deeper to find out the truth underlying the spirit of literature in relation to the culture. The main aims and objects of both are same, both endeavour to seek the form and structure, but while the formalists look for the meaning through the physical structure, the structuralists would go for the meaning of meaning. Thus Vladimir Propp turned to structuralism.

Application of structural theory

Being tired with the formalists, Vladimir Propp engaged himself in the morphological analysis of Russian folktale and published his famous book *Morfologiya Skazki* in 1928. It is unfortunate that the western scholars did not even notice the importance of this book for thirty years. Dundes has rightly remarked, "Since the appearance of the English translation of Vladimir Propp's *Morphology of the Folktale* in 1958, there has been an ever-increasing interest in attempting structural analyses of various folklore genres. In view of the enormous impact Propp's study has had on folklorists, linguists, anthropologists and literary critics, one can only regret that there was a thirty year time lag between Propp's completion of the morphology in 1928 and the time that most European and American scholars read it." (Dundes, 1965, 11).

In botany the term morphology means the study of the characteristics and functions of the different parts of the tree or plant. In folklore the term morphology is used almost in the same manner. This is true about linguistics as well. Propp was the first folklorist to observe that the structure of a folktale is like the structure of a sentence which has a set of words arranged in a strict methodical order. "He wants a sweet mango," never becomes "sweet he a wants mango". Cottage cheese does not become cheese cottage. In similar manner, the folklates contain the motifs arranged in order—the story of a tale always brings the events one after another in accordance with the requirement of the tale so that it may take a full shape. Every tale has two aspects—the variables and the constants. The *dramatis personae* and their attributes change, but the actions and functions do not. With these observations Propp goes on to say, "The number of functions is startlingly small, compared with the great number of *dramatis personae*. This explains the two-fold quality of a folktale: it is amazingly multiform, picturesque and colourful and to no less a degree, remarkably uniform and recurrent" (Propp 1958, 20-21). The role of *dramatis personae* is only to support the functions. A function is expressed simply by the name of an action: interdiction, flight, villainy and so forth. The sequence of functions in a tale is constant. In this respect, all fairy tales are of one type in regard to their structure. According to Propp, the number of functions in a complex tale is limited to thirty-one altogether—it may be less if the tale is a simple one. Besides, the functions implicate one another with logical and artistic necessity, they belong to the same axis so that any two functions are never mutually exclusive. So far as the *dramatis personae* are concerned, Propp notes seven protagonists: the villain, the donor, the magical agent, the sought-for person, the dispatcher, the hero and the false hero. In addition, Propp also suggests two non-functional categories, the 'connectives' and the 'motivations'. 'The connectiye serves to establish some immediate relation between two characters or between character and an object, whereas circumstances in the story would have made possible only an indirect relation". (Levi-Strauss 1973 : 122-23)

By motivations are meant all reasons and aims of characters which give rise to their deeds. Propp concludes that when the motivations exist, they may result from a secondary formation.

Propp's endeavour is a step forward from the diachronic

to a synchronic approach. Stith Thompson's emphasis on 'motif of a tale, which means the smallest unit of the story, such as magic bird's heart, resuscitation, suitor's tests, and so on was completely ignored by Propp who stressed on the functions of a tale rather than on motifs. Dundes suggested that motifeme be used in place of function in the new index as an extension of motif. The 31 functions Propp enumerated are "Initial Situation, Absentation of a Person, Interdiction, Violation of Interdiction, The Villain's Reconnaissance, The Villain Receives Information About His Victim, The Villain Attempts to Deceive His Victim, The Victim Submits to Deception, The Villain Causes Harm to the Members of the Hero, The Members of the Family Lack Something, Misfortune or Lack is Made Known to the Hero, Preparation of the Seeker for Revenge, The Return Journey of the Hero, The Hero's Test and Achievement of Magic Object, Hero's Reaction about the Future Donor, The Use of Magic Object as a Means of Help, Arrival of Hero to a Place Where the Object or Person of His Quest is Staying, The Villain and the Hero Join in Direct Combat, The Hero is Branded With a Mark, The Defeat of the Villain, The Initial Lack of the Hero is Liquidated, Hero's Return, The Villian's Pursuit of the Hero, Rescue from Pursuit, The Hero's Unrecognised Arrival, False Hero Establishes Him as a Hero, Diffl-cult Task to Hero and His Success in Performing the Task, Exposure of the False Hero, Transfiguration of the Hero, The Villain is Punished, Marriage and Achievement of the Throne."

The French anthropologist Claude Levi-Strauss accepted Propp as a pioneer and introduced a new pattern of structural analysis. In his paper on "Structural Study on Myth" (1955), he won considerable interest in its presentation of a structural model for mythological narratives. While Propp's model was syntagmatic, Lévi-Strauss's analysis was paradigmatic. The functions in this process are to be arranged in a binary opposite form and set in a perpendicular or vertical order. Myths are still widely interpreted in conflicting ways: as collective dreams, as the outcome of a kind of aesthetic play or as the basis of ritual mythological figures are considered as personified abstractions, divinized heros, or gods.

Whatever the hypothesis, the choice amounts to reducing mythology either to idle play or to a crude kind of philosophical speculation. Hence, Levi Strauss clarifies :

> In order to understand what a myth really is, must we choose between platitude and sophism? Some claim that human societies merely exist through their mythology, fundamental feelings common to the whole of man-kind, such as love, hate or revenge or that they try to provide some kind of explanation for phenomena which they cannot otherwise understand astronomical, meteorological and the like. But why should these societies do it in such elaborate and devious ways? When all of them are also acquainted with empirical explanations? On the other hand psycho-analysts and many anthropologists have shifted the problems away from the natural or cosmological towards the sociological and psychological fields. But then the interpretation becomes too easy. If a given mythology confers prominence on a certain figure, let us say an evil grandmother, it will be claimed that in such a society grandmothers are actually evil and that mythology reflects the social structure and the social relations, but should the actual data be conflicting, it would be as readily claimed that the purpose of mythology is to provide an outlet for repressed feelings. Whatever the situation, a clever dialectic will always find a way to pretend that a meaning has been found. (1963 : 207-208):

Regarding the characteristics of myths, Lévi-Strauss states, Mythology confronts the student with a situation which at first sight appears contradictory. On the one hand it would seem that in the course of a myth anything is likely to happen. There is no logic, no continuity. Any characteristic can be attributed to any subject, every conceivable relation can be found. With myth everything became possible. But on the one hand, this apparent arbitrariness is belied by the astounding similarity between myths collected in widely different regions. Therefore, the problem: if the content of a myth is contingent, how are we going to explain the fact that myths throughout the world are similar. (1963, 208).

Levi-Strauss terms the constituent units in myth as mytheme, as in a language there are phonemes, morphemes or sememes. He suggests that we should look for the mythemes on the sentence level. He also suggests that "analysing each myth individually, breaking down its story into the shortest possible sentences, and writing each sentence on an index card bearing a number corresponding to the unfolding of the story. Practically each card will then show that a certain function is, at a given time, linked to a given subject, or to put it otherwise, each gross constituent unit will consist of a relation." (1963, 211)

Levi-Strauss feels that the true constituent units of a myth are not the isolated relations but bundles of such relations. He cites some examples and suggests that to make the study meaningful one may read the mytheme diachronically along one axis, that is, page after page and from left to right; and synchronically along other axis, all the notes written vertically making up one gross constituent unit, that is one bundle of relations. The kind of logic in mythical thought is as rigorous as that of modern science and that the difference lies not in the quality of the intellectual process but in the nature of things to which it is applied. "What makes a steel ax superior to a stone ax is not that the first one is better made than the second. They are equally well made, but steel is quite different from stone". (1963, 230)

Levi-Strauss takes major functions of the myth into his consideration and divides them in columns. According to him, these functions are the mythemes. Then he arranges these columns vertically and decides, "column four is to column three as column one is to column two. The inability to connect two kinds of relationship is overcome (or rather replaced) by the assertion that contradictory relationships are indentical in as much as they are both self-contradictory in a similar way". (1963, 216)

I would now apply Levi-Strauss's method on an Oriya myth and analyse its structural pattern. The myth *Deul Tola* (construction of a temple) has been taken from a booklet written in poetry and published in the name of poet Krishnadasa. The story of the myth goes like this :

The king Indradumna of Puri wanted to construct a temple of Lord Jagannatha. But the statue of the Lord must be found out. He sent people in all directions in search of the Lord. After seventy one years all came back to report that they could not succeed except the one who went to the east. He was Vidyapati who took shelter in a savara village in the house of Basu Savara. Here he fell in love with Lalita, the daughter of Basu Savara. Basu Savara wanted his daughter to be married to Vidyapati who refused on the ground that he was a Brahmim. Basu Savara became angry and narrated a story of his forefathers. Jadu family was ruined because of the poisonous effect of *kadamba* juice which the members of that family joyfully drank. Krishna was shocked and went to the forest where he started swinging in a rocking cradle of *shari* plant. On that very day Savara Basu, who was a hunter, did not get any hunt. On seeing the swinging legs of Krishna he thought that those were the ears of a deer. He threw his arrow which struck Krishna's legs. Savara Basu was ashamed and repentant. But Krishna consoled him, as it was not his fault. Krishna advised him to call Judhisthira and Arjuna. Both Judhisthira and Arjuna decided to bury the body of Krishna. Then through a revelation Krishna desired to float away his body in the ocean so that He would come back once during *Kaliyuga* floating over the sea as a piece of wood to be installed in the temple of Jagannatha. This Savara Basu was the ancestor of Basu Savara and hence as a descendant Basu Savara could rightly claim to be the disciple of Lord Jagannatha. Vidyapati was convinced and married Lalita. After becoming a family member Vidyapati observed that Basu Savara went out every morning for worship. On an enquiry he came to know that there existed the temple of Jagannatha where Basu Savara paid his homage every morning. Vidyapati wanted to go there. Basu Savara became angry at this proposal and at first did not agree to take him. Later on because of the persuasion of Lalita, Vidyapati was taken to the temple with his eyes covered by a piece of cloth. While being escorted to the temple, Vidyapati, as advised by Lalita, took a handful of mustard seeds which fell all the way. Later on Vidyapati went to the temple guided by the fallen seeds and located the place. He then fled away to the king Indradumna and informed him of the location of the temple. Indradumna at once felt proud as he was the only king in the world who knew about the location of Lord Jagannatha's statue. He made an expedition with his army to bring the statue. But when he reached the temple, Jagannatha disappeared—Indradumna's boast did not please the Lord. Angry, Indradumna attacked the Basu Savara village and ransacked the whole area killing hundreds of innocent people. Then a revelation dawned on Indradumna to build a temple on the seashore at Puri, where, the Lord promised, He would come in the shape of a piece of log floating over the sea. A beautiful temple was erected as desired by the Lord by Indradumna. But after the completion, the question arose, who would sanctify the temple. The king went to Brahma who was engaged in a meditation. In a minute, of course, he completed his meditation and appeared before Indradumna. But a minute in heaven is equivalent to nine ages each covering the length of period as long as *Kaliyuga* on the earth. When Indradumna came back with Brahma, the temple was under the possession of Gala Madhaba, a king. While King Gala Madhbaba had been passing through something hard struck the legs of his horse. The place was dug up and a beautiful temple was discovered. Thus, Gala Madhaba claimed in front of Brahma that he was the founder of this temple. Brahma wanted Indradumna to bring proof to refute the claim of Gala Madhaba. Indradumna took Brahma to the oldest crow Bhusundu who rebuked both Brahma and Indradumna as he had seen Brahma take birth from the navel of Krishna. Then they went to an old pond where dozens of tortoises fell into the water after they saw Indradumna. They declared that they were the labourers who built the temple. Brahma was covinced and then sanctified the temple. But he prophesied that there would be a statue of Gala Madhaba on one side and of Indradumna on the other side of the temple, but they would never be worshipped. Brahma also asked Indradumna to establish Purikshetra. After Purikshetra was set, Indradumna prayed to the Lord to appear so that he would have the statue installed in the temple. But there was no revelation. The disappointed king took to his bed of straw and remained unfed for days together. Then there was a revelation from the Lord that Indradumna should go to the seashore and bring Him from there to the temple —He would appear on the water as a piece of wood. Indradumna at once went there and found the Lord floating as a log with the marks of a conch shell and wheat shaped missile. He then immediately engaged five thousand elephants, 13 lakhs army, 120 wrestlers—all of them tried to pull the log to the shore with a thick rope, but failed to move the log an inch. The king then again took shelter on the straw and vowed not to take anything. Again a revelation came. Even if all the people of the kingdom try to pull the log out of water they would not succeed. The king must bring the savaras to pull the log. Then the savàras were brought and the log was held on one side by the savaras and on the other side by the king and his people. The log was easily brought to the temple. Then came two lakh carpenters to work on the log to give it the shape of Jagannatha. They tried for four days in vain— they could not put their chisels on the body of the log. Then the Lord Jagannatha Himself came in the disguise of an old carpenter, so old that he could not even stand the force of a finger. But when he put his chisel on the log, it worked. The old carpenter desired that the temple be kept closed for 21 days while he would be engaged in work. He was allowed to do that. After the expiry of 14 days, the Queen became restless—she asked the king to open the door of the temple as there was no sound from within the temple. The chief minister opposed this idea. But ultimately the door was opened and it was found that the old carpenter had left the temple keeping the wooden statue half incomplete. The Lord had hands but not fingers and His body was complete only up to the waist. Being greatly shocked the Queen took the bed of straw and remained without food and drink. Then the Lord told through a revelation that the Lord would settle on

The Structural analysis of the myth

I	II	III	IV
7. God disappeared when king Indradumana boasted	2. Savara* as the killar of Hindu God Krishna	3. The God asked to let afloat Krishna's body in the ocean	1. Indradumna sent messengers in search of the Lord
10. The king went to Brahma to have the temple sanctified	6. The Brahmin, Vidyapati was married to the daughter of Savara Basu	9. The Lord asked the king to establish His temple who engaged himself in killing the Savaras	4. The Savara worshipped the Lord
12. The crow and tortoise told the truth	11. Galamadhava claimed that the temple belonged to him	13. The Lord came floating as a log with the marks of conchshell and wheet-shaped missile.	5. Failure those sent in other directions for the search of the Lord except the one who went to the east—the man who went to the east succeded.
16. The image remained incomplete as the king broke his promise	14. The log of wood could not be pulled without the participation of the Savaras		8. Indradumna ravaged Savara village and killed many of them (enmity)
18. The king begged to be childless	15. Savara and Brahmin joined hands to pull the log of wood.		
	17. Both the Savaras and brahmins employed in temple servlce		
↓	↓	↓	↓
I Overrating the Hindu sense of sanctity	II Underrating the Hindu sense of sanctity	III Denial of Savara origin of Lord Jagannatha	IV Savara origin of Lord Jagannatha

*Savaras were a non-Aryan tribe who lived on hunting. Most of their descendants have gradually turned to agriculture.
From the columns glven above, it appears that I : II : : III IV.

the very incomplete statue of the temple. Henceforth, He would receive worship as a Buddha—the joint management and service-system by the savaras and the Brahmins would continue for all time to come. Then the Lord asked Indradumna to express his desire for a reward. Indradumna prayed that he should have no children so that his descendants may not have any claim for ownership of the temple. The temple would belong to the people. He also desired that the temple would remain closed from midnight till early dawn when it would be opened. The Lord granted the prayer of Indradumna.

As in almost every myth and tale, here in this myth of the Jagannatha temple, there are two opposite parties and conflicting functions :

Parties

a. Hindu force

b. Savara force

Functions (F) :

x The acceptence of the concept that Jagannatha was a Hindu God

y The concept that Jagannatha was a Hindu God is denied —He was a Savara God.

It thus follows

$$Fx(a) : Fy(b) :: Fx(b) : Fa^{-I}(y).$$

Structurally, the Jagannatha myth revealed the truth that in India the brahminical concept of God which originally belongs to the Aryan concept has been mixed up with the non-Aryan concept of God. Thus Lord Jagannatha in the shape of a log of wood floating over the water could not be pulled over only by the brahmins—the hands of the Savaras were required. Last of all, Lord Jagannatha arranged that the temple services must be done jointly by the brahmins and the Savaras and He would be worshiped as Buddha. This myth is thus the product of a cross-cultural social order. Besides, this myth, like many others, proves that the mythical thought always progresses from the awareness of oppositions toward their resolution. To clarify this, I would add more structural analysis of the myth. The contrast between the columns, if graphically shown, will stand like this :

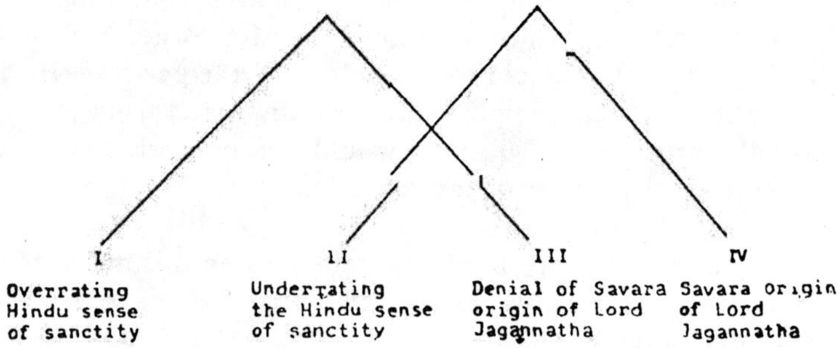

The whole columns are paradigmatically arranged according-ing to Levi-Strauss. If we change this arrangement, the myth cannot stand. Thus the columns are the logical conclusion of the myth. Now we can say that this myth, like all myths of the world, is not the product of the savage minds. At every step, it follows certain norms and proceeds towards reasonable aims and objectives. This is true about all myths, all aspects of folklore. We can find that deeper meaning only through the structural analyses of which Levi-Strauss provides a major one before us of the genres of folklore.

Let us see how binarism works in this myth. The opposite forces in culture help the growth and progress of values and through them the culture as a whole is reshaped. This is true about folk culture. In this myth, as in all myths, we get some opposing forces and their functions. They come in binary form, such as nature and culture, savaras and aryans, king and queen, father and daughter, earth and sky, ocean and forest, hero and god. If we consider them on high and low order, there also we get some separate sets of binarism, such as sky and earth, aryans and savaras, pride and humility. These binary sets opposing each other would be better understood by the following graphic arrangements.

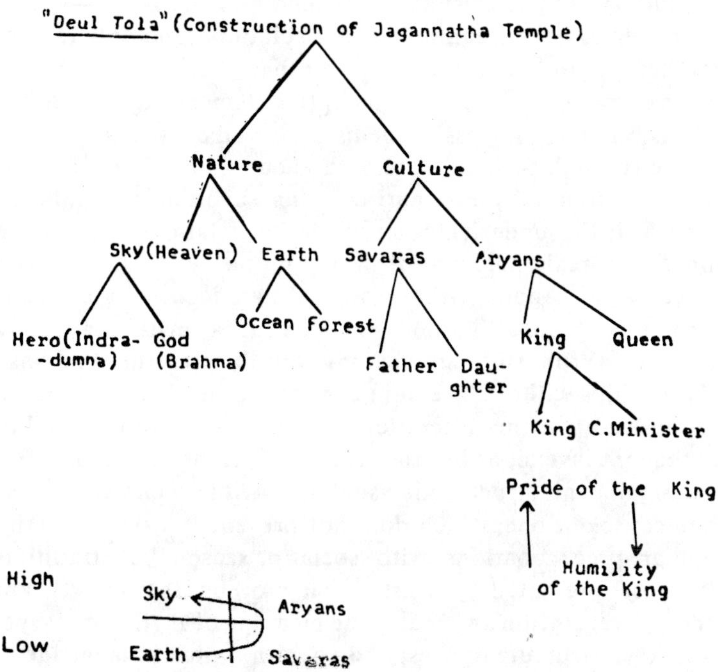

That some fundamental contradictions exist and work in a culture are better revealed through the structural analysis in the pattern of Levi-Strauss. The analysis of this Oriya myth has been helpful to prove that the myths are created to express some meaningful language of the traditional society—which is, of course, true about all materials of folklore.

There have been three major developments in the modern study of myth. The first was the realization, associated specially with Tylor Frazer and Durkheim, that the myths of primitive societies are highly relevant to the subject as a whole. The second was Freud's discovery of the unconscious and its relation to myths and dreams. The third is the structural theory of myth propounded by the great French anthropologist Claude Levi-Strauss. The essence of Levi-Strauss's belief is that myth is one mode of human communication—economic exchange, and kinship exchanges by means of women, being others. It is a product of language, which itself together with music and rhythmical sound, form a fourth or auditory mode. Just as the elements of language—sounds or phonemes—are meaningless in isolation, and only take on significance in combination with other phonemes, so the elements of myth, the individual narrative elements, the persons or objects, are meaningless in themselves, and only take on significance through their relation with each other. But it is not the formation of mere narrative as such that is significant; rather it is the underlying structure of relations that determines the real meaning of a myth, just as it is underlying structure of a language that gives it significance as a means of communication. Variant versions of a myth may show changes in the surface meaning, but the structure and basic relationships will often remain constant, indeed may even be emphasized by the alteration of the overt symbols and by consequent inversions or other forms of transformation. Yet this significant structure is usually, in tribal societies at least, an unconscious one, which does not prevent it from reflecting popular preoccupations with social or seasonal contraditions like those presented by a sister-in-law or by the growth and decay of vegetation and men. The meaning of myth is conveyed by its own structure, corresponding with syntax in language.

Levi-Strauss goes further to say that a structure can reveal itself at different levels, or by means of different codes. Among South American myths he distinguishes a sociological, a culinary or techno-economic, an acoustic, a cosmological, and an astronomical code. Any one myth may contain all or most of these. In The Story of Asdiwal he writes of reaching rock bottom at the sociological level of meaning, and in his provisional interpretation of the Oedipus myth he uses the sociological code as a means of revealing something about the origins of men on the cosmological level (1963: p. 213). His interpretations of the myth's implication is 'summarized in these words: "Although experience contradicts theory, social life validates cosmology by its similarity of structure. Hence cosmology is true." (1963, p. 216). Similarly, his analysis in the same article, of the Puebto creation myth claims to reveal a message concerned with the relation of life and death: namely that some mediation is possible between the two, in this case through the concept of hunting as a way of getting food. Hunting is a mean between agriculture (which furthers life by producing good without killing) and warfare (a special kind of hunting which causes human death). This mediation is confirmed by a further one: for if grass-eating animals are on the side of life and predatory animals on the side of death, there is a third kind, namely, carrion-eaters, which mediate between the two because they do not kill, but eat raw animal food all the same. In other words, a kind of logic is being elicited from certain relationships in nature—one that makes death appear as an acceptable element in human experience. Mythical analysis, he writes, cannot have for its object the demonstration of how men think in their myths, but how myths think themselves in men, and without their awareness. All his analyses demonstrate that the differential distinctions exploited by myth consist not so much in things themselves as in a body of common properties that can be expressed in geometrical terms, and transformed into each other by means of operations that are, already, a kind of algebra ("Du Miel aux Cendres", (Mythological vol. II, Paris, 1966).

At certain points, according to Levi-Strauss, the Greek mythology turned into philosophy. By spirit he seems to mean the very structure of the human mind, which is the same all over the world, among illiterate tribesmen and the supposedly civilized, an innate tendency to work in certain ways, notably by a process of binary analysis. In this respect, he concludes, the meaningful content of myth is entirely abstract, it cannot be expressed algebrically, it is not about any particular aspect of the world or human life—about sociological problems or contradictions, for example, rather, it is about the human mind as such, and man's general qualities as an entity involved in an environment. Thus, Levi-Strauss feels that the myths of primitive peoples are really going to reveal a kind of truth about the nature and working of the human mind, and hence they are valuable indeed and their study should be pursued at all costs.

Many of Levi-Strauss's interpretations of the ultimate meaning of myths, from the South American Indians as well as those of the Nothwest, end up with the question of the tensions brought about by different systems of giving in marriage, or the exchange of women; and there is no doubt that in exogamous tribes, specially matrilineal ones, the proper interchange of women is a subject of abiding interest and enormous potentiality for social stress. He deals with a hundred and eighty-seven myths in the first volume of *Mythologigues*, almost as many again in both the second and the third. All these myths are held to be interconnected in one respect or another, so that the interpretation of any one of them can only be understood in relation to the unfolding interpretation of the rest. We may not agree with many analyses or methods of interpretations propounded by Levi-Strauss, but the contribution he has made to the structuralism of folklore in general and myths in particular, has its great value.

After Levi-Strauss, P. Maranda, E.K. Maranda and Alan Dundes proved their efficiency in the structural analysis of folklore, E.K. Maranda and P. Maranda's book, *Structural Models in Folklore and Transformation Essays* (1971, Mouton, The Hague) has introduced the new formula of Quasi Solution: Quasi Result: Final Solution: Final Result. This can be successfully applied in riddles, proverbs and many other aspects of folklore. The Marandas have also applied the transformational method in some items of folklore with success. Alan Dundes has applied the Propp's method in the tales of American Indians and invented the word motifeme in the light of morpheme in linguistics (1963, FFC 195). My recent book *Folklore Charchaya Rupatattic Bisslation Paddhoti* (Morphological study in folkloristics, Loka Laukik, Calcutta, 1982) elaborately deals with the methods of structural analysis followed by Propp in folkltales, N. Chomsky in linguistics and Levi-Strauss in anthropology. In the fourth chapter of this book, I have morphologically analysed the Indian myths, tales, legends, proverbs, riddless and folk songs.

The concept of structuralism as a special doctrine has been questioned more than once in its short history. Even then the tremendous popularity this theory has gained cannot be underestimated. In spite of its many drawbacks, its philosophical strength and social fervour have already gained momentum among the folklorists all over the world. Pierre Maranda rightly pinpoints the state of structural analysis, "in folkloristics the approach has gathered momentum in the present decade. After the earlier pioneerial works of Vladimir Propp, Claude Levi-Strauss, and Thomas A Sebeok, a relatively large array of articles on different folkloristic genres has now appeared". (1971, p. 19). Dundes writes, "The reason why folklorists should adopt a pattern (structural) approach to folklore is not simply because the approach has been successfully utilized in other disciplines, but rather because of the nature of folkloristic materials that is, because the materials of folklore are structured and patterned." (1963, FFC No. 195, p. 6). So far as the Indian sub-continent is concerned, Dr. P.R. Subramanian has done some structural analysis of Tamil lullabies (1969: unpublished doctrol dessertation), Dr. Jawaharlal Handoo has applied this method on *Cilapattikaram*, a Tamil epic (1978, *Current Trend in Folklore*) and Dr. Nirmalendu Bhowmick has made some wonderful experiments of structuralism on Bengali rhymes (1386, Bengali era). My recent work on morphological analysis of folklore written in Bengali is perhaps the first elaborate attempt made in the Indian subcontinent where Propp, Chosmky, Levi-Strauss, Marandas, Dundes, Henricks have been thoroughly discussed and the applications of their methods have been successfully done on different materials of folklore besides myths and folktales. I have proved that this method can profitably be applied to Indian folklore belonging to different languages and regions.

I have made a short survey of the theories of folklore and put forward some arguments in favour of their applicability on folklore of the Indian subcontinent in this paper. I am convinced that the theories of folklore are our proud possessions and we must work hard for their successful application on all genres of Indian folklore, their necessary modifications and further development.

APPENDIX

In search of Indian archetypes

I. Folktale types indexed in the Aarne-Thompson compendium that are linked exclusively to South Asian sources

Ordinary Folk Tales

302B Hero with Life Dependent on his Sword.
306A The Pursuit of the Heavenly Maiden.
315A The Cannibal Sister.

369	The Youth on a Quest for his Lost Father.
411	The King and the Lamia.
413	Marriage by Stealing Clothing.
433C	The Serpent Husband and the Jealous Girl.
450A	The Brother Transformed to a Snake.
459	The Make-Believe Son (Daughter).
462	The Outcaste Queens and the Ogress Queen.
465D	Animal Brothers Help the Hero.
467	The Quest for the Wonderful Flower (Jewel).
516A	The Sign Language of the Princess.
516B	The Abducted Princess.
534	The Youth Who Tends the Buffalo Herd.
535	The Boy Adopted by Tigers (Animals).
546	The Clever Parrot.
567A	The Magic Bird-Heart and the Separated Brothers.
612A	The Ungrateful Wife Restored to Life.
622	The Talking Bed-Legs.
653B	The Suitors Restore the Maiden to Life.
655A	The Strayed Camel and the Clever Deductions.
670A	The Woman Who Understood Animal Languages.
674	Incest Averted—Talking Animals.
709A	The Stork's Daughter.
780A	The Cannibalistic Brothers.
855	The Substitute Bridegroom.
856	The Girl Elopes With the Wrong Man.
$875B_2$	Converting a Moslem into a Hindu.
875_3	Moving the Well.
875E	The Unjust Decision: The Oil Press Gives Birth to a Colt.
881A	The Abandoned Bride Disguised as a Man.
888A	The Wife Who Would not be Beaten.
896	The Lecherous Holy Man and the Maiden in a Box.
897	The Orphan Girl and Her Cruel Sisters-in-Law.
910H	Never Travel Without a Companion or Stay Alert.
910J	Never Plant a Thorn Tree.
923B	The Princess who was Responsible for Her Own Fortune.
926A	The Clever Judge and the Demon in the Pot.
926B	The Ring to be Cut in Two and Divided Equally Between Two Quarrelling Persons.

934D[1] Outwitting Fate.
939 The Offended Deity.
949 The Faithful Servitor.
951C The Disguised King Joins the Thieves.
976A The Thief Exposed by a Story.
977 The Eloping Couple and the Robbers.
978 The Youth in the Land of the Cheaters.
1152 The Ogre Overawed by Displaying Objects.
1164D The Demon and the Man Join Forces.
1168B The Tree-Demon Pays the Man to Save the Tree.

Jokes and Anecdotes

1250B The Fool Dangling from the Elephant's Tail.
1295B* Man on Camel has Doorway Broken to Down Ride in.
1331B* Letters too Small.
1409C Obedient Husband Walks Slowly.
1511 The Faithless Queen.
1525N The Two Thieves Trick Each Other.
1525Q The Two Thieves Married to the Same Woman.
1532 The Voice from the Grave.
1534A The Innocent Man Chosen to Fit the Stake (Noose).
1633 Joint Ownership of the Cow.
1646 The Lucky Blow.
1653E The Entrails Dropped from the Tree.
1685A The Stupid Son-in-Law.
1692 The Stupied Thief.
1693 The Literal Fool—the Burning of Lanka. Posts Broken; Fire Set.
1707 The Noseless Man.
1962A The Great Wrestlers.

Animal Tales

56C
58
59
64
68
122G
122H
122Z
131
157A
170A
176
178B
223
233A
233B
239
241
243
248A

Formula Tales

2013	2034D
2023	2034E
2028A	2042
2029A	2042B
2029B	2042C
2029C	2042D
2031C	2042A
2031A	2045B
2031B	2047

II. Most extensively indexed motifs in the Thompson-Balys volume on Indic Folktales

(The column on the left indicates the number of lines devoted to listing sources: Roughly three sources are cited on each line.)

No. of lines required to list sources	*Motif No.*	*Motif description*
13	N 451	Secrets overheard from animal (demon)
12	L 161	Lowly hero marries princess
11	Z 71.1	Formulistic number; seven
10	D 231	Transformation: man to stone
	E 80	Water of life
	K 1811	Gods (saints) in disguise visit mortals
	S 31	Cruel stepmother
	S 143	Abandoned in forest
9	D 721.3	Disenchantment by destroying skin (covering)
	E 631	Reincarnation in plant (tree) growing from grave
	J 1172.3	Ungrateful animal returned to captivity
	K 842	Dupe persuaded to take prisoner's place in sack
	K 1715	Weak animal (man) makes large one (ogre) believe he has eaten many of the large one's companions

	K 2111	Potipher's wife : Woman makes vain overtures to a man and then accuses him of attempting to force her
	K 2211	Treacherous brother (usually elder brother)
8	B 491.1	Helpful servant
	B 571	Animals perform tasks for man
	H 335	Tasks assigned suitors
	H 1385.3	Quest for vanished wife (mistress)
	K 2115.2	Slander. Woman has given birth to objects
	Q 115	Reward : any boon that may be asked
	T 11.4.1	Love through sight of hair of unknown princess
	W 154.2.1	Rescued animal threatens rescuer
7	B 216	Knowledge of animal languages
	B 360	Animals grateful for rescue from peril of death
	B 505	Magic object received from animal
	D 630	Transformation and disenchantment at will
	D 1812.3.3	Future revealed in dream
	G 84	Fee. fi-fo-fum: cannibal returning home smells human flesh and makes exclamation
	K 1051	Diving for sheep. Dupe persuaded that sheep have been lost in the river
	K 1335	Seduction (or wooing) by stealing clothes of bathing girl
	K 1911	The false bride. An impostor takes wife's place without detection
	K 2213	Treacherous wife
	N 681	Husband (lover) arrives home just as wife (mistress) is to marry another
	N 683	Stranger accidentally chosen king. Picked up by sacred elephant
	N 711.1	Prince finds maiden in woods tree and marries her
	N 817	Deity as helper (usually in answer to prayer)
	Q 241	Adultery punished
7	S 260.1	Human sacrifice
	S 262	Periodic sacrifices to a monster

	S 451	Outcaste wife at last united with husband and children
6	B 41.2	Flying horse
	B 244.1	King of serpents
	B 450	Animal nurse
	C 331	Tabu : Looking back
	C 611	Forbidden chamber
	D 191	Transformation : man to serpent (D 391 = serpent to person, 4 lines)
	D 621.1	Animal by day; man by night
	D 672	Obstacle flight
	D 1076	Magic ring
	D 1470.1.15	Magic wishing ring
	E 30	Resuscitation by arrangement of numbers
	E 113	Resuscitation by blood
	E 761.3	Life token : tree (flower) fades
	F 582.1	Serpent damsel
	F 913	Victims rescued from swallower's belly
	G 530.2	Help from ogre's daughter (or son)
	H 94	Indentification by ring
	H 171.1	King selected by elephant bowing to him
	H 346	Princess given to man who can heal her
	H 931	Tasks assigned in order to get rid of hero
	H 1212	Quest assigned because of feigned illness
	H 1235	Succession of helpers on quest
	J 163.4	Good counsels bought
	J 1112	Clever wife
	K 511	Uriah letter changed. Order of execution
	K 512	Campassionate execution: servant charged with killing hero (heroine), arranges escape of latter
	K 522	Escape by shamming death
	K 543	Biting the foot : fox to bear who is biting his foot 'you are biting the tree root'
	K 941.1	Cows killed for their hides when large price is reported by trickster
	K 1837	Disguise of woman in man's clothes
	K 1911.2.2	True bride pushed into water by false
	K 2212.2	Treacherous sister-in-law

M 370 Vain attempts to escape fulfilment of prophecy
N 812 Giant or ogre as helper
N 831.1 Mysterious housekeeper. Men find their houses mysteriously put into order (by a girl)
S 165 Mutilation : putting out eyes
T 11.2 Love through sight of picture
T 15 Love at first sight
T 16 Man falls in love with woman he sees bathing
T 24.2 Swooning for love
T 211.2.1 Wife throws herself on husband's funeral pyre
T 511.1.3 Conception from eating mango
T 548.1 Child born in answer to prayer
W 154.8 Grateful animals : ungrateful man
B 422 Helpful cat
B 431.3 Helpful tiger
B 469.9 Helpful parrot
B 552 Man carried by bird
B 582.1.1 Animal wins wife for his master
D 185.1 Transformation : man to fly
D 610 Repeated transformation
D 615 Transformation combat
D 700 Person disenchanted
E 0 Resuscitation
E 670 Repeated reincarnation
E 715.1.3 Separable soul in parrot
E 728 Evil spirit possesses person
F 303 Wedding of mortal and fairy
5 F 772.1 Tower of babel : remarkably tall tower designed to reach sky
G 72.2 Starving woman abandoned in cave eats newborn child
G 530.1 Help from ogre's wife
H 11 Recognition through story-telling
H 11.1 Recognition by telling life history
H 175.1 Recognition of son by gushing up of milk in mother's breasts

H 324	Suitor test=choosing princess from others identically clad
H 133.5	Quest for marvelous flower
H 1385.4	Quest for vanished husband
J 1191.1.1	The sea is on fire—not more absurd than the decision about the colt
J 2233	Logically absurd defenses
J 2415	Foolish imitation of lucky men
J 2511	The silence wager (one becomes angry, scolds and loses the wager)
K 11.1	Race won by deception : relative helpers
K 335.1.1.2	Cow-hide falls on robbers from tree
K 553	Wait till I get fat—captive persuades captor to wait and fatten him before eating
K 941.2	Dupe burns house because trickster reports high price paid for ashes
K 1321.1	Man disguised as a woman admitted to woman's quarters
K 1715.1	Weak animal shows strong his own reflection and frightens him
K 1836	Disguise of man in woman's dress
K 2112	Woman slandered as adultress
K 2248	Treacherous minister
L 10	Victorious younger son
L 111.4	Orphan hero
L 162	Lowly heroine marries prince (other way around has about ½ the entries)
M 21	King hears judgement. King flattered by elder daughters and angered by seeming indifference of youngest banishes her and favours eldest
N 7	Trained rat upsets pieces in gambling game
N 101	Inexorable fate
N 111	Luck thought of as a goddess
N 347	Innocent man accidently suspected of crime
N 451.1	Secrets of animals (demons) accidentally overheard from tree (bridge) hiding place

N 452	Secret remedy overheard in conversation of animals (witches)
Q 112	Half of kingdom as reward
Q 211	Murder punished
Q 285	Cruelty punished
Q 431	Punishment : banishment or exile
R 10.1	Princess (maiden) abducted by monster (ogre)
S 146.1	Abandonment in well
S 161	Mutilation : cutting off hands (arms)
S 411	Wife banished
T 69.1.2	Seven princesses sought by seven princes
T 143	Infant marriages
T 511.1	Conception from eating fruit

REFERENCES

Abraham, Karl 1913 *Dreams and Myths*; *A Study in Race Psychology*, Trans. by WA White, Nervous and Mental Disease Monograph Series No. 15, New York.

Anderson, Walter 1923 "Kaiser Und Abt" *Folklore Fellows Communication* (FFC), No. 54, Helsinki.

———— 1959 Review of W Roberts. "The Tale of Kind and Unkind Girls," *Febula* 2307-10.

Barthes, Roland 1967 *Elements of Semiology*, Trans. by Lavers and Smith, London.

———— 1972 "To Write: An intransitive verb," in Macksay and Donato, *The Structuralist Controversy. The Language of Criticism and the Science of Man*, Baltimore.

Bascom, William R 1954 "Four Functions of Folklore," *Journal of American Folklore*, (*JAF*), 66, 283-90.

———— 1953 "Folklore and Anthropology," *JAF*, Vol. 66, pp. 283-90.

———— 1955 "Verbal Art," *JAF*, 68, 245-52.

Baughman, EW 1966 Type and Motif Index of the Folktales of England and North America, *Indiana University Folktale Series*, No. 20, Mouton, Thc Hague.

Beardsley, MC 1958 *Aesthetics*: *Problems in the Philosophy of Criticism*, New York.

Beardsley, MC and Schucller, HM (eds) 1967 *Aesthetic Inquiry, Essays on Art, Criticism and the Philosophy of Art*, Belmont, California.

Beck, Brenda EF 1974 "The Kin Nucleus in Tamil Folklore," in Thomas Trautman (ed), *Kinship and History in South Asia*, pp. 1-27, University of Michigan Center for South and Southeast Asian Studies, Ann Arbor.

Benedict, Ruth 1935 *Zuni Mythology*, 2 Vols. Columbia University Contributions to Anthropology. Abridged in Margaret Mead, 1959, "An Anthropologist at Work. Writings of Ruth Benedict," 226-245, Houghton-Mifflin, Boston.

Bhowmick, Nirmalendu 1986-1386 (Bengali Era): *Bangla Chodher Bhumika*, Calcutta.

Boas, Franz 1981 "Dissemination of Tales among the Natives of North America," *JAF*, 4, 13-20.

Bodker, L 1957 "Indian Animal Tales, A Preliminary Survey," FFC, 170, Helsinki.

Breal, Michel 1877 "Melanges de mythologie et de linguistique," *Librairie Hachette*, pp. 163-185.

Brooks, Cleanth 1967 *Modern Poetry and the Tradition*, Chapel Hill.

Brown, W Norman 1920 "Escaping One's Fate," in *Studies in Honor of of Maurice Bloomfield*, Yale University Press, New Haven.

Campbell, Joseph 1949 *The Hero with the Thousand Faces*, Pantheon, New York.

——— 1959 *The Masks of God : Primitive Mythology*. Viking, New York.

——— 1961 *The Masks of God*: *Oriental Mythology*. Viking, New York.

Casey, John 1966 *The Language of Criticism*, London.

Cassirer, Ernst 1953 *The Philosophy of Symbolic Forms*, Vol. II, *Mythical Thought*, (Eng. trans.), New Haven.

Caudwell, H 1951 *The Creative Impulse*, Macmillian and Co. Ltd, London.

Christiansen, Raider 1957 "Introduction," *Febula*, 1, 1-2.

Claus, Peter J 1975 "The Siri Myth and Ritual: A Mass Possession Cult of South India," *Ethnology*, Vol. 14, No. 1, pp. 47-58.

Culler, Jonathan 1973 "The Linguistic Basis of Structuralism," in David Robey (ed.), *Structuralism: An Introduction*, Oxford.

Cushing, FH 1931 *Zuni Folktales*, New York.

Dollard, John 1939 "The Dozens: Dialectic of Insult," *American Imago*, 1, 3-25.

Dorson, Richard M 1959 A Theory for American Folklore, *JAF*, 72, 197-215.

——— 1960 Replies of Questions on "A Theory for American Folklore," *JAF*, 73, 327-30.

——— 1961 (ed.) *Folklore Research Around the World*: *A North American Point of View*, published jointly as Vol. 74, No. 294 of *JAF* (with an index), as No. 16 in the Indiana University Folklore Series, Bloomington.

——— 1963 "Current Folklore Theories," *Current Anthropology*, Vol. IV. Chicago.

———— 1963 (ed.) *Studies in the Japanese Folklore*, Indiana University Folklore Series No. 17, Bloomington.

————1978a "American Folklore vs. Folklore in America," *Journal of the Folklore Institute*, (JFI) Vol. 15, pp. 97-112.

Dundes, Alan 1963 "The Morphology of North American Indian Folktales," FFC No. 195, "Structural Typology in North American Indian Folktales," *Southwestern Journal of Anthropology* (SWJA), Vol. 19 (1963), 121-130.

———— 1963 "Toward a Structural Definition of the Riddle," *JAF*, 67.

———— 1965 (ed) *The Study of Folklore*, Prentice Hall Inc. Englewood, Cliffs. N.J.

———— 1971 "The Making and Breaking of Friendship as a Structural Frame in African Folktales," pp. 171-188 in Pierre Maranda and Elli Kongas Maranda (eds) *Structural Analysis of Oral Tradition*. University of Pennsylvania Press, Philadelphia.

———— 1975a "From Etic to Emic Units in the Structural Study of Folktales, "(reprint of 1962) in *Analytic Essays in Folklore*, Mouton. pp. 61-72, The Hague.

———— 1975b "Structural Typology in North American Indian Folktales, (reprint of 1963) in *Analytic Essays in Folklore*, Mouton, pp. 73-79, The Hague.

———— 1975c "The Study of Folklore in Literature and Culture: Identification and Interpretation," (reprint of 1965) in *Analytic Essays in Folklore*, Mouton, pp. 28-34, The Hague.

———— 1975d "Thinking Ahead: A Folkloristic Reflection of the Future Orientation in American Worldview," (reprint of 1969) in *Analytic Essays in Folklore*. Mouton, pp. 226-38, The Hague.

Elliot, TS 1948 *Notes Towards A Definition of Culture*, London.

Emeneau, MB 1940 "A Classical Indian Folktale as a Reported Modern Event, The Brahman and the Mongoose." *Proceedings of the American Philosophical Society*, Vol. LXXXIII.

———— 1941 "The Faithful Dog as Security for a Debt," *Journal of the American Oriental Society*, Vol. 71.

Feldman, Sandor S 1947 "Notes on the Primal Horde" in *Psycho-analysis and Social Sciences*, Vol. I, (ed) G. Roheim. International University Press, New York.

Freud, Sigmund 1900 *Interpretation of Dreams. The Basic Writings of Sigmund Freud* (Trans. and ed.) AA Brill, Modern Library, 1938, New York.

———— and Oppenheim, DE 1958 *Dreams in Folklore*, New York.

Fromm, Erich 1949 "The Oedipus Complex and the Oedipus Myth" in *The Family: Its Function And Destiny*, (ed.) Ruth N. Anshen, Science of Culture Series, Vol. 5, Harper and Row Publishers, New York.

Hallowell, AI 1947 "Myth, Culture And Personality," *American Anthropologist*, Vol. 49, 544-45.

Hand, Wayland D 1946 *Nazi Use of Folklore* (manuscript).

Handoo, Jawaharlal 1978 *Current Trends in Folklore*, Institute of Canada Studies, Mysore.

Hart, George L III 1975 *The Poems of Ancient Tamil*, University of California Press, Berkeley.

Herskovits, Melville 1958a *Dahomean Narrative, A Cross-Cultural Analysis*, Northwestern University Press, Evanston, Illinois.

Herscovits, Melville and J and Frances Herkovits. 1958b "Sibling Rivalry, The Oedipus Complex and Myth" *JAF*, 71, 1-5. Abridged in *Dahomean Narrative*, 85-95 as "Sibling Rivalry and the Oedipus Theorem".

Hori, Ichiro 1959 "Japanese Folkbeliefs", *American Anthropologists* 61: 405-424.

———— 1958 "Sibling Rivalry, the Oedipus Complex and Myth," *JAF*, 71, 1-15.

Ishida, Eiichiro 1950 "The Kappa Legend" *Folklore Studies*, 9, 1-52.

Islam, Mazharul 1982 *Folklore Charchaya Rupatattik Bisslation Paddhati* (Morphological Analysis of Folklore), written in Bengali, Loka Laukik, Calcutta.

———— 1974 (2nd edition) *Folklore Parichitio Loka-Sahityer Pathon Pathon* (The introduction and Study of Folklore), Dacca.

———— 1970 *History of Folktale Collections in India and Pakistan*, Bangla Academy, Dacca, 2nd enlarged edition, 1982, Panchali Prakasan, Calcutta.

Jack, Philip 1960 Questions on "A Theory for American Folklore," *JAF*, 73, 325-27.

Jackobson, Roman and Levi-Strauss, Claude 1962, Charles Boudelaire's "Les Chats", "L'Homme" 2., reprinted in Michael Lane (ed.) *Structuralism A Reader*, 1970, (Trans) Katie Furne's Lane, London.

Jacobs, Melville 1958 *The Content and Style of an Oral Literature*, Chicago University Press.

———— 1959a "The Content and Style of an Oral Literature," *Clackamas Chinook, Myths and Tales*. University of Chicago Press, Chicago.

———— 1959b *Folklore in the Anthropology of Franz Boas*, (ed) W. Coldschmidt, pp. 119-38, Memoirs of the American Anthropological Association, 89.

———— 1959c "Review of V. Propp's Morphology of Folktales," JAF, 72, 195-96.

———— 1960 *Humor and Social Structure in an Oral Literature in Cultural History*, (ed) S. Diamond. pp. 181-89, Columbia University Press, New York.

Jones, Ernest 1930 "Psychoanalysis and Folklore," Jubilee Congress of the Folklore Society: Papers and Transactions, London. Also in Essays in Folklore, *Anthropology and Religion*, 2: 1-21 of *Essays in Applied Psycho-analysis*, 1951, Hogarth Press, London.

———— 1959 "The Connections Between the Nightmare and Certain Medieval Superstition," *On the Nightmare*, Part II, 55-239, Evergreen Edition; First Published in 1931, New York.

Jung, CG 1956 "On the Psychology of the Trickster Figure" Paul Radin, *The Trickster, a Study of American Indian Mythology*, pp. 195-211, (Trans) R.F.C. Hull, Philosophical Library, New York.

———— 1958a "The Psychology of the Child Archetype" *Psyche and Symbol, A Selection from the Writings of CG Jung*, (ed) VS Laslo, pp. 113-131, Doubleday Anchor, New York.

———— 1942 *Psychology of the Unconscious*, Dodd Mead and Co, New York.

———— and Kerenyi, C 1949 *Essays on a Science of Mythology* (Trans) RF Hull, Pantheon Books, New York.

———— 1958b "The Spirit in Fairy Tales," *Psyche and Symbol*, pp. 72-86.

Katzer, J (ed) 1959 *Russian Decorative Folk Art*, Foreign Language Publishing House, Moscow.

Keri, Hedvig 1958 "Ancient Games and Popular Games," Psychological Essay, *American Jamago*, 15, 41-81.

Kramer, SN 1903 *The Sumarians*, Chicago.

Krohn, Kaarle 1926 *Die Folkloristiche Arbeitsmethods*, Oslo.

Langer, Sussanne K 1953 *Feeling and Form*, London.

———— 1957a *Problems of Art*, Routledge and Kegan Paul, London.

———— 1957b *Philosophy in a New Key*, 3rd edn. Cambridge, Mass.

Leach, ER 1970 Levi-Strauss, Fontana, London.

Leach, Edmund 1967 (ed) *The Structural Study of Myth and Totemism*, ASA Monograph, Vol. 5, London.

Lessa, William 1956 "Oedipus-Type Tales in Oceania," *JAF*, Vol. 69, 63-73. Reprinted as "Tales from Ulithi Atoll" of Calfornia Publications, Folklore Studies 13, 1961, Berkeley.

Levi-Strauss, Claude 1963 *Structural Anthropology* (trans) C. Jacobson and B.G. Schoept, New York (Original French edition, 1962), (Harmondsworth, 1972).

———— 1964 *Totemism*, Lonodon (Original French edition, 1962).

———— 1966 *The Savage Mind*, London (Original French, 1962).

———— 1969 *The Elementary Structures of Kinship*, (trans.) JH Belle and J.R. Von Strumer, (ed) R. Needham. Boston (Original French, 1949).

———— 1971 *The Story of Asdiwal in the Structural Study of Myth and Totemism*, (ed) E Leach (original French edition, 1958).

Lord, AB 1960 *The Singer of Tales*, Cambridge, Mass.

Luomala, Katharine 1955 *Voices on The Wind*, Berniel P. Bishop Museum, onolulu.

Maranda EK and P Maranda 1971 *Structural Models in Folklore and Transformational Essays*, Mouton, The Hague.

Malinowski, Bronislaw 1926 *Myth in Primitive Psychology*, WW Norton, New York.

———— 1927 *The Father in Primitive Psychology*, WW Norton, New York.

Messenger, John 1959 "The Role of Proverbs in a Nigerian Judicial System," *South Western Journal of Anthropology*, 15, 64-73.

Munden, Kenneth J 1958 "A Contribution to the Psychological Understanding of the Cowboy and His Myth," *American Imago*, 15, 103-48.

Naumann, Hans 1922, 2nd ed 1929 *Grundzuge der deutschen Volkskunde*, Quelle and Meyer, Leipzig.

Nygard, Holger Olof 1958 "The Ballad of Heer Halewijn, Its Forms and Variations in Western Europe," *FFC No. 169* and University of Tennessee Press.

O'Flaherty, Wendy Doniger 1973 *Asceticism and Eroticism in the Mythology of Siva*, Oxford University Press, Oxford.

Ortutay, Gyula 1955 "The Science of the Folklore of Hungary between the Two World Wars and During the Period Subsequent to the Liberation," *Acta Ethnogaphica Academiae Scientiarum Hungaricae*, 4, 6-89.

Palumer, Frank (ed) 1913 *National Proverbs, Russia*, London.

Piddington, Ralph 1970 "Action Anthropology," *Applied Anthropology—Readings in the Uses of the Science of Man*, Clifton (ed), Houghton-Mifflin Company, Boston, New York.

Propp, Vladimir J 1928 *Morfologiya Skazki*, Leningrad, *Morphology of the Folktale* (trans) L. Scott, Indiana University Research Centre for Language Sciences, 1958.

Ramanujan, AD 1971 "The Indian Oedipus," *Symposium on Indian Literature*, Indian Institute of Advanced Study, Simla.

Rank, Otto 1929 *The Trauma of Birth*, Harcourt, Brace and World, Inc. New York.

———— 1932 *Modern Education*, (Trans) Mabel E Moxon, Alfred A Knopf, Inc, New York.

Richards, IA 1926 *Principles of Literary Criticism*, 2nd ed. London.

———— 1929 *Practical Criticism*, London.

Riel, WH 1858 "Volkskunde: Die Volkskunde als Wissenchaft," in *Ein Handbuch Zur Geschichte Chrer probleme*, (ed) Gerhardlotz, pp. 23-37, Erich Schmidt, Berlin.

Roberts, Warren E 1958 *The Tale of the Kind and Unkind Girls. Aa-Th. 480 and Related Tales*, W. De Gruyter, Berlin.

Roheim, Geza 1945 *The Eternal Ones of the Dream*, A Psychoanalytic Interpretation of 'Australian Myth and Ritual' International University Press.

———— 1952 *The Gates of the Dream*, International Universities Press, New York.

———— 1942 "The Primal Horde and Incest in Central Australia," *Journal of Criminal Psychopathology*, Vol. 3, 454-60.

Roy, Nihar Ranjan (ed) 1969 *Introductory Address, Urgent Research in Social Anthropology*, Indian Institute of Advanced Study.

Runciman, WG 1969 "What is Structuralism?" *The British Journal of Sociology*, 20, 253-65.

Sebeok, Thomas A 1955 (ed) "Myth, A Symposium," *JAF* 68. Reprinted 1958, Bloomington, Indiana University Press.

———— 1960 "Recording a Text, Levels and Aspects in a Cherimis Sonnet," *Style in Language*, New York.

Sebeok, TA and Francis J Ingemann 1956 "Structural and Content Analysis in Folklore Research," *Studies in Cherimis, the Supernatural*, New York.

Shirer, William 1962 *The Rise and Fall of the Third Reich*, Fawcett Publication, Greenwich Conn.

Shulman, David 1978 "The Tamil Flood—Myths and the Cankam Legend," *Journal of Tamil Studies*, Vol. 14, pp. 14-31.

Spier, Leslie 1921 "The Sun Dance of the Plains Indians: The Development and Diffusion," Anthropological papers of *American Museum of Natural History*, Vol. 16, No. 7. New York.

Sterta, Richard 1941 "A Dutch Celebration of a Festival," *American Imago*, 2, 205-8.

Subramaniam, PR 1969 *Folklore of South India*, an unpublished doctoral dissertation.

Taylor, Archer 1928 "Precursors of the Finnish Method of Folklore Study," *Modern Philosophy*, 25, 481-91.

———— 1948 "Folklore and the Student of Literature", *The Pacific Spectator*, Vol. 2, 216-223.

———— 1959 "All is not Gold that Glitters", and Hypothetical Reconstructions, *Saga Och Sed*, 129-32.

Thompson, Stith 1955-58 *Motif Index of Folk-Literature*, 6 Vols, Revised and enlarged, Indiana University Press, Bloomington.

———— 1953 "The Star Husband Tale," *Studia Septentrionalia*, 4, 93-163.

———— 1955 "Myths and Folktales," *JAF*, 68, 482-88.

———— 1951 *The Folktale*, The Dryden Press, New York.

———— 1961 *The Types of the Folktale*, 2nd revision (based on original work by A. Aarne), *FF Communications 184*, Helsinki.

Thompson, Stith and Jonas Balys 1958 *The Oral Tales of India*, Bloomington.

———— and WE Roberts 1960, "Types of Indic Oral Tales," FFC No. 180, Vol. LXXIII, Helsinki.

Todorov, Tzvetan 1972 "Language and Literature" in Macksey and Donato, *The Structuralist Controversy*, Baltimore.

Vidyarthi, LP 1978 *Rise of Anthropology in India* (2 Vols.) Concept Publishing Company, New Delhi.

———— 1979 *Trends in World Anthropology*, Concept Publishing Company, New Delhi.

Von-Sydow, Carl Wilhelm 1948 "Selected Papers on Folklore," (ed) L. Bodker, Copenhagen: Rosenkilde Og Baggers Forlag.

Williams, PH 1938 *South Italian Folkways in Europe and America*, Yale University Press, New Haven.

Wimsatt, WK 1970 *The Verbal Icon*, London.

——— and Beardsley, MC 1949 "The Affective Fallacy," *Sewanee Review*, 57. Reprinted in *Wimsatt*, The Verbal Icon.

Yanagita, Kunio 1954, 1958 *Japanese Folklore Dictionary; Studies in Mountain Village Life; Studies in Fishing Village Life*, (Trans) Masanori Takatsuka, (Ed) George K Brady, University of Kentucky, Micro card series, Lexington.

3

A MORPHOLOGICAL ANALYSIS OF A BENGALI FOLK SONG

BENGALI folklore has a rich component of folk songs in it. Among many gems of these songs, Baul songs occupy the position of the central jewel. These songs have a touch of Tantricism in them and are distinguished, at the same time, by a fine literary quality and musical appeal. These qualities of the Baul songs have been discussed in the past and are being studied even now. Rabindranath was attracted to Baul songs by their distinctive aesthetic qualities. An article of his on Baul songs appeared in the *Bharati* (Baishakha, 1290 B.S.) in 1883, when he was 22 years of age. He said, later on, that his acquaintance with Baul songs helped him to discover his own poetic gifts and to realize that he was a Baul in spirit from his birth. His acquaintance with Baul songs even before he came into close contact with the Upanishadic ideas played a significant part in the development of his own poetry. Even those with an adverse view of the aesthetic qualities of folklore must perforce agree that songs that made a significant contribution to the development of Rabindranath's poetical genius cannot be lightly dismissed as trash.

The philosophy underlying these songs or their mystic significance is not proposed to be discussed here except as an introduction. These songs have two meanings, one appearing on the surface and the other underlying it. The Upanishads speak of the Purusha that is to be known and realized, while the Bauls speak of the Loved One dwelling in the mind of man. The One, according to the Upanishads, has to be realized in the mind and not in the world outside it. So do the Bauls want to realize Him as the One within the mind. "O where shall I find Him, the Loved One of my mind?", says the Baul. Here lies the basis of the Baul's philosophy. But the mind and the body are not mutually exclusive entities. In the process of the Baul's realization, the body plays a significant part; it has a distinct role. Many Baul composers have compared the body to a temple or mosque. There are others who have compared it to a boat, house or bark. I am now entering into the structural analysis in which the human body, or the human being as a whole, has been compared to and designated a bark. The composer Pagla Kanai (*kanai*, the demented) was born sometime in the first or second decade of the nineteenth century at Berubari of Jessore district, Bangladesh, and died on Thursday, 11 July, 1889, Bengali era being 1296, Asharh 28. His probable date of birth is 10 March, 1811 (Falgun 24 to 28, 1217). He was a contemporary of Lalan Fakir but differed from him in this that while Lalan carried on his *sadhana* (spiritual endeavour) in silence, Kanai was a bard, singing to gatherings of the people. He was, in other words, more of a *kabiyal* (a village bard) than a Baul, while Lalan was a Baul, pure and simple. Even then, Kanai's songs, composed extempore and sung to gatherings of people, are sung by many today and are greatly valued as Baul songs. I have collected and published some songs of this Muslim bard in a book* Even as a composer of Baul songs he could be compared with none other than Lalan.

The life of a Baul song is provided by its inner meaning. Many more things than those that are said in the song lie hidden inside it. To understand the real meaning of a song one has, first, to discover the hidden truth. Most Baul songs have as their inner meaning the playful and sweet relation that binds the Creator to the created. The Baul song that I propose to discuss has the same theme as its structural basis. The Creator has sent out a bark to the earth, but, bewildered by the earth's allurements, it has forgotten its Creator. Then in the end, it wends its way back to the Creator. Let us now examine the song.

*"Kabi Pagla Kanai" in A History of Folktale Collections in India, Bangladesh and Pakistan, Mazharul Islam, Panchali Prakashan, Calcutta, 1982.

A translation of a Bengali folk song of Pagla Kanai

Peculiar a bark was made
And then the Creator sent the bark on the earth
It does not glide on water
But floats on soil surface
Its helm is in the hands of the mind-helmsman
It moves by two rows.

What a miraculous mechanism is there in the bark
It floats on the ground, but within it is the water
Besides water and fire there are valuable contents in it
O brother helmsman ! Be alert and upright,
Do not loose your grip
The bark may sink under water any moment.

Pagla Kanai is deeply concerned
As to what will happen to the bark
When it will lose its strength
The joints of the bark would be loosened too
And the water will enter into its body
The six senses as the oarsmen would take leave
And then the bark will get drowned even in the ground,
(Then the bark will go to eternity)

Special mention may be made about three aspects, among others, of this song:

I. *Narration:* Ordinarily a story is narrated in sentences indicating functions and in these sentences, the object is closely related to the subject, while the functional portion is less closely so. In other words, a sentence has, in the main, two component parts—the subject and the predicate. In the sentence "The boy went to the field", 'The boy' is the subject and 'went to the field' is the predicate. Similarly, in the structural build of all that is comprised in folklore, there is a subject and a predicate. In the song under discussion, too, there is a subject and a predicate; and the whole narration mainly aims at developing the functional aspect of it which often indicates a movement from good to evil and, finally, a return from evil to good. The song under discussion has the same structure. But there may be movements quite dissimilar to these. The Creator makes a bark with a noble end in view and sends it out to the earth. But evil influences set to work on it and it founders on land that is dry. But the foundering of the bark does not constitute the journey's end. It forces its way out through the wall of evil and is then on its way to good. In all popular Bengali songs, there is this conflict between good and evil which always ends in the conquest of evil by the powers of good.

II. *The composer's personal opinion :* The composer of a verse or song may often interpose his own views among the words of his composition. This is a distinctive feature of Bengali songs. He seeks to express his own views and personal preferences intermittently throughout the narration. In the song under discussion the bard calls out to the helmsman "Heigh, brother don't let go your hold on the helm! Control the bark, howsoever you can." He adds that Pagla Kanai is now wondering what will happen to the bark.

III. *Details describing the surroundings*: The bard goes beyond the essential limits of the tale and describes in his song some details of the surroundings, as also of nature. There is some elaboration of the functional aspect as well. In the song, there lies the picture of a floating boat in riverine Bengal, looming behind the story, the presence of a river is hinted at, and the bark moves on its way through land that is dry. The picture of the bark moving on two oars recalls the sight of a plying boat. The descriptive details relate to the surroundings but they are not always confined to the surroundings or the scenery. They may also elaborate the functional aspects of the story. There is, for example a description, in the song of the bark moving on its way on two oars, of its admitting water into it on running into a tidal bore and the leaving of the bark by its six oarsmen.

IV. *The description and the instances cited, sometimes create dramatic developments in the story :* This song has a dramatic development. It begins, as it were, in the middle of the story without any introduction to it. It starts with the making of a strange boat, the boat then enters an area where it receives endless buffeting, and is threatened with the loss of its oars and helm. With dramatic swiftness, the composer comes to the end of this part of the story and begins to hint at his own misgivings. He relates how the bark ran into a tidal bore, admitted water into it and was about to meet with a disastrous end. The six oarsmen, who were friends in times of happiness, bid adieu to the bark now that it has fallen on evil days. The Bengali saying "many are the friends in prosperous times, but, alas, in days of adversity, there are none" is reflected in the verbal picture drawn by the bard. We see, with our mind's eye, the wreck of the bark through the dramatic narration of the event. A deep tragedy of human life is pictured herein. Bengali songs are not always characterised by this dramatic intensity. But some songs are marked by it.

In the structural analysis of the song, in my own way, I have evolved a pictorial representation of the story. It is made up of the characters, the words of the song and their functions, and the agencies that intervene in it.

The first stanza: The numbers indicate the number of sentences

The main character	*The functions of the characters*	*The main linking force*	*The functions of the sentences*	*The negativity of the sentences*
The Creator	1, 2		1, 2	0
The bark	4, 6	The earth	4, 6	3
The mind-helmsman	5		5	0

The second stanza: The numbers indicate the number of sentences

The main characters	*The functions of the characters*	*The main linking force*	*The firm position of noun*	*Indicative sentences*	*Compound sentences*
The bark	2		2, 3, 4		Otherwise
The mind-helmsman	5	The mechanism		5, 7	(not expressed but implied)
The earthliness	5 (The implied function)		7 (The function is dormant but steady)		

The third stanza: The numbers indicate the number of sentences

The main characters	*The fuuctions of the character*	*The main linking force*	*The functions of sentences*	*The inner structure of the sentences* Anxiety	Doubt
The poet	1, 2	Lack of :	2	2	1
The bark	3, 4, 6	(a) power	3, 4, 6		
Six oarsman	5	(b) the faithfulness of friends	5		

In the first line the words indicate the function of the characters. The fact that there is no water for the bark to ply on creates an atmosphere of negativity. In it the world or its earthliness provides a connecting link. But, in the second line, it adopts the rọle of a party to the story in a veiled fashion. Here, it plays an important part but its whole function lies concealed. In the second line the action lends strength and a position of preeminence to the subject. In referring to the bark, a compound sentence is brought into use and the word "or" has to be understood in construing it. The total meaning is, "Take care, or the bark will sink." The words convey a direction for the man at the helm of the bark. The helmsman is cautioned and asked not to let go his hold on the helm. In the inner structure of the sentence is another meaning concealed below the surface. It is that, when the helmsman withdraws his controlling hand from the helm, the boat sinks. Similarly, in the seventh sentence, there is a direction and within its inner structure, there is another sentence which is this, "The boat may sink all of a sudden." It may be said, following Chomsky that the grammatical form of the two sentences (5 and 7) upholds the surface structure of the song. But they are both informed with a deep meaning and there is another sentence concealed in the inner structure of each.

The surface structure and the inner structure are now placed side by side. The meaning of the given words: the grammatical form : the surface structure.

(Second stanza)

Sentence 5 : O brother helmsman : Be alert and upright
Do not lose your grip
" 7 : The bark may sink all of a sudden.

The inner meaning : The reasonable form : Deep structure:

Sentence 5 : The bark whose helmsman loses his grip over the helm, is drowned.
" 7 : It is true that the bark sinks all of a sudden.

The third line has within it a sense of anxiety. There is a sense of misgiving and, to use the language of Propp, the functional part of the song tends to become complex. The song is led towards a dramatic end by the atmosphere of want, portrayed by the language. The words convey a sense of inadequacy in the surroundings and the song is led to a dramatic end.

Even if the song is judged from the viewpoint of the literary critic, its literary value cannot be missed. Composers of folksongs are naturally a little lax in building up the structure. Restraint is a desirable quality in literary creations, but there is often a lack of it in the compositions of folksingers. This lack of restraint is noticeable not only in the use of words but also in the ideas. A looseness is noticeable in the substance also, it is marked by a lack of cohesion. It is not perceptiveness that is lacking in the compositions. What is lacking is restraint. The structures of folksongs and folktales are hardly ever well-knit. Pagla Kanai was, however, an exception to the general rule and so is the song now under discussion. The composer here displays a remarkable brevity and restraint and achieves greatness as an artist. In a few words, with a faultless rhythm and a pleasing repetition of sounds in them, he creates an atmosphere of suggestiveness of a very unusual quality. The endings rhyme beautifully and add to the beauty of the song. The inner meaning, above all, adds to the depth of its appeal. In a few words, the composer delves into the depths of human life and seizes upon the message of profound sorrow, lying at the bottom of it. The song should, in this view, be assigned a high position as a literary piece. Qualities such as these distinguish many other compositions of Pagla Kanai.

It is clear from what has been stated before that there may be different methods of structural analysis. But in spite of this difference they have the same end in view—a deeply introspective interpretation. Propp has separated the functional aspects from one another and based his analysis on the individual sentences of the composition. Levi-Strauss has, on the other hand, devised a method of analysis based on the formulation of words or on words and their derivatives. A method based on progression and regression, evolved by Chomsky, has been followed by others in their analytical study of folklore. In analysing the song of Pagla Kanai, I have applied, with reasonable success, the systems advocated by the scholars like Propp, Levi-Strauss, Chomsky, William Hendricks, and later the methods of analysis developed by the Marandas and Alan Dundes. It will be seen that the methods of analysis used by them all are not the same. But they all seem to be very earnest and sincere to make the methods used by them thoroughly scientific and totally based on reasons. I have tried to realize the main approaches behind these methods, and in undertaking an analysis of the song of Pagla Kanai. I have applied some of these methods with as much care as possible highlighting my own modes of interpretation. When it is found possible to apply such scientific methodologies to a song based on an idea, not on the narration of a story, it goes without saying that it should be possible to apply them, with more remarkable success, to our myths and tales. There is no doubt that those who will make good use of this possibility will assume a leading part in our folklore studies in the future.

The method adopted by me in the following analysis will, I hope, explicate the different meanings in a Baul song.

I would like to find out the inner meaning of the song in the following process:

The Creator creates the bark He gives favour to the bark	:	a { C, B }
The Creator sends the bark on earth—it leaves the Creator	:	ā { B, C }
The bark likes earthly things	:	d { B, E }
The bark is in the company of evils	:	c { E, B }
The bark has no purpose, it is misled by earthliness	:	m { E, B }
The Creator is mysteriously inside the bark	:	a {°C, B }
The bark loses its strength, it gets old	:	c {E°, B }
The Creator calls the bark from within	:	i {C°, B }
Earthly things leave the bark	:	ā { B, E↑ }
The bark returns to the Creator	:	ā { B↓, E }

a {C, B} = The Creator or the power of good is in the ascendant. The notation 'a' has been used throughout to indicate that some good influence is at work. That is why the Creator is in the front and the

{Abbreviations of letters inside bracket : C=Creator, B=Bark, or worldly affairs.

bark lies behind Him. The notation ā signifies that the influence of good is about to be exhausted. The subtraction mark may indicate abondonment of the bark by the powers of good or of evil. Now, the bark is in the front and the creator is behind it.

d {B, E} = The earthly powers exercise their influence on the first character that is the bark. But even then, the bark is in the front and the earthly powers are behind it, indicating the departure of the bark from the blessed world of God to the earthliness after having his first introduction with the earth, which interests him to a great extent.

c {E, B} = Following Propp's method of analysis, it may be said that the earthliness or powers of evil have strengthened their hold on the bark and are trying to dominate it fully. Here, earthliness is in the front and the bark is behind it. This is the first order of reversion, having earthliness in a forefront position.

m {E, B} = The position now is, simply, not that of earthliness being in the front and the bark behind it. Earthliness has now assumed full control of the bark. The bark is vanquished and earthliness is the victor.

a {°C,B}= Earthliness has conquered the bark but the Creator is still in it, hidden in its depth. But His influence is less effectual, since earthliness has weakened the bark. Now, the Creator is in the front and the bark is behind Him. The Creator, however, is largely passive. That is why the notation C has been used.

c {E°,B} = The letter c is used before bracket to indicate the stage, preceding total destruction. As in c {E, B} used before, here, too, earthliness is in the front and the bark is behind it. But earthliness has established itself firmly as the victor and is sure of the bark's destruction. As a matter of fact, earthliness here is more determined and powerful than in m {E, B}.

i {C°, B} = The Creator here extends His influence to the bark, sends out his call to it, and draws it to Him. The bark responds. Here, the Creator is in the front and the bark is behind Him. But the full impact of the Creator's influence is yet to be felt. The earthly powers still control the movement of the bark. To denote the difference from a {°C, B}, the notation used here is C which indicates that the Creator now exercises a far larger degree of influence on the bark, who is impelled by consciousness. 'i' is implied here as an inner call.

ā {B, E ↑} = The influence of earthliness has now completely ceased, that is, the man, who functioned as the bark, is now dead. He is now of no significance to earthliness. Earthliness attaches no value to a man, once he is dead. It has drawn into itself all that was vital in the man and cast off the fibres as trash. That is why B is in the front and E is behind it, being on its way out. It is because of this that the notation E ↑ has been used. It means that the earthly powers are now on the wane, have changed their course, and are making for a different destination.

ā {B ↓, E} = Earthliness and man, in the guise of the bark, have now parted company with each other. Does this mean that the being of man has now reached its ultimate end? No, says the bard. He does not believe that death spells an end to man's existence. His real life—a life that knows no end, begins after his death. It is through death that man establishes his victory over earthliness. He now goes back as the victor to the protection of his Creator. That is why here B ↓ is in the front and E is behind it. B ↓ is now on its return journey. Thus the notation B ↓ has been used to indicate the homecoming of the bark.

The letters to the left of the brackets indicate the functional significance of the characters, denoted by the first letters inside them. They indicate the respective functions of the Creator, the bark, and the powers of earthliness. The function of the second letters inside the brackets is less direct and more or less secondary.

The above analysis of the song's aesthetics leads to the conclusion that man has been created by God out of love and sent out to the earth. Man has the same special features as a ship. A ship depends for its power of movement on the water and fire inside it and so does man. But man, upon his journey to the earth, tends to forget his links with his Creator and falls prey to earthliness. He enters a circle, where Satan or the powers of earthliness rule, and surrenders himself to them. The Creator, however, continues to caution him through the agency of his mind which acts as helmsman to the bark. He cautions him against involving himself in earthliness. The bark does not heed the cautions of the Creator and the victorious forces of evil gradually establish their hold on the bark. The Creator notices this and the vitality of the bark suffers a decline. The six oars, that were close associates of earthliness, abandon the bark. Then there is the journey's end or death of the man. But man's existence does not come to an end with death. Then the powers of evil suffer a defeat and the Creator draws man towards Him and establishes His own victory and also the victory of man over them.

The above discussion shows that behind all functions the Creator is the only agent of power. There is, first, the victory of His will, and man in the form of a bark is sent out to the earth when earthliness and the powers of evil appear and extend their influence over him. Finally the Creator appears and conquers them. There is, first, the appearance of an agent which controls the functions, followed by the appearance of a rival agent, opposing it, and then there is a conflict between the two, ending in the victory of the agent that controls. All branches of folklore, particularly folk songs and folktales have the same structural characteristics. But there is little chance of finding them in songs based on abstract ideation without any story in them. Even then, one may notice this conflict in quite a few songs through an aesthetic and morphological analysis. I believe, quite a new vista will open up as the result of analysis of the structure of Bengali songs.

The song under discussion may also be interpreted in another way following the Lack (L) and Lack-Liquidated method.

1 (a) Want of barks in the world—want—L (Lack)
  (b) The all-merciful God sends a bark—want removed=LL (Lack Liquidated)
2 (a) A bark cannot steer its course on dry land=L
  (b) The bark steers its way on dry land=LL
3 (a) A bark does not usually ply on two oars=L
  (b) The bark plies on two oars=LL
4 (a) If one lets go one's hold on the helm, the bark sinks, want of the helm=L
  (b) The helm is held fast, the bark does not sink=LL
5 (a) What will happen to the bark? Lack of a s e of security=L
  (b) Pagla Kanai is full of misgivings,—lack of a sense of security=L
  (c) There is no controlling power on the bark. The tidal bore has no opening in it. Water cannot be withheld from pouring into the bark=LLL
  (all the three are symbolic of want).
  (d) The six foes disappear=L
  (e) The bark sinks on dry land—lack of strength =L

The above formulation of wants and their disappearance may be caste into the frame of a chart in the following manner.

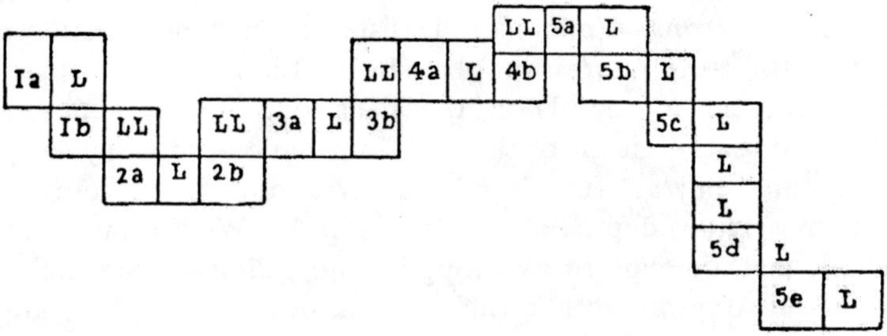

The chart shows the ups and downs in the movement of the bark and the development of the incidents related there, to judged by the norms of good and bad, earthliness and godliness. The foundering of the bark becomes inevitable because of the preponderance of evil. There is steadiness upto I(a) and 2(b) and an upward movement from 2(b). The acme is reached in 5(c). There is no likelihood of the want being remedied after 5(a). So there is a quickening of movement in the opposite direction, that is, on the downward path. As man advances in years his body develops deficiencies of kinds. The bark develops similar deficiencies. The upward and downward movements in this formula indicate youthfulness and physical decline, bodily power and the lack of it. The structural analysis at least in the present instance has, for its basis, the body of man. The outer structure may be interpreted by this formula of lack and its liquidation, but it will not be of much help in interpreting the inner structure. A want has a rational form based on material standards, and its remedy, too, has perforce to be material. A material want would hardly admit of an idealistic interpretation. The hero wants a wife, he marries. The want is removed. But the inner structure of the story remains unaffected.

I have said above that it is possible to explain the various materials that go into the composition of folklore by following the method evolved by Propp. Propp evolved his system of analysis mainly for the interpretation of fairy tales. That is why his method may be applied to fairy tales and certain other kinds of folktales. But the following morphological analysis will prove that it may be applied, with satisfactory results, to the interpretation of folksongs as well. It may of course be applied to other branches of folklore in a somewhat limited fashion. Folksongs are mainly idealistic in substance and there is very little story interest in them. In Baul songs, in particular, the interest centres mainly on the ideas contained in them and other thoughts related to them. They have hardly any story interest and they are sustained by a narration of the journey to the mysterious depths of man's existence. Would this mean that the method evolved by Propp has no validity in the analysis of Baul songs and other kinds of folksongs of the Bengali-speaking people? I would firmly disagree and say that it has its validity. As I have said before, in structural analysis, we should reach down to the inner structure by following Chomsky's system; discover the conflict lying within, and the chain of reasoning that supports it, by following the system of Levi-Strauss; and then try to find out the truth, or the lack of it, that lies beneath. That is why I think that the analysis of aesthetics need not be confined to folklore with a story in it and that it may be applied to other branches of folklore, both material and non-material. We may now analyse Pagla Kanai's song following Propp's method. The principal characters that emerge from the analysis of the song are the bark as representing man, earthliness or the powers of evil and the Creator.

The initial situation : (X)[12]

A. (i) The Earth Has No Bark In it.
The Creator Feels That He Should Build One :
Absence : (b^1)

(ii) The Want Of A Bark Creates A Vacuum : A State Of Vacuity : (b^2)

B. The Creator Builds A Wonderful Bark And Sends It Out To The Earth To Make Good The Vacuity : Introduction : C

(i) He creates the bark and sends it to the earth (c^1)

(ii) That the bark moves not on the water but on the dry land (c^2)

C. Interdiction : (Y)

(i) The Creator determines certain norms (y^1)

(ii) Interdiction is addressed to the bark, the bark is told of the danger being ahead (y^2)

D. Violation : (d)

(i) The interdiction is violated and the bark comes closer to worldly affairs, pays no heed to the warning and begins to be influenced by earthliness (d^1)

E. The Villain's Reconnaissance :

Reconnaissance (e)

(i) A preliminary survey by earthliness to know the features of the bark : (e^1)

(ii) The satan starts functioning in the guise of worldly affairs-earthliness assumes a disguise and conducts the survey (e^2)

F. The Villain Receives Information About His Victim : Delivery (f)

(i) Earthliness starts to acquire knowledge of the bark. That is, earthliness begins to display curiosity about man, since it needs man and other beings of the animal world. Man, too, begins to co-operate with it (f^1)

(ii) The villain or satan in the guise of worldly affairs gathers direct information of bark's weakness and attracts the bark (f^2)

G. The Villain Attempts to Deceive His Victim In Order To Take Possession Of Him : Deception (n)

(i) The Villain starts to deceive the bark and makes an attempt to take away the bark's best assets, the good qualities (n^1)

(ii) The villain slowly persuades the bark (n^2)

(iii) Employment of magic powers by earthliness—a seeming indication of the use of magical tools. (n^3)

(iv) Other ways and tricks of earthliness. The earth does not enchant man through the sight, the taste and the smell alone. It gets the better of him through his craze for enjoyment of worldly things. It exercises a dominant influence on him through his material and bodily needs. (n^4)

(v) The villain (earthliness) proceeds with utmost carefulness (n^5)

H. The Victim Submits To Deception And Thereby Unwittingly Helps His Enemy : Complicity : (z)

(i) The bark accepts all the conditions imposed by earthliness (the villain) and becomes a worldly figure. (z^1)

(ii) The bark favourably reacts to all the alluring acts of the villain (z^2)

(iii) The bark mechanically reacts to the employment of the magical or other means and helps its adversary, earthliness, through its own deeds. (z^3) (z^4)

I. The Villain Causes Harm Or Injury To The Members Of The Bark, The Propensity Of Earthliness For Mischief : Villainy : (a)

(i) Taking advantage of the old age of the vessel or the bark, the villain causes loosening of the screws of the joints and eats up the edges of joints of the bark (a^1)

(ii) The six comrades of the bark are allured by the villain, the earthliness drives out, with calculated steps, six of the bark's associates—they abandon the bark (a^2)

J. The Members Of The Family Lack Something : Deficiencies That Beset The Bark And Others Of The Party: Lack: (i)

(i) The screws lack strength (i^1)

(ii) So long the six comrades received some advantages, but now the advantages are lacking, so they leave (i^2)

(iii) The bark experiences lack of strength and admits water into it being struck by a tide (i^3)

K. Misfortune or Lack Is Made Known To Bark Through Caution. Caution : (b)

(i) A call for being careful of the villain is given, the bard announces the evil development to the bark (b^1)

(ii) Besides the announcement, the story of its misfortune is sung in a dirge—e.g. 'What will the bark come to?" Misfortune is predicted. (b^2)

L. The Villain And The Bark Join In Direct Combat: Conflict: (h)

(i) The bark starts conflict with the help of mind-helmsman, which means the conflict in the mind acting as helmsman (h^1)

(ii) Time and old age of the bark join hands with earthliness, the defeat of the bark becomes inevitable: (h^2)

M. The Victory Of The Villain, Destruction Of The Bark: Defeat : (m)

(i) Earthliness drowns the bark on dry land (m^1)

(ii) The Creator lives in the vessel as a dormant force (m^2)

N. The Ultimate Victory Of The Bark : Victory : (r)

(i) Death is not the end, it marks the victory of the spirit. The Creator comes to the rescue of the bark and saves it from the clutches of earthliness (r^1)

(ii) When the worldly things leave the bark, the villain is defeated and the bark gets back to its original abode (eternity) to live there in peace. In the end, man declares his victory over earthliness. He passes through the portal of death, rends the ties that bind him to the world of matter and enter the supreme life. Earthliness is now a vanquished power. (r^2)

The abbreviated letters used here may differ to some extent from Propp. This is because Propp used the abbreviations in the analysis of folktale, while I have used them for analysing a folksong. One may differ from the procedure I have followed above in analysing this song. But it is evident from this experimentation that Propp's method is applicable to folksongs besides the tales.

As a formula the above model summed up below :

(x^{12}) A.$b^{1\cdot2}$ B.$c^{1\cdot2}$ C.$y^{1\cdot2}$ D.d^1 E.$e^{1\cdot2}$ F.$f^{1\cdot2}$ G.$n^{1\cdot2\cdot3\cdot4\cdot5}$ H.$z^{1\cdot2\cdot3\cdot4}$ I.$a^{1\cdot2}$ J.$i^{1\cdot2\cdot3}$ K.$b^{1\cdot2}$ L.$h^{1\cdot2}$ M.$m^{1\cdot2}$ N.$r^{1\cdot2}$

The model may be represented in the figure given below :

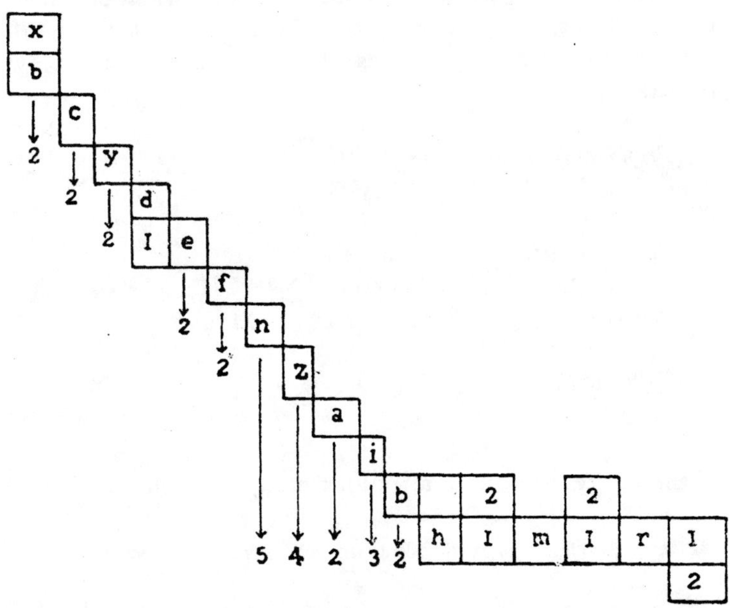

I hope I have been able to establish that Propp's system can be applied also to songs, based on ideas, without any story-content in them.

Nikiforov of the USSR almost a contemporary of Propp, evolved a system of analysis of the functional aspects of folklore on a grammatical basis. He analyses by a linguistic formula based on the position of words. We may apply this formula to the song of Pagla Kanai. There are, according to Nikiforov, three kinds of actions in a composition—prefix actions, root actions and suffix actions. According to this system, the root actions are to be found in the middle of the story and their chief ingredients are violation and surrender. The ingredient of rendering assistance to the adversary without one's knowledge or in other words the functional aspects of the bark will be found in this part of the story. If the story starts with the aspect of violation the root actions will then be found in the beginning. This system of analysis may be applied to other branches of folklore as well. Nikiforov's system is based mainly on Propp's, but the linguistic element is of utmost importance in it.

Thus the figures may be shown also in the manner as suggested by Nikiforov*. This gives an analysis of actions (functions) on the linguistic model of word formation, that is, prefix actions, root actions and suffix functional actions. If we extend this scheme to the present data, we get the following results:

Prefix actions :

(x^{12}) $A.b^{1\cdot 2}$ $B.c^{1\cdot 2}$ $C.y^{1\cdot 2}$

Root actions :

(a) $D.d^{1}$ $E.e^{1\cdot 2}$ $F.f^{1\cdot 2}$ $G.n^{1\cdot 2\cdot 3\cdot 4\cdot 5}$ $H.z^{1\cdot 2\cdot 3\cdot 4\cdot}$

(b) $I.a^{1\cdot 2}$ $J.i^{1\cdot 2\cdot 3}$ $K.b^{1\cdot 2}$ $L.h^{1\cdot 2}$ $M.m^{1\cdot 2}$

Suffix actions :

$N.r^{1\cdot 2}$

If the figures are put in a rough sketch, they will stand like this:

*Please see references at the end of this chapter.

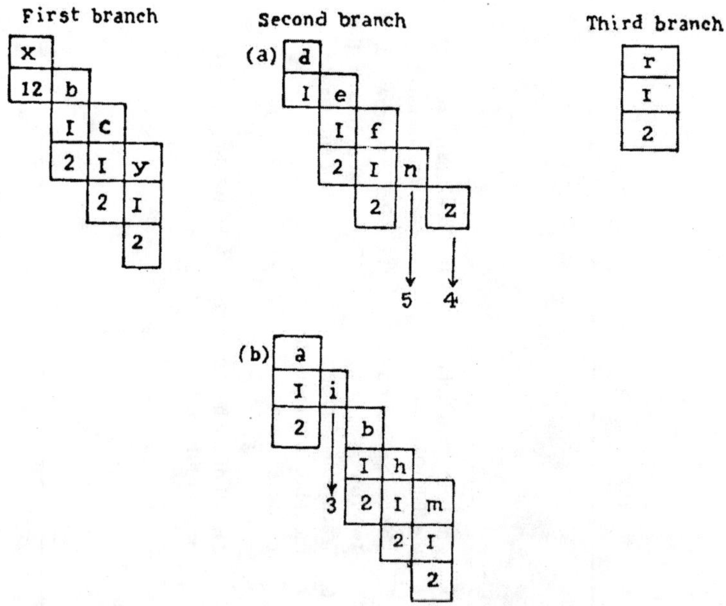

Let us now revert to the main discussion. If the system of Levi-Strauss and the Marandas is now applied to the structural analysis of Pagla Kanai's song we shall have applied almost all the methods of analysis to a Bengali song. This would establish the possibility of assessing the aesthetic quality of our songs by the application of scientific methods of analysis. The fact that we have not so far applied these methods only proves that we are lacking in interest in matters of science. The song may be analysed following the system of Levi-Strauss since it speaks of two distinct parties, the bark and worldly allurements to earthliness.

Two opposite parties :

(a) : The bark
(b) : The earthliness

Functions (f) :

z. To float over the soil
y. To get drowned in the ground

Thus it follows :

$$fx^{(a)} : fx^{(b)} :: fx^{(b)} : fa^{-1} (y).$$

To be more clear, the motifs of the song can be arranged in a paradigmatic order which would help us to understand the forces opposed to each other and their functions :

2. The bark does not get drowned on the soil, 4. It moves on the soil but within it remain the water and fire	7. It is drowned on the soil	3. The helmsman holds the helm 5. The bark glides on the two rows 6. Water enters through the small holes caused by loose screws	1. The creator sends the bark on the earth 8. After it is drowned, the bark goes back to the creator (implied)
↓	↓	↓	↓
Overrating the earth	Underrating the earth	Denial of the heavenly origin of the bark	Heavenly origin of the bark

The contrast between the columns, if graphically shown, will stand like this:

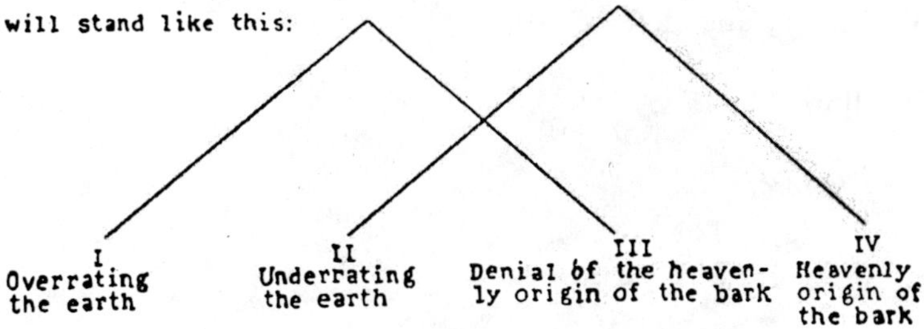

Out of these eight motifs as arranged in the columns, of which one is not expressed but implied, we get two clear opposing forces which may be shown in the following figures:

Forces :

(a) : The earthliness, the bark is of earthly origin.
(b) : Non-earthliness—the bark is not created by earth.

Functions (f) :

x. That the bark is earthly origin, his physical being gives an evidence to this.

y. The gradual wearing out and final annihilation of the physical being of the bark denies its earthly origin—it returns to heaven which proves that it is of heavenly origin.

Thus it follows :

$$fx^{(a)} : fy^{(b)} :: fx^{(b)} : fa^{-1}(y)$$

Because of the existence of two opposing forces, the figures may be arranged in a more clear term in the following diagram:

$$\left[f^{(a)} \right] \quad \left[fx^{(b)} \right] \rightarrow fa^{-I}(y)$$

The conflict may be pointed in the following manner:

$$fx^{(a)} : fy^{(b)} :: fx^{(b)} : fa^{-I}(y)$$

Yet the conflict between the two forces may be explained in a different perspective by putting an emphasis on the functions like victory and defeat.

It follows like this:

The forces :

(a) The bark
(b) : The earthliness

Functions (f) :

x. The defeat of the bark, victory of the earthliness.
y. The defeat of the earthliness, victory of the bark.

Therefore :

$$fx^{(a)} : fy^{(b)} \qquad fx^{(b)} : fa^{-I}(y)$$

Let us see how binarism works in this song. The opposite forces in culture help the growth and progress of values and through them the culture as a whole is reshaped. But the opposing forces in a culture is found, almost with no exception, to appear in a binary form. It is interesting that even in a mystic song like the one under our discussion here, follows this process of human thought. The binary sets opposing each other in this song may be better understood by the following graphic arrangements:

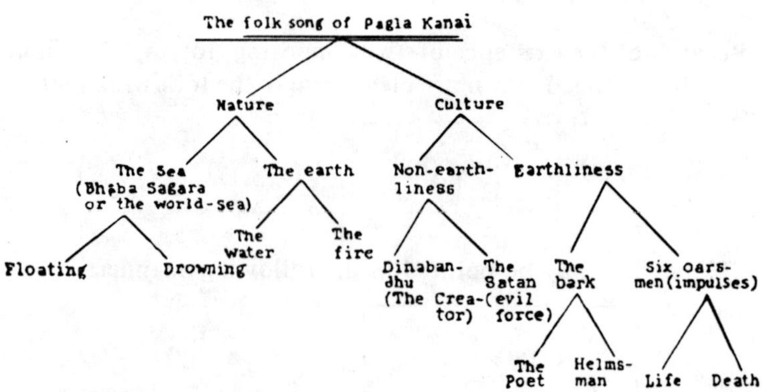

Of the two, the second analysis brings the inner meaning into clearer relief. In the first, the bark is floating about and, in direct opposition to it, is the possibility of its being drowned. Though we feel that this possibility is the result of a conspiracy hatched by earthliness, there is no mention of the victory of the bark over it. In other words the first analysis confines itself to the outer structure, while the second goes deep into the inner structure of the song. The two forms of analysis are, however, complementary to each other. The full meaning of the song will elude us if we accept one of these and reject the other. If we apply the formula of Levi-Strauss elsewhere there may be the same problem for us. That is why I would like to place the results of the two forms of analysis alongside each other. I shall now try to explain the position by referring to the following diagrams:

The arrival of the bark on the earth The passive acceptance of the earthliness	The eagerness of the bark to live on the earth for good The disapproval and opposition of the earthliness

—	+
—	+

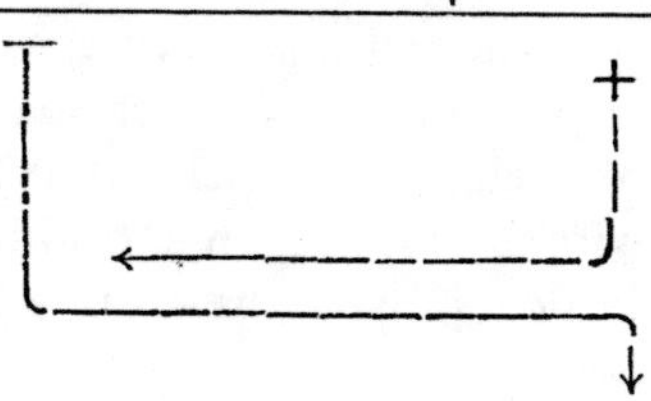

There are some elements in the song which remain unchanged while others change. Let me put them in a diagram:

A.

	The parties	Unchange-able	Changea-able
Given (The changeable force is implied, not expressed)	Bark (a)	floats (c)	Water (d)
Underlying	Man (e)	floats (c)	Soil (c)

B.

	The parties		
Given (The changeable force is implied, not expressed)	Bark (a)	drowns (b)	Water (d)
Underlying	Man (e)	drowns (b)	Soil (c)

(a) Under a given meaning, the bark is very much known to us. But in this song it has been used allegorically in a figurative meaning. The image is symbolical which acts as a starting force.

(b) The main theme has been presented centering around two unchangeable elements—in the case of one it is a verb, namely, 'float' and in another the verb is 'drown'. Both have set a link between the main forces—the bark (the man) and the objects. These unchangeable elements signifying action are engaged in the act of changes.

(c) Soil has appeared as an inner changeable element, which has helped the expression of an ideated concept. The symbol of personification of man through the bark has been made possible by using this element, which acted like a riddle and created a mystic environment. As in a riddle, it has been declared that the bark floats over the soil and also gets drowned in it.

(d) Water as the changeable element has not been mentioned. But since it has a close relation with a party namely the bark and the unchangeable elements, the two verbs, this has been shown here as an implied object. Although water is not an expressed object, but its presence is being felt through its absence and thus the mystic atmosphere of the song has been deepened.

(e) Man is an underlying force in this song. In the riddle, the answer lies in the underlying element which is kept concealed in a roundabout way. Likewise, man, in the symbol of a bark, is hidden here and it is for the listeners of the song to trace it out.

The song could be structurally analysed also on the basis of Quasi Solution (QS) and Quasi Result (QR), Final Solution (FS) and Final Results (FR). It is given below:

QS = Bark, as accepted generally, is sent on earth with a purpose to serve the Creator.

QR = Allurement of the earthliness, which the bark is obliged to accept.

FS = Man is symbolised as the bark. Ultimately he surrenders himself completely to the influence of earthly attraction, the force which leads him to utter destruction.

FR = Although the bark succumbs to the earthliness which brings his ruination, he comes out victorious, as through his bodily extinction, he is released from earthly bondage and returns to the Creator.

Since this paper deals with the structural and morphological analyses of a Bengali mystic folksong and I have tried to make them quite exhaustive, some of the themes, motifs and points have been repeated time and again, which seemed unavoidable to me in the interest of the methods used as well as of the inner meanings of the song analysed on the basis of those methodologies. In the mystic songs, with almost no exception, the three distinct forces play the main role—the Creator, the man and the earthliness, often called *Bhabanadi* (world as river) or the *Bhabasindhu* (world as sea or ocean). The interactions through the functions of these three forces are the major concern of all the songs. The functions and interactions are presented in the song with a cloud of mysticism, while the forces are symbolised in the forms of some objects or ideas. The cloud is not an imaginary one—it is real in the sense that many portions of our life are shrouded with cloud and we do not know where their meaning lies and how they would look like if brought to light. The mystic songs attempt to highlight them through their words, rhythm and melody. I hardly need to emphasize that my analyses endeavour to unfold that meaning through interpretations, sketches and diagrams.

REFERENCES

Barthes, Roland 1967 *Elements of Semiology*, Boston.

Bascom, WR 1953 Folklore and Anthropology, *Journal of American Folklore* (JAF), 66, 283-90.

———— 1954 "Four Functions of Folklore," *JAF*, 67, 333-49.

Bloomfield, L 1933, *Language*, Holt, Rinehart & Winston, New York.

Chafe, WL "Language as Symbolization," *Journal of Linguistic Society of America* (*JLSA*), Baltimore 43, 57-91.

Chomsky, N 1957 *Syntactic Structure*, Mouton, The Hague.

———— 1965 *Current Issues in Linguistic Theory*, Mouton, The Hague.

———— 1965 *Aspects of the Theory of Syntax*. MIT Press, Cambridge, Mass.

———— 1968 *Language and Mind*, New York.

Cox, Howard L 1948 "The Place of Mythology in the Study of Culture", *American Imago*, 5, 83-94.

Culler, J 1967 *Structural Poetics*, Cornell University Press, Ithaca, New York.

Dorson, RM 1959 "A Theory for American Folklore," *JAF*, 72, 197-215.

———— (ed) 1961, *Folklore Research Around the World*, published jointly as Vol. 74 No. 294 of the *JAF* and (with an Index) as No. 16 in the *Indiana University Folklore Series*, Bloomington.

Dundes, Alan 1962 "From Etic to Emic Units in the Structural Study of Folklore" *JAF* 75, 95-105.

———— 1963 "Structural Typology of North American Indian Folktales", *South Western Journal of Anthropology*, (*SWJA*).

———— (ed) 1965 *The Study of Folklore*, Prentice-Hall Inc., New Jersey.

———— 1968 "The Morphology of North American Indian Folktales" (Ph.D.Thesis, 1962, Indiana University), *Folklore Fellows Communications* (FFC), Helsinki.

Durkheim, E & Mauss, M 1963 *Primitive Classification*, (trans) R. Needham, Chicago (Original French edition 1901-1902).

Elemendorf, WW 1960 "The Structure of Twana Culture (with) Comparative Notes on the Structure of Yuruk Culture by A.L. Kroeber" *Research Studies Monographic Supplement*-2.

Elson, B & Pickett, VB 1962 *An Introduction to Morphology and Syntax*, Summer Institute of Linguistic, Santaana, Calif.

Fischer, JL 1960 "Sequence and Structure" in Folktales, *Men and Culture* A.F.C. Wallace (ed) University of Pennsylvania Press, Philadelphia, pp. 442-46.

Fodor, JA & Katz, JJ 1964 *The Structure of Language*, Prentice-Hall Inc.

Fortes, M 1949 "Time and Social Structure," *Social Structure Studies* presented to A.R. Radcliffe-Brown, Meyer Fortes (ed), Oxford.

Friedman, Albert B 1961 "The Formulaic Improvisation Theory of Ballad Tradition—A Counter-statement," *JAF*, 74, 113-15.

Hall, M & Chomsky, N 1968 *The Sound Pattern of English*, Harper & Row, New York.

Halliday, MAK 1961 *Categories of the Theory of Grammar*, Ward Journal of the Linguistic Circle of New York.

Handoo, Dr Jawaharlal 1978 *Current Trends in Folklore*, Mysore.

Harris, SZ 1957 "Co-occurrence & Transformation in Linguistic Structure, *JLSA*, Baltimore, 33, 283-340.

Hendricks, WO 1973 *Essays on Semiolinguistics & Verbal Art*, Mouton, The Hague.

Herskovits, Melville J & Herskovits Frances 1958 *Dahomean Narrative—A Cross Cultural Analysis*, North Western University Press, Evanston, Illinois.

Islam, Mazharul 1959 *Kabi Pagla Kanai*, Rajshahi University Publication, Bangladesh.

———— 1974 *Folklore Parichiti Lok Sahityer Pothon Pathon*, 2nd edn. Bangla Academy, Dacca, Bangladesh. (An elaborate introduction and a scientific study of folklore).

———— 1982 *A History of Folktale Collections in India, Bangladesh and Pakistan*, enlarged second edition, Panchali Prakasan Calcutta.

———— 1982 *Folklore Charchaya Rupatattik Bisslation Paddhati* (The Morphological Analysis of Folklore), Lok Laukik Prakasani, Calcutta.

Jacobs, Melville 1959 The Content & Style of An Oral Literature: *Clackamas Chinook Myths and Tales*, University of Chicago Press, Chicago.

———— 1959 *Review of V. Propp, Morphology of the Folktales*, *JAF*, 72, 195-96.

———— "Humour and Social Structure in Oral Literature" in *Culture in History*, S. Diamond (ed), Columbia University Press, New York.

Klagstad, HL Jr 1958 "Great Russian Charm Structure," *Indiana Slavic Studies 2*, 135-144.

Katz, JJ & Postal, PM 1964 *An Integrated Theory of Linguistic Description*, MIT Press Cambridge.

Krohn, Karrle 1926 *Die Folkloristiche Arbeits Methode*,' H. Aschehong, Oslo.

Ladefoged, P 1973 *Preliminaries to Linguistic Phonetics*, University of Chicago Press, Chicago.

Leach, Edmund 1961 "Levi-Strauss in the Garden of Eden : An Examination of Some Recent Developments in the Analysis of Myth", Transactions of the *New York Academy of Sciences*; Series 2 Vol. 23, 386-96.

Less, William 1956 Oedipus-type Tales in Oceania," *JAF*, 69, 63-73.

Levi-Strauss, Claude 1955 "The Structural Study of Myth," *JAF*, 68, 428-44.

———————— 1960 "L'analyses morphologique descontesrusses," *International Journal of Slavic Linguistics and Poetics*, 3, 122-49.

———————— 1963 *Structural Anthropology Vol. I.* (trans.) C. Jacobson & B.G. Shoepf; New York.

———————— 1973 *Structural Anthropology Vol. 2.* (trans.) Monique Layton; Penguin Books, London.

———————— 1964 *Totemism*, London.

———————— 1966 *The Savage Mind*, London.

———————— 1969 *The Raw & the Cooked*, (trans.) J & D Weightman; New York.

———————— 1969 *The Elementary Structure of Kinship*, (trans.) J.H. Belle & J.R. von Sturmer, (ed.) R. Needham; Boston.

———————— 1971 "The Story of Asdiwal," *Structural Study of Myth and Totemism*, E. Leach (ed), London.

Lildgren, EJ 1939 "The Collection and Analysis of Folklore" *Study of Society—Methods and Problems*, F. Bartlett et, al. (ed.)

Longacre, RE "Some Fundamental Insight of Tagmemics," *JLSA*, 41, 65-76.

Lord, Albert B 1960 *The Singer of Tales*, Harvard University Press, Cambridge, Mass.

———————— 1962 "A Comparative Analysis"—Introduction to Umbundu—*Folktales from Angola* : collected & translated by Merlin Ennis, Beacon Press, Boston.

Lyons, J 1970 *Chomsky*, Fontana Collins, London.

———————— 1970 *New Horizons of Linguistics*, Penguin Books, England.

Malinowski, B 1962 *Myth in Primitive Psychology*, W.W. Norton, New York.

Maranda EK & Maranda, P 1971 *Structural Models in Folklore & Transformational Essays*, Mouton, The Hague.

Marx, Karl 1967 *Das Capital*, (ed) F. Engels, New York.

Needham, Rodney 1958 "On Wallis Review of Levi-Strauss," *American Anth.* 6:163.

Nikiforov, AI 1928 K Voprosu morfologicheskom izucheni norodnoy skazki (Morphological Research of the Folktale) in *Festchrift for A.I. Sobolevsky*, Leningrad.

Oinas, Fellx J 1961 "Folklore Activities in Russia" in *Folklore Research Around the World*, R.M. Dorson (ed).

Parry, Milman 1930 "Studies in the Epic Techniques of Oral Verse

Making" (Vol. I: Homer & Homeric Style), *Harvard Studies in Classical Mythology*, 41, 73-147.

Propp, VJ 1968 *Morphology of Folktale*; 2nd Edition, Revised and edited with a preface by Louis A. Wagner, New Introduction by Alan Dundes; University of Texas Press, Austin.

Radcliffe-Brown, AR 1958 *Method in Social Anthropology—Selected Essays*, (ed.) M.N. Srinivas; Chicago.

Radin, P 1933 *Method and Theory of Ethnology*, New York.

Roberts, Warren E 1958 *The Tale of the Kind and the Unkind Girls, Aa-Th840 and Related Tales*, Berlin, W. de Gruyfer.

Rosenbaum, PS 1967 *The Grammar of English Predicate Complement Construction*, MIT Press, Cambridge, Mass.

Saussure, F de 1959 *Course in General Linguistics*, (ed) W. Baskin & C.A. Sechehaye; (Trans) W. Baskin with A. Reidlinger, New York.

Sebeok, T A & Ingemann, FJ 1956 "Structural and Content Analysis in Folklore Research", *Studies in Cheremis : the Supernatural*, New York.

Sokolov, YM 1950 *Russian Folklore*, (Trans) Catherine R. Smith; Macmillan, New York.

Tawney, CH 1859 *Kathasaritsagara or Ocean of the Stream of Stories* (2 Vols.), London.

Taylor, Archer "Folklore and the Student of Literature", *The Specific Spectator*, Vol. 2.

Thompson, Stith 1955-58 *Motif-Index of Folk Literature*, 6 Vols; 2nd edition, Indiana University Press, Bloomington.

———————— 1956 *The Folktales*; The Dryden Press, New York.

4

STRUCTURAL ANALYSIS OF TWO SANTAL MYTHS OF THE BAHA FESTIVAL

LET me now turn to the Santals. The Santals are no longer indifferent to agriculture. In ancient days they were hunters and forest-dwellers, but now most of them depend on agriculture and their boys and girls are gradually adopting themselves to the modern situation. They are believers of spirits (*Bongas*) and their religious faith is predominantly animistic. The house has a spirit, the spirit dwells in the forest, the hills, trees and rocks, their ancestors have spirits—thus they locate spirits almost in every spheres of their life and world around them. A few of these are also the guardian spirits such as Moreko Turuiko though meaning five-six deities, they are single in power, Marang Buru, Jahenera and Gosainera—these four are the main spirits or deities of the Santals. Many ceremonies and festivals including sacrifices are connected with the spirits and during these ceremonies and festivals both men and women dance and drink the home-made beer prepared from rice. Baha festival is one such festival. It is the festival of flowers. Like many of the Santal festivals, Baha reveals the high aesthetic taste of this tribal group.

Santals are fond of tales and stories. Many folktales including myths and other types of stories of Indian origin have originated from them since ancient times. All their ceremonies and festivals have myths or tales behind them with many variations. I have collected from the Santals of Rajshahi two myths connected with Baha festival which are different from those prevalent in the districts of Birbhum, Bankura, Burdwan and Midnapur of West Bengal. Let me narrate those two myths in short.

Tale I. The shepherd and the Baha festival

There was a servant, a shepherd, who lost a calf one evening. He was afraid of being scolded by his master and went out in search of the calf. He failed to find it even till night time. Instead of returning home, he thought it safe to go to Jahirstan where More Turuiko might give him protection. There he climbed upon a tree with his bow and arrows still in his hand. This tree was the abode of a spirit. At dead of night many women from the nearby villages came and assembled at Jahirstan, and were none but witches. They called up the *Bongas* and also summoned two tigers, one was male and the other female. All of them including the two beasts started dancing. While taking rest, the witches called More Turuiko to appear before them. The witches, the *Bongas* and More Turuiko danced together, while the tiger and tigress remained observers. The boy was very much frightened all this while. But suddenly he thought that since the tigers were not taking part in dance, it was the right time to kill them with arrows. He at once took his bow and shot the two tigers. The male died after some roaring, but the female one attacked the women witches thinking that it was because of the jealousy of these women and through their conspiracy that her husband had been killed. So she retaliated by killing them all and a short while after she herself also died. Her roaring was so terrible that the lost cows and calfs rushed to the villages for safety and the villagers also could not sleep. The boy came down at dawn and went back to the village.

After coming back home in the morning, the boy found the calf in the cowshed and was bold enough to face his master, who asked him "where did you pass the night and why." The servant replied that he was in Jahirstan. The master was angry. But at the same time he was worried too as his wife was found missing since dinner time last night and their only baby was crying for its mother. The servant could understand the situation as he knew that one of the women killed last night as a witch was his master's wife. He felt pity for the master and told him that he would give him a clue to his wife, who was but a witch, on condition that henceforth he would not scold him for little things or faults. The master became angrier and attempted to hit the boy. The shepherd now resisted and in a loud voice of protest said, "I pity you, I pity you, your wife is a witch, she is killed, her dead body is lying at Jahirstan." Meanwhile, the other people assembled there and the boy related the whole story. Then it was revealed that a few other wives of the well-to-do men of this village and of some other villages were also found missing since last night. The boy took them all with him to Jahirstan where the women including the tiger and tigress were lying dead. The villagers were convinced that the women were really witches and expressed that the boy did not do any wrong by killing them all. Then the bodies were burnt to ashes. After the burning was over, a saint appeared there and proposed that he would plant a sal tree over the ashes of the witches to have a festival. But the people were so annoyed with the witches that they did not allow the saint but they themselves planted a sal tree on the ashes. Within a year the tree became grown up and it was full of flower. The people decided to have a festival under the tree with garlands of sal flower on their head and neck and dance on that occasion during the Spring. So the men and women, little and old, assembled there on one day in the spring and danced with flowers of sal over their head and neck and drank the rice beàr for the whole day and night. At night a dozen *bonga* girls joined them and danced till morning. These girls suggested, before disappearing, to repeat this festival every year, which the people had already decided to do before the celebration. The people named this festival as *Baha Parab* (festival) to be observed every year during Spring. Then they returned home.

Tale II. The Girl and the Baha Festival

There were seven brothers who excavated a large pond but

could not reach water. They were very sad. One day a saint came and advised them to sacrifice a woman who must be their sister born of the same mother. They had only one sister whom they requested to have a new dress and bring rice to them in the field next day for lunch. Their mother sent their sister with food and she was well-dressed. After taking food, the brothers sent her to fetch water for them from the same tank nearby. When the girl reached the bank of the tank she found little water at the bottom of the tank. She went near the water when the water began to rise up from the bottom to touch her feet. She bent down to fill her earthen pot, which, in spite of her repeated endeavours, did not fill. On the other hand, the water rose higher and higher and apprehending a danger, she cried for the help of her brothers, who did not respond. The girl was drowned.

The marriage of this girl was fixed up earlier and the wedding day was not far away when she died. The betrothed bridegroom on his way to the bride's village along with his relatives on the day fixed earlier, was attracted to see a beautiful flower near the tank. He asked the bearers to stop the *palki* (palanquin) and sent a boy to bring the flower. The boy went near the flower, but the flower moved away. It was strange. The bridegroom came on the bank of the tank himself and wanted to pluck the flower. Now the flower came closer and was plucked by the bridegroom. When the groom entered the *palki* with the flower in his hand, the flower became the same bride for whom the marriage party was going. Being surprised with what had happened, they returned back with the bride who was married to the bridegroom and was happily accepted as the wife.

The seven brothers were cursed by the Marang Buru and as a result they soon became very poor. Some of them became beggars and some leaf-sellers. One day all of them came to the same village where their sister was married and living happily. The sister recognised them and took them to her home. She prepared nice food for them and while serving the food, she told them, "Do you recognize me? I am your sister whom you sacrificed". The brothers were ashamed and looked down to the earth. The earth at once split open and swallowed them all. With utter surprise next morning people found that a sal tree has grown on the same spot and it was full of flower. Marang Buru told the priest of the village on the same day to arrange a festival there at night. But the people of the village decided to wait for the spring season to come, which was not far away. During Spring a festival was arranged and the people named it as the Baha Festival.

Tale No. I is a variant of the tale entitled *The Herd Boy and the Witches* translated by Bompas (1909, *Folklore of the Santal Parganas*, David Nutt, London, p 440) except that the last part of Tale I is completely different. The saint and the *bonga* girls in the last part of the myth wanted to play an important role and set the story towards the introduction of Baha Festival among the Santals. But the people did not allow them to do so and they themselves caused the introduction of Baha Festival. This is also true about Tale No. II which resembles the tale entitled *How Sabai Grass Grew* translated by Bompas (op. cit. p. 102). Marang Buru wanted to turn the tale from its last portion towards Baha Festival with the help of the village priest. But the people decided to have the festival by themslves.

Myth is like the language that speaks out the inner feelings of man and it speaks the truth felt by the ancient people. In both these tales related with the Baha Festival the evil forces are destroyed and on their ruins grows a sal tree. In the conflict betcen the evil and good forces, the good force not only wins and establishes its victory, but it releases the inherent love for beauty hidden in the deeper mind of man. Love for beauty creates the aestheticism, which the Baha Festival embodies in it—aestheticism is an important aspect of the Santal community as a whole. The myths related to Baha may differ from one another in their form structure, spirit and even theme but in one respect they have a surprising similarity—all the tales release the sense of man's aesthetic taste through their narration. The victory of good over evil, the establishment of love for beauty on a common platform seem the real purpose of all the Baha myths. Apart from this, the socialization of aesthetic taste is also a forceful aim and object of all their narrations. The two myths collected by me reveal that it is not an individual, but the society as a whole which closely related with whatever is good, and all that is beautiful. Along with these comes the soothing effect of music on the human mind as can be noticed particularly in myths related to Baha Festival. Dance and music are the two forerunning performances of this festival since the day of its origin.

Both the tales could be analysed structurally in the pattern of Levi-Strauss with a slight deviation in the arrangement of columns. This is required as it seems to me that there are some missing links in the last portions of the tales. Since they have been collected from oral sources the missing out of a portion here and there appears to me quite natural. But, in spite of this minor deviation in the arrangement of columns, the mythemes have been accurately identified from both the myths and the main patternistic approach of Levi-Strauss is fully preserved in the analyses of the two tales that follow.

It is obvious that like almost in all the elements of folklore, there are opposing forces in the two tales of the Santals cited in the foregoing pages for interpretations. The opposing forces and their conflicting functions in these two tales can be shown in the following figures:

Tale. I. The Shepherd and the Baha Festival

Forces :

(a) Witches representing evil forces

(b) Shepherd representing goodness

Functions (*f*)

x The witches control the events : heavenly origin of Baha Festival

y Shepherd controls the events—witches are destroyed and Baha originates as a social festival.

Thus it follows:

$fx^{(a)} : fy^{(b)} :: fx^{(b)} : fa^{-I}(y)$

The above interpretations clearly show that in spite of their

Tale I : The Shepherd and the Baha Festival

Column I	Column II	Column III	Column IV
1. The servant is afraid of his master ↓ Overrating the society of master	4. The servant comes out victorious and pities upon the master whose wife is a witch ↓ Underrating the society of master	2. The boy climbs upon a tree being afraid of witches ↓ Denial of goodness by evil forces	3. The boy hits the tigers who in return kill the witches ↓ Goodness comes out victorious

Column V	Column VI
5. The saint wants to plant sal tree by himself 7. The *bonga* girls advise the people to observe a festival ↓ Denial of social origin of Baha Festival	6. The people ultimately plants the tree 8. The people already decided to have a festival before being advised by *bonga* girls 9. The people decides the timing and the title of the festival ↓ Social origin of Baha Festival

The last four columns may be reduced to two in the following manner

1. The servant is afraid of his master	4. The servant comes out victorious and pities upon the master whose wife is a witch	2. The boy climbs upon a tree being afraid of witches 5. The saint wants to plant sal tree by himself 7. The *bonga* girls advise the people to observe a festival	3. The boy hits the tigers who in return kill the witches 6. The people ultimately plant the tree 8. The people already decided to have a festival before being advised by *bonga* girls. 9. The people decide the timing and naming of the festival
↓	↓	↓	↓
Overrating the society of master	Underrating the society of master	Denial of goodness by evil forces : Denial of social origin of Baha Festival	Goodness comes out victorious : Social origin of Baha Festival.

Tale II : The Girl and the Baha Festival

1. The brothers agree to the saint's proposal to sacrifice their sister	2. The girl becomes a flower and attracts her betrothed groom 3. The brothers are swallowed by the earth when the girl reminds them of their sin	4. The sal tree grows over the ruins of the brothers in a miraculous way—Force of heaven 5. The *bonga* asks the village-priest to have a festival.	6. The people decide to have a festival in Spring and name it Baha in their own way
↓	↓	↓	↓
Overrating the evil force of the society	Underrating the evil force of the society	Heavenly origin of Baha Festival	Social origin of Baha Festival

adherents to the spirits of different kinds, their social attitudes are very strong and deep rooted. Society, rather than the individual, plays an important role in the creation, distribution and preservation of Santal folklore. The witches have been destroyed by an individual in this particular tale, but when the question of festivity arose, the society came forward to the forefront. Faith in supernatural being is also shattered when the question of community became a matter of consideration. Apart from this, the Santals are a docile people, their sense of value in terms of society is very forceful. Thus, they seek goodness whenever they are confronted with a problem leading to a conflict between good and bad as determined by the society. They have a clear conception of what is an evil force and what is goodness in the eye of society and they abide by that conception in their day-to-day life. Thus the women, although they are the wives of masters and important people of the society, have been killed by the shepherd in this myth as they represent the evil force, the witchcraft. However important an individual might be, he must bow down before the society and shun whatever evil and wrong designs he might have in him. The wives have been killed by an ordinary boy and the poweful masters have accepted this killing without uttering a single word of protest because the action taken by the shepherd is the action of the society—he has a strong social sanction behind him. Thus, on the ashes of the wives of these poweful men grows a tree of beauty, an embodiment of goodness and truth. The beauty is truth and truth beauty, is not only a mere proverb, but a conviction of the Santals. Truth and beauty evolve out of the ashes and ruins of the opposing forces that deter their existence and effectiveness. This is the main objective of the Baha Festival as enunciated by the two myths under analysis.

Tale II. The Girl and the Baha Festival

The two opposing forces and some conflicting functions can be clearly conceived of in this myth also. The following figures will analyse these elements in a distinct way:

Forces:

(a) Brothers representing the evil force
(b) Sister representing the goodness

Functions (*f*) :

x. Brothers win over the sister
y. Sister wins over the brothers, the brothers are destroyed and the Baha is originated as a social festival.

Thus it follows :

$$fx^{(a)} : fy^{(b)} :: fx^{(b)} : fa^{-I} (y).$$

The analysis given above proves beyond doubt that the evil force which is opposed to goodness, however strong it might be, must succumb to the far less stronger force which represents goodness. The superior evil force is thus inferior to an inferior good force. Apart from this, the theme of the story moves in a planned way to introduce a social festival over the ruins of the undesirable elements of society. Here also the sal tree embodies in it the goodness and beauty which proves the fact that beauty is good and good is beauty. To them, the beauty reflects the truth in a very bright manner.

In the functions of the two myths, the binary opposites are also active through interactions. The conflicting binary forms may be understood in the graphic order arranged below:

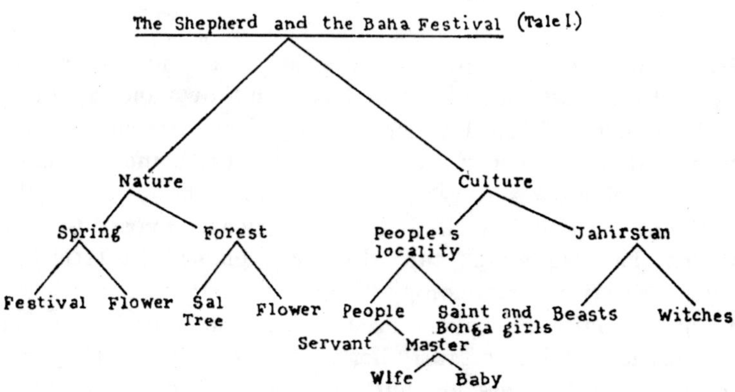

Apparently it appears that there exists no conflicting binarism between festival and flower, between tree and flower as well as between husband and wife and mother and baby. But within the deeper structure of the narration, the flower invokes the festival which remains dormant all the year round—it dces not come wilfully and spontaneously. Hence it is opposed to flower—like a snake-charmer, the flower makes the festival rise its head up and function. On the other hand there is also a binary opposition between the sal tree and flower as during the festival the flowers receive more honour and care than the tree. The tree remains where it is, but the flower is plucked and taken away to be used in the garland and in decoration.

The Girl and the Baha Festival (Tale II)

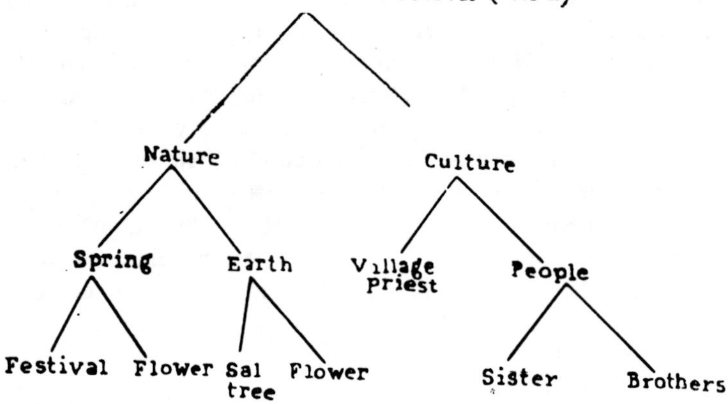

The binarism existing between the Sal tree and flower and also between festival and flower has been shown and explained in the analysis of Tale I. Other binary forces are clear in this graphic sketch except in the two pairs, the earth and spring.

The spring takes away the beauty from the body of the earth and garlands herself. Naturally they are opposed to each other. The two myths can also be explained in terms of psychoanalytical methodology. From the trend of the narration it may be construed that the master's wife had a desire in her subconscious mind to satisfy her sexual thirst by the shepherd boy who was her servant, but the shepherd did not agree. Hence she went out at the dead of night to meet and have a sexual relation with the servant. But the servant who represented goodness had no other alternative but to kill her. In the similar manner it may be said about the second myth that the six brothers had sexual weekness for their own sister—but since they were six and the sister, who represented goodness, was not found to be agreeable, they had to kill her. Up to the last moment, when they found that their sister could not be seduced and no intercourse with her was possible, they entered the earth. Entering the earth is equivalent to intercourse with their sister, as the earth represents eternal womanhood. Thus, the sexual impulse, hidden in the subconscious mind of man, is released in these two myths of one of the ancient peoples of this subcontinent. The way the tigress behaved is also an indicative factor. She killed the women as they were jealous of her—she guessed that perhaps the women were keen to have sexual intercourse with the tiger, her husband, which she was not ready to allow. She supposed that that was the reason for which the women killed the tiger and tigress—hence in retaliation she killed the women. Sex is no doubt a very powerful force in man and animal. This can bring a disastrous effect when it is suppressed. Many of the actions and functions of folktales, specially the myths, could be connected with the suppressed libidinous and lascivious emotion of human beings. Overfull of sex desire suppressed by social sanctions in ancient days found its way out through some motifs of folktales. The sexual relation between man and animal was not an unusual affair in the primitive society which the folktales and myths have retained in some of their motifs.

Baha Festival has some ritualistic importance in the Santal society. Since Baha is the festival of flowers, the men and women in the community do not use flower unless the festival is held. The Sal tree as well as its flower play an important role in Santal life. The ritualistic functions during the festival include the worship of several gods in the sacred grove. People of all walks of life collect flowers and make a flower-mound in front of which they offer goats and fowls in the name of Gods, specially the *Moreko* or 'five'. After the ritualistic functions are over, flowers cease to have the religious importance any more—then comes the aesthetic part and flowers of *sarjam* (sal), *matkam* (mahua) and *murup* (polas) are used specially by the women for their physical decoration. As a race, the Santals love flowers. Thus, through Baha, a religious social sanction is made to cover that love. A close socio-religious link has been established since long past between faith and aesthetic pleasure which the Baha manifests in it as a festival. Apart from this, the Baha Festival annually commemorates the divine contact of the people. The memory of *bonga* girls who danced with the people on the opening day of the festival long time ago, is evoked through the rituals, songs, tales, dances and other performances. Baha is a socio-religious festival blended with aesthetic love for beauty and deeper respcet for truth.

REFERENCES

Bodding, Paul Olaf A Note on the Wild People of the Santals, *Journal of Asiatic Society of Bengal*, XXVII (n.s.) 241-263.

——————— 1924 *A Chapter of Santal Folklore*, Krishiana, A.W. B B, A-S, 119.

——————— 1925-29 *Santal Folktales*, 3 vols, Oslo and Cambridge, Mass.

Bompas, CH 1909 *Folklore of the Santal Parganas*, David Nutt, London.

Boyler, IA 1874 "Telugu Ballad Poetry," *Indian Art*, Vol. III.

Campbell, A 1891 *Santal Folktales*, Pakhuria, Manbhum, Santal Mission Press.

——————— 1899 *A Santal-English Dictionary*, Pakhuria, The Santal Mission Press.

Cole, Ev FT 1875 "Santali Folklore", *Indian Antiquary*, IV, 10.

Dundes, Alan 1963 "Structural Typology of North American Indian Folktales, *South Western Journal of Anthropology*, (SWJA).

——————— 1968 *The Morphology of North American Indian Folktales*, Folktale Fellows Communications, Helsinki. (FFC)

Elwin, Verrier 1944 *Myths of Middle India*, Oxford University Press, London.

Fontenrose, Joseph 1966 *The Ritual Theory of Myth*, Berkeley.

Grierson, George 1885 *Bihar Peasant Life*, (revised, 1926), Government Printing Press, Patna.

Handoo, Jawaharlal 1978 *Current Trends in Folklore*. The University of Mysore, Mysore.

Hendricks, William O, 1973 : *Essays on Semiolinguistic and Verbal Art* Mouton, The Hague.

Islam, Mazharul 1982 *A History of Folktale Collections in India, Bangladesh and Pakistan*, (2nd enlarged edition). Panchali Prakasan, Calcutta.

Islam, Mazharul 1982 *Folklore Charchaya Ruptattik Bisslation Paddhati*, Lok Laukik, Calcutta.

Leach, ER 1970 *Levi-Strauss*, Fontana, London.

Levi-Strauss, Claude 1955 "Structural Study of Myth," *Journal of American Folklore*, Vol. 68.

———— 1966 (Eng. trans.) *The Savage Mind* (*La Pausee Sauvage*, Paris, 1962) Weidenfield and Nicolson, London.

———— 1969 *Structural Anthropology*, Allan Lane, The Penguin Press, London.

Maranda, E. Kongas and P. Maranda 1971, *Structural Models in Folklore and Transformational Essays*, Mouton, The Hague.

———— 1971 *Structural Analysis of Oral Tradition*, University of Pennsylvania, Philadelphia.

Parsons, T 1960 *Structure and Process in Modern Societies*, Free Press, Chicago.

Propp, Vladimir 1958 *Morphology of the Folktale*, Bloomington: Indiana University Research Center in Anthropology, Folklore and Linguistics Publication No. 10. (First published from Leningrad in Russian in 1928).

PART II

5

SOCIAL CHANGE AND FOLKLORE
(In the Context of the Indian Subcontinent)

EVERY culture in a human civilization has its infancy and growth, comparable with man's life-cycle. Each culture has its childhood, youth, manhood and old age. The analogy of life-cycle of the stages of cultural growth took deep roots even in the mind of Toynbee, who was influenced to a considerable extent by a study of Greece and Greek thought. He remarks about the development of western society in the following manner:

> The germ of western society, first developed in the body of the Greek society like a child in the womb. The Roman Empire was the period of pregnancy during which the new life was sheltered and nurtured by the old. The Dark Age was the crisis of birth, in which the child broke away from its parent and emerged as a separate, though naked and helpless, individual. The Middle Ages were the period of childhood . . . . The fourteenth and fifteenth centuries . . . stand for puberty, and the centuries since the year 1500 for our prime. (1921, 290).

The stages of development of social order is also accepted by the Marxists. We need to turn to the programme of the Communist Party in the Soviet Union, published in draft form in 1961 to learn that "the epoch-making turn of mankind from capitalism to socialism, initiated by the October Revolution, is a natural result of the development of society . . . the highroad to socialism has been paved. Many peoples are already marching along it, and it will be

> taken sooner or later by all the peoples .... Harmonious relations (in future) will be established between the individual and society .... Family relations will be freed from material considerations and will be based solely on mutual love and friendship. (1962, 107, 118, 160).

Human society, since ancient time. has been subject to change and development. Considerable time and thought have been devoted to trying to understand why and how change occurs in the social actions of men. What specific societal forms seem disposed to facilitate or encourage changes in behaviour? What are the factors associated with bursts of inventions that radically change the behavioural complexion of an entire society in a relatively short period of time? What are the conditions associated with the cessation of innovations? What are the biological characteristics of those who invent? What particular biological characteristics of population, if any, differentiate those that undergo relatively rapid change in behaviour from those that do not? Does change follow any definite course? Is this course linear or cyclical? These and numerous similar questions have been asked from time to time and answers to them sought. Besides, sociologists, like other scientists, have been worried with various substantive and methodological difficulties in the analysis of social change.

Social change is the most important aspect of group existence. Being social beings, men express their nature by creating and recreating an organization which guides and controls their behaviour in numerous ways. This organized society, liberates and limits the activities of men, sets up standards for them to follow and maintain. Whatever the imperfections and tyrannies it has exhibited in human history, it is a necessary condition of every fulfilment of life. Society is a system of usages and procedures, of authority and mutual aid, of many groupings and divisions, of controls of human behaviour and of liberties. This ever-changing, complex system we call society. It is a web of social relationships. And it is always changing. (MacIver and Page, 1957 : 5)

When we speak of social relationship, it signifies something different from the relationship existing between a plant and the tub, fire and smoke, between the sun and the earth. Each of these is affected by the existence of the other, but the relationship is not a social one. The physical condition is lacking. Their relationship is not determined by mutual awareness. Without this recognition there is no social relationship, no society. Society exists only where social beings behave toward one another in ways determined by their recognition of one another. It is evidenced in man's reflection on society ever since the beginnings of recorded thought, the reflection that it was not good for men to be alone. Thus, Aristotle called man a social animal. Man is dependent on society for protection, comfort, nurture, education, equipment, opportunity and the multitude of definite services which society provides. He is dependent on society for the content of his thoughts, his dreams, his aspirations, even many of his maladies of mind and body. His birth in society brings with it the absolute need of society itself.

Society is thus based on individual relationship of man with man and their mutual actions and interactions. The seed of social change lies in these relationships. Society in a sense, is the changing pattern of social relationship. The relationships which are central to sociology are those which involve mutual recognition, the sense of something held or shared in common, or, we may call it a sense of belonging together, and the conflicts of individual or community interests—a sociologist studies both the conditions that unite and those that separate human beings. Whether social units are viewed as "structural functional equilibria" in Talcot Parsons sense or as "quasi-stationary equilibrium process" in Kurt Lewins sense, social change, as stated before, is the most constant aspect of group existence. Social change may start in any part of the system, through changes in the external system for pattern of the group, alterations in its physical environment, technical organisation, or even in its internal system, and will, of course, have back effects of a greater or lesser order on all of these. Both immanent and external factors are important in the changes of social systems, their birth and their death. Once in existence a social system. "cannot help changing, even if all its external conditions are constant" (Sorokin, 1957, 633).

Social systems, thus, provide many sources of change, on the basis of which two broad areas of theoretical study have been evolved. The first is concerned with the factors or mechanisms which produce change. The second is concerned with general characteristics of the course of social change. The conceptions of society and culture seem to fall into five principal categories: (1) It is possible to conceive society to have always been just as we see it presently. The characteristic of constancy may often be accompanied by the notion that society was a sudden creation. (2) Another view, essentially nostalgic, looks upon the present form of society as manifestations of trends towards degeneracy. Such a view is based upon the assumption that in the past society and, consequently, the social actions of man were more effectively conducive to human happiness. Thus the golden age of man, the millennium, is a thing of the past, and the future holds nothing but further degeneration. (3) Societal forms and culture may be conceived as manifestations of a progression. Beginning in simplicity, with little or no differentiation and, consequently, with gradual transformation led to greater and greater complexity, and improved adaptation to the environment. Such a view would suggest an upward trend essentially based upon the creation of societal forms suited to human happiness and achievement. (4) Another view would make society go through a cycle analogous to that followed by man himself, that is, birth, infancy and childhood, adolescence and youth, maturity, old age and senility, and finally death or dissolution. (5) Society, lastly, may be conceived as tending to change from one extreme to another, going up and going down, more adapted and less adapted to insuring human happiness, but following no consistent plan or pattern, and rendering impossible attempts to predict its most probable state at any period in the future. These views, of course, are all essentially evaluative, intimately associated with man's hope and aspirations. There are diverse opinions about the social changes and the theories relating to that change, but my task would be to summarize and to contrast in short some of the leading thoughts on the subject of social change. My object is to indicate how we may approach the solution of problems posed by the mechanism and factors responsible for and the general characteristics of the course of social change. The best known explanations of social change in terms of a single or dominant factor, which may be called as theories, are: the technological theory, the economic theory, the conflict theory, the ideation theory and, finally, the cultural interaction theory. Before entering into the theoretical discussion on social change, it occurs to my mind, what really prompts the change? How does it begin in the first place? It may be said that innovation and diffusion were important sources of change for any society, although the latter probably accounts for a much greater share of it. To those two, we may also add crisis and conflict as a significant source. Each is discussed below.

Innovation and the technological theory

Innovation in the form of invention is one obvious source of social change. Innovations introduced new elements, or new combinations of old elements into the cultural accumulation. If the new element is truly new it may be called a discovery if it involves a new combination or use of cultural elements already known, it will probably be called an invention. Einstein's theory of relativity and the germ theory of disease were discoveries, the automobile and the computer were inventions. Both inventions and discoveries can be either material or non-material. The discovery of the New World by European explorers was a true discovery for them. The inventions and discoveries, both in material and non-material forms, are responsible to a great extent for bringing about the change in society. If a pre-literate society that uses stone-tools discovers a new type of stone, more easily worked and more durable than the old, this new and better material will probably replace the old stone.

Another type of innovation comes about from putting already known materials to new uses. Gun powder, for example, was an amusement in Chinese culture a long time before it was put to use as part of a weapons system. Sometimes it often happens that things that have just been lying around are put to new uses that have a radical impact on cultural change. Innovations are also made by recombining elements into new complexes, or by inventing new processes, new ways of doing things. Giving the existence of the boat and the steam engine, the invention of a steamboat was inevitable.

The saying that 'necessity is the mother of invention' does not always hold up well under the weight of empirical evidence, for most inventions come about by accident, rather than by discovery through conscious efforts. The antibiotic properties of penicillin were accidentally discovered by Alexander Fleming and Charles Goodyear hit upon the process of vulcanization, which prevents the deterioration of rubber, also by accident.

An interesting aspect of innovation is that important discoveries are made, more often than we might expect, in different cultures independently or in the same culture by different and independent sources. This phenomenon, called polygenesis, a theory in folklore, which has been explained before, is illustrated by the invention of several important items, ideas and processes independently in the old and new worlds. A calendar for computing the passage of time, the mathematical concept of zero, and the domestication of plant for food resources are examples. The invention of calculus by Newton in 1671 and by Leibnitz in 1676, the invention of photography in 1839 by Daguerre, Niepce and Talbot, are some striking examples of polygenesis.

Whether it is wise to tag the innovation concept with the technological theory, may be a matter of dispute. Some would disagree to put the two under a same theory on the basis that innovation includes both material and non-material inventions and discoveries, while the technological theory emphasizes only the technological inventions, achievements and progress. Others would tend to argue that all inventions, discoveries, in the form of innovations, be they material or non-material, belong to the technological category, as all of them introduce a technique of change in the society. Thus the new ideas, thoughts, knowledge, machines or equipments, systems, achievements both material and non-material forms, all are armed at reaching the same goal—the advancement and progress of society, which means, the society, as a result of that discovery or invention, steps forward or moves from its previous position. Accepting this view it may be said that the innovation (and the concept of innovation) falls within the technological theory.

The technological theory is true in one respect and false in others. Any technological change which is great enough will produce some other social change as a correspondence. For example, new techniques of manufacture are bound to affect social relations as can be found in modern industrially developed societies—its tensions, conflicts, forms of mental illness, the failure of social organisation to keep pace with technological change and so on. This, however, does not mean that the technological change alone can produce social changes of all types, nor is this always a necessary condition for other social changes. Here lies the shortcoming of this theory.

Even then, it cannot be denied that man's utilitarian devices, are thus, in many ways, responsible for social change. In order to apply these devices effectively, it is often necessary to establish new social relations. Every change in the process of production, every new attempt to utilize means either for private or for public gains, involves a new alignment of the human beings engaged in it. With the gaining of the advancement in technology, we can see that a new invention is suddenly introduced and rapidly developed. We can see how it brings a specific social change. We can see how the radio sets up common standards of speech or how it creates the interest amongst the people of the remotest village or even the tribal areas, who are gradually influenced by the cultural dominance of the city life. We can see how the technical conditions of the modern factory tend to strengthen industrial unionism and to weaken the older type of craft unionism or craft-based community feelings, the feelings which have penetrated in all sectors of labour forces even in the agro-based societies of the Indian subcontinent. Thus, the technological factors of social change are concrete, measurable, demonstrable and therefore are the forces that offer greater prospects to the scientific mind.

It is also true that the rapid changes of the societies of the developed world, and to some extent of the developing world, including countries of the Indian subcontinent, are related to and somehow dependent upon the development of new techniques, new inventions, new modes of production, new standards of living. Besides, attitudes, beliefs, traditions, which once were thought to be the very expression of human nature, have crumbled before the technological advance.

Monarchy, the prestige of birth, the divine ordering of social classes, traditions regarding the spheres of the sexes, regarding religion, regarding politics, have felt the shock. Thus, a true sociologist would not deny the impact of technology over human societies, rather he would, in all fairness, concentrate his study, in the light of technological development since the past, specially in the last one century on the aspects such as mechanization and social changes, mechanization and changes in values, direct and indirect effects of technological change, how technological advance initiates social change, new agricultural techniques and social change, advances in communication and social change, specialization and last of all the modern significance of the technological factor. It is true that technological advancement cannot alone initiate all the changes in a society, but the significant changes caused by it in the vast and major part of a society can never be undermined. In this sense, it may be regarded as a vital theory of social change.

Of all the areas of culture, folklore has been tremendously affected by the technological factors. Not to speak of the European or American folklore, where special features like industrial lore, factory lore, coalfield lore, and so on have been brought under the study of folklore; even the Indic folklore, viewed in the perspective of the last one hundred and fifty years has undergone a remarkable transformation. It has been, in the main, a transition from the great traditions, to modernity with its inexorability in the context of technological change, leading to shrivelling of the dimensions of time and space. Changes were, at first, slow, imperceptible and less pervasive, but since the fourth or fifth decade of the present century they have been rapid and sweeping. Thus a Bangladesh folkbard of the remotest village composes his song about an airplane, which, within a short span of time, is widely accepted by the folk of almost all the areas of present-day Bangladesh; the Patuas of West Bengal, who maintain their livelihood by drawing a series of pictures on papers from 20 to 26 cubits in length. They fabricate a story in lyrical form, based upon the drawn pictures and song showing that the illustrations in villages, particularly in the districts of Birbhum, Murshidabad and Burdwan, have changed some of their motifs from the *Ramayana*, *Mahabharata* and *Puranas* to the speedy train or motorcar or even a man coming down from a helicopter. Their counterparts in Orissa have stopped drawing pictures and have become folk-singers taking their themes from modern novels.

Agrarian changes caused by technology have also a great impact on folklore, specially on beliefs, customs, festivals and so on. Let me cite an example from Thanjavur, a district in Tamil Nadu. Thanjavur's rice production increased by 164 per cent between 1950-51 and 1973-74. Production fell by 12 per cent because of drought in 1974-75, but rose by 2.8 per cent in 1975-76 showing an overall increase of 139 per cent since 1950-51 and of 44.5 per cent since 1961. In Kumbapettai the main change induced by the Indian Agricultural Development Programme is that all of the paddy-land is now potentially doublecrop land, whereas 19 per cent of it was single crop in 1952. Some fields even now produce a third paddy crop in June, between the months of March and October. (Kathleen Gough, 1977, 260). This agricultural development becomes a major source of social change in that particular district. For the purpose of more effective cultivation, the Harijans of Kumbapettai have increased by 21 per cent since 1952. Among the dominant sub-caste of Brahacharanam Smartha Brahmins and among the hereditary temple priests of Siva (Kurukals) more people have left for professional, clerical or service work in cities reducing this sub-caste population by 31 per cent. Six new families of non-brahmin salaried workers have recently moved in Kumbapettai. Since only the brahmin street contained middle class housing, and because brahmins were short of money, these newcomers were allowed to buy or rent houses in the *agraharam.* Their arrival in the 1960s ended the age-old ritual seclusion of the brahmins and has helped to relax rules of religious pollution throughout the village. Once the *agraharam* had been polluted, the village headman went further and brought two of his non-brahmin servants to live at the eastern end of the street, one from the very low-caste of ambalakkar or fisherman. Spatial relations in Kumbapettai, therefore, no longer reflect the ritual hierarchy of caste as closely as they did in 1952. Similarly, whereas it has always been common for men of higher castes to have sexual relations with women of lower caste, one brahmin woman has now gone to live openly with a non-brahmin lover in a nearby village (Gough, 1977, 266-67).

More elaborate discussion on the impact of the technological aspect on folklore would be followed in this chapter and the chapters following this.

The economic theory

Owing largely to influence of Marx and Marxism, the economic theory of change occupies a major place in the discussion of social scientists and historians. The fundamental assumption of this theory is that the changes in the economic infrastructure of society are the prime-movers of social change. This infrastructure consists of 'forces' and 'relations' of production, the 'super-structure' consists of those features of the social system such as the judicial, political, and religious institutions, which serve to maintain the infrastructure and which are moulded by it. The social stress of the industrial revolution led in the nineteenth century to a revival, restatement and sharper formulation of the theory that the structure of society is an economic creation, and its changes essentially the sequel to economic change. In this, we begin with the power of economic production as the determinant of primary economic relationships—given the stage of productive efficiency, these relationships are "indispensable and independent of men's will" (Marx, N.I. Stone, trans 1904, 11). In other words, the stage of technological development determines the mode of production and the relationships and institutions that constitute the economic system. This set of relationships is in turn the chief determinant of the whole social order or as Marx puts it in the same work, "the sum total of these relations of production constitutes the economic structure of the society—the real foundation, on which rise legal and political super-structures and to which correspond definite forms of social consciousness" (Stone, 1904, 11-12). The cultural life of man, his intellectual, aesthetic, spiritual life, his creeds and his philosophies, and the social forms which are their vehicles, are the reflection of the economic order. Here is the material reality which comes to consciousness in our ideals.

This theory has been heavily criticised for ignoring or underestimating the causal significance of ideas and political processes as such. Economic determinism, in other words, does not solve the major problem of social causation. Its attempted solution rules out the influence of too many other factors. Economic influences are certainly powerful and penetrating. But the relation of the economic to the cultural, and to its social embellishment, is less clear and less conclusive. Our cultural interests are, to be sure, affected by our economic interests. It is not difficult to establish correlations between social changes and economic changes, though it is harder to interpret them. But it is hardly possible to pass from these indications of interrelationship to the simple causal priority asserted by Marx. Closely bound with the economic are the other aspects of civilisation. The economic system, with respect to the distribution of property and the relation of producers to owners, may be revolutionized, as in Russia, while the technological system associated with the former order may endure and develop. As Veblen puts it, "Man is what he does. As he acts, so he feels and thinks. The forces which have shaped the development of human life and of social structure are no doubt ultimately reducible to terms of living tissue and material environment" (1922, 189).

In spite of some of its drawbacks, as pointed out by many scholars from different angles of view, one of the great merits of the Marxian theory of change (Economic Theory), as opposed to the technological theory, is that it is truly sociological. It seeks to explain social change in terms of inner processes of social system as such.

If we try to analyse the elements of folklore in the light of economic theory, we find some relevance. Let me cite an example :

Since ancient time, Mandala has been regarded as the most important and wise man of the village. In olden times all the village affairs were settled and managed under his directions. There is a saying in Sanskrit *Gramasya mandalo raja*, that is, the headman is the king of the village. In course of time, Mandala also became the chief of Gambhira, a popular form of Shaiva cult in eastern India, specially of its administrative and financial side. Besides, if one died without an heir, the Mandala used to make over his property to the Gambhira. This financial factor ultimately caused feuds among the followers and on such occasions, among other things, the Gambhira also turned out to be an apple of discord. The villagers also sided with the contending parties, and thus there arose a necessity for the establishment of separate Gambhira for the seceding branch of the Mandala family and its supporters; and they had to forgo their claims to the old Gambhira. In this way there sprang more than one Gambhira in almost all the villages. (Sarkar 1972 : 66-68). Thus, even the folk festival, which is a part of folklore, is within the fold of economic influence.

The conflict theory

Another fundamental perspective on the process of social change, as also formulated by Marx, is the conflict theory. In general all conflict theorists maintain that the competition between groups for scarce resources inevitably produces divergence, opposition and conflict. The enduring struggle of these social groups or forces makes the continuing change. Although conflict is not necessarily turbulent, and may in fact be well-organised, as is, for example, collective burgeoning; occasional eruptions of violence do indeed flare up between various contending groups. As regimes succeed one another, those in power, attempt to implement their ideas and impose their values on the rest of their society, and those subjected to their domination, in turn, inevitably rise up and oppose the people in power. Once the formerly subordinate group assumes control, it is likely to be opposed by those among the vanquished, thus completing the cycle of conflict and change.

Max Weber believes the social conflict to be an action-oriented process and says, "intentionally to carrying out the actors own will against the resistance of the other party or parties". (1947: 132). Coser has termed social conflict thus : "Social conflict may be defined as a struggle over values or claims to status, power and scarce resources, in which the aims of the conflict groups are not only to gain the desired values, but also to neutralize, injure or eliminate rivals" (1967, 232). Coser's definition has the advantage of being more in line with the everyday usage of the word conflict than Weber's definition. Nevertheless, a theory of conflict ought also to encompass situations in which divergent interests and disagreements over values can be resolved without necessarily intending or bringing injury or harm to one's opponents. Social conflict arises from the structured arrangement of individuals and groups in a social system—from the very fact of social organization. In every social organisation, as Dahrendorf has pointed out, some positions are entrusted with a right to exercise control over other positions and to ensure compliance with authority through coercion. (1962 : 165-66). In other words, there exists a division of authority such that there are individuals and groups who are subject to authority rather than participants in its exercise. In Marx's theory economic change only occurs and produces other change through the mechanism of intensified conflict between the social groups and different parts of the social system. Recently, social theorists have suggested that conflict, in its broadest sense, must be the cause of social change. The reasoning behind this is that if there is a consensus in society, and if the various sectors are integrated, there is little pressure for change; therefore, change must be due to conflict between groups and/or between different parts of the social and cultural system.

The contention that group conflict is a sufficient condition for social change cannot always be accepted as true, though, in some cases, this may be the cause. There is no society which does not have conflict of some kind, so, obviously, all social changes are associated with conflict in some way or another. But the real social change, which affects society at large, is, in most cases, the result of the intensification of this conflict, which, this theory did not emphasise.

Ever since Marx, there has been a continuous debate by historians and social scientists on what are the precise links between economic change and social conflict, in particular revolutionary outbreaks. There is ample literature on topics such as short and long-term economic trends, particular sequences of short and long-term up and down swings, migration patterns, rural-urban demographic shifts, the effects of the introduction of new technologies and novel modes of production and other structural economic changes, changes in the cost of living, of wages, of the cost of basic foods and a host of other economic facts and processes. Besides, not only changes in absolute terms, but relative gains and losses, the concepts of relative deprivation, rising expectations, or some other social psychological concepts such as hope and cramp, reactions of various groups and social classes to absolute and relative economic gains and losses, have received close assessment from the students of social conflict. The conclusion that several diverse patterns of economic change must bear some direct and indirect links to social disturbances, and that this link is mediated by some intervening social psychological processes, is inescapable. Mancur Olson Jr., a famous economist, writes on this point, "Economic growth . . . can significantly increase the number of (economic) losers" (1963 : 529-52) and such growth might be associated with changes in the relative economic position of social strata and other population groups.

Marx thought that conflict stemmed from the clash between different economic interests, as represented by the proletariat and the bourgeoisie. Some recent theorists have attempted to refine Marx's economic and conflict theories in the light of the changes taking place in post-capitalistic societies. Ralf Dahrendorf, for instance, points to authority relationships, rather than economic interests as the fundamental point of cleavage in contemporary industrial society. Dahrendorf sees conflict arising when those who possess authority seek to maintain the *status quo*, while those who lack it attempt to expand their powers (1959 : 24). Other conflict theorists apply the dialectic in still different ways, conceiving of revolution as a rejuvenating response, promoting renovation and renewal of an otherwise decadent and perverted social order that has over-extended its ideals and authority.

When we think of a society, we form certain primary concepts about the community, associations, institutions, customs and mores. A serious discussion about society includes topics like interests and attitudes, individual and society, environment and life, geography and people, the total environment and accommodation, the social structure, the mores and social control, the major social codes, social codes and the individual life, types of social groups, the family, the community; city, country and region, social class and caste, ethnic and racial groups; herd, crowd and mass communication; associations and interests; political associations; economic associations; the cultural associations; cultural, functional systems and some other minor ones.

The life of human beings, in all ages and stages of culture, is primarily controlled by a vast mass of folk ways handed down from the earliest existence of the race, related to the ways of other animals, only the topmost layers of which are subject to change and have been somewhat modified by human philosophy, ethics and religion, or by other acts of intelligent reflection. Underlying and sustaining the more formal order of institutions and associations there exists an intricate complex of usages or modes of behaviour. The socially accredited ways of acting are the customs of society. Like folk ways and customs, folklore is also an important aspect of society—it reflects the creativity of man. When we talk of society, we must consider. among others, folklore as a very significant part of its culture which fulfils the demands of human mind and covers a vast area of folk life.

Every society has a structure and that structure is subject to incessant change, growing, decaying, finding renewal, accommodating itself to extremely variant conditions and suffering vast modifications in the course of time. Its contemporaneous aspects hold and hides the secret of its past. We know its nature, as we know the nature of a living person, only in the comprehension of it through a time-span. Its meaning is never revealed in any moment of its existence, but, finally and fully, only in the whole process through which it passes. To understand the social structure we must, therefore, view it in the historical process, seeking countinuity, observing also how differences emerge. We must, in other words, discover the direction of change, or all is meaningless.

The present is based upon the foundations of the past.

which has a great bearing not only upon man's present activity but also upon his future. Each fresh day creates a new climate of existence, albeit in doing so many past values have to be destroyed, but the past also enables man to follow his many potentialities. Thus the changes and the retentions play an important role in the society of man. The states of existence, the past, present and future—within the relative notion of time are not static entities and there is no movement through the passage of time from fixed positions. Therefore, the states of existence are really qualities of activity processes which have their relationship to present existence alone. This suggests that man's existence is always within the framework of a dynamic and creative present. The Indian civilization, if analysed in the context of this proposition, will show how structural transformations from one configuration to another have taken place and this will enable us to base our findings not merely on contents, chronology, or other narrative descriptions of historical and archaeological evidence, but on its structure and change. Change and continuity are twin fundamentals of the dynamics of human societies.

There is a tendency among Indian scholars to concentrate more on the continuity aspect of tradition in India in their interpretations of Indian civilisation than on change, associated with conflict and tension, which is considered a newer concept to view the past, present and future. The goal of understanding past socio-cultural and economic processes and patterns is of great utility than that of mere description and the historiographical pursuit of piecing together the past heritage. We tend to follow a methodology that seems to be a continuation of the narrative method of myths, legends and other elements of folklore emphasizing the ideal norms of Indian religion and philosophy. But this approach neglects the other aspect which may seem more dynamic—the change of the social structure through constant conflict and tension from within the society which shaped Indian civilization. Thus the study of our heritage, specially embodied in Indian culture as a whole which is mainly folk-oriented, may have to be viewed from the point of view of change, conflict and tension by seeking meaning not only in the contents alone, but also in terms of contemporary meaning and intelligibility, which will enable us to explore the enduring content of Indian civilization and to see how it has been transmitted to its various parts. It will also help us to find out the rates of social change, the kinds of changes and the agencies of change underlying in the diversified patterns of Indian culture having a strong and regulating force of unity inherent in them.

The idea that folklore belongs to the past and savage origin has been long discarded. It is a dynamic force in the sense that with the change of social structure and cultural pattern, folklore also takes a new shape and form and adopts a new spirit. Since it is a very important part of folk culture or the culture as a whole, as in culture, there exists in folklore the constant and variable elements which provide its strength to retain the traditionalism on the one hand and accept the change on the other. India has one of the richest treasures of folklore in the world, but little attempts have so far been made to analyse the vast materials of her folklore in the context of social change and its reflection on folklore vis-a-vis the impact of folklore on bringing about the changes in the society. The seeds of conflict, tension and change are also the regulating forces in folklore and they can be traced back from Indian society, if viewed from sociological standpoint, since ancient past.

Social conflict forms one of the basic characteristics of many elements of folklore. The Secret Tale of Golden Commander, a Russian legend, gives us a good example.

> Golden Commander is the pseudonym of Stepagovis Plotnikov, a farmer. While working in a factory as a labourer, he organized a gang of dacoits under his leadership and killed Shirayev, the mill-owner in 1771. The niece of the deceased millowner became the owner of the mill. Once, when a follower of Plotnikov betrayed the cause of the labour-gang—the dacoits, Plotnikov killed him with his own hand. Gradually, this beautiful woman, the owner of the mill, attracted Plotnikov and related a secret chant to him which gave Plotnikov the information of a huge wealth hidden in a cave. This was enough to degenerate Plotnikov from his own ideals. Being enchanted with the ownership of this wealth, Plotnikov lost his proletariat

character and was killed by his followers. He then became the hero of a fighting-legend.

Biryukov (1937) presents us this legend from his own collection and indicates that, even in pre-Revolution folklore of Russia, there exists a class conflict, a thirst for freedom from economic exploitation and a struggle for the equitable distribution of wealth.

Indic folklore is full of conflicts reflecting the caste-oriented classes, the religions, gods and tribals and non-tribals. There has been a multiplication of gods and goddesses of the Hindu pantheon during the successive ages of Indian history. The folklore, literature and art of each age reflect the inventiveness of folk-imagination as displayed in the creation of new orders of deities to help man in the solution of new problems of life. The rivalries of the devotees of these gods have been embodied in the elements of folklore in various ways. Here is a legend :

Usha, daughter of king Vana, a staunch Shaiva, fell secretly in love with Aniruddha, a grandson of Sri Krishna, king of Dwaraka. Enraged at this, high-souled Vana imprisoned Aniruddha in an iron cage. The latter implored the assistance of Kali, of complexion dark as collyrium, and, pleased with his devotion the goddess released him at dead of night on the fourteenth day of the black half of the month of Jyaistha (May-June). On the following night, a formidable conflict took place between king Vana and Krishna, in which, as soon as Krishna lopped off the arms of his opponent with his discus named Sudarshana and prepared himself to cut off his head, Samkara (Shiva) cried out : "Don't, oh don't behead my Vana; don't cut off his head, rather withdraw your Sudarshana". At this Lord Krishna said, "Let then your Vana live. Here do I recall my discus." Then with gracious words, Nandi, the gate-keeper and constant attendant on Shiva, advised Vana to rush to Shiva and dance before Him to save his life. Vana followed this and was saved with the blessing of Shiva.

There are hundreds of legends and tales, myths and proverbs, ballads and songs, where social conflict can be traced to prove the strength of this theory. Besides, conflict is also hidden within the structure of the genres of folklore, such as one Bengali proverb I have mentioned to illustrate the structural theory of folklore *Nachte Na Janley Utthan Banka.* It is possible to trace two conflicting forces from the structure of almost all genres of folklore.

The malintegration theory

The complexity of modern social organisation gives peculiar significance to the various ways in which the interdependent parts of the inclusive system fail to function harmoniously together, the discrepancies and disparities of means and ends, to the fictions and checks that impede the working of the system, to the clashes and conflicts that lower its efficiency, disturb its co-ordination, or confound its service. Ogburn distinguishes between material and non-material culture and says, when changes occur in the material culture, these in turn stimulate changes in the non-material culture, particularly in what he terms the adaptive culture or the ways of utilising, exploiting or rendering more serviceable the material changes. He further directs attention to the role of two major categories of factors that may be and have been responsible for change—namely, man's biological heritage and man's social heritage. "Theoretically, cultural changes may be accounted for in terms of changes in the biological nature of man or in purely cultural factors" (1927 : 61). A review of the data of cultural development or evolution leads him to reject the hypothesis of any consistent or close relationship between biological and cultural changes. The total accumulation of additional knowledge and techniques has a great deal to do with both the quantity and the kind of innovations that are devised. This cultural repository limits the range of all inventions. Leonardo da Vinci sketched many machines—the airplane, helicopter and submarine among others—that were workable in principle, but the technology of his was inadequate for building them. Without the necessary preliminary innovations in metallurgy, the internal combustion engine, advances in electricity had to be postponed until later. Thus, inventions tend to stimulate still more inventions. This is one aspect, on the other hand, as the culture base expands, there are likely to be increases in rates of change. The greater the number of elements in a given culture, the greater the number of possible combinations and recombinations. For example, glass gave birth to costume jewellery, window panes, lenses, test-tubes, X-ray tubes, electric light bulbs, and so on.

Costs are another important factor influencing the willingness to accept change. In 1932 August Dvorak developed a new keyboard for the typewriter which was superior to the existing typewriter. But because of the cost involved, it could not be manufactured. Change also affects people differently. Some individuals and groups are likely to lose more benefits. and privileges from change than others. Those who benefit from the status quo often have a vested interest in maintaining it, and are likely to mount considerable opposition to change when it threatens to diminish their power, rewards and esteem. In traditional peasant societies, for example, native medical curers and midwives are likely to resent modern medical programmes; large landlords are likely to oppose too much education for peasants for fear it may promote unrest and demands for land redistribution.

Sometimes the new technology is introduced from without into a community or country where culture is wedded to a quite different system. In primitive societies culture and civilization are peculiarly interdependent and inseparable. This harmony is destroyed when an alien technology is imposed on them. The situation, on the other hand, is different when the alien technology is introduced to or imposed upon peoples of relatively high culture, but here, too, serious disturbances are apt to occur. Since Chinese culture has been peculiarly attached to family institutions and since industrial development limits the functions of the family and its social role, there has been strong cultural resistance to the new technology and a danger of cultural disintegration where it has been introduced. This may in large measure explain the slow industrial development of China in the period prior to the Japanese invasion and the long civil war. In India, on the contrary, the new technology was associated with alien domination and incurred widespread resistance. Our poets, folkbards painted the contrast between the old order and the new. One is quoted below :

I look for the goats coming home in the haze of evening,
I see the trams jerking down the streets crowded with tired workers
I look for the blue threads of smoke rising from the huts at the cooking of the evening meal
I see the tall chimneys of the factories sending forth black clouds.

Sometimes it so happens that the two cultures (one being alien) are brought rather abruptly into contact, and under these conditions, one of them appears to be a threat to the very existence of the other, specially the original one, which is associated with a dominant group. Culture clash may broadly be said to exist wherever two ways of life or modes of thought within the same community are so opposed that they cannot exist side by side, in such wise that the very presence of the one implies the suppression of the other. The most serious of such clashes since World War II is that between the communistic type of totalitarianism and democracy. This culture clash is a sword of division within many countries, both in the East and in the West, provoking civil wars and revolutions.

Thus, closely allied to the conflict theory is one which explains change in terms of incompatibilities or malintegration between different parts of social systems. There are a number of sources of inconsistency within social systems. The most obvious is the possible tension between personality and the demands made upon it by social institutions. The second source of incompatibility is inherent in the nature of role expectation. Thus, this theory explains change in terms of the conflicting pressures or demands of different sectors of a society or culture. The assumption underlying this is that if actions in one sphere inhibit those in another, then, one or the other must change.

This theory is as plausible as the group conflict theory; and the two together seem to account for a good deal of social change. But it is also true that incompatibility is not always a necessary condition for change. The two forces in the society remaining compatible for long cannot be incompatible gradually or even suddenly unless there is some change or reason responsible for it. Thus the social change caused by the incompatibility between the two forces is responsible not to incompatibility itself as such, but to the cause behind it. This is the main weakness of this theory.

The Indic folklore provides materials in support of this theory. The Bengali rhymes still retain the resistance to English culture and eulogise some of the heroes who took the lead in resistance. On the contrary some rhymes denounce those who worked as the henchmen of the British. I quote

> Ali Naki was a brave man with a turban. He binds his sword by his turban. And looted the market of Calcutta within a moment.*

It is said that Ali Naki Khan, the prince of Rajnagar, worked for some time under Siraj-ud-daula, the last ruler of Bengal. On receiving the news that the Englishmen, who were allowed the business at Calcutta, were preparing for an attack, Siraj marched to Calcutta and crushed that movement. Ali Naki was one who accompanied Siraj and proved his gallantry. Till now, the Muslims of Lucknow use a piece of cloth, named as 'luter kapra' during Muharram and tie it with the Tajia. This cloth is the remnant of the cloth looted by Ali Naki from the defeated Englishmen.

> A man named Kanta became docile and struggled to escape
> something.
> But he was clever enough to retort and cause to split
> Even he succeeded in overcoming Hastings
> Is there anybody second to him in Bengal ?**

This is connected with an historical event Hastings came as Governor in 1772. A man named Kanta, who had business at Calcutta, became the henchman of Hastings. Hastings became Governor-General of India in 1774 and

* Translation by author of the Bengali original by Harekrishna Mukherjee, 1323 Bengali era, 243-46.

** Author's translation of the Bengali original by P. Mallick, Prabashi, 1328 Bengali era : 883-884.

hanged King Nanda Kumar in a conspiracy case, in which Kanta was one who was a witness against Nanda Kumar. The general condemnation against this man is still remembered through this rhyme. Bhawmick quoted both these rhymes (1979, 206, 207), but without reference to this theoretical relevance.

The sense of resistance can also be traced from within the cultural context of India. Here is a myth about death :

> The Gadaba of Koraput, partially Hinduized, say that the Gods were responsible for bringing about death to the human world. In ancient days there was a God called Kalanka Deota who had had many lesser gods as servants. In those days man did not die and the Gods would not work properly as they could not eat the human corpses. Kalanka Deota refused to accept the proposal of the Gods to bring death to human beings. The Gods went hungry. Even then Kalanka Deota did not yield. The Gods became weak and failed to administer the world properly. One day, Kalanka went to his sister who had just given birth to a daughter and was lying exhausted and helpless. His sister's condition really hurt him and being angry with the child, the Deota picked it up, ground the bones to powder and made it into bread. In the guise of an old mali woman, he went from village to village peddling the bread. Whoever took the bread died. In this way death came to the world and the gods were satisfied. (Elwin, 1954, 509).

This myth clearly demonstrates that the Godaba of Koraput resisted the advent of Hindu culture, which, even today, has not been able to spread all its wings amongst that tribe. Such examples are not hard to seek from the culture as well as folklore which is called Indic.

The adaptation theory

Oscar Lewis, from his Mexican experience, points out that "culture change may not be a matter of folk-urban progression, but rather an increasing or decreasing heterogeneity of culture elements. For example . . . the incorporation of Spanish rural elements such as plow . . . did not make Tepoztlan more urban, but rather gave it a more varied rural culture." (1951, 432-440). This gives a clear example of how a culture from outside is adapted by a society to suit its own genius. Sorokin distinguishes the cultural integration from change by two major methods of approach—the methods he calls the causal, functional and the logico-meaningful. He states that the diagnostic criteria of the functional relationship of the parts of the cultural configuration are "the tangible, notable, testable, direct interdependence (mutual or one-sides) of the variables or parts one upon another and upon the whole system (1937, 15). One of his many statements about the nature of the logico-meaningful integration through adaptation is "the ordering element is not uniformity or relationship between fragmentary variables, but identity of meaning or logical coalescence. Hidden behind the empirical difference, seemingly unrelated fragments of the cultural complex lies an identity of meaning, which brings them together in consistent styles, typical forms and significant patterns." (1937, 23): Sorokin continues with this statement of the basic difference between the two views : "If, therefore, uniformity of relationship is the common denominators of causally knitted phenomena, in the logico-meaningful union, it is identity of central meaning or idea." (1937, 23).

According to Talcot Parsons, society is a system, composed of a set of interrelated parts of structures that are integrated with one another, functioning so as to promote over-all social stability. Every society must provide for five basic needs if it is to endure: (a) member replacement, (b) member socialization, (c) production and distribution of goods and services, (d) preservation of order and (e) provision and maintenance of a sense of purpose in order to assure committed participation in group activities. These needs tend to give rise to the development of a set of accommodative structures. The family provides for replacement, the educational system for socialization and so on.

Functionalism does not or cannot explain social change, yet it may assume to be a theory of change if it is also a theory of social persistence. Besides, what some proponents of this theory have in mind is the process of adaptation of social systems to one another. Thus one can explain changes in the economy as adaptations to other economics or to the polity, or changes in the family structure in terms of adaptation to other institutions, and so on.

The weakness of this theory lies in the fact that the terms like 'system', 'environment,' 'differentiation' and 'adaptation' can always be defined in such a way as to demonstrate the truth of the theory. But to do this one does not need a complicated theory of adaptation. As for example, the differentiation may, in some circumstances, characterize the process of adaptation effective and in others it may not. Then again, it is much simpler to analyse changes in business organizations, the armies and the structure of 'command' economics in terms of adaptation then it is to analyse changes in the structure of families, religious organizations and non-command economics.

A little explanation may not seem out of place here. There remains a group of terms which signify not the change of one object or system in itself but the changing relation of two or more objects or systems to one another. These terms are often wrongly quoted with the terms of the last two groups. They are 'adaptation', 'adjustment', 'accommodation', 'assimilation' and their negatives. To these such vague terms as harmony may be added. It may by noted that the positive terms cannot as such mean either evolution or progress. They signify merely that the two objects conform to one another within a common process, but whether that process should be named evolution, or progress or something else altogether remains thereby undetermined. Adaptation, for example, does not mean evolution. There is not the slightest reason to regard the lowest forms of life as less adapted to their environment than are the highest form. A small lice can certainly claim to be as well adjusted to his life conditions as is civilized man to his. But the underlying force of this theory lies in the fact that human beings are rationally prone to adapt themselves favourably within their own societies as well as adapt the culture alien to them for harmonious accommodation and beneficial adjustment.

Since plurality is one of the main characteristics of Indian civilization, its culture is divergent in nature, it may be called the culture of adaptation and integration, the process which is still in vogue. Indian culture has been stabilized through diversification, strengthened through assimilation and nourished through amalgamation. This has been considerably reflected in Indic folklore.

Under the long rule of the Pala kings, ostensibly Buddhist, were really eclectic in matters of faith, the people of Bengal became accustomed to the performance of both Buddhist and Hindu rites. This hybrid trend of socio-religious life became so well-established that Brahmanas of the orthodox school could not, with all their efforts, stamp it out to any appreciable extent. Hence they thought it more expedient to incorporate the deities of the Buddhist Viharas, either as they were or in some modified form, with those of their own religion, and these borrowed divinities were allowed the same rank as the deities of the Hindu Tantric school. Thus, this provides one aspect of adaptation. But long before this, when Buddhism was spread, the Buddhist festivals had adapted themselves to the form the society of those days had assumed and the rites and ceremonies of the Mahayana school had become greatly Hinduised to suit the social organism of the time. Even the little vows and observances practiced by tender boys and girls were in keeping with that transformation.

The process of adaptation had been in operation even when culture from outside India penetrated deep in the society of this vast subcontinent, specially the western and eastern zones. Bengal was then connected in various ways with Tibet, China and the adjacent countries. Owing to this foreign intercourse many a god of the Chinese, the Mongols, the Huns and the Burmese also found its way into the Hindu pantheon. The Tantric deities of the Buddhist Viharas having been recognized by the Hindu Tantric school, the people in general began to forget even the existence of the Viharas. Thus, Vishnu, Shiva, Surya, Tara and the other gods and goddesses, with their various festivals, became firmly established in Bengal.

Let me cite one more example of adaptation. Satya of the

Hindus and Pir of the Muslims were combined to give birth to a powerful deity named as Satya Pir for the welfare of both the communities. *Satya* means truth, but in Sanskrit God Vishnu was called Satya. *Pir* means old or a preceptor who founded a Muslim religious sect in Persian, Satya Pir in Bengal, Bihar and Orissa became a monk whose worship was popular in the last quarter of the seventeenth or the beginning of the eighteenth century. Poet Krishna Hari Das has depicted the life and performances of Satya Pir in his long narrative poetry named "Malanchar Pala." Satya Pir appeared before the people sometimes as an old brahmin, an *avdhut* or a *faqir*. This has been described in *Skanda-Purana* and in the Palas of Srikavipandit, Sitaram Das and Kavikarna of Orissa.

Matsyendranath and the heroic Pir named Sasdeala in course of time became one Matsandali Pir. Matsyendranath, Goraknath and Satyendranath became Trinath. People accepted Satyanarayan as one of Trinath. Later on he was identified with Jagannath. This was done purposefully by the devotees to enhance the glory of Satya Pir. He has been described in Kavi-Karna's Pala as a log of wood floating on the waves of the sea out of which the image of Jagannath was built and instituted in the temple. The function of the Great God was not only to do away with the difference existing between the two main communities of India but among all sects and sections of the world. The Brahmin did not hesitate to take Mahaprasad with Sudras. His message was that Ram and Rahim are one. *Quran* and *Purana* are one. Jagannath after becoming a God of the Sabaras, Jains, Buddhists and Hindus became a joint God of the Hindus and Muslims and a God of the whole world. (Kunjabehari Das, 1953, 76).

Twenty-six Satya Pir folk dramas (*Pala*) containing songs and dances have been discovered so far, sixteen of them are attached to the name of Kavikarna who has written in a mixed Oriya-Bengali and Persian dialect. The name of Kavikarna is very popular in Orissa, though not known in West Bengal or in Bangladesh. Most of his stories are fantastic and adapted from folktales. The story of Janma-Pala of Kavikarna and Malancha Pala of the Bengali poet Krishna-Hari Das is almost the same. The stories of Kalburia Pala, Madan Sundar Pala, Sadananda Saudagar Pala are well known in Bengali folklore. Satya Pir's worship is in practice in South India as well as in the Punjab.

There are hundreds of themes in Bengali literature, both in the written and oral tradition, where the mutual influence of Hindu culture, Buddhist culture and the Muslim culture has been distinctly accepted, adapted and integrated. Folklore's attempt and success in this respect is unique, where the genuine feelings of the peoples of this subcontinent have been truly reflected.

The ideation theory

The innovation in the shape of inventions and discoveries play an important role in changing the social pattern. The innovation may be classified as material inventions, such as the bow and arrow, telephone or airplane and social inventions, such as the alphabet, constitutional government, or contract bridge. In each case, old elements are used, combined and improved for a new application. Invention is thus a continuing process, with each new invention the last in a long series of preceding inventions and discoveries. In some rare cases, of course, the innovation could be absolutely new.

New ideas belong to the non-material category, but it is purely social. Since ancient time, along with material and other social inventions, the ideas, be they new or based on older ones, have been the very significant and effective cause of socio-cultural change in human civilization.

It has been long argued that discovery, invention and diffusion are processes of change. But what causes them to happen? This cannot be answered without first examining the meaning of the term cause. A cause is sometimes defined as a condition which is both necessary and sufficient to produce a predictable effect. It is necessary in that this effect can never be achieved without the said cause and sufficient in that this cause alone, always, produces this effect. Does extraordinary love for research cause a scholar to be indifferent towards his wife? There are some, of course, who might be like that, but, obviously, the love for research is neither a necessary nor a sufficient condition to produce this apathy. Most causation in social science is multiple—that is, a number of factors interact in producing a result. What factors interact in producing a social change?

First of all, it may be noted that the factors in social change are predominently social and cultural, not biological or geographic. Not everyone accepts this view. Some people would attribute the rise and fall of a great civilization to changes in the biological characteristic of nations. Often these theories have a racial twist; a great civilization is said to arrive from a vigorous, creative race, and falls when the race mixes with lesser breeds and dilutes its genius. According to an opposite version, a great burst of creativity follows a fortunate intermixture of races and dies out as the hybrid strain runs out. Most scientists reject all such theories. There is no convincing scientific evidence that any race differs from any other race in its biological basis for human learning, or that man's biology has changed during the last twenty-five thousand years or so. During the period of recorded history, man's biological attributes appear to have been, a constant, not a variable in his behaviour. Compared to all these, the theory about ideas being the force of social change seems to have more solid ground and validity.

Aside from its general attitude toward change, each society has many specific attitudes and values which cling to its objects and activities. When government agents introduced hybrid corn to the Spanish American farmers of the Rio Grande Valley, they readily adopted it because of its superior yield, but within three years, they had all returned to the old corn. They did not like the hybrid corn because it did not make good tortillas (Apodaca: 1952 35-39). Thus if an object or an idea has a purely utilitarian value, that is, if it is valued because of what it will do, change may be accepted quite readily. Even in the USA, the new farm practices, as studied by Fliegel and Kivlin (1966: 253-248), are readily accepted by the farmers if they find that those are perceived as most profitable and least risky. The same may be true about ideas. The average American, who usually takes a coldly rational, thoroughly unsentimental view of economic activities, finds it hard to appreciate the sentiment and values of non-western peoples. He is irritated by the *Boiga* of Central India, who refused to give up their primitive digging sticks for the far superior mold beard plow. Why? The Boiga loved the earth as a kindly and generous mother. They would gently help her with the digging stick to bring forth her yield, but could not bring themselves to cut her with knives (Elwin, 1939 : 106-107).

The ideational theory of social change could take one of the three forms. First, it could assert that all social change is ideational. Second, it could assert that the ideational changes are necessary conditions of social change. Third it could assert that ideational changes are important contributory factors to many or most types of changes.

The first objection against this theory is that it can be shown that certain ideas which are thought to reflect the underlying social structure have themselves developed independently of those structures and sometimes have preceded that historically. Certain myths can be shown to have existed before the rituals with which they later become associated. Secondly, it can be shown that a number of different sets of ideas can co-exist with the same social structures while the number of different social structures can coexist with the same sets of ideas. Thirdly, the sociology of knowledge is itself an idea which is either a social product or must be an exception to the rule.

In the Indic context, as is evident in so far as other theories of social change are concerned, which I have indicated and analysed in short along with those theories, the ideation theory also seems quite relevant, specially in the vast field of Indic folklore. Let me cite an example from Vaisnava and Baul songs, both are precious folk songs in the Bengali language.

The Vaisnava Sahajia cult is based on the impulsive love for the beloved. In Vaisnava philosophy and religion love is the eternal force. This love-impulse is sometime humanly, sometime mystically depicted through the episode of Radha and Krishna. The dedicated feeling, intense emotion and yearning for the beloved, as narrated in the Radha-Krishna episode, are the basis of Vaisnava philosophy and religion, which have been expressed, in many forms, themes and styles in Vaisnava literature. The religious sentiment based on the Bhakti cult, aesthetic love expressed through emotion and eroticism arising out of physical desire, have been combined and through a process of metamorphosis, elevated to the sublime in Vaisnavism.

Sufism, which is a Persian product under the banner of Islam, is also concerned with love, a love for Allah, the God. The Sufis believe not in relgious regularities and performances, but on having a direct relation with God like the one between male and female human lovers, which can be attained through a process. It is the intense love that can lead man nearer to God, not the day-to-day religious formalities. God does not live over the sky, but in the body of the human being. Poet Jalaluddin Rumi thus says:

> The mosque that is built in the hearts of the saints
> Is the place of worship for all, for God dwells there.

This Sufism, when brought to India by the Persian Sufis, found an easy access—the ideas of the followers of the Vaisnava cult and the Sufis found a common way. A new pattern of folksong, based on mainly these two streams of ideas, found its creation in the name of Baul songs in Bengal. The beliefs, customs and religious practices of the Baul sect hold to some extent the heritage of the Buddhist Sahajiya cult, Tantricism and Sufism. The Baul cult has certain similarities with these schools, but as a religious cult, it is more a product of Persian Sufism than of the others. The cult does not have a formal religious way to follow strictly through worship, ceremonies and rituals. It incorporates the yogic practices, which by way of the concentration of mind through the full control of sensual organs lead to the subjective idealistic love of the sublime plane to realise the absolute, the eternal true existence dwelling in the human body. Their religious attitude is purely a subjective psychological discipline. Like Sufis, they also feel that "it is only after the melting away of the human personality that the door is opened and the screen before our eyes is removed leaving the lover and the beloved unified in a bond of infinite love" (S.B. Dasguta, 1962: 180). The Baul songs, a powerful stream of Bengali folk songs, reveal this truth of life in the context of rural Bengal. The Baul community is equally dedicated to uphold their cult and to demonstrate the underlying ideas embodied in it through innumerable songs, and mostly songs with dance. In this sense, the Bauls conform more to a music community than, strictly speaking, any formal religion.

I have brought forward this issue only to focus on the acceptance of ideas for a happy and harmonious coherence. This has been possible in a considerably wide manner on the vast canvas of Indian culture. The Baul community is one such example.

The cultural interaction theory :

W.L. Warner and P.S. Lunt defined society as "a group of mutually interacting individuals" (1941, 13). Contacts between individual groups and cultural communities lead to some constant interactions, which, according to this theroy, produce change. Professor Morgenthau observes : "The pluralism of domestic groupings and conflicts tend to impress upon the participants the relativity of their interests and loyalties and thus to instigate the clashes of different groups" (1963, 503). This pluralism causes an interaction bringing about a clearly identifiable economy, which must be spread wide in order to provide every group its contended share. This expresses the integrative role of groups and leads us on to the consideration of interaction, which is like tension, a personal, an inter-personal and also an inter-group phenomenon.

In most cases, the disruptive consequences of change are manifold. Introducing new elements into a culture whether they be social, physical or ideational—often may promote or intensify social interaction. As for example, India, with its vast historical past and peculiar geographical conditions, has become a home of multi-religious, multi-lingual, multi-racial and multi-caste groups of society. But there exists unity in diversity there is a culture which is predominently Indic and a civilization called the Indian civilization. This has been possible only through actions and interactions between the groups, societies and peoples for more than the last two thousand five hundred years. Constant change and adjustment, adaptation and assimilation, conflict and coherence, tension and interaction, are the processes that moulded the social structure in this subcontinent. As I have reviewed in short, the basic condition s to which social change in the Indian subcontinent, and for that matter in all countries of the world, is responsive. It became manifest that the change must be explained as a process contingent on the interaction of numerous factors. Any instance of social change in the countries of this subcontinent is the resultant of a specific and probably unique conjunction of a considerable diversity of conditions. The continuous interaction always intensified these conditions, and it still does.

It is, of course, true that no society is exculsively competitive or exclusively co-operative. The very existence of very highly competitive groups implies co-operation through interaction within the groups. Both competitive and co-operative habits must exist within the society. There is furious competition among the ranking chiefs, but within the household of each chief, co-operation is mandatory for the amassing of the wealth that is distributed or destroyed (Mead, 1937, 360) Thus, competition and co-operation both are mostly guided by social interaction.

The development of city-life has increased the mobility and tension and has multiplied the interaction. When people lived in rural areas, the circle of their activities was limited and only a handful of persons could meet each other. But the cities have brought a large number of people to a concentrated area and opened enormous opportunity to come in contact with different types of people. As a result, the scope of intense interaction has become wider, which, in itself is a force to initiate change in the society directly or indirectly. A village tailor comes to the city and happens to have interactions with his city-counterparts. He goes back and tries to introduce the city's latest style in his cuttings, which the village-people readily accept. This is only one aspect, there are hundreds of such activities, which, being inspired and accelerated through the effect of interaction, are causing change in the agro-based rural societies. The superfast trains, as I find around Calcutta, have attracted even the tribals, who were previously home-keeping people by nature. Mobility amongst them has become a factor in their livelihood which deserves consideration. Their whole culture is exposed to constant interaction. And the inevitable change has already started to find its root.

Socially, the present duality of city and countryside of the Indian subcontinent has started to give place to a continuum, in which agricultural development regenerates the villages, small-scale and medium industries are located in the towns and large-scale industries that necessitate heavy inputs of capital and high technical efficiency are located in the cities. As such a fusion and interaction between industry and agriculture has started to take place gradually. Further intermediate links in this continuum—rural social structures in towns, urban amenities in villages are being developed, thus combining the best traditions of both rural and urban life and producing a composite and integrated culture through interaction. Our towns and cities are not the same as in Europe and America—many portions of them both physically and culturally are village-oriented. On the other hand, our villages are no longer the villages of vedic or Ramayana ages, though not much, at least some signs and touches of the modern township can be found therein. Thus, the interaction between the two is slowly heading towards a synthesis.

In this manner the cultural interaction theory suggests to explain change in simple societies and some historical societies. When the members of two cultures, or of the same culture placed in two different situations interact, there is a tendency for a cultural change to occur or for an acceleration of cultural change, as a result of influence of either one over the other. Cultural interaction might also be used to explain change in simple societies in another way. Such interaction, often, though not always, results, in new forms of social relationship, particularly in the form of conquest. The theory also stimulates thought on the causes of change in the complex societies. The different parts of complex societies constitute to some extent separate sub-cultures, which, when they interact, stimulate change.

In spite of some merits, this theory has been regarded as an ingenious one, as the cultures in the same social structure or when the two cultures of two separate social structures come closer to each other, do not always interact.

What Vicente Rivera (1953:9-10) has said about Manila is more or less true about Calcutta:

> For Manila is a city like all cities—changeless and changing. Giving and taking back. Harsh and yet tender as a

> child's caress. And unlike other cities, it is the east and the west meeting at last. It is the Malay and the Latin. The American and the Chinese. . . . The city of the strident voice and the brick and cement jungles, and the city with the hidden lullabies and the warm hand—Cankered by ugliness and evil, spiked with violence and sudden death, it has its moments of breathless beauty and primal innocence. And if a man could see his way clear through to the very core of the city, he might yet apprehend the final meaning which could be the germ of his fulfilment.

But Calcutta's striking difference lies in her glorious tradition of cultural heritage comparable with a very few cities in the world. Of many reasons of multiplicity of interaction in and around Calcutta, the attraction of various cultural activities also plays a significant role, which bears a considerable impact on folklore of and around Calcutta. I would deal on this point with more detail.

According to two Planning Commission consultants, India's urban population is concentrated in the old cities and towns, new urban settlements having grown only marginally. This pattern will have to change since the thrust for the latest plan is to take the pressure off the cities by encouraging a flow to new townships. For this, Rs. 4.20 crores have been allotted for 35 towns including Calcutta. There is no option, with overcrowded metropolitan cities bursting at the seams. Calcutta has for long been the model for all that a city should never become; even Bombay, once held as an example of civic achievement, is heading inexorably in the same direction. Housing, watersupply, power, transport and crime, which grow apace with congestion, have become major problems in Calcutta. While the urban population in Calcutta has increased more than ten times in the last half a century, facilities have often remained archaic. Calcutta is still dependent on an eighty-year-old sewage system and hope to get a Metro, which, if considered the answer to growing demand for transport, should have been built when its population was one-eighth the present figure. The main difficulty with Calcutta lies in the fact that this city cannot become a substitute for rural areas covering vast localities adjacent to its suburbs. Urban facilities, however generous, can never cope, if neglect of the rural sector all around Calcutta suburbs continues to be perpetuated and increases migration which, at last tally, accounted for 40 per cent of the urban explosion.

When we speak of migration, we face the enormous propensity of population-movement in and around Calcutta. As one of the largest cities of the world today, its peculiar characteristic is that almost half of its population who live outside Calcutta and her suburbs, rush to Calcutta everyday for economic, cultural and other reasons. Mobility of a huge section of the population thus provides potential frequency and multiplicity of social as well as cultural interaction in Calcutta and this has its greater impact on folklore including the folk arts.

Through the inter-continental migration and continuous diffusion, folklore assumes a new dynamism acceptable to a situation different from the place of its origin. This is also true about the folk arts. Because of wider urban spread and multiplicity of socio-cultural interaction taking place in Calcutta, the themes and forms of the folk arts are undergoing constant changes, except, of course, lhe motifemes selected by the artists in different patterns of art, which remain unaltered. The changes occurring in the socio-cultural and ethno-social patterns of the society of Calcutta through an uncommon mobility of human beings, demand certain new themes and forms which the folk artists and craftsmen are obliged to fulfil. Thus the public plays an important role in bringing about change in the folk arts. Their participation, indirect though it is, cannot be overlooked. Since the folk arts are saleable items, the market controls to a great extent their patternization and shaping—the demand and supply process rules the imagination of the artists in a considerable manner. Specially the past several decades since the independence of India have witnessed a significant expansion of popular interests in the folk arts and crafts.

The living traditions of the arts of Bengal as handed down to the people from the remotest antiquity are imbued with many ancient forms and motifs which speak of their early beginning. Their antiquity goes back a "botanic age" beyond the ages of iron and bronze. As a matter of fact a pre-metal cane-bamboo-wood age gave birth to many techniques and methods, many forms and motifs which continued till now with modifications throughout the ages. Certain forms and motifs which are found in the living traditions of the folk arts of Bengal at the present day furnished fairly convincing evidence in support of the view that the basic traditional culture of Bengal is a living and unbroken continuation of the preryan civilisation. The folk arts that survive in Bengal are, in the opinion of some scholars, directly descended from the arts of at least five thousand years ago. Keeping these in view if due emphasis is given on the structural and socio-cultural analysis of the folk arts of Calcutta and nearby areas in particular and of Bangladesh and West Bengal in general to understand the nature of changes reflected in the arts through interaction varied characters caused by population-movements in relation to the structural and formaic patterns of the main-stream of folk arts, some interesting features may be revealed to us, such as the happy combination of old and new motifs, ready acceptance of the changing patterns in the artefact, socio-cultural consciousness of the artificer reflected in the arts, his skill in the process of assimilation, all of which seemed to have taken ingredients directly or indirectly from Calcutta-based interaction. If we concentrate our focus mainly on alpana, dolls and toys, clay works, painting, metal and cane works, embroidery and textiles, minor arts like mask, *sika* (a reticulated bag made of jute strings or wires, which is kept hanging usually from the walls), blocks for making cakes from mango-juice or rice or sugar, *sara* and *chat*, pottery, and so on, we will find that for untold generations the people have delighted in these arts which are the expressions of the Bengali people themselves, the flow of tradition by which it is still carried on in the mass consciousness has undergone a change. Thus, the present folk arts of Bengal should be judged not by its age but by its mode of expression. It has been an art transmitted from generation to generation without much essential change of structure, the roots reaching deep into the soil, but since the last few decades, specially from the time of independence, they have embraced some potentiality, keeping pace with the modern trend of Calcutta arts. This has been so because of the interaction in enormous scale. It is true that the Bengalis are a race, in which there is a great admixture of non-Aryan elements—these elements have ever been active to preserve the traditional culture which has not been disturbed by any other foreign ethnic element down to the present day. Thus the worship of the Mother Goddess Manasa, Kali and some others, the Harvest Goddess, the Vana-Durga Goddess, the God of Tiger, and so on are still so popular in West Bengal and to some extent in Bangladesh, they are no doubt the significant survivals from ancient days. The nature of the land with its flora and fauna a whole in itself without detaching the individual from his surroundings, helps the people to inherit a common traditional culture which has essentially a folk origin. It is obvious that the folk culture of Bengal is a spontaneous expression of the life of the people themselves and is an inseparable part of that life. All these are dynamic forces, and this being so, social change through interaction based in Calcutta, has exerted its influence over the mainstream of folk arts, including these gods and goddesses. The images of gods and goddesses have not been spared. Their structure remaining the same, shape, style the main motifs have been thoroughly re-oriented. These changes towards modernity are implemented on the images in the spirit of competition every year. Some of the images of goddess Durga provide the best examples of refined sculptor.

Concentrating on the potential frequency and multiplicity of social as well as cultural interaction in Calcutta, an endeavour to explore the impact of this interaction on the spirit, form and structure of folk arts, thus, may prove a profitable one. The evolution of the main forms and motifs and the erosion of their authentic contours in the course of untold centuries, must be treated in the context of past history and present conditions responsible for the creation of folk arts. Art can only be interpreted with understanding of the artificer.

The interaction may be viewed from another angle. Calcutta, a city about two hundred years old, is one of the largest cities of the world today. It was once the capital of India. The growth of the city in size was accelerated during the last three decades, particularly after the independence and the partition of Bengal. The influx in population was due to the settlement of persons from East Bengal, usually belonging to rich and middle classes, and the refugees clustering in and around Calcutta, on the one hand, as well as a large number of migrating people from the hinterland of the city and also from other states in search of jobs. Urbanization has been made in Calcutta due to circumstances, the situation of people living in the city, and the reason is primarily economic. The sophisticated urban culture is almost absent among the people of the city at large.

The causes of emigration in the city of Calcutta are of two types, the 'push' and the 'pull' phenomena. The spread of education in the rural areas without corresponding employment facilities and the development of researches 'pushed' the migrating people to the city. Increase of population in the villages and dearth of sources of income also 'pushed' the people to the city. The 'pull' process of the city is mainfested first and foremost in the possibility of economic gain and the dream of better living with modern gadgets. The industries are located in and around Calcutta, so a large number of people as industrial labourers live in the metropolis.

The urban culture, therefore, could not encompass the people living in the city and the urban mind could not develop, in spite of its striving for sophistication, in the manner as is expected from a city dweller because of the agelong traditional influence. The people who are living in the city for more than one generation migrated from the villages and their mind still holds the traditional heritage. The 'urban mind' and the 'traditional mind' are interwoven and there is continuing interaction of these two. In the socio-cultural as well as religious life in particular the conflict and contradiction is significantly manifested.

This inner-conflict inherent in the minds of the city-dwellers which is the result of the interaction between the traditionalism on the one hand and sophistication on the other, has influenced the folklore of West Bengal to a great extent. The whole socio-cultural set up of Calcutta is patterned through the compromise between these two ends and the co-existence of the two cultures. A close analysis of the reflection of these aspects in the ethno-cultural behaviour and socio-religious performances guided by beliefs and customs, will provide some basic information, which a true folklorist will earnestly seek to understand folklore truly in social context. A village-bard belonging to the Baul cult, even goes so far as to compare Calcutta with the human body. One such song says :

> O, Calcutta is a human body, whose style is really
> fascinating
> O brother, the water of Laldighi, I am told, is very sweet
> Some, of course, says, her sweat is salty
> And it is lost for nothing
> He who has tasted this sweet, would indulge in frolics and
> find the goal
> Wonderful style really !
> If you happen to be at Bagbazar
> O brother, you would be involved in so many affairs
> Bring the head of Hari-name
> And eat at ease
> Then when you would be in trouble at Bagbazar
> You would harldy escape
> O, what a style really !
> Calcutta has hundreds of markets and thousands of lanes
> Where you are caught
> And may even be driven to the butcher-house
> There are Sonagachi, Maniktala, Jora-Sanko,
> What a variation of beauty every where
> Style, O the fascinating one !
> Your abode on the bank of the Ganges trembles
> And within it exists the wonders of caprices
> The magic drop in the guise of stupidity deprives me
> As if I swim in the forest of reedy grass
> What a wonderful style !*

Folksongs of these pattern are the product of Calcutta-based interaction, which has some strong bearing in the process of social change both in Calcutta and the rural areas on her outskirts.

I have tried in my humble way to present some of the answers to the complex and oft-recurring questions how and

* *Translation is mine.* Quoted by Barun Chakravorty, 1980, 36.

why society changes and undergoes transformations. Hundreds of opinions have been expressed and answers given. To review and assess all of them is beyond the scope of my present work. There is no question regarding the fact that confusion and conflict exist in this field. The whole branch of contemporary sociological theory is experienced by many sociologists as in crisis. They feel that the theory of social and cultural change is in a great need of re-examination than any other branch of the discipline. The idea that sociology can provide a single theory of social change has been regarded by many as a myth.

Some more thoughts : theoretical and conceptual

There could be some conceptual frameworks for the understanding of the social change on the true perspective of thoughts, both theoretical and process-oriented. Linton and Parsons were concerned with the relation between individuals, which they thought was a useful way of looking at social structure. Nadel advanced our understanding of the internal structure of an individual's roles and their interrelations and tended to conceive of role as an allocation made by the society as a whole. Some of the approaches tend to select behaviours, influences, structures and variables from everyday life emphasizing the element of continual flux of human behaviour and social life. But of late, two major levels of analysis of social change have been current in sociological theory, structural and organisational. Firth, who distinguishes between the two, felt that the former meant a change in the form of realignment. He further recognised the intimate relationship between social structure and social organisation and between structural and organisational changes. Barth, on the other hand, developed the analysis of social organization for a fruitful investigation of the process of social change. The concept of network as formulated by Barnes in an attempt to distinguish different kinds of social fields. A.J. Mayer has attempted to characterize a less structured social situation in terms of action set. In complex societies it is difficult to identify areas of social relations in terms of groups.

In the world of the social scientists, change is important

from three points of view. As an active human being he thinks of a desirable future society and would like to know how to bring it about. As a reflecting intellectual, he would like to know how society has come to be, what it is now. As a scientist, he is interested in the study of change as a means of discovering causal interrelations and lawful regularities. The study of social change can be sketched on a broad canvas, transition from one historical phase to the next, general principles of stability, changes in the relations between economic and cultural factors can be made the objects of enquiry. But one can also approach the problem of change on a microscopic level. How do people make up their minds on a particular subject, how are saving and employment related, how has a specific piece of legislation been passed—these, too, can be made the objects of empirical investigation.

The special change is a process responsive to many types, to changes in the man-made conditions of living, to changes in the attitudes and benefits of men, and to changes that go back beyond human control to the biological and the physical nature of things. To understand how special change takes place and why it follows certain trends it is necessary to investigate its relation to the three great orders, the biophysical, the cultural, and the technological. These three orders and the concepts related to them could be profitably taken into consideration to demonstrate their relevance to the study of social change and the position of folklore in the Indian subcontinent. It may be further specified that the dimension of empirical reality to be explored in such a study for investigation of the problem may be directed to know intimately the people and their social relationships; since, according to some scientists, the study of society is different from the study of culture or of civilisation. The latter, as they emphasise, embody themselves 'in products which persist and exercise an influence by their continued presence, while the society in which they arose lives on only as a changing equilibrium of present relationship. Thus the direct concern of our objectives, from both sociological and folkloric standpoints, could be with social relationships. It is the change in social relationships alone, as mentioned before, which could be regarded as social change. When we speak of a social evolution, perhaps we should not mean human evolution, but only an aspect of it, nor should we mean cultural evolution, but only a concomitant of it. This view still persists strongly in the domain of the study of society.

The crisis in the explanation of social and cultural change has arisen from the fact that although the progress-evolution theory collapsed, the contemporary positions have not been altogether satisfactory. The culture-log theory rested on a distinction between material and non-material culture and the notion that inventions in the material realm are progressive, while those in the non-material realm are not. As a crudely accurate description of contemporary scientific civilization, the culture-lag theory was plausible. When one examines the distinction between material and non-material culture carefully, it tends to melt away. The idea of a technical process, for example, is no more material than the idea of a new school curriculum. Furthermore, when one studied other cultures, it quickly became apparent that many waves of civilization have formed without an appreciable change in the basic material culture. One can explain classical Greece as a good example of the 'lag' of material culture behind and inventive non-material culture. Thus, it is obvious that there are both theoretical and empirical problems for the culture lag theory.

The functionalists, who were the heirs of the positivistic organicists, found themselves in a rather curious predicament. Their organismic theories of society inclined them to the position that functionally interrelated social wholes were the primary causal factors in interhuman behaviour. From this standpoint social and cultural change could have one of two possible origins : from intrusive events outside the organismic system or from the imminent evolution of the forces within the system itself. The fact that contemporary functionalism did not embrace until very recently, imminent evolutionism can only be explained by the historical disaster this theory of change suffered in early sociology. Hence, by fairly general admission the single most significant difficulty with contemporary functionalism has been its failure to develop an adequate theory of social change.

The social behaviouristic theory of social and cultural change

Social systems are directly or indirectly the creation of human behaviour based on cultural values. Every change in valuations on the part of social groups registers itself in institutional change. In this respect Max Weber's position is justified. But, unfortunately, the correspondence, though complete, is also complex. The unity of the social structure corresponds to the diversity of social attitudes and interests. But, in spite of that we may agree with Hobhouse that there is "a broad correlation between the system of institutions and the mentality behind them." (1924, Chapter XII). This uniformity of behaviourism leads us to believe that human beings want to exist in this earth within well-defined and well-meaning society against all natural and supernatural odds and calamities.

Behaviourism may be of various types, but the theorists stress upon the collective behaviour, which in its simplest way, means that a group action that occurs having no definite or clear-cut direction from culture. The events may occur, and their consequences are somewhat surprising to participants and observers, as in the case of the war of liberation of Bangladesh in 1971. Independence was declared by the great revolutionary leader Sheikh Mujibur Rahman without any armed preparation. The powerful as well as barbarous, highly trained army of Pakistan jumped upon the innocent people. There was heavy upsurge of the people, who were thoroughly determined, a huge section of young men took up arms. Ultimately, the revolutionary spirit, determination, guerilla type of warfare adopted by the people of Bangladesh, combined with the armed intervention and huge material help of India, the independence of Bangladesh was achieved within a short span of nearly nine months, shorter than the people of Bangladesh could ever imagine. The events at least have been in part unplanned and their outcomes unforeseen. The most heinous genocide was let loose upon the people by the Pakistan armed forces, resulting in the massacre of about three million people. A compact society of ninety million people was thoroughly affected and changed by this upheaval and war. From this example, we may say that the patterns of behaviour when they emerge spontaneously in the process of people interacting together (rather than stemming from the norms and patterned roles that ordinarily direct behaviour) we come to a situation affecting society, which may be called the collective behaviouristic situation.

The historical cases have been the basis for this theory. There have emerged two theories that attempt to account for much of it. These are the explanations of James C. Davies and Neil Smelser. These two theories are not really alternatives, but represent different approaches to this complicated field. Davies wanted to explain political turmoil of a rebellious or a revolutionary kind (1962, 5-19). Smelser's theory of collective behaviour is more ambitious, as he recognizes the value of earlier theories, but felt that they tended to define behaviourism by essentially incidental characteristics, such as size of the group, violence of event and so on. He defines it more broadly as the mobilization on the basis of a belief which redefines social action. He is concerned with the process of collective behaviour, how they are motivated and involved or mobilized by beliefs that then redefine social action (1963, 31). Social behaviourism is the view that at the bottom level all human social events may be reduced to inter-human behaviours which are meaningful to the parties involved. It assumes that the peculiarity of man is his lack of instincts and correspondingly expended capacity for learning. Man is not born social, he learns to be social. He is so dependent on others for survival that he is unavoidably shaped in terms of the particular patterns of the social unit which rears him. Everything he does or becomes is through learning and the modification of one learned pattern by another. Though men have an almost endless capacity for modification, the collective survival of any plurality of men requires that some more or less consistent systems of inter-human behaviour exist at various levels of generality: social groups and institutions, communities and civilizations. The upholders of this theory assert that two fundamental problems must be solved if men are to survive: the mastery of nature and the establishment of working arrangements of man with man. The three major subforms in which these two general problems are encountered are socialization, the mastery of nature and social control.

Community

The theory of community is the accord of the process involved when the various specific groups which represent first-order structure to social life are formed into more or less consistent total ways of life. The three processes at work to bring communities in existence are stability, consistency and completeness. The social behaviouristic theory of civilization accounts for the manner in which the total stock of cultural forms of a people is woven into more or less consistent systems complementary to the community. While every man, according to social behaviouristic theory, is a potential innovator, the formation of communities which reconstruct first-order institutions and integrates them into the completed set, making up a total way of life, casts into central consideration those persons who operate, not in the social institutional areas, though they may have an anchorage in a particular institution, but who act to bring about the integration of the total set. Thus, the formation of communities is particularly significant for the theory of social change since no community can arise without the reconstruction of basic institutions. If one is to study the interrelations between community, the intellectual, and civilization, his empirical examples must be of sufficient scope to comprehend the wave of development which covers the rise and decline of a community. Communities are slow to form and hard to destroy. The total process may extend over centuries.

The social behaviouristic theory of community formation seeks to establish as precisely as possible the relation between intellectual activity, community formation and civilization synthesis. Four hypotheses concerning these relations could be advanced:

1. Creative epochs of mankind are the periods of formation of new communities. At such times the spheres for manifestation of individuality is widened and its products are rewarded.

The creative periods of human culture

There are evidences of great creative periods in human culture

—sometime between 14,000 and 8000 B.C. mankind moved out of a world of tribal communities of hunters and food-gatherers into a world of peasant village within which active food-production was carried out. In these peasant villages of the Old World the domestication of plants and animals was carried out, pottery-making was discovered, a great advance in the manufacture of textiles was made, social units of larger size than hitherto were created and a new differentiation was achieved.

A second great creative period of human culture, one conventionally identified with the rise of historical civilization, was carried out between 5000 and 3500 B.C. when the first cities of the ancient world were formed as new kinds of communities on a foundation of neolithic peasant village. A new specialization of institutions produced city-religions, city governments, complex economic institutions and social classes.

Civilization gradually passed through its formative period to next steps in Egypt, Middle-East, Greece, India, Middle Asia, China and other places.

2. The quality and quantity of creativity are related to the type of community in which they occur. In general, the brilliant creative periods of human culture have coincided with the creation of the more complex human communities.

The relation between community type and kind of creativity

While creativity occurred for the same general reason in the main cultural areas of the ancient world, the milieu were distinct. Chinese creativity in the late feudal period was provided by the courtly society of the feudal princes; that of the ancient Indians by the cities and seats of the patrimonial princes; that of Palestine by the royal cities and rural towns of the monarchy; that of the Greece by the autonomous city-states. The milieu for the creative activities of the recent west was provided first by the western city and the nation-state.

3. During the period of maturity of a community the encouragement of free creativity declines. The sphere of social life left open for the free construction of individuals is narrowed, and a restrictive array of intellectual forms is fixed.

Community stability and cultural stereotyping

In the final phase of a community's development the hardening of forms is often, though not always, brought about by the development of forces internal to the community itself. The internal hardening of its structure exposes a community to some outside forces. If it comes, that blow from outside only accelerates forces already in motion.

4. The standards of the acceptability of thought or truth in the restrictive sense varies as between the creative and conformist epochs of human civilization. (a) during creative epochs there is a strong tendency to determine truth in terms of standards and criteria established in the proper conduct of the thought process; (b) during conformist epochs of human civilization there is a tendency to establish socially acceptable truth by institutional procedures.

The changing criteria of thought

The establishment of truth in the sense of acceptable or authoritative knowledge varies between creative and conformist epochs. In the creative epoch, the very free space for individuality inevitably leads to a plurality of points of view. In all the main areas of the ancient world during the creative period, the problem of truth was raised, though in quite varying degree. The recent west took over the problem of truth from the Greeks, and carried it to undreamed of lengths. The extent to which the determination of truth in the recent west will, if at all, be shifted from logical and scientific to institutional grounds, can not yet be known. The two major poles, continue to be humanism and science; philosophy and technology, I am afraid, will remain as they are now or grow wider during the last decades of the present century.

When we talk of theories and thoughts of social change we have to take into consideration some major concepts or theories as the process or directions of social change such as the cyclical process, the evolutionary process, diffusion process.

These three concepts, of course, received the status of theories. We can not deny that in all the societies hundreds of processes of change are working with simultaneous effects. If in one part there is conflict, in other parts there may be adjustment. Of all the concepts, the cyclical process, greatly contributed by P. Sorokin, is perhaps the oldest.

The theories of inevitable social development have been, of late, discredited. But the tendency to accept certain broad notions of the general trend exists amongst the sociologists and there is still a feeling that the concept of stages is useful or even, some feel, indispensable.

The first usage treats stages as necessary steps in the process of change of all societies. An assumption underlying this usage is that each society contains inner mechanisms which ensure that it must change only in one way. The second usage treats stages in terms of the total history of human society. This assumption does not concede that mankind in general or a particular society could have leaped from primitive agriculture to industry. But in practice it may be possible for societies of a low level of agricultural development to become industrialised without passing through all the stages of later agricultural and early industrial development. A third usage applies the concept of stages to the study of particular historical processes. In this case there may be no assumption that one stage necessarily precedes or succeeds another. The stages are simply ways of characterizing actual processes of changes and classifying them in some sequence.

The first usage has been almost totally abandoned, because a particular society or societies need not traverse the same path of development of others, especially when they may benefit from the experience of these others. The second usage is still retained by some social scientists, but treated with caution or scepticism by others. The third usage has been subject to some criticism and it is sometimes suggested that particular schemes of development are highly arbitrary constructions and are no truer than a host of others.

According to Sorokin, many phenomena, having similarity with human society and nature, are thought of as cyclic course. The variations of business activity are frequently referred to as the economic cycle. The economic cycle formulated for urban communities by R.E. Park describes a succession of events adequately enough to make possible the prediction of the most probable next state in the cycle. The work done by Park indicates that urban centres undergo cyclical phases that are predictable and accompanied by specific categories of social actions (1925). Somewhat similar in character are studies of cycles in economic activities. In this respect the illustrations offered by nature herself are perhaps more convincing—the orbital motions of atoms, the regular sequence of the seasons, are some of the many examples. Sometimes the term 'cyclical' is applied to the process that the individual organism reveals from birth through to maturity and then to decline and death, and there have been many thinkers who have regarded societies and civilizations as pursuing a similar course. We have in Ogburn's work a cycle theory of human cultural development based upon the nature of invention and culture. In his theory, the two, culture and invention, are interwoven to produce a pattern of change, which follows a sequence of jump acceleration and stability which is repetitive in nature. Ogburn observes "the general reason why the adaptive portions of the non-material culture lag behind the changes in the material culture is the fact that the relationship between the adaptive culture and the material culture is not very close, but several steps removed. Thus the form of city government is not so close to industry as the corporate organization of industry itself" (1927, 261).

Sometimes this concept, to many it is a theory, is applied to the rhythm of successive ups and downs that repeats itself without definite beginning or end, like that of the waves, and this pattern, too, many thinkers have thought they discovered in human affairs in political movement of conservatism and radicalism, in long-range change of population in the tides of fashion, in the moves that are by turn more repressive and more free. (Sorokin, 1947 : Part VII). Besides, Sorokin contended that cultures tend to be characterized by one or two dominant themes: sensate cultures stress values based on the importance of sensory experience, while Ideational cultures give priority to spiritual and metaphysical values (1941). Once a culture tends to emphasize either extreme, it begins to revert back to its polar opposite. Because of this swinging nature, culture reaches at a point where a mixture of both sensate and ideational values prevail.

Both O. Spengler and Toynbee hold that all cultures pass from childhood to maturity and ultimately are destined to die. According to Toynbee, climate plays a great role in the birth and nourishment of a culture. The frigid climate and scarce resources of the Arctic region have greatly limited the cultural response and development of Eskimo people. Conversely, the vast abundance of assets and good weather of the south Pacific islands have effectively reduced initiative among the Polynesians. But when the challenge is powerful enough to stimulate without being overwhelming, as it is in the Nile river basin, the culture develops. The ancient Egyptians developed an elaborate and complex civilization (1935-1961).

Diffusionism asserting stages of development

One of the earliest critiques of the stage theory of social development came from the diffusionist. In its most reasonable form—and the diffusionist ideas were far from reasonable—they asserted that since societies often obtain cultural traits from others, they could not be said to develop them spontaneously, in these cases societies could possess characteristics which they ought not to have according to some scheme of social development. This argument is unassailable, but it only dispenses with the first doctrine of stages and does not affect the second and third ones. Another argument against the diffusionists is that no society can obtain a cultural item from another unless it is ready to use it. The third and final argument against diffusionism is that it can not explain why certain items organize in the first place except by assuming that at least one society has reached a certain stage of development.

According to diffusionists, diffusion operates both within societies and between societies. This has been one time a major theory of folklore/folktales originated in India and gradually became diffused to the areas and societies within India. Later it spread to the societies of China, Russia and Europe through a ~~east~~ne-bound journey, and to the societies of Persia, middle-eastern countries, Spain, Italy, whole of Europe, and later, America through a west-bound journey by way of Iran. Thus diffusion takes place whenever societies come into contact. Linton gives an interesting but thought-provoking information to substantiate his views on the theory of diffusion:

> Our solid American citizen awakens in a bed built on a pattern which originated in the Near East but which was

modified in Northern Europe before it was transmitted to America. He throws back covers made from cotton, domesticated in India or linen, domesticated in the Near East, or silk, the use of which was discovered in China. All of these materials have been spun and woven by processes invented in the Near East. He slips into his moccasins, invented by the Indians of Eastern woodlands, and goes to the bath room, whose fixtures are a mixture of an European and American inventions, both of recent date. He takes off his pajamas, a garment invented in India, and washes with soap invented by the ancient Gauls. He then shaves, a masochistic rite which seems to have been derived from either Sumer or Ancient Egypt.

When our friend (American) has finished eating, he settles back, to smoke, American Indian habit, consuming a plant domesticated in Brazil in either a pipe, derived from the Indians of Virginia, or a cigarette, derived from Mexico. If he is hardy enough he may even attempt a cigar transmitted to us from the Antilles by way of Spain. While smoking he reads the news of the day, imprinted in characters invented by the ancient Semites upon a material invented in China by a process invented in Germany. As he absorbs the accounts of foreign troubles he will, if he is a good conservative citizen, thanks a Hebrew deity in an Indo-European language that he is a 100 per cent American" (1936, 326-27).

Theories of social development (Methodical)

The burden of the criticisms of some of the functionalist anthropologists has been that the evidence of existence of primitive societies cannot be used for establishing the characteristics of earlier stages of development on the grounds that these contemporary societies have had long histories of their own and may be quite unlike historically extinct simple societies. One can hazard a reasonable guess that early hunters and gatherers lived in small bands or even in separate family units, depending on the kind of foraging and hunting that was engaged in, and one could not be far wrong in assuming that foraging and hunting represented an earlier stage of human history than agriculture. This does not mean that one can also assume that the earliest forms of religion were totemism or ancestor worship simply because such religions are found in fairly simple contemporary societies.

Popper, a logician, thus directly argued largely against Hegel, Comte, Marx, J.S. Mill, and Arnold Toynbee. He makes a distinction between two kinds of historicism: 'anti-naturalist' and naturalist and refutes the doctrine that there are laws of social development with the following arguments. First, historicism makes false claims for natural science and, therefore, for social science. He maintains that the theoretical science does not assert the existence or occurrence of any particular event; it is not its intention or purpose to state that events of type x or y do occur, but only that events of type x cannot occur without being followed by events of type y, or that events of type y cannot have occurred without being preceded by events of type x. But the so-called laws of social development do state that certain sequence of stages occur according to a law. This may be true to the laws governing the growth of organisms, of the movements of planets where the systems are relatively closed and the sequence of events are recurrent, the conditions of such changes or movement can be stated as precise and constant factors. Some of this applies to societies or social institutions, which do not move like planets or grow like organisms, because the conditions of change within them also change.

The German diffusionist school championed by Fritz Graebner, Father Wilhelm Schmidt and Wilhelm Koppers, is considered by Lowie "in the range and solidity of their knowledge incomparably superior to their British counterparts" (1937, 177). The Graebnevian school again conceived of man as naturally uninventive. They argue that "Losses and modification (since primitive age) were inevitable, but they do not preclude identification of the cultural totalities even today (quoted by Lowie, 1937, 179). On the basis of this kind of reasoning Graebner and his followers are able to detect all sorts of similarities in cultures the world over which to them suggest a common origin of the [cultures within which the similarities are observed. Even if we accept this proposition, diffusion is always a two-way process. It is also a selective process. A group accepts some culture traits from a neighbour, at the same time is rejecting others. Then again, diffusion generally involves some modification of the borrowed element. Endless examples could be cited to show how diffusion has been operative through a two-way process, how people has been selective and how traits are nearly always modified as they are diffused.

These arguments cannot be lightly dismissed and have a bearing on a number of live issues in historical interpretation. But on the whole, the diffusionist critiques are treated as true, but trivial.

Secondly, the analogies between social entities or physical or organic ones, according to Popper, are misleading and are partly responsible for absurd historicist claims. Third, large-scale social changes are logically unpredictable. Fourth, the role of ideas makes social knowledge and social prediction different from physical knowledge and prediction. These arguments are connected with one another. The third argument, linked to the two, is that large-scale changes in social systems are, in a sense, logically unpredictable. Every change in social structure is the product of intersecting causal chains which are, to some extent, independent of one another, and whose convergence is, therefore, in an important sense partly accidental.

The counter-argument against Popper is that every major historical development may involve the conjunction of separate causal processes, but that such conjunctions are themselves inevitable and, therefore, predictable. According to the Marxist view, the breakdown of feudal agrarian society, resulting from an internal contradiction, gives rise to the beginning of capitalism. The opposing view would be that had it not been for the development of trade and the possibilities of centralization of power, which are by no means predictable within a feudal system, feudal agrarian society would not have changed in the way that it did. Besides, this is like saying that if two objects are moving towards one another, one can safely predict that they will collide. Some social changes are possibly of this kind, rather like those studied by meteorologists: here there is a probability that independent causal chains will intersect, but though there are always a number of unknowns that may alter the nature of the interaction. Few major social transformations are even as simply contingent as they result from so many different causal chains, that the outcome cannot be determined in any meaningful sense. Popper's ultimate argument seeks to undermine any remnant of defence of historical determinism: for, he insists that changing ideas and growth of knowledge must, to some extent, affect social development; but future ideas and states of knowledge cannot be predicted in advance. If they were predictable they would be present conditions not future ones. One can have no theory how ideas will affect social development, and so one cannot know what future cases of social development will be. This being so, there is no logical defence of the doctrine that past stages have been part of an inevitable development. He defends the view that there can be sociological theories which simply makes conditional statements, such as: if governmental activities increase, then bureaucratic organizations increase. "There general theories do not state that one stage of social development will necessarily succeed another, or that one set of conditions will necessarily occur; they only state which will occur if certain conditions arise." (Cohen, 1968, 214).

Evolution process: evolution of development doctrine

When Charles Darwin wrote *The Origin of Species*, he traced a process by which the multiplicity of organic types emerged from earlier, fewer, less differentiated forms of life. The particular mechanistic explanation of this process offered by Darwin may or may not be valid, but the scheme of evolution which he so clearly traced does not stand or fall with any theory of the manner in which it has come about. Even then, a great deal of thought has been devoted to this process by a host of a social scientists who cannot be overlooked. In the late nineteenth century there was considerable interest in the evolutionary theory of change. The first assumption of this doctrine is that some stages of development must be achieved for human society as a whole, before others are achieved. This suggests that the change tends to be cumulative. The early thinkers were convinced that change inevitably brought about improvement. For Lewis, H. Morgan, change meant the passage from savagery to barbarism, and ultimately to civilization. For H. Spencer, it meant the replacement of military-religious societies by industrial orders. For August Comte, change meant the passage from what he called the theological stage of social organisation to a scientific stage. It may, however, be argued that it is scarcely disputable that agriculture must precede industrialization. But this may not be true to other areas of culture. Totemism or ancestral cults may precede the development of polytheism and monotheism, but whether they are necessary preconditions for them is another matter. Much that is objectionable in developmental doctrine result from the confusion of actual historical sequences with theoretically necessary sequences: it is hardly disputable that feudalism preceded the modern nation state in most western Europe, but it is by no means clear that feudal structures are a necessary precondition for 'the development of a nation state. Thus, it may appear that most of the early thinkers offered very limited, highly selective, and sometimes inaccurate information to subtantiate their claims.

The second assumption is that some stages are more likely to precede others because they are more easily achieved. This does not assert that one stage is a necessary basis for another, but simply that it is a more likely occurrence in particular conditions. The third assumption is similar to the second, it is that in any given conditions certain developments are more likely than others. The limitation of the likely form of development is bound to be greater in very simple societies: the lower the level of technology, the greater the influence of physical environment on social structure; and the simpler the social structure, the narrower the range of developments which can occur within it.

Of course, two of the offered viewpoints that contemporary social scientists still find useful, one by E. Durkheim and the other by Ferdinand Tonnies. Not only have the latter-day social scientists found Durkheim's and Tonnies, procedures more consistent with contemporary scientific practice, but their viewpoints seem to describe rather well the trends observed in today's complex societies. Durkheim argues that change tends to transform the basis of social cohesion in society from a mechanical solidarity, characteristic of so-called primitive societies, to an organic solidarity, found in complex industrial societies. He held that as change brings increased technical progress, it also tends to weaken the rational bonds among members of society (1933, part IV). Tonnies' has the same view. He feels that the individualism and struggle for power characteristic of the urban world could result in cultural disintegration; as people become more socially fragmented, isolated and independent of communal and institutional bonding, the integration and stability of traditional societies weaken. For both Durkheim and Tonnies, change did not inevitably bring progress, it had varied consequences, some positive and some negative.

The chief fault of most earlier developmental 'theories' was that they overemphasized the 'limitation principle' in tracing the emergence of one type of social system from another; that is, they operated with a rather closed model of the social system and of the mechanisms whereby it changed its form. Max Weber, of course, sought to analyse the structural changes which were discernible in historical processes, he also tried to show how and why a certain trend of development was started and maintained, particularly in the history of European societies. Finally, he aimed to explain how one set of conditions of social structure and culture could set limits to the possible changes which could emerge from them. Weber also recognized the possibility of combining a genuine historical interpretation with a sociological analysis of the emergence of one type of system from another. To do this he made use of what he called 'ideal types'. Among his best-known ideal types of social structure are those of patrimonialism, feudalism and the rational-legal bureaucracy. Weber also sought to link changes such as these with the major forms of change in the economy, and, in particular, with the growth of impersonal markets, the use of money and the rational calculations, and the gradual 'liberation' of economic relations from the influence of traditional obligation. (1961, 162)

Weber is commonly criticized for not recognizing the importance of informal, personal-relationships in bureaucracies which are thought to be necessary for their functioning.

But while this objection may pinpoint a defection, Weber's model of how bureaucratic organization works, does not weaken his explanation of a developmental process from feudalism or patrimonialism to bureaucracy.

In spite of some very substantial contributions by both Durkheim and Tonnies, during the early part of the present century, evolutionary concepts were subject to increasing criticism. A few new evolutionary theories have been elaborated during this period. The armchair techniques and ethnocentric excesses of early exponents let others shy away from this perspective. Since World War II, however, there has been a resurgence of interest in evolutionary thought among sociologists and anthropologists, frequently called neo-evolutionism.

If, of course, there is to be any progress in analysing the course of social change in a developmental manner, this will have to be done by constructing models using a small number of factors at a time. The assumption of linking these factors would not necessarily be applicable to all or even a great number of the developmental stages, though a scheme of this kind would certainly make use of certain very general assumptions about the nature of social interaction the characteristics of social systems and the likely courses of social change.

From simple to complex social systems

One of the most influential ideas in contemporary sociology which has survived from the nineteenth century is that human society has developed from simple to more complex forms and that this development has been accompanied by certain qualitative changes in the nature of social and cultural life. This view was in the past, closely linked with two assumptions: (i) that social evolution is a continuation of biological evolution, (ii) that the mechanisms of social evolution are the same as those of biological evolution. Assumption (i) seems to be either meaningless or wrong. There is no law of biological evolution which describes and explains the actual process of increasing differentiation, specialization and adaptability. The second assumption is equally unnecessary. Of course, human procreation is affected by genetic laws, but the transmission of social characteristics occurs through the process of social interaction itself. Besides, the argument of greater adaptability to explain the greater survival value of social systems is clearly indefensible. The evidence in favour of this does not exist. A thermonuclear conflict may destroy all societies, or at least all complex ones.

Emile Durkheim, in his book, *The Division of Labour in Society* has given a most valuable analysis and interpretation of the process of increasing social complexity. He argues that primitive societies have little division of labour, a point agreed upon by Comte and Spencer. Such societies, according to Durkheim, consist of a number of homologous units, such as families or clans; they have a segmental structure. These are bound together solely by their uniformity or practices and beliefs. This, Durkheim calls a mechanical solidarity. The measure of this form of solidarity is a type of social control which is largely punitive; there is a great reliance on repressive law. As the division of labour progresses, a number of things occur, the 'segmentary' structure of homologous social units is replaced by an increasing differentiation of units, which are interdependent; and, in addition, the uniformity of ideas, including moral ideas, decreases. He also holds that the growth of the division of labour; closer to the views of Comte and Spencer, brings with it the new form of social solidarity to replace the older forms which disappears with the breakdown of the segmentary structure of society; 'organic' solidarity meets certain needs (or fulfils a particular function) which were previously met by the mechanical form.

Though the boldness and ingenuity of Durkheim's conception is unrivalled, there are a number of defects in his arguments. Firstly, he does not treat the classification 'segmentary—differentiated' as simply dichotomous. Simple societies do not consist of a number of distinct, homologous units, with scarcely any links between them. Even when they are divided into segments, such as lineages, the numbers of different segments are linked together by ties of affinity, and, therefore, of kinship, since affinal ties in one generation create kinship links in the next—of ritual participation, and by political alliances.

Secondly, Durkheim over-emphasizes the punitive nature

of social control in simple societies and, in some ways, misinterprets it. He insists that such measures are a collective expression of disapproval of or horror of some moral delict. They sometimes are; but not when they are taken against some other group.

Thirdly, Durkheim is probably also wrong in thinking that the division of labour is necessarily accompanied by a decline in the significance of punitive law even in industrial society. With the increasing centralization of power, the dogmatism finds its stronger roots in the society, as in Iran under Khomieni.

Fourthly, he assumes that the growth of contract is an expression of a new moral basis of social life. But, on the other hand, the expanding trade makes it necessary for contracts to be made and honoured and that the growth of contractual relationships itself contributes to the formation of some morality of contractual obligation.

This brings us to his fifth defect as he refers to the 'needs' of society and emphasized on the state as a coordinating agency which is required because of the growing complexity of social life. Even if it is accepted, it does not follow that the State simply reflects the moral basis of social life. The powerful one can, to some extent fashion morality and they can also act in defiance of public morality.

Many of these defects are related to the sixth, the tendency of his treating society as organic entities. The statement that the 'segmented' structure is replaced by a differentiated one is almost tautological. The cultural uniformity is replaced by increacing diversity, but, to say that the emergence of the latter performs a function for the social system is almost meaningless, for the characteristics of normative uniformity or diversity are simply aspects of social system.

It is usually asserted in social study that man, in modern industrial societies, is alienated from himself. It is misleading to generalize this statement. There is a greater likelihood that the individual may in certain circumstances, feel that he is isolated from others and 'alienated' from himself. The theory tends to exaggerate or dramatise the rather tortured sense of identity which results from this type of upbringing and this form of participation in the social system: the transitions are not usually so sudden, nor do we know that the effect is really to create an experience that different persons are imposed upon one another.

The process of development from the simple to more complex forms of society has no doubt brought with it many changes in the quality of social relationships, in the structure of personality and in the nature of the relationship between the personality as a system and the social system. "The speculations of Durkheim and others have contributed greatly to our understanding of these things. But what is called for is a readiness to treat these ideas not as received wisdom, but as theories to be tested. Durkheim was almost alone among theorists in trying to do this." (Cohen, 1968; 234).

Leslie White was one of the first to revitalize evolutionary theory. White's general neo-evolutionary view held that as culture evolves, there is a progressive increase in the amount of energy placed under human control. In his conception, the idea of progress is confined to greater mastery of the environment (1949).

Robert Redfield's work on folk-urban drift (1941) established a new variant of the neo-evolutionary theory. He built his conceptual scheme on the pioneering work of Durkheim, Tonnies and others. After conducting research among several communities in Yucatan, Mexico, Redfield concluded that social change tends to result in a gradual shift away from the folk or traditional community to an urban society, where the values, the quality of life and the social organizational features sharply diverge from traditional forms. Urban society represents a fundamental contrast with its folk antecedents.

The state is the last stage of social organizational development, characteristic of industrial societies. The distinguishing characteristic of the state is more effective control by the leadership over the members of the society. The state contains a police or military body, the only group legitimately empowered to exercise force. A tribal chief might hold the advantage of force, but this differs from the monopoly of force available to leadership in the state. (Service, 1962).

Along with this development, a new trend has raised its ugly head. The military power, maintained for the defence of the society from foreign invasion, tends to invade its own people. Taking advantage of its armed strength, it topples down the peoples' elected government and captures the state power through bloody or bloodless coup. Sometimes the military junta calls it a revolution. Once this force occupies power, it hardly finds it congenial to go back to barracks. At first the army chief or a chosen leader of the revolting group, who usurps power, as it happened in many or most cases, promises to return the power to the elected government of the people, but after the country is settled down, he defers the process on this or that plea for years together. This has become a frequent event world over, specially in the underdeveloped and developing countries of the Third World since World War II. Democracy is a process which needs the test of time. But due to military take-over, sometimes over a number of times disturbed in the same country, this process is seriously disturbed and a damaging set-back is brought upon the normal social progress initiated through democracy and large participation of the people motivated through democratic order. A social scientist cannot overlook this situation, as I feel, the military take-over in any country, hampers the social change towards progress or it may be put the other way round that a social change process is being retrieved in the reverse. It may be true that a civilian government elected by the people may become thoroughly corrupt and there may remain no other alternative for the armed forces of the country than to take the power in the hand of the military regime. But it is evident from the history of many countries for the last few decades that the military people, ambitious for power, use this as their pretext, almost in all cases of coup, to put themselves on the saddle of power. Besides, who would guarantee that the junta itself would not be corrupted, as it happened in almost all countries falling under military domination. Military rule cannot be an alternative to a democratic set up of the government. It has to be condemned as a great impediment to social progress.

CONCLUSION

I am not a sociologist, nor do I pretend to be one. I have

Folklore and social change

I have selected the heading here in a reversed order to distinguish between how social change affects folklore and how folklore affects social change—obviously the two are not the same, though the goal, change, is common. It is a continuous process that folklore causes change in the society as the society causes the change in folklore. Though this mutual relation between the two is inseparable, folklore is the product of society, society is not and cannot be the product of folklore. Naturally so, influence of society over folklore is far greater than the influence of folklore on the society. Nevertheless, folklore is one of the many forces created by the society, but sometimes, this force acts so powerfully that the whole society is directly moulded by it. This is historically true so far as the ancient and primitive societies are concerned. The role of myths, the functions of proverbs, tales, riddles, the influence of epics in oral forms, are no less important than any written literature of the past. Let me cite an example :

The Goolwa clan of the Narrinyeri Tribe of Australia did not have a sense of justice among them. One deprived the other in one way or other whenever such occasion arose. Then a mythological legend was created, and as the legend was popularly accepted, the sense of justice prevailed strongly upon the people. This is a good example of how folklore affects social change. The legend goes like this :

> Ngurundere had two wives who caught a large fish and a small one. They gave him the small fish to eat, and baked the large one for themselves, when he ate his, he saw the large one and became very angry and said to them, "you shall die for that and all the Tanganarin shall die, and there will be fighting and sickness and evil spirits until then". Ngurundere, after creating them, made everything for their use and taught them to use their implements and weapons in hunting, fishing and fighting. But after the sentence of death by him for deception practised by his wives, he deprived Tanganarins of knowledge and power and, in his anger, left them and ascended to *Wyir* (their heaven). They were then ignorant and powerless and they

> lived like the beasts of the field. After a long time there was born of a virgin, a good and wise man, who was named Wyllngare. He returned to them their lost wisdom and power and taught them sorcery. When this great teacher had regenerated them, he was taken up to *Wyir* by Ngurundere, where, he is now the second king of that place; and when Tanganarin dies Wyungare takes his spirit up to *Wyir*, and gets him a fine place in that country from Ngurundere. (Taplin, 1879, 51-52).

In a Baul folk song, it is said, "There are four moons in the world of *sadhana*, as austere practice for God. Two of them are known to all. He who knows the rituals of four moons possesses great power. He can catch the Moon (the real lover of the mind meaning Almighty God) through ritual of the moon". Another Baul folk song says "O my mind ! see through the spiritual vision and you will find that the four moons sparkle in the jewel chamber. The seat of the Moon is surrounded by moons. One can realize the Moon only after performing the ritual of the moons." The four moons are the four elements of the human body, semen, ovum, stool and urine. Thus the songs have tremendous influence not only on the Bauls, but over the larger communities of the districts of Kushtia, Jessor, Pabna and Faridpur, the areas where Baul communities are found more in number than in any other district. The regulation of these four elements of body are strictly observed in most of the societies of this area and preservation of semen in the body is considered as highly desirable. Some elderly people regard semen as precious as gold, they used to spend it very cautiously in their youth days by having intercourse with wife only once in a month.

When we look back to the situations prevailing in the Indian subcontinent, we find that the geographic and climatic conditions played a role in the major cultural discontinuities of Indian development extending as far back as the middle pleistocene. Periodically, waves of men penetrated India through the mountain passes of the north-west and north-east. They came in contact with each other and a process of amalgamation continued since then. By 3000 B.C. agricultural communities of a peasant-village type were forming in northwestern India. Then the movement of Indo-European peoples continued down into historical times and through conflicts with the non-Indo-Europeans and assimilation process from within the societies, a new generation with an Indian social structure gradually sprang up. When, as a product of increasing conquests of the states, of the policies of the princes who found it advantageous to play the Brahmins off against the urban masses which were formulated in Hinduism in an orthodox manner, the caste system emerged as the definitive Indian community. The neo-orthodox Brahminism and the caste system represent a comparatively complete synthesis of a variety of cultural phenomena arising from social historical peculiarities and a variety of adjustments to different social conditions and natural environments. Pluralism and diversity are two basic characteristics of Indian societies and culture. But even then the unity is there, where folklore has a distinct place. It narrates the tales of unity and sings the songs of brotherhood.

It is interesting to note that throughout this long period of syntheses and adjustments, Indian folklore contributed to an enormous extent, to the stabilization and change of the societies, both rural and urban. Indian myths and legends and folktales of various kinds bear clear testimony of how they influenced the social values which helped the progress of the society forward. While the myths provided the inner truth of the social characteristics, keeping in view the vision for the future, the proverbs presented the beauty of the truth acquired through experience. Folklore, thus, helped the social change from within the structure of Indian societies, and at the same time got itself changed with the changing pattern of the societies.

Tension and conflict are the two seeds of Indian societies. Many cultures, many ethnic groups, many languages, many religious cults have been, through the ages, merged in the societies of the Indian subcontinent. Thus, conflicts and movement for and against, social tensions and disturbances have been, and still are, the results of social change. On the other hand, they have been, as they are today, the usual ways in which changes are brought about. It is, of course, true that change occurs rather as a response to cumulative pressures and social forces whose results benefit some groups while it creates misery and hardship for others. After a period of social tension and conflict the imbalances are redressed somewhat, but newer processes of change, equally poorly designed, are initiated and call forth yet further tension and conflict. This has been the fate of Indic societies at large.

The traditional Indian society has from the very beginning been a dynamic society and has seldom refused spontaneous changes from within. In the meantime it has also borrowed influences from outside, both through raiders as well as through rulers provided they had settled down in the country and had a continuous interaction with the people. The whole Indian history is a saga of this multifarious influences, interactions, adjustments and readjustments in Indian society at different times. Whereas, structural changes have occurred at many times and are still occurring, there was seldom a functional loss or variation in the traditional order of Indian society. A series of hypotheses concerning the importance of social factors in social change in the Indian subcontinent as related to the possibilities may be and have been developed. In the case of these changes, Freedman's concept that the "individuals of lower prestige accepted culture traits from those of high prestige more readily than the reverse" (1952, 319), seemed to have acceptable relevance. But at the same time the argument that the reverse also might have happened, cannot be altogether ruled out. Similarly, other hypotheses also seemed to have held well with the Indian situation, such as the better a cultural trait is understood, the easier it will be to introduce the change. If two cultural items are available, the one which costs the least in effort and yields the greatest satisfaction, will be accepted (Parsons, 1951, 499), or greater the functional need of a system for a trait the easier and more rapid will be its acceptance (Freedman. 1952 : 317). These references have been brought in here to substantiate my objective that folklore helped as a bridge between the two cultures of high or low prestige, or a bridge in understanding the cultural traits in a better manner or in the realisation of the functional need of a system. The Aryans accepted many of the occult practices of the non-aryans in the form of folklore, as is evident in some of the Vedas. P.K. Bhowmick cites an interesting example: There was "a man belonging to the Namasudra Caste (lowest caste in West-Bengal whom some consider as *khadal* or *chandal*) who having acquired occult powers did cut across the traditional caste inhibitions. He knew the art of healing snake-bites. His method consisted of puffing a number of times into a pot of water and loudly uttering some incantations with the object of investing the water with magical potentialities. To make the process most effective his sputum got mixed with the water which was drunk very devoutly by the patients of higher castes also." (1978, 14). Bhowmick goes on to say, "Low caste persons are found to practice sooth-saying and such other things to help to solve the predicaments of the afflicted and the victims of various diseases in rural society all over India" (1978, 14).

According to R.C. Majumdar, a great historian of Bengal, some of the major elements which are found in Hinduism like the faith that the consequence of one's actions of a previous life governs one's weal or woe, the belief of the doctrine of rebirth, the worships that were not prescribed in the Vedas beyond an oblation of fire, Vedic sacrifice and so on, the great Gods like Shiva, The Goddess of Power, Vishnu and many stories narrated in the Puranas have been taken from the non-Aryans. Many tales, the practices, customs, festivals, the use of turmeric powder during the marriage ceremony, use of vermilion on the women's forehead, the use of boat, garments like the dhoti and sari, were adapted from those who were not Aryans (Dr. Ramesh Chandra Majumdar's *Bangladesher Itihash*, 1949 p. (12, the History of Bengal written in Bengali).

Examples of other influences are innumerable. Thousands of non-Aryans came within the fold of the Aryan civilization and culture. So far as Bengal is concerned, "the Aryanization of Bengal may be said to have commenced in right earnest from the closing centuries of the first millennium B.C. (Majumdar, *History of Bengal*, Vol. I, 1942, ch. 12, p. 876). The two great epics, *Ramayana* and *Mahabharata* having a rich store of folklore, attracted the rural and simple people to the Aryans. Folklore was thus instrumental in developing a gradual and healthy understanding between the two societies having distinctly separate culture.

Family is one of the oldest institutions of human societies. It has four very major functions to play. First the family produces children. Second, it provides nourishment and maintenance for its members, a function of special importance while children are still young. Third, it provides the individual, of one generation with most important linkage with the social and cultural systems of previous generations, permitting him to internalize, for example, the ends, norms, status-roles and authority patterns of these systems. In other words, it provides situations, experience and affectual relationships whereby socialization may take place. Fourth, it provides each member with an important reference, indentification or placement, ascribing, at least during the early part of life specific status-roles and social rank not only in the family, but also in society. Thus Murdock says, "no society, in short, has succeeded in finding an adequate substitute for the nuclear family" (1949, 11). These are more true about the Indian family structure, because it not only involves and includes children, but other near ones within the fold of a joint family system. Joint family is the classical form here. Levi-Strauss' assumption of the joint family concept is, of course, different. He does not support the term joint family. He objects to the term 'joint' being used with family and points out that it is erroneous to think of joint families as being made up of smaller (nuclear) families which are joined together as it were, into a larger grouping. Levi-Strauss also disregards the usage of the term 'extended family', suggesting the adoption of the term 'restricted family' for the nuclear family to emphasize that the socalled extended family is not made up of smaller units. The Indian joint family is neither smaller families joined together, nor extended from smaller ones, it is, in a sense, restricted. That is why one of the qualities of the Indian joint family more commonly agreed is stability. The recent changes, of course, in the family in the context of urbanization, industrialization and modernization have tended to break up the joint family structure with some exceptions here and there. The caste system which introduces unusual rigidities into the social order, supported the joint family, but with the gradual eradication of this system, the joint family structure is also losing its strength. Whatever may be the case, throughout the long history of India, the family has been a strong aspect of social system upon which Indic societies have most consistently relied for the nurturing of some meaningful affectional relationships so necessary in the development of stable personalities and the transmission of this family-based kinship-influenced culture from one generation to the other. A lovely and affectionate family is the desire of all people of this subcontinent—he who deviates, repents. Thus, in folklore, a tribal wife of Kuilipal, of West Bengal, laments :

I have not obeyed the father-in-law
I have not obeyed the elder brother-in-law
Now I will have to suffer
I will tear away my hair
And dance like a mad woman by swinging my head.*

This song explains how folklore could be a balancing and educative force in society. A good family relation is essential for mental as well as physical health. Songs of this type work as an eye-opener to others and provide ample inspiration to the society for its equilibrium and sustenance.

All great religions emphasize on familial bond. According to Islam, raising children is equivalent to the worship of God. In the Indian tradition the analogy of intercourse with plowing is an ancient theme, which also directs to family life. "Your women are lands (*earth*) for you, so plough them as you wish", says the *Quran* (11, 223). But the religion in the scriptures and the religion in folklore are not the same. Two examples of folk beliefs relating to family bondage and fertility are cited below representing two communities, one Hindu, the other Muslim :

A Hindu myth explaining the origin of rice goes like this :

Narayan and Lakshmi, his consort, while travelling overhead one time, heard the lamentations of a poor cowherd boy, who asked for their help. Lakshmi asked Narayan to give help but he replied that it was she who had power to do so. Thus fortified with her consort's permission,

*Translation by Islam, quoted in Bengali by Banerjee, 1969, 228.

> Lakshmi came down to earth and handed some paddy seeds to the boy and advised : 'Take these, and poverty and sorrow will remain away from you. When the rains set in, go and sow these seeds in your field. The plants will grow up and bear numerous fruits. When they take on the colour of gold like that of my body, and a sweet-smelling odour as of my person comes out of them, you reap the fruits and bring them home." When the seeds sprouted and the grain ripened, behold, it was lit with the colour of gold like Lakshmi herself, and had a heavenly fragrance as of the person of the goddess who was manifest in it (Krishna Basu, 1962, 21).

In this myth, although Lakshmi had the power, she sought the permission of her consort for that power to be released. This indicates familial love. Here, in a popular belief, goddess Lakshmi has been personified as the generative force, but that had to be released by the male.

Muslim peasants in Bangladesh believe that the earth is uniquely powerful, strong, and productive, because it produces food. Adam and Haoya were caste out of heaven after they ate the forbidden food because they began to urinate and defecate and were smelling up heaven. But earth is the agent that purifies these products. When someone dies and his soul returns to Allah, the body is buried in earth so that the decay may be concealed. The strength (*Shakti*) of the surrounding earth quickly reduces the cadaver back to its fundamental state, which is ordinary productive earth (Thorp, 1978, 6,9).

There is also a general belief that one who owns land and subsists from it, benefits from its special *shakti*. Only one who owns land is a *malik* in the full sense that Adam was, and he, his family members and those who are provided with food through his cultivation (the household members) share directly in the earth's strength (Thorp, 1978, 23,28): indeed, it is sometimes said that only those who eat the food from the land of a village can learn the particular dialect of Bengali spoken there.

These beliefs, whether emanating from myths or folk religion, have been set deeply in the root of society and they play a dual role: help the society from disruption and manifest the slow but steady change by acquiring new beliefs through the process of diffusion and variations from the old ones. In many primitive cultures, besides various kinds of beliefs, songs are thought to have a supernatural origin, or some function connected with the supernatural. Consequently, the songs are not to be changed, else the whole effect of an elaborate ritual might be marred or vitiated. Among the Navaho Indians the fact that some ceremonial cures happen to prove ineffective is taken to mean that in the performance of these cures some mistakes must have been made; either in details of the ritual procedure, or in the hundreds of songs which form an essential part of each of these rites.

The vital literature in British social anthropology, specially relating to East Africa and South Africa, that emanated so largely from the influences of Malinowski and Radcliffe-Brown and that was highlighted by its explicit studies of the impact of European on African native, may provide some guidelines to us. It cannot be denied that social change in Indian society is marked with the western education, emancipation of women growth of modern technology, social mobility towards industrial and urban settings, political consciousness, westernization both in thought and external behaviour and so on. The new movements also touched a more considerable bulk of population than did direct westernization. The new awakening in the realm of literature, the movement of social renaissance by progressive politicians, the religious movement of the Arya Samaj, the humanistic approach to religious system and a secular outlook and many other reformative steps helped Indian societies to accept some of the changes. But even then, functionalism as the agent of change cannot be repudiated. For all its mistaken emphasis on social systems, rather than social behaviour, and for all its mistaken predication of change as an immanent process, there is none the less much to be learned from functionalist studies of culture, groups and customs. The phenomenon of continuing persistence and inertia even when a given way of behaviour is subjected to events and intrusions, which of other times, or other places plainly lead to change. The best of functionalism lies exactly in its emphasis upon those processes, which are, as the beliefs and customs, or any element of folklore, as we have seen in some of the representative examples cited in the foregoing pages, involved in equilibrium and stability. For these are real and powerful agents and processes in the conduct of human behaviour. While we bring folklore within the gamut of functionalism, which in my view, is absolutely in the right order, we have to be alert that social change, by the very nature of social reality so well illuminated by functionalists in their empirical studies of social stability and fixity, is not inextricably involved only in the historical processes of event and external impact, but also assumes processes of immanent developmentalism.

So far as the Indian tribes are concerned, their proximity to Hindu society, is an agent for change. The tribal societies in immediate contact with the Hindu society are also changing. Opening up of new industrial centres in the tribal areas of Bihar, West Bengal, Orissa, Madhya Pradesh causes acculturation and subsequent adoption or assimilation. A common interactional contact is also caused in tribal societies by Christian missionaries.

The Indian situation is both interesting and full of paradoxes. India is an old society, but a new nation, and her aspirations for a future image are promising and brilliant. But the paradox of the situation is that it cannot move much forward without looking back. The modern intellectuals are not totally cut off from the traditional background. There is a continuity between the tradition-oriented common mass and the intellectual or modernizing elite. Since folklore is the wealth of the common mass and inspiring traditional heritage to the intellectuals, its force in the societies of the Indian subcontinent is beyond any dispute. The Indic literary tradition in written form goes back to 1200 to 1000 B.C., the tradition we find in Vedic literature. More than hundred books, mainly to be divided into four categories, form this literary stream. They are *Samhita*, *Brahmana*, *Aranyaka* and *Upanishada*. *Samhita* contains mainly the songs, hymns, charms, and so on; which have formed the four vedas, *Rigveda*, *Samaveda*, *Yajurveda* and *Atharvaveda*. *Brahmanas*, linked with *Samhitas* but unlike the Vedas, are written in prose form, relating to performances of religious oblations and offerings. *Aranyaka* is a type of literature that seeks for the mysteries and meanings of life and world. Almost similar type of literature are the *Upanishadas*, which are mostly written in *slokas* (couplets). A table given below might help us to understand the main stream of this literature.*

Samhitas	*Brahmanas*	*Aranyakas*	*Upanishadas*
Rigveda	Oitorio, Kaushitoki	Oitorio Kaushitoki	Oitorio Kaushitoki
Samaveda	Panchabimsa or Tandyo Maha Sarbingsa, Jaiminio	Aranyaka Samhita, Aranyaka Gan, Jaiminio Upanishad, Brahmanas	Chhandyogya, Keno
Jajurveda	Koth, Toittirio, Satapatha	Koth, Toittirio Satapatha	Katha, Toittirio, Maitraonio, Svetasvara, Brihadaranyaka, Isha
Atharva-veda	Gopatha		Manduka, Mandyukya, Prosno

This great stream of literature was not written even in one century. According to scholars, the *Rigvedas* period was between 1200 and 1000 B.C., while the *Samhita's* period was during 1000 to 800 B.C. and the others are presumed to have their origin within next two hundred years. These literatures, though were supposed to be in written form, but many elements in them, as they appear, were taken from the oral tradition and by their characteristics, many of them could be termed as folklore. Besides, the most powerful and almost unique in the world folklore tradition, what we call the Indic folklore, was created during later periods on this very tradition established by the vedic literature. The appearance of *Brihat Katha* and *Panchatantra* goes back to first century or during

*This diagram has been translated from the author's work in Bengali.

the life-time of Christ. Johan's Hartle holds that the tales of the *Panchatantra* were in oral tradition during the second century B.C.—the basis of his very exhaustive research is *Tantrakshayika*, a Kashmiri version of the *Panchatantra*. Keith objects to this opinion, as he finds a latin word 'denarius' used in *Panchatantra* and thus he decides that it could not have been before second century A.D. In one of the Sanskrit versions of the *Panchatantra* once there is a reference of Chanakya and from this, it is supposed by some scholars that it cannot go beyond the first century A.D. Whatever may be the time, the tales of *Brihatkatha* and the *Panchatantra* have been accepted as one of the oldest and richest specimens of folktales of the world. The influence of Vedic literature over them has been considerably great.

It is interesting how the *Panchatantra* starts the origination of the tales. In the south, there was a city named Mahilarapyang. The king of the state Amarsakti, who was a scholar and also unmatched in power, lived in this city. The king had three sons, who were completely illiterate. The king Amitasakti was very unhappy about it. One day he consulted his ministers who suggested him to invite Vishnu Sharma, a great scholar and a genius, and engage him as a teacher to the princes. Vishnu Sharma was invited. The king promised him a huge property and requested him to teach his three sons. The Pandit accepted. Next day he started with a couplet. The substance of which is "a great store of learning in the form of an elegant piece of literature is now introduced in the world."*

The *Panchatantra*, which inspired the German scholar Theodor Benfey to declare a theory of folklore, namely Indianist origin of the world folktale, and the diffusionist theorists to postulate the age-area concept, the concept of folklore origin, presents a great example of how folklore could be educative as well as an ardent agent of social change. Indian tales as narrated in the *Panchatantra* conformed to the world view of the ancient man everywhere. *Panchatantra* means the five *tantras* or sections or scriptures. The first *tantra* where the question of enmity is prominent, is about the tales of Karatak-

*Translated by the author.

Damanak, which contains the tales mostly of animals and birds like the tales of Kilotpatak money, the jackle dunduvi, the crow-black snake, the crane-cuckoo, the blue jackal, the tittive husband and wife (birds), the three fishes, the elephant and chataka, the god who is yet to arrive, and so on. Among the tales relating to human beings are the city-captain Tantil and Gorombho, Deva-Sama, the traveller, Kaulik and Rathakar, the businessman, the thief and Brahmin, and others. The second section's main title is the end of enmity and it contains the tales of crow-tortoise-deer-rat relationships where the tales of animals as well as human beings, have been closely connected. In the same manner the other three sections have also been arranged. The *Panchatantra* deals with philosophy, economics, palmistry, astrology, humanities, and so on. From the sociological point of view, these tales are immensely valuable, as they depict the picture of Indian society of more than two thousand years ago. The narratives also directed their most sobering influence on the society to bring about the changes. In some of the stories, as in the tale of a princess having three breasts, it is clearly suggested that the social wrong can be repudiated not only by using the morals or practicing the higher values, but sometimes it necessitates the wrong to counter it effectively.

Hitopodesh is almost another version of the *Panchatantra*, compiled by a scholar named Narayana. According to Keith, *Hitopodesh* was compiled sometime between the thirteenth and fourteenth centuries. In spite of many similarities, *Hitopodesh* has added some new motifs and types which are no less important than *Panchatantra* or some later products in the study of Indian folklore in general and folktales in particular. The women depicted here many of them, seem to have better talents and thirst for life than those of the *Panchatantra*. Its objectives to moral teaching is more prominent and pointed and as such its role in maintaining the social equilibrium as well as initiating some changes seemed to have better effect. The characteristics and social or environmental conditions as reflected in the tales, almost confirm that Narayana was a man of Bengal—the mention of Bikrampur, now in Bangladesh, makes a strong ground that he was from present Bangladesh.

Both *Panchatantra* and *Hitopodesh* aimed at preaching

morals through the tales, though their entertainment value thereby cannot be undermined in anyway. But so far as the importance of story and entertainment is concerned, *Brihatkatha*, linked with the name of one Gunadhyaya as the writer, seems to have greater value. This may be regarded as the source of later tales found in Kshemendra's *Brihat Kahamanjuri* and Somdeva's *Kathasaritsagara*. Gunadhyayas *Brihatkatha* cannot be traced, but the latter's, specially *Kathasaritsagara*, have been collected and edited. *Kathasaritsagara* means the ocean of stories—it really is an ocean. While *Brihat Kathamanjuri* has only 7,500 couplets containing innumerable tales, *Kathasaritsagara* has 22,000 couplets, all of which narrate tales. Besides, the tales of Gunadhyaya, the tales from the *Jataka*, and *Abadansutaka* have also been narrated in the Ocean. Being attracted by the excellence of the tales of the *Panchatantra*, *Kathasaritsagara* and other Indian classics containing tales, many western scholars came forward to have them translated into English. Thus "Margaret Noble or Sister Nivedita published, *Cradle Tales of Hinduism* (London, 1907), a pleasant selection of tales from the older Hindu literature, distributed into eight cycles occuring in *Ramayana* and *Mahabharata*. John Mandeville Macfie's *Myths and Legends of India* (Edinburg, 1924) is also a selection of myths and legends from the *Ramayana*, *Panchatantra* and the *Mahabharata*. The two volumes of *The Panchatantra Reconstructed* (Connecticut, 1924) by Franklin Edgerton (Vol. I, Text and critical apparatus; Vol. II, Introduction and translation) fulfilled the long-felt desire of the English world to have the *Panchatantra*, the mother of tales, in their own language, in a scholarly form. Translated from the Sanskrit into Pahlavi, it passed through Persian into Syriac, Arabic Latin, German and most other western languages. The reconstructed form of Edgerton's *Panchatantra* to the English world was of immense value." (Islam. 1982, 116).

"But the ten volumes of *The Ocean of Story* (London, 1924-1929), being Charles Henry Tawney's translation of Somadeva's *Kathasaritsagara*, edited by Norman Mosley Panzar, surpassed all previous translations. Charles Henry Tawney (1832-1922) translated these volumes from Somadeva's *Kathasaritsagara*. Tawney occupied the chair of history in the

Presidency college, Calcutta from 1866 to 1872, succeeding Professor E. Byles Cowell, the editor of Jataka, and later the Registrar of Calcutta University (1877-89). An equally strenuous and laborious job was the scholarly work performed by Norman Mosley Panzer in the editing of these stories in *The Ocean of Story*. The first volume contains a foreword by Temple, while the second contains a preface by Grierson. After serious criticism of volume I (*Folk-Lore*, XXXV, 1924, pp. 399-406) and volume II (*Folk-Lore*, XXXVII, 1926, pp. 105-108) by W.R. Holliday, Panzer provided more annotation of stories from India than from Europe in the rest of his volumes. His later volumes may be regarded as ideals for the annotating of Indian tales. He has cited parallel Indian as well as European tales on almost every page, and no main incidents of his tales have gone without parallel. Thus he has been able to make *The Ocean of Story* the Ocean of scholarship as well. Helliday very truly comments on the later volumes (II to VIII) "while the oriental information remain full and excellent, the references to European folktales have been greatly strengthened". (Islam. 1982:117).

Short description of the contents of *Kathasaritsagara* may not be regarded as out of place here. It contains eighteen *lambhakas* (volumes), each having several *tarangas* (the chapters, sections or streams). The first *lambhaka*, named as "Kathapitha," contains the stories supposedly composed by Gunadhyaya, the second *lambhaka*, named as "Kathamukh," has *Udayan-Katha*, the third has the tale of Udayana and Padmavati and the fourth gives the tale of the birth of Narabahana Datta, who is the hero of the episode. From fifth to eighteenth, the tale of Narabahana Datta and of his wives receives prominence. In these volumes have come the tales of the *Jataka* (eighth), Betalpanchavimsati (twelfth), king Bikramaditya (eighteenth) and so on.

Next to *Sagara* come the tales of *Betalpanchavimsati* which contains 25 tales, all concern king Bikramaditya. The man who took down or wrote these tales is Shivadasa. Keith considers its time as twelfth century. But there can be no doubt that its tales are far older than that. The tales not only give the description of the social conditions, but they narrate the story elements with humour and intelligence of extraordinary order. The influence of the tantric cult is distinctly visible in these tales.

Datringsha Puttalika, which narrates thirty-two tales of bikramaditya, specially how he was crowned, was written by the great poet Kalidasa, it is said. But this presumption, as many scholars believe, is not correct. Chintamoni Bhatta's *Sukasaptati* contains seventy tales related by a bird named Suka, a kind of parrot.

These tales from great collections, mixed up with the tales of two great epics, the *Ramayana* and *Mahabharata* and the southern epic *Cillapattikarama*, provide the major motifs and types of not only Indic folklore, but also the folklore of the world. I have, in my book *A History of Folktale Collections in India, Bangladesh and Pakistan*, (1982, Calcutta) mentioned and analysed in short the large collections and English translations of Indic tales done by British administrators, their relatives and European missionaries and scholars.* But there are hundreds of such collections collected and published in the Indian languages; and the huge quantity is still scattered all over the subcontinent which is yet to be collected. If one goes through the *Motif Index of Folkliterature* (6 vols.) by Stith Thompson, *The Aarne-Thompsons Type Index, The Oral Tales of India* by Thompson and Balys, *Types of Indic Oral Tales by* Thompson and Roberts, one would at least be surprised to see what a flood of material the Indic folklore has supplied to these volumes, specially when one knows that the materials in these volumes have been incorporated only from English translated sources.

Folklore and economic action

While focussing the effect of folklore on the Indic society, I have given a brief description of our stock of folklore that our forefathers generated for us a few thousand years ago. Did they do it for nothing or only for entertainment? The underlying truth in all folklore elements tells us that their originators had combined in them the entertainment with some functional aspects of social education. They were the great

*Those interested, may please read this book for further elaboration of this chapter.

teachers and philosophers of our society, they provided ideals before the people to pattern the society through folklore and people accepted them and constituted and changed their societies accordingly. The entertainment value certainly made folklore as well as their underlying truth for human society and philosophy of life readily acceptable to the people. As for example, the myth of Indra relates the conflict between drought and rain, rain is essential for an agrarian society. Thus Indra is the king of gods and drought the demon named Vritta. "In the early ages," Muir says, "when the vedic hymns were composed it was an idea quite in consonance with the other general conception which their authors entertained to imagine that some malignant influence was at work in the atmosphere to prevent the fall of the showers, of which their parched fields stood so much in need. It was but a step further to personify both this hostile power and beneficent agency, it was at least overcome. Indra is thus at once a terrible warrior and a gracious friend, a god whose shafts deal destruction to his enemies, while they bring deliverance and prosperity to his worshippers. The phenomena of thunder and lighting almost inevitably suggest the idea of a conflict between opposing forces even we ourselves, in our more prosaic age often speak of strife of the elements". (*Muir's Oriental Sanskrit Text*, vol. 5, page 98. Also quoted Hangsanarayan Bhattacharya, 1977, 194). Among the Murngin, an exogamic partilineal aborigine of Australia "a man of religious knowledge and his understanding of the sacred totemic lore, with associated myths and rituals, are dependent upon how far he has been initiated into the sacred mysteries. The initiations elevate him from a lower and more profane existence to a higher and more sacred plane and mark his transition from one age grade to a higher and older one". (Warner 1937, 131). Thus all myths have some functions both economic and social, in society,—the myth of Indra, as quoted above relates to human necessity in relation with his economy, while the knowledge of myth in the Australian aborigine elevates one's social status, which, also, is linked up with his economy.

Folklore, thus becomes a guiding factor also in matters relating to the economy of the society. Let me cite another example from Tikopia, a Polynesian group of people. As in most societies, food is a primary goal of production in Tikopia, and therefore a prime factor in the economic process. This follows from the commonsense and pragmatically obvious notion in order to live one must eat. However, beyond this, not only is the Tikopia economy related to food; the social system itself is so oriented, where folklore plays a dominant role. The reason is not far to seek, taking into account several situations. It is not the nutritional value of the food which plays such a vital role. It is rather that food is necessary for hospitality, in a culture given to dancing, singing and narrating tales, while visiting. The Tikopian folklore, the proverbs, the tales, the ballads, direct that food must be the main item of hospitality when one visits other. It is a means for repaying obligations of various kinds, for showing respect to one who sings folksongs or narrates tales or to a chief. It not only binds kinship units, but honors folklore, the treasure of this culture. It is furthermore, a means of making religious offerings (Firth, 1939, 33). These are, of course, not simply religious beliefs. I should make it clear that, at no point is the thesis maintained and tenable that "social action is basically religious." This view is notably inaccurate even in the Indian context and at several stages of my discourse, care has been taken to insist that at the various levels of social action some elements of religious beliefs and emotions do play a significant part, but linking folklore always with it would be erroneous.

From the information provided by Firth about Tikopia, it may be said that, it is at this point, the system of ultimate values of a society, makes a pronounced impact through folklore. For, just as in case of a Dahomey king, who annuls an ordeal both as a supreme political head and as possessor of superior magic, (a power vested in him by the people because of their adherence to folklore) (Le Herisse's notes quoted by Herskovits, 1933, 75), the folklore elements impinge on the economic system through the socio-cultural order. Here the emphasis is on the non-nutritional aspects of food offering, exchange, and distribution, as well as the conditions surrounding all these. That is, the folkloric obligations and ritual rules, the value obtained, through folklore and beliefs the impulses, set certain ends, and aid in fixing means and conditions to these ends. This is also applicable in the case of Indic societies.

Folklore, through the ages, has set certain ends, has established certain values and norms, which are still forceful. Some fishermen in Bangladesh, as I have seen, perform certain ceremonies and utter some chants, (though as Muslims they are strictly prohibited to do this), before going for fishing and if the catch is not good enough, and specially to get a large fish, the ceremony is again performed. This also supports the relation of folklore with social economy. The ritual and folkloric sanction furnishes a strong reason to perform the rites prescribed by folklore with dispatch. This has another implication, as in the case of the people of Uta, the most sacred area in Tikopia, who also perform ceremonies, though different from those performed by the fishermen in Bangladesh, before going fishing. The ceremonies depend, in both the cases, upon the allocation of time and energy as well as equipment and rituals to fishing. The deities will not be satisfied unless proper offerings are made, and therefore fishing will be poor. These can be made only if the necessary repairs of the net and canoe is made, work is expanded on fishing, and many members of the clan or the group co-operate and compete to achieve these goals. Besides, God or gods approve the efficiency and admire a fast worker. And the competitive context of the ceremony induces a greater expenditure of labour. Thus the act which initiate the period of excitement, hard work, routine as well as dependence on rituals and the folkloric inspiration, constitute both an economic and socio-religious act.

While I worked in Visva-Bharati University, Santiniketan, I used to travel occasionally by train to cover the distance between Bolpur and Calcutta. Some of the Bauls, of this area, sing songs in the train and the travellers pay them some coins, which, I am told, sustains the Bauls and their family. Once I saw a blind Baul led by his old mother. He was reluctant to sing, but being pressed by his mother, the blind fellow presented two songs. There was however, no response from the travellers. Being annoyed, the Baul remarked, "mother, you insisted and I had to sing, but you see the result. Did I not tell you that the mood of the travellers and God is not favourable today?" The old mother smiled and with humour uttered a proverb which loosely translated means:

"A lock is on the door of mind, The song and its melody is thus neglected". This had a magical effect. The blind Baul earned the best on that trip. Thus, folklore has the potentiality to direct economic action favourably!

I may cite one more example from my own experience. I made a comparative study between a group of farmers who work in the field and sing songs of labour or their favourite songs while working; and the group who also does the same work, but does not sing at the time of working. The group which worked and sang, had a better output and yield than the other. Besides, the day labourer in the village who can sing well is in popular demand than one who does not sing. Folklore here serves as the best means of earning. It can even compete with expertise and skill, and provide more economic scope.

The coincidence of wealth and rituals is seen in the element of economic achievement during ceremonies of the Zuni tribe. Although the technological development of the Zuni lies somewhere between that of the Dahomey and the Tikopia and considerably above that of the Manus, their orientation toward economic affairs is not strong. But the centre of their tribal attention lies in the area of their adherence to ceremonies and folklore. As for example, some of most elaborate of ritual food and gift distribution takes place during the dance of the Kianakawa, following the dances for thanks giving. Since these occur in the fall after the harvests, there is more food available. The contributions for this begin to arrive at the gathering during the dances. The offerings are carried in blankets and the men bring theirs in through the hatchway. The women hand theirs into the gathering. Usually an aged man of the gathering receives these gifts. Thus, economic action is tied up with folk ceremony and dance.

But most interesting is their making of a mask and its ownership, the task which is significantly linked with economic action directed by folklore. A more direct motivation to work hard in the fields or at shepherding is to be found in the desire of a man to have a mask, that would give him the right to the folkloric performance like the dance, drama, song and so on or specially when he does not have any other sacerdotal relationships or objects to protect him. In former times, the good hunter could obtain a mask through his ability to provide feasts and skins for payment. One cannot be poor and acquire a mask. And he may be even driven to selling his beads for sheep to make a feast (Bunzel, 1929-30: XLVII). A native account of this situation and the religious motivation for the economic activity, is significant: "So if a man wants to have a mask made he will work very hard in the spring. He will plant a great deal and he will work very hard all summer so as to have good crops. Then after the crops are gathered in, he will say to his wife, "Now I want my mask made. 'He will say this to his wife and his people'. 'That is why I have worked so hard'. No one will say to him, 'Do not do it, we are poor people and cannot afford it'. No one will tell him that. They will be glad because they want something very valuable in the house to pray for "(Bunzel, *ibid*). Now that buckskin and buffalo hides are not obtainable as they once were, tanned leather from the store must be bought. After the headmen have titled it, and finished the sewing and ritual for making the mask sacred, the man must furnish a feast for the members of kiva. All the man's female relatives grind corn this feast. All his people prepare for the occasion. He brings wheat and corn, and slaughters eight or ten sheep as well. On the other hand, the mask itself is valuable, including even the point used for colouring it.

It is thus seen that even in this society of little intensity or interest in economic affairs, the patterns of their religious activities, social commitment and adherence to folklore, have a concrete, as well as indirect and less tangible effect on production and distribution as well as exchange. The demands of the rituals and sanctions connected with folklore and folk-religion, help to motivate as well as shape such economic activities.

From some examples cited, it has been seen that this is absolutely true also for the folk of the Indian subcontinent—this is true even for some of the Indic tribes, who are at a very low level of technological development.

In a recent study, "Concept and Treatment of Diseases in West Bengal", it has been revealed that the majority of the people attribute the causes of some chronic diseases, madness and nervous disorder to some evil potentialities and to get recovery from these, they seek advice from the temple priests.

Kalighat, Tarakeswar, Ghuriari Sharif, Pir Sharif of Hatiara, and so on are widely known sacred places in and around Calcutta, where people go in thousands for cure from various ailments (Bhowmick, 1978: 149).

On the Bengal-Orissa border there is a famous temple of Siva as Chandaneshwar where the phallic symbol of Lord Siva is worshipped regularly and the place is frequently visited by the people of the adjoining areas including the district of Midnapore, for seeking therapeutic advice. The priests offer worship to the deity on behalf of the devotees and give suggestions along with amulets, talismans and consecrated water to the afflicted. In rural areas of Bengal, more than 90 per cent of the local population think that child diseases are generally caused by the evil eyes of witches. This is locally called as *Bataslaga*, that is, influence of the evil wind. Most of the cases of paralysis are also considered to originate from *Banmara*, that is, shooting of an arrow for causing physical affliction by charm and look. So to cure such diseases, the folk medicinemen and sorcerers are consulted. The notion is still in vogue, but it may assume different forms due to the changing situation (Bhowmick, 1978, 149-50).

I have mentioned these to substantiate two important factors: one, the beliefs, costoms, ceremonies, the way of treatment and different manner through which people try to get rid of their diseases, are social affairs and these forces, emanating from folklore, have retained the society on its traditional footing; two, these are linked up with economic actions. In every action and interaction of the types mentioned above, there are two parties, one is the believer, who is paying in kind of money or some gifts in exchange of something that the believer is seeking for, and the other is the receiver, who is receiving and delivering the goods. This payment and receipt of it is in one way or other affecting the society economically. Folklore has its economic potentiality in Indic societies, which deserves a thorough and careful study.

The process of continuity of the secret institutions propagating occultism from ancient times to the modern period, specially in the Indian situation, including Bangladesh and Pakistan, has its importance. Let me again quote from Bhowmick, who rightly says:

> The physical background of the area surveyed along with the population structure has also been studied and examined for ascertaining other, associated interactions. A group of persons in different compelling social situations and demands, received training in occult practices from the adepts in guarded sorcery to deal with mysterious happenings and diseases. This resulted in the growth of some specific institutional formalities for occult practices and these were considered indispensible for eradication of human misfortune, as other social agencies are unable to solve such problems. These institutions came as a great hope to the common people. Besides, when confronted with intractable problems, human beings generally suffered from maladjustments and mental coniflcts. In that situation, the institutional procedures were thought effective and appropriate and also provided some sort of emotional compensation and relief. So one cannot ignore the spontaneous nature of the growth of such institutions, which are necessary adjuncts to the demands of overall human culture. (1978, 147-48).

Thus, occultism, a part of folklore has been institutionalised in Indic societies and these institutions play some role in the economic action of the society. It cannot be denied that the people of ruder cultures have to accept magical procedures as part of their life style and even today, after enormous development of civilization in all spheres, the dependency on those has not decreased. There are evidences that the magicians also sometime work as priests, pirs or thakurs. They usually tackle every odd situation or problem that is faced by an individual or a society by charms or administering magical drugs and puffs or soothsaying and thus play the quack or, may be termed as an empty pretender to knowledge or skill of healing or driving misfortune. This, perhaps, compelled them to acquire and master some traits of trickery and some craft by which they differentiated themselves from the rest of the people and thereby commanded their faith and respect. With the detailed ritual performances, as I have seen some of the so-called pirs of Bangladesh among the vast Muslim community (though Islam does not sanction occultism), with locally available rare ingredients or materials and utterances of long-winded magic lores and incantations (the pirs would say that they utter from the *Quran*), in sonorous high-pitched tone they treat the patients or sufferers and advise their devotees, who are in trouble, and thereby they succeed to create an aura of reverence and mystery around themselves, which separate them and raise their prestige, dignity and social status to a very distinct level of rank, hierarchy and privilege. Some of them have become materially so rich that their position can be compared only with a few rich persons of their own country, be it in Bangladesh, India or Pakistan.

Other areas of society

Folklore has its limitations. It is not a major or only force to initiate change in the society. But I have tried to locate its position as an active agent which has a role in bringing about change in the society it belongs to. Thus I have enumerated in short, with a few examples, how folklore can create the norms, values as well as preserve them against sudden onslaught and help maintain an equilibrium. I have also described the position of folklore in the economic persuits of society. These are all related directly or indirectly with the functional aspects of folklore. As in so many areas of anthropological concern, functionalism, either of the sociological sort associated with the name of Radcliffe-Brown or of the social psychological sort associated with Malinowski, has tended to dominate recent theoretical discussions of the role of folklore and religion in society. Steming originally from Durkheim's *The Elementary Form of the Religious Life* (Glencoe, 1947) and Robertson-Smith's *Lectures on the Religion of the Semites* (Edinburgh, 1894), the sociological approach, or as the British Anthropologists prefer to call it, the social anthropological approach, emphasizes the manner in which folklore, including beliefs, customs and rituals, reinforces the traditional social ties between individuals, stresses the way in which the social structure of a group is strengthened and perpetuated through the folkloric, specially of its mythic or ritualistic symbolization of the underlying social values upon which it rests. The socio-psychological approach, of which

Frazer and Tylor were perhaps the pioneers, but which found its clearest statement in Malinowski's classic *Magic, Science and Religion* (Boston, 1948) emphasizes what folklore and religion do for the individual, how they satisfy both his aesthetics cognitive and affective demands for a stable, comprehensible and coercible world, and how they enable him to maintain an inner security and mental health in the face of natural contingency. Together the two approaches have given us an increasingly detailed understanding of the social and psychological functions of folklore and religion in a wide range of societies.

But even then, it is true that the functional approach with regard to folklore has not been as impressive so far as is desirable, in dealing with social change. As has been noted by several scholars, the emphasis on systems in balance, on social homeostasis, and on timeless structural pictures, leads to a basis in favour of well-integrated societies in a stable equilibrium and to a tendency to emphasize the functional aspects of a people's social usages and customs rather than their dysfunctional implications (Leach, 1954, Merton, 1949). In the socio-cultural analyses of folklore, this static historical, approach has led to a somewhat overconservative view of the role of folklore including ritual and belief in social life. Despite cautionary comments by Kluckhohn (1944) and others on the gain and cost of the various folkloric practices such as witchcraft, soothsaying, chants and the use of folklore, the tendency has been consistently, specially by most of the scholars of the Indian subcontinent, to stress the harmonizing, integrating and psychologically supportive aspects of folkloristic patterns, rather than the disruptive, disintegrative and psychologically disturbing aspects, to demonstrate the manner in which folklore preserves social and psychological structure rather than the manner in which is destroys and transforms it. Where change has been treated, as in Redfield's work in Yucatan, it has largely been in terms of progressive disintegration : "The changes in culture that in Yukatan appear to go along with lessening isolation and homogeneity are seen to be chiefly three : disorganization of the culture, secularization and individualization" (1941, 339).

In this connection the view of M. Fortes may seem more

enlightening. One of the major reasons for the inability of functional theory to cope with change lies in its failure to treat sociological and cultural processes on equal terms; almost inevitably one of the two either is ignored or is sacrificed to become but a simple reflex, a mirror use of the other. Either culture is regarded as wholly derivative from the forms of social organization—the approach characteristic of the British structuralists as well as many American sociologists—or the forms of social organization are regarded as behavioural embodiments of cultural patterns—the approach of Malinowski and many American anthropologists. In either case the lesser term tends to drop out as a dynamic factor and we are left either with an omnibus concept of culture or else with a completely comprehensive concept of social structure (1953 : 17-41).

A profitable example from the situation of Indonesia might help us understand the role of folklore in social change. "In the villages and small towns (of Indonesia) the major ideological changes appeared largely in the guise of a widening split between those who emphasized the Islamic aspects of the indigenous religious syncretism and those who emphasized the Hinduist and animalistic elements. It is true that some difference between these variant sub-traditions has been present since the arrival of Islam; some individuals have always been particularly skilled in Arabic chanting or particularly learned in Moslem law, while others have been adept at more Hinduistic mystical practices or specialists in local curing techniques" (Geertz, 1975, 148-49).

"However, the appearance after 1910 of Islamic modernism (as well as vigorous conservative reaction against it) and religious nationalism among the economically and politically sophisticated trading classes of the larger cities strengthened the feeling for Islam as an exclusivist, antisyncretic creed among the more orthodox element of the mass of the population. . . . On the one hand, there arose a more self-conscious Moslem, basing his religious beliefs and practices more explicitly on the international and universalistic doctrines of Mohammad; on the other hand there arose a more self-conscious 'nativist' attempting to evolve a generalized religious system out of the material—muting the more Islamic elements

—of his inherited religious tradition. And the contrast between the first kind of man, called a *Santri*, and the second called an *Abangan*, grew steadily more acute, until today it forms the major cultural distinction in the whole of the Modjokuto area. ... Of this complex of political parties and modalities only two are of immediate concern to us. Masjumi, a huge Islam-based political party; and Permai, a vigorously anti-Moslem politico-religious cult. ... Masjumi's enemies accuse it of pressing for an intolerant, medievalist theocracy in which abangans and non-Moslem will be persecuted and forced to follow exactly the prescripts of the Moslem law. ... Permai's most notable characteristic is its strong anti-Moslem stand. Charging that Islam is a foreign import, unsuited to the needs and values of the Javanese, the cult urges to return to pure and original beliefs, by which they seem to mean to the indigenous syncretism with the more Islamic elements removed." (Geertz, 1975, 149-52).

Geertz cites an example of a crisis over the funeral of a boy of a man's family, who was a leader of the Permai cult, in 1954, when Geertz was on the spot. After a long hurdle the corpse was washed and wrapped in the Parmai way, but was buried in an Islamic order, but when all returned to the house—"it was now well in the afternoon—the slametan (*intended to be both offerings to the spirits and commensal mechanisms of social integration for the living. A special food is also offered, as in Milad prevalant in the Indian subcontinent*) was finally served, and Paidjan's (*the name of the deceased boy*) spirit presumably left the kampong (*place*) to begin its journey to the other world." (Geertz, 1975, 160).

After relating the story of the funeral crisis Geertz very rightly comments :

> A case such as that described above clearly poses some difficult problems. Not only was the victory of tradition and culture over thwarted instinct, a narrow one at best, but it seemed as if the ritual were tearing the society apart rather than integrating it, were disorganizing personalities rather than healing them. ... For both *santris* and *abangans* in the Kampongs the slametan maintains a force as a genuine sacred symbol; it still provides a meaningful

framework for facing death—for most people the only meaningful framework. We cannot attribute the failure of the ritual to secularization, to a growth in skepticism, or to a disinterest in the traditional 'saving beliefs', any more than we can attribute it to anomie.

We must rather, I think, ascribe to a discontinuity between the form of integration existing in the social structural (causal-functional) dimension and the form of integration existing in the cultural (logico-meaningful) dimension—a discontinuity which lead not to social and cultural disintegration, but to social and cultural conflict. In more concrete, if some what aphoristic terms, the difficulty lies in the fact that socially Kampong people are urbanites, while culturally they are still folk (Geertz, 1975, 163-64).

He further goes on to argue :

> The rituals themselves become matter of political conflict; forms for the sacralization of marriage and death are transformed into important party issue. In such an equivocal cultural setting, the average Kampong Javanese finds it increasingly difficult to determine the proper attitude toward a particular event, to choose the meaning of a given symbol appropriate to a social context. . . . The way Kampong people go about maintaining solidarity in everyday life is quite different from the way the slametan insists that they should go about maintaining it. . . . Thus when an occasion arises demanding sacralization—a life-cycle transition, a holiday, a serious illness—the religious form which must be employed acts not with but against the grain of social equilibrium. (Geertz, 1975, 163-168).

Geertz concludes with a remarkably suggestive comment :

> The disruption of Paidjan's funeral may be traced to a single source : an incongruity between the cultural framework of meaning and patterning of social interaction, an incongruity due to the persistence in an urban environment of a religious symbol system adjusted to peasant social structure. State functionalism, of either the sociological

> or social psychological sort, is unable to isolate this kind of incongruity because it fails to discriminate between logico-meaningful integration and causal-functional integration, because it fails to realize that cultural structure and social culture are not mere reflexes of one another but independent, yet interdependent, variables. The driving forces in social change can be clearly formulated on by a more dynamic form of functionalist theory, one which takes into account the fact that man's need to live in a world to which he can attribute some significance, whose essential import he feels he can grasp, often diverges from his concurrent need to maintain a functioning social organism. A diffuse concept of culture as a 'learned behavior', a static view of social structure as an equilibrated pattern of interaction, and a stated or unstated assumption that the two must somehow (save in disorganized situation) be simple mirror images of one another, is rather too primitive a conceptual apparatus with which to attack such problems as those raised by Paidjan's unfortunate but instructive funeral (1975, 169).

I have given a good many and long quotations from Geertz certainly not without a meaningful purpose. What Geertz has observed in Kampong, a town in Java, Indonesia, is more or less true for the social and cultural position as it exists in all the three countries of this subcontinent, India, Bangladesh and Pakistan. And the observations and analyses he has put forward, as quoted above, are almost equally applicable to the socio-cultural conditions of the three countries. There are hundreds of small and medium-size towns, all the cities of the three countries, where we find a large number of people, who claim to be urbanites, 'while culturally they are still folk'. So, folklore has a persisting and significant role in the socio-cultural interaction taking place in these towns and cities. It is true that folklore's effect directly or indirectly acts as a balancing force to preserve the equilibrium of the social structure. But this assumption holds well with the rural and completely agro-based society, where the interactions and the resultant conflicts have not yet reached a point leading to the disintegration of the social order. But this may not be the case in some of the towns and most of the cities where folklore is a force that works toward the achievement of disintegration by providing the inequilibrated pattern of interaction, as it happened in Paidjan's funeral. The conflict between the orthodox and liberal Muslims of Bangladesh has been and still is reeling around this point. The orthodox ones want to impose everything Islamic, things from Arabian and Persian cultures over the Muslims of Bangladesh and shake off everything relating to Indian and Bengali culture, which is impossible. On the contrary, the liberal people and the upholders of secularism, believe that the elements of culture which we have inherited over thousands of years, which are still preserved among the Muslim peasants and labourers all over the country, cannot be thrown away. They hold that it is quite possible for a man to be a true Bengali and a Muslim and there is no conflict between the two. Hence the rivalry, and historically it will not be wrong to say that this conflict and rivalry, along with financial exploitation, was the root cause for the disintegration of Pakistan. Though not evaluated yet, the contribution of folklore to the cause of liberation of Bangladesh, judged from this point of view, is considerably great.

Folklore has not been sociologically studied in India. Had it been so, the causes of many of the unrests in India since the last one decade or more, could have been scientifically located, 'the incongruity between the cultural framework of meaning and the patterning of social interaction' would have been truly realized. The rituals, beliefs, customs and many other aspects of culture emansting from folklore, are 'tearing the societies' of India (specially in the underdeveloped areas), 'rather than integrating them'. They are disorganizing personalities rather than healing them'. Why is there unrest in the tribal belts of the North-East, Bihar and Orissa? Why is there demand for a Jharkhand state? Is it all political? Some would answer that the rapid social change has disrupted the backward, less developed and tribal societies and this is reflected in a disintegrated culture; as the unified state of traditional village society mirrored in its beliefs, customs and rituals, so that the breaking-up of society in areas demonstrating unrest is mirrored in the broken rituals, customs and beliefs of that society, and the result is unrest, which may be viewed as within the jurisdiction of the normal process of social change. Or in alternate terms, cultural decay has led to social fragmentation; loss of a vigorous folk tradition and folklore has weakened the moral ties between individuals. This answer, I am afraid, may be wrong for two reasons: it identifies social or cultural conflict with social or cultural disintegration; it denies independent roles to the cultural and social structures, regarding one of the two as a mere epiphenomenon of the other.

Pandit Nehru realized this point through his extraordinary vision and prophetic mind and was deeply shaken by his experience on the Linguistic Committee, and with the candor that made him virtually unique among the leaders of the new states, he admitted it :

> (This inquiry) has been in some way an eye opener for us. The work of 60 years of Indian National Congress was standing before us, face to face with centuries old India of narrow loyalties, petty jealousies and ignorant prejudices engaged in mortal conflict and we were simply horrified to see how thin was the ice upon which we were skating. Some of the ablest men in the country came before us and confidently and emphatically stated that language in this country stood for and represented culture, race, history, individuality, and finally a sub-nation." (Quoted in Harrison, 1956, 3).

The issue is thus clear before us that the differences in customs, beliefs, rituals and some other cultural phenomena produced by folklore, do form the basis for a certain amount of national disunity in India, and are of special prominence in those cases in which an intellectually and/or artistically rather sophisticated and enlightened group sees itself as the bearer of real cultural heritage amid a largely folklore-oriented rural peoples or a tribe who would be well-advised to model themselves upon it, as the Arabs are doing in Morocco, Amhara in Ethiopia. New orientation is certainly desirable, technological, scientific, political, economic, agricultural, educational advancement through modernization is the primary need for the people of all areas of the Indian subcontinent, but those who are taking the lead in these activities, must step forward with wisdom and caution. The attempt to kill folklore would never succeed—rather it will resist. In the name of integration folklore cannot be tamed, rather the effect would be reversed, it will tear apart the society and cause serious disintegration. The folk and folklore must be won over through closer understanding and acceptance of their right place in society and the nation.

I hope, I have been able to throw enough light on how folklore acts and reacts under social conditions and how it helps integrate and disintegrate a society towards change. Now I pass on to the next point: social change and folklore. I would try to understand some of the problems, such as, when a society is changed from a primitive to modern state, what happens with its folklore, does folklore die with technological and scientific progress, if folklore is changed with the modernization of society, how does it do so.

Social change and folklore

Social change and folklore is one of the main subjects of our considerations. I have, thus, from the beginning of my discourse, tried to say in connection with other topics, that the inner potentiality and dynamism of folklore saves its existence and vigour from death and extinction.

Folklore refers to people's creative knowledge of things which is frequently invested with some normative functions. Many anthropologists equate folklore with oral literature or verbal art but folklore is actually much more than that. Any spontaneous response of the people of physical and social environment that goes into the making of material and nonmaterial aspect of cultural heritage is folklore. It is continuously in the making and not just a thing of the past. It follows from the living nature of folklore that frequently it serves as an instrument of social change. Again it is often the mirror of the changing society. Examples could be cited from *Ramayana*, *Mahabharata* as well as from the source materials in different countries including USA to show the impact of folklore in generating and perpetuating social values. The universal appeal of folklore is something which proves its dynamism and strength.

The question of anonymity in folklore was raised and discussed before in detail. A folk creation did not cease to be so, if it was documented in written form or if the name of the author was known. The distinguishing feature of folklore is that it draws upon a deeper substratum of the collective memory and perceives the phenomena as a resolution of conflicting dualities. Even in sophisticated societies folklore is in the making. These draw upon the psychic need of interpreting the uncanny experiences in terms of more shared knowledge of the community and of expressing the same in archaic idioms of the specific culture. Folklore is not only a form of communication it is also a form of communion. And as it happens in every communion, it has embedded in it, the elements of identification and distantiation; of acceptance and rejection. Several illustrations from India and the USSR can be shown to draw the attention to the utilitarian value of folklore studies particularly in the fields of adult and non-formal education as well as participatory social development. Besides, the new impetus to folklore as a sequel to changes taking place in the process and scope of industrialisation may be referred to assert folklore's enormous ability to adjust with the changing patterns of society. Until recently industrialisation was a process of disruption of physical and social environment. It was a journey to the wasteland; but to day there is a growing global awareness that industrial development can be promoted through harmony with nature; with the psychic needs of individuals and collectivities. In this milieu of new consciousness, folklore is not to be looked upon only as vestiges of the old world; but also as harbingers of the new.

According to Louis Wirth, modern society exhibits two major aspects. On the one hand it consists of organized groups, ranging from informally constituted intimate groups to highly formalized organizations, such as the modern corporation, the union, the church and the state. On the other hand, there are the detached masses that are held together. If it all, by the mass media of communication (1948,5).

The mass media and communication system in the subcontinent has been considerably developed and as a result the social gap between peoples has been greatly narrowed down. Mobility has been increased and interaction is intensified between various groups of people. From the point of development in all the three countries of the subcontinent, the objective to decentralize industrial development and its location, so that the urban growth becomes complementary to rural development and enhances employment and incomes of the poor strata, has not yet achieved success. It cannot be denied that the main casualty of the long colonial period was a whole range of rural and semi-rural industries and a number of non-agricultural occupations that provided livelihood to large sections of the people, and which in fact made for a society that was far less unequal and unjust than is the case now. It may not be possible and necessary to provide a new basis for fulfilling the same economic functions, namely, making available work other than farming. But the encouragement of self-employed artisans, the cultivation of the finer arts and crafts in the line with our rich and complex folk traditions, and the growth of new and small-scale industries for the manufacture of goods needed by the local people can certainly provide the basis for this regeneration. Besides, we cannot either by-pass the enormous number of landless peasants, which is growing at an unusual speed. But this is, of course, beyond the scope of my present study.

The overall development of all the three countries may not have reached the desired goal since their independence; but the economic growth, material progress and achievements in all other fields of national life, specially in India, cannot be undermined. The societies are not the same societies of the colonial period—even the Bondos are not the same people as Elwin saw them in 1950: "The Bondos spend a great deal of time on their religion, and the feasts and holidays are an important part of Bondo life, which can hardly be understood apart from them. They express and fulfil the Bondo's love of relaxation, his delight in gorging himself with meat and drinking with his cronies, his excited interest in ceremonials, his sense of the need to protect himself against the unseen powers" (1950, 172). The current of progress has touched the remotest rural areas and the communities who had, since ancient time, purely relied on fate and tended to lead an idle life. They have started to work hard and find their livelihood. The Bondos or the Santals are not an exception.

With the mobility of the folk either in the village or in the town, the nature and characteristics of folklore have also undergone a change, except those which have been handed down to us since the past from generation to generation. Even some of the old folklore elements have made necessary adjustments to cope with the present situation.

Passin and Bennet, in their joint article, "Changing Agricultural Magic in Southern Illinois: A Systematic Analysis of Folk-Urban Transition" have examined the social change and its effect on the magic of the illinois-folk (1943-98-106). This study may serve as an interesting example of social change and its impact on folklore. Even if we generalize the folk-urban continuum, it necessary to conceive it as a transition from greater to lesser homogeneity. The basic idea of this approach has been more or less accepted by scholars like Redfield, Durkheim, Tonnies, Becker and Sorokin. With this conception the difference between such transitions in primitive and modern societies becomes merely one of degree. In the community, of Stringtown, Illinois, and its immediately adjacent area, the historic process of adaptation to expending urbanism has involved a change from a folk-like-homogeneous community to a heterogeneous town-country type. In 1939, this town and its outskirts became economically dependent upon the wider American scene. Even one decade prior to that Stringtown was almost similar to primitive society. It was believed that, lettuce and certain other garden crops must be planted on February 14. St. Valentine day. Cucumbers must be planted on a dark moon and in the zodiacal twin sign. Potatoes and corn must be planted in the dark of the moon. Beans should be planted on Good Friday. Failure to observe the prescription will automatically result in a bad crop.

The signs are also significant in respect the care of stock. Hogs should be slaughtered in the dark of the moon when the sign is between the thighs and the knees. Otherwise the meat swells up. Similarly soap must be made in the dark of the moon. Planking and house building must occur in the appropriate sign, or the roofing will curl upwords. The coming weather can be predicted from a variety of sings, astral, floral, and faunal. The magical prescriptions carry their own sanctions. Failure to comply results in unfortunate consequences, even diaster, for the skeptic or forgetful one. What is of crucial significance, however, in determining the role of magic, is that magical and rationalistic agriculture were not practised disjunctively, side by side as it were, but were both articulated in a consistent body of practice. It is important to note that observance alone could not guarantee success, but transgression could assure failure. Thus, failure, despite observance, could be explained by many factors within or without the system.

With urbanization, a cash crop economy was the concurrent need for a more rational and efficient agriculture. Failures have immediate consequences and money places a premium on success. The individual must pay attention to scientific practices and not let tradition interfere with sound practice. With the general turning of the community to urban influences and the increasing differentiation which followed, people began to accept secular and rational modes of thought from the urban models along with other urban values. The decline of the church contributed to the secularizing tendency by virtue of the elimination of sacred ways of thought from the minds of most inhabitants. Reciprocally, of course, its decline was affected by the general change.

Finally, the appearance on the scene of alternate and competing systems of thought and behaviour, fostered by urban values, hastened the destruction of the older system. With this situation' all evidence goes to show that there has been a catastrophic decline in the total number of persons who believe in the magic. This is of fundamental importance, for now instead of a community of believers, a community is found in which believers and non-believers are sharply distinguished, and all the intermediate stages are discernible.

Is the magic dead now? It would be, of course, very misleading to leave the impression of complete disintegration of magic in the community. The empirical case of Stringtown covers but a limited segment of the logically possible continuum. In its earlier phase it was only relatively homogeneous; at present it is only relatively heterogeneous. But then, at present there are islands of homogeneity within the general disorganization. These result from the dual processes of: (1) persistence of older elements for a veriety of reasons, and (2) the adaptation of old elements to the new conditions—an important phase of cultural creativity. With respect to the latter, genuinely novel elements may develop in accommodation to the new cultural conditions.

The writers argue that these foci of the folk quality may be ranged in three categories: (1) the persistence of the old, (2) the conflict area, and (3) the new emergent patttern.

(1) It is not in magic alone that the older pattern has persistence-power, but rather in the whole social structure. Indeed, it is here proposed that the persistence of the earlier magic is associated with the partial-carryover of the earlier social categories into the urbanized stage. Exhaustive analysis of the area has demonstrated a division, amounting to a dual status system, between those most affected by the economic changes and those least affected.

(2) The area of conflict here concerns the element of risk or luck which attends human endeavour. Many persons are torn between their rational doubt and the traditional impulsions which they acquired in the younger days. While they may feel the need for experimental evidence, they hesitate to accept a negative result as conclusive. They seem to fear to take the risk of non-compliance. There is one further aspect of the intermediate conflict area which seems to be achieving a satisfactory solution. The planting of gardens is still more subject to the observance of signs than is the planting of cash crops. Corn, bean, and hay crops are almost entirely free from magical control.

(3) The adjustment to the rational atmosphere is, however, taking somewhat different lines. The most significant readaptation, however, is in the reduction of the importance of the sign so that it becomes only one among a number of other important elements. Here there is a basis for a new magical theory. The sign is important, but so are the rains, the condition of the soil, the season, the temperature, and so on. Besides, the final discernible mode of adaptation is a strictly individual one. Certain deviant personalities, queer in the conception of their neighbours, deliberately seek to cultivate past and exotic values, and by way of compensation for their

present unadjustment, become extraordinary repositories of the magical cult even adding to the stock of traditional magical content by bringing in ideas from other sources.

It is clear, then, that some of these magical attitudes never completely disappear. They constitute residues in the culture that are never completely eradicated as a result of urbanization.

Stringtown's case is not an isolated one. In the countries of the Indian subcontinent, wherever urbanization is penertrating, the situation there present the same picture. The observations made by Passin and Bennett are applicable in our situation where the heuristic conditions which satisfy the proposed variables may be found. These may be found in three general types of institutions: (a) in a comparison of two or more societies that come from discrete historical traditions, where differences in respect of isolation and homogeneity can be shown, (b) among two or more societies within a historical continuous culture areas, but where differentials in the historic process have brought about type-differences in the isolation-homogeneity range, as in Redfield's study; and (c) in the historic course of change in a given society, where the change has been in the direction of the mobile heterogeneous pole. Passin and Bennett's study exemplifies this latter type.

The historic course of change, as it happened in Stringtown, may be effective in such areas of our subcontinent from relative isolation and homogeneity to relative external contact and heterogeneity, as a consequence of economic change. It is also to be noted that reintegration may occur as precisely those points where some equilibrium was being achieved within the changing culture, whether as persistence or readaptation of entirely new elements. Thus, folklore has the potentiality to adapt the changing situation of a society.

Dundes makes an intimate observation of the said article of Passin and Bennett and remarks : "The problem, in part, concerns the fate of folklore when function is changed or lost. If the folklore survives, it generally fulfills a function other than that which it originally fulfilled. One reason for the persistence of folklore is that old form can be used to fit new functions. A sacred American Indian myth may be used as a bed time story, a song sung by a dissident minority group engaged in a street demonstration can serve as entertainment at a teenage hootenanny, and so on.

In the case of the southern Illinois community examined by Passin and Bennett, it is clear that the superstitions will continue to be known for sometime to come. However, knowing them is not the same as believing them, which in turn is not the same as practicing them. Some individuals may believe the superstitions to be true but may be too ashamed to practice them, others may both believe and practice. The present article provides an important contrast with most collections of superstitions in that the latter rarely give any information about belief and practice. The collector does not indicate whether the informant believes the superstition he relates or whether he practices it. Without this kind of informant contextual data, it is virtually impossible to discuss the function of a superstition in a given community, and further, it is equally difficult to see the changes in folk attitudes towards its folklore. Yet these attitudes and the historical changes in them can be equally as interesting as the folklore itself (1965, 314).

I have willfully selected an example from an American situation, the ideal place for urbanization, so that my argument that with change in society folklore does not vanish, but makes an adjustment, may be better and firmly established. Even in the USA, where urbanization occurs in the true sense of the term and the area of conflict is more wide, folklore constitutes the residues in culture that are never completely eradicated as a result of urbanization. This single example, I feel, will enable me to make my further discussion precisely short, for in our subcontinent also, specially in India, with the technological and educational development, agricultural improvement and urbanization, three dominating factors are working, (1) persistence of older elements of folklore for a variety of reasons; (2) the adaptation of old elements of folklore to the new conditions—an important phase of cultural creativity and (3) the new emergent pattern through interaction and conflict.

To elaborate these points a little further, I would first turn towards Calcutta, one of the largest cities of the world. Some rich and enlightened people started settling in Calcutta by the end of the eighteenth century when Calcutta assumed a metropolitan character. For the entertainment of this section a new pattern of song was developed named *Kabi* song which combined the sense of humour of the newly urbanized people and the attitudes of the real folks. The *Kabiwallas*, the composers and singers, became tremendously popular." *Kabi* songs were not art songs in the proper sense of the term, but some popular lyrics rendered into music. It was a very lively pattern since it was in the form of a musical duel. Such boisterous songs and music were liked by the people of the eighteenth century. Music did not lack in varieties, but there was not so much of refinement. Calcutta society was more or less the same old village society where different village patterns gathered in a concentrated form and from Calcutta one could guess what was the general mental make up of the whole country. It was the mentality of somewhat contented people who were rehabilitated in peaceful surroundings after an irksome period of insecurity and fear. The enlightenment of the modern age, however, did not yet cast its gleam on these people although worn out ideas and practices of the mediaeval ages were being given up by degrees". (Mitra, 1972, 207).

Thus, when urbanization started in Calcutta, folklore was predominantly present in her song, drama, dance, painting, sculpture and so on, sometimes in an unchanged form, which justifies my point about the persistence of older elements of folklore for a variety of reasons. But *kabisongs*, *jatras*, *panchali* songs, *kathaks*, *dhaps*, *tappas* were not the same as which emanated from the pure folk. They present examples of the adaptation of old elements of folklore to the new conditions—an important phase of cultural creativity.

Most of these songs and folk dramas gradually became obsolescent, but a number of them were modernized during the early twentieth century. "Lyrics and dramatic songs were variegated and elaborated. Several distinct forms of the city's own culture began to grow and the old unostentatious forms came to the field of theatre and other musical trades. The Gramophone Company started with utmost public support and enthusiasm. There was altogether a new awakening in musical appreciation while the catholic instinct still persisted" (Mitra, 1972, 209).

What Mitra has termed as catholic instinct, I would consider as a most normal traditional instinct, the instinct of folk music, which persists still today in the realm of our music through adaptation. Tagore himself adapted many elements of his very famous songs from folklore and that was certainly not done by this great poet because of his catholic faith in the tradition, but a deeper love for it. Of course, Mitra also admits this truth in his analysis in the concluding paragraphs of his article. A synthetic innovation certainly worked throughout the nineteenth and twentieth centuries where folk song, with its forms and tunes, influenced Calcutta music which was reflected in the songs of many artists who became immensely popular. Mitra very rightly says, "Why was it that some types of Baul, Bhatiali and so on, became popular while *jatra*, *panchali* of the older days went out of favour? It was because the universal appeal of these songs was recognized and a new value was attached to them" (1972, 210). *Kirtan*, a typical folk song about the love of Krishna and Radha could not make much headway in Calcutta even up to the Thirties of this century. But when some synthetic innovations were introduced by Krishna Chandra Dey, his *kirtan* was readily accepted by the people of Calcutta and he became very popular during the thirties and Forties, while the classical *kirtans* were forgotten.

Though the process of urbanization was started in Calcutta by the end of the eighteenth century, the picture this city still presents, is different from the large cities of Europe and America. Asitkumar Bhattacharya gives an interesting description of Calcutta in 1971 in Bengali which is translated below :

> There is no arrangement in this city of the electricity and gas for day-to-day cooking. Thus, both in morning and evening, each of the small or big rooms or the roads and streets, become miniature inferno. Although it has not been possible to construct a circular railway, the rails around the city exist like a noose. And there is no end of the laboured breathing of the old and wornout vehicles,

> whose speed is very often towards the back, but they discharge the smoke as much as to substantiate their right to become the master of Vesuvius. (1971-1377 Bengali era: 49).

It is true that Calcutta, the largest city of India and the Indian subcontinent, is the city of coexistence. This is also true about the cities of all the three countries of our subcontinent. Modernization in any of these cities has never gone up to that extent as to destroy the rural base and folk orientation from the physical and cultural spheres of the cities. A process of synthesis, innovation of the new and coexistence of the old and new traditions are going on still today. In this situation, if one says that folklore ceases to exist any longer in our cities, he will not be regarded as a sensible and rational man. The spirit of urbanization here has been to accept the old elements of our culture, traditional aspects of our society and agro-based economy of our people, along with modernization. This, of course, gives birth to a lack of coherence between various ethnic groups, their economic action, their culture, which, obviously becomes a factor in our cities and that requires a close study. Professor Nirmal Bose, in his pioneering survey of Calcutta, raises some fundamental issues and also provides clear guidelines for a major area of investigation, which may be profitably quoted below to understand this problem:

> It can be said that the diverse ethnic groups in the population of the city have come to bear the same relation to one another as castes do in India as a whole . . . Actually the superstructure that coheres the castes under the old order seems instead to be re-establishing itself in a new form . . . In Calcutta the economy is an economy of scarcity. Because there are not enough jobs to go around, everyone clings as closely as possible to the occupation with which his ethnic group is identified and relies for economic support on those who speak his language, or his co-religeonist or members of his own caste and or fellow immigrants from the village or districts from which he has come. By a backwash reliance on earlier modes of group

identification re-inforces and perpetuates differences between ethnic groups. (1965, 102).

This 'backwash reliance on earlier modes of group identification', today, is still one of the factors that acts favourably in retaining infact the folklore elements brought by members of groups from villages or small towns, or even from languages other than Bengali.

Our urban situation, as I have cited before, also helps give a new impetus to folklore. Thus, a women of a village of Bankura, West Bengal, whose husband works in Calcutta and provides her enough to live happily and gives here ornaments up to her satisfaction; but he comes to the village to meet her after a long gap. The woman laments:

> You stay in Calcutta for twelve months
> 'Here grows grass around the building'
> O, my beloved Moina bird
> I have not seen the husband like this
> Who deprives me from real pleasure
> which a wife would expect from her husband
> And instead, he gives me the ornaments
> (*Pata Nacher Gan*, B. Chakravorty, 1980, 31)

Similarly, a woman of a village of Pabna, expresses her frustration in a proverb ;

> He stays in Dhaka, brings taka (money)
> But does not see my heart which is barren (*faka*)

These are few examples of many elements of folklore which are taking shape everyday as a new emergent pattern to keep pace with urbanization and modernization. Social change, thus, does not uproot folklore, and makes it more adaptable.

When we come to the point of faithful reliance on group identification vis-a-vis folklore, it reminds us of the concept of *gemeinschaft*, meaning traditional communal grouping, and *gesellschaft*, meaning large-scale associational grouping stated by a german sociologist Ferdinand Tonnies, more than a century before. The *gemeinchaft* is a society in which most relationships are personal or traditional, and often both, as can be found among the ethnic groups of our cities. Tonnies named these two opposite types of social structure, the one *gemeinschaft*, usually translated into English simply as community, rural, or folk, is based on the natural will of human beings and people relate to one another as total personalities within a communal context. Each person is bound strongly to the community and does not pursue private interest at its expense. Social life is governed by tradition and custom, rituals and beliefs which go unchallenged. This is a natural solidarity, not deliberately willed but springing from the fundamental social character of man, the unity of those bound by the instinct of the family and common blood. People's positions, based on family and community ties, are stable and secure, although not equal. The preliterate tribe and the medieval European agricultural village would be classic examples of *gemeinschaft*. Tonnies regarded that historical process of society as a passage from the solidarity of the community, so understood, to the more varied, more superficial and less unified attachments of the civilized life. This parallels Durkheim's social organization based on mechanical solidarity.

The other, *gesellschaft*, has replaced the society of traditions with the society of contract. Thus *gemeinschaft* is shattered by the emerging urban-industrial-capitalist order. At the core of this new social structure is the rational will of human beings. The rational will is calculative and examines all practices with a view toward the *gemeinschaft*, based on customs, rituals and community, comes under rational scrutiny. In this society neither personal attachment nor traditional rights and duties are important. The relationships of men are determined by bargaining and defined in written agreements. Relatives are separated as people move about and live among strangers. Commonly accepted codes of behaviour have less force than rational or cold-blooded calculation of profit and loss. Individuals begin to pursue private interest at the expense of others and of the community's general interest; relations among people are increasingly based on calculation of private advantage. Social relations narrow in scope and become more specific and purposeful. These tendencies give rise eventually to a new form of society, the *gesellschaft*, a type approximating urban industrial society. The *gesellschaft*, flourishes in the modern metropolitan city.

Our community in the villages which depends purely on agriculture and is cut-off from the towns and cities, may be termed as *gemeinschaft*, where kinship and social relationships are personal, informal, traditional, sentimental and general. Folklore in this community is functional as well as the source of entertainment. Mostly, old elements of folklore are still persisting here, but folklore also finds a best breeding ground in this community. Among some of these societies, folklore is regarded as personal property, which stands in the way of change. Herzog gives a good example:

> There may be ostensible impediments of change, for instance, a proprietory feeling for song. On the Northwest coast of this continent (North America), on many islands of the pacific, and elsewhere, certain types of songs are individual property. That a man owns a song or songs; may add considerably to this prestige and social status. it may accompany and validate certain prerogatives. Thus it is important that the identity of the song be preserved. The owner alone may have the right to sing it, and other may share this privilege only after his permission has been granted. With a limitation on the number of performers and performances through which the song can pass, there is naturally less opportunity for change. Experience with traditional music has shown, however, that a proscription of change, for whatever reason, is no guarantee against it. Nor does the lack of special ideas militating against change necessarily make for greater fluidity (1938, n.p. 1940, 71).

We have our primitive societies. Because of their approximity to .some other culture, culture of the majority, some of the primitive people have lent many elements of their culture to the majority groups, as well as absorbed the culture of the majority in their own. This mutual adaptation process seemed to have a stronger ground in West Bengal than in Assam, Orissa, Bihar and Madhya Predesh, where the *gemeinschaft* or the primitive groups, have retained their identity more or less intact. The Lodhas and Saveras, who were isolated from the main groups of Bihar and Orissa and settled in the region of south-western border of West Bengal, have contributed to, as much as they have adapted from, Bengali folk culture of that area, and thus was formulated there a regional culture of West Bengal. Both of these groups of the tribal community are mainly dependent on agriculture and they lack in many respects the plurality of culture. Even then, the Patua songs as well as folk dramas with pictures, present a very healthy tradition. The singers and the actors are known as *Patuas*. It seems that the tradition of drawing pictures and presenting them with songs or play acting has come from these two tribes the Lodhas and Saveras, whose major population is still living in Orissa and has retained this practice among them; but the contents, which they usually narrated and pictured before coming in contact with the Hindus, have gone completely into obsolescence. Now the contents and themes, both in Orissa and West Bengal, are being taken from *Mahabharata*, *Ramayana* or some motifs of the folk tales of the Indic classics. The songs are of two types, *padabandia* and *arthabandi*, the first is in simpler form and does not require to be explained to the audience, the latter has a deeper meaning and is shrouded in a jugglery of words. This requires an explanation from the *gayak*, a singer, who must possess an oratory power and knowledge. The first type is accompanied by a *drum* and the second type by a *mrudanga* which is adopted from *palawallas*. There are six or seven members including *gayak* and *bayak* (one who plays on the *mrudanga*) in a *Patua jatra* or folk drama. There is one *rautani*, a male member who puts on the dress and ornaments of a female borrowed from women of rich family. He breaks the monotony of the *jatra* with occasional dances.

It is interesting that four best forms of arts have been combined in Patua drama, the painting, the music, the drama or acting and the dancing. The story is dramatic and poetical. We may apply here R.G. Moulton's remark about classical drama . . . "a story of poetical conception, is at one and the same time versified, chanted and conveyed in gesture" (1890, 4).

Both Patua songs and Patua dramas are examples of folklore which sustains the cultural interaction and opens an important phase of cultural creativity. The process of adaptation of old elements to the new condition has been pursued by both sides, the Hindu community on the one hand, and the Lodhas and Saveras on the other. In this case, as in many others, social change has not been an impediment for folklore to be adapted into a new social situation, rather it tended to be very helpful to formulate a new synthetic pattern. It is further gratifying that the people of towns and cities have developed a likeness for Patua pictures which is proved to be of great financial help to this community of folk artists. Urbanization and modernization, in a way, have appeared in case of Patuas not as a curse but as blessings.

While *gemeinschaft* is still a reality in the Indian sub-continent, its gesture to adjust with *gesellschaft*, the other end, has been effectively started since the second great war. The societies of our metropolitan cities are not truly *gesellschaft*, or we may say that the *gesellschaft* has not yet been able to flourish successfully in the modern metropolitan cities of this subcontinent. In spite of full-scale urbanization and modernization in some areas of our cities, the alienation process of the individuals as conceived of in the concept of *gesellschaft*, is not found to be in practice even in those areas. Even if it happens to be so in future, as could be found in some American cities, folklore has nothing to fear. It will sustain any amount of social change and emerge as folklore of the changed society, folklore of the true *gesellschaft*.

The fear concerning the future of folklore, which is looming large over the mind of many scholars, is not a healthy sign. It is evident that even in highly industrial society, the migrants prefer to retain their tradition brought from the homeland. A.C. Mahr (1945: 1-32) has enlightened us with such a fascinating information about the Pennsylvania Dutch community migrated from Europe:

The Pennsylvania Dutch are quite unique in this country, in that they have tenaciously clung to a great many of the peasant tradition which the ancestors had brought with them from the Old Country. Again and again they migrated in larger and smaller groups from the same parts, mostly the upper Rhine, the Rhenish Palatinate (*Rheinfalz*) and Switzerland, but also from other West and South German states. They are further unique in that they maintained their communal form of life in the new world, both to their own benefit and that of William Penn and his Quaker associates. The greater number of these so-called 'Palatines' (*Pfalzer*) landed, mostly in the harbour of Philadelphia, between 1710 and 1775 (cf. R.B. Strassburger, 1934).

This adherence of the Pennsylvania Dutch, for more than two centuries to the native peasant customs of their German forefathers can only be explained by the fact that they did not lose their original group consciousness after they had settled in America. Instead of being readily absorbed by the new environment, as were the countless individual settlers from other German, and non-German peasant communities in Europe, the Pennsylvania Dutch possessed in the peasant traditions of their old homeland a cultural force that was sufficiently strong to shape their new environment into a peasant community of distinctive character (1945:5).

The migrants from the East Pakistan (now Bangladesh) who have settled in the outskirts of Calcutta, have, similarly, retained the pattern of housing, some names of the places they have left and some other aspects of their culture as the memory of their motherland.

The adaptability of folklore, like culture, is substantially great. Like the old god, it never dies, but changes to suit the new situation.

Folklore not only changes because of social change; but because of travel and transmission as well. In this, Von Sydow's concept of active and passive bearers, deserves consideration. He holds that the active bearers are those who narrate the tale or sing the song or ballad, while the passive bearers are those who listen or observe. Folklore migrates from one place to another through these active bearer—it does not move in a massive way. Besides, when an active bearer migrates, if there remains no other active bearer in that place from where he migrates, the particular tales may gradually go into obsolescence. Sydow also believes that since the folk, are governed by some laws, so there were also laws governing the transmission of folklore forms. We, of course, do not agree with Sydow, because in the Indian situation folklore is transmitted not only by the active bearers, but also by those who are listeners. Besides, there are, of course, active narrators of tales, singers of songs, actors of drama, but those who listen and observe, they are not completely passive, specially in the case of songs, the listeners are almost as active as the main singers. Then again, when an element of folklore migrates, it does not leave behind vaccuum, many persons remain there to relate them to others in that particular locality.

But there is certain truth in what Sydow says:

> In speaking of mutations I have confined myself to the more sweeping changes resulting from intentional remodelling. A good many changes are, however, brought about in a different way. Every receiver of a tale tradition will always make a few alterations in some motifs partly on account of failing memory, partly in order to make the story conform better to his own view and tastes, or to kindered motifs in such other tales as he may know.. All these questions about hearers of tale tradition, of the cases in which a tradition is applied and can be transmitted, the changes that may be brought about by various kinds of mutation, and by oiko typification, are naturally of the greatest weight for a scientific study of folktale, and the results of such study cannot, even by the best of methods, be correct unless they are based on a right knowledge of the life of the folktale and the laws by which it is governed (1948, 105-107).

Change is within the body and spirit of folklore. Not to speak of its compatibility to fit in with social change or the changed conditions of a society or with the new society where it is transmitted or migrated, it has to adjust with the change caused by individual narrator or the active or non-active bearer and nourish itself for existence. When a particular element of folklore becomes different from person to person in the same group, community or society, it does not forgo the right of its existence. Rather it derives strength and a vitality of regeneration through its variants. Mutilation of the elements of folklore by the folk does not cause them death, rather it invigorates them to a new lease of life. This being so, those who are afraid of folklore's bleak future because of urbanization, industrialization and modernization; are perhaps not truly aware of its vital dynamism and love for life. Folklore is the creation of the human mind—society is also the creation of the human being—so there cannot be any ill-feeling between the two that one would change and the other would remain static.

Folklore of the industrial belts of Europe and America has been thoroughly studied by some scholars and through them we have been enlightened about the condition of folklore prevalent in those areas. All of them have, mostly after an on the spot study, opined that with the industrial and technological advancement, folklore finds a new way of expression and exists in a new order. Thus the term industrial lore has been invented and a systematic study of these has received a new impetus. Here also we find three major processes, the persistence of old elements, the adaptation of old elements to the new conditions, and the new emergent pattern through interaction and enormous mobility of the people.

The old occupational structure in Orissa and South Bihar was shaken with the implementation of irrigation schemes, multi-purpose river valley projects (Hirakund Dam in Western Orissa, the hydro-electric power project of Muchhkund Dam and Balimela Dam in southern Orissa), establishment of heavy industries in Jamshedpur, Bokara in Bihar, in Rourkela in northern Orissa, development of an industrial belt near Cuttack in Orissa and Ranchi in Bihar, and the coal-mining in Bihar. These industrial and development projects brought the technological advancement along with modernization to the doorsteps of the tribes such as Kond, Santal, Hill Saora, Gadaba, Bhuiyan, Juang, Bondo, Binjhwar, Koya, Gond, Oraon, Munda, Lodha, Savera, and so on. Naturally their social structure has been affected, though a huge majority of these people are still dependent on agriculture, many of them have got employment in these industries or other projects. People are gradually coming forward to accept education and technical know-how. The process of social change among the tribes has been in practice during the last phase of the British rule, specially initiated by the missionaries, but this has been accelerated in a more systematic order since independence. This has influenced their folklore. Let me cite an example from a Mundari song:

Original

Megha comes and goes
To come again,
We know then
It will come again,
But O my friend
Where have you gone away,
The phalsa tree stands
Dressed up in flowers
Mahul has thrown up new soft leaves,
Rightly megha will come again
But where did you go away
My dear, dear friend.

The new variant

Megha has come like the deep smoke of chimneys,
Megha goes to come again
But not the smoke,
We know then
Megha will come again,
But smoke will not go
It stands between you and me,
When you go to Jamshedpur
It takes you from me,
Megha does not,
Where have you gone my friend

The phalsa tree stands
Dressed up in flowers,
When you are in the smoke of engine's fire
Mahul has left the leaves,
As you have left me,
I am also shrouded by smoke,
Will the megha come again

And remove the smoke of our life?
Jamshedpur I love, it gives me money,
Jamshedpur I hate, it brings me smoke.
(*Collected by a teacher of Bengali, Ranchi College*).

A riddle of Bangladesh, original

Her four sons are khatur khutur
(*making sound by woodlike hard thing*)
Her four sons are sweet like honey
Her two sons are dry wood
Her one son is mad like Siva.

The meaning is cow. First four sons are legs having hoops below, which makes sound while the cow walks. The next four sons are the milking teats of the cow. The two sons are the horns, and the one is the tail that always drives madly the flies away.

A variant from Dhaka

Her four sons are the types of the car
Her two sons are torch light
That burns at night
Her four sons are hanging, but lick when you press
Her one son does not allow anybody to come
(*both the riddles are collected by me in Bengali*)

In this riddle, the horns have been omitted, but two eyes have been added. Obviously, it reflects the modern situation, as it has the references of car and torch light.

Load-shedding has become a perennial problem lasting throughout the year in West Bengal and Bihar causing a set-back to industry and serious discomfort to the people. Hundreds of songs, proverbs and humorous anecdotes have been created and spread among various sections of people of these two states. Since the Hon'ble Chief Minister's name in West Bengal is Sri Jyoti Basu and *Jyoti* means light in Bengali, a proverb *Jyoti elo Alo galo* meaning 'jyoti', the light, has come and the light has gone, has become a very off-quoted proverb even among the educated sections of West Bengal. There are many small booklets in Bengali on load-shedding sold in the trains, bazars and *melas* by the village bards. Thus, a new theme of folklore about modern technology and its failure, has been in vogue because of a changed social condition, which could not have been even dreamed of two decades ago.

With the change of social structure a significant change in some of the ceremonies in Bangladesh has taken place. The serpent worship and boat race, the coincidence of the two, has helped both the ceremonies merge into a single ceremony in the Sylhet area of Bangladesh, specially after the migration of a huge Hindu population from those places after 1947. Bhattacharya writes: "The special feature of the serpent-worship in this part of the State (Sylhet) is the rice-paste drawings (alpana). The entire venue of worship is decorated with these drawings representing serpents. Around this serpent drawing other drawings illustrating the chief incidents of the legend of Chand or the principal serpent story are also made. Coloured powders are used in such drawings. The entire floor of the room appears to be a picture gallery. From the first day of the Bengali month of *Sravana* until the day of the worship, the legend of Chand is sung in part after nightfall before the assembly of villagers. The immersion ceremony of the deity takes place on the day following the day of her annual worship. This occasion is marked by a special national festivity, namely the boat race. It is very difficult to say how the boat race has come to be associated with the immersion ceremony. It may be that these two distinct festivals have by chance coincided together". (1977:161). In Sylhet and other adjoining districts of Bangladesh, the boat race is an annual festival held during the Bengali month Sravana. Because of coincidence, both have merged into the annual serpent worship adding to it additional force. But after the heavy migration of people, these areas have become predominantly. Muslim-populated localities, and as a consequence, the Monosha Puja or Worship of the Serpent-goddess Monosha is hardly held now. But the boat race ceremony is still observed during the rainy season and it is interesting that most of the boats are decorated with the paintings of serpents—some might even have the dual paintings, the face is that of goddess Monosha, the tail is of a snake. The social change has changed the structure of the festival. The major change has also been effective in the content of the songs sung by the oarsmen at the time of the boat race. Previously, mostly Radha, Krishna, Nimai were the main figures in the theme of the songs all over Bangladesh. Now the subject-matter has been modernized to a great extent and along with Radha, Krishna and Chaitanya, have come Ali, Hassan, Hussain, Jainab (wife of Hassan), Jainal, Hanifa, Yazid, and so on. The boat race songs are known as *Sari* songs. I cite two examples from my recent collections from Bangladesh: (giving only translation):

1. O my sweet confidante
   Do not wave the water
   Let me look on and see
     the image of the black
   With my eyes fully enamoured

This indicates Radha's dedicated love for Krishna.

2. Jainal weeps and says
   Only Allah is above my head.

Jainal, as depicted in the popular Karbala theme, was the only member of Hussain's family who was not killed but was kept in the prison of Yazid.

Even myths take a new shape and meaning in the context of social change. Let me cite an example from Japan's present technologically developed society and the myths.

> Mt. Keito is a steep peak in front of Mt. Hayachine. The people in the village at the peak refer to it as Mae-Yakushi. In fear of the *tengu* or long-nosed goblins, that live there, even those who climb Mt. Hayachine do not climb Mt. Keito. The master of the Haneto household in Yamagachi, was an intimate friend of Mr. Sasaki's grandfather. He was an eccentric fellow, who in his youth would do such things as cut grass with an axe or turn up the ground with his sickle. He was known also for his rowdy behaviour. One day he made a bet and climbed Mae-Yakushi all alone. Upon returning he told the story of how there

was a huge rock on the top of the mountain and three gaint men were on it. In front of them there were piles of gold and silver. Seeing him approaching they glared frightfully at him. When he said that he had lost his way while climbing Mt. Hayachine, one huge man replied, "If so, we should see you off," and they led him down to a spot near the foot of the mountain. They told him to shut his eyes and after a bit, the Ijin suddenly disappeared.

Another goes like this: A man from Oguni village went to gather same bamboo on Mt. Hayachine one day. Amidst the thick short bamboo plant he found a large man sleeping all alone. The man had taken off his meter-long bamboo sandals and was lying on his back snoring loudly.

(*Both the legends taken from Yanagita, 1975, 29-30*)

Who is this Ijin? It could have several meanings seventy-five years ago when Yanagita collected the myths from his single informer Sasaki, a great story-teller. But now the people of the same locality that Sasaki has come from, would no longer consider Ijin as *tono* who has the *kami* to guard home, hearth and privy, as goblin creatures like Kappa and Tengu, as rich men or *Choja* who encounter fortune and misfortune, as evil foxes with powers of transformation, as spirit of the dead and of the mountains, who blend with the *kami*, or as warriors and fools who make magic, but simply as foreigners or a man from other land. Since World War II, after the greatest human tragedy at Hiroshima, inflicted upon the people by men coming from a faraway country, the old animistic folk beliefs about the mysterious strangers encountered beyond the village boundary, have turned, in some cases, and instead signify the man from other land beyond Japan.

Towards the end of 1961 several distinguished scholars, headed by Bikram K. Roy Burman, undertook experiments in various types of social study to go into great depth over specific problems of social change. In one of the monographs, the final draft of which was prepared by Roy Burman himself, an interesting aspect of cultural assimilation has been revealed. This is regarding the observance of *Muharram* not only by the Shia and Sunni communities of the Muslims of two cities, Delhi and Lucknow, but also by some Hindus of these two cities. At Pahari Dhiraj area of Delhi, a Hindu cloth merchant every year participated in the ceremony. "In a Shia procession in Delhi the drummers were found to be Sunni Muslims. Similarly, in a Sunni Akhara some Hindu participants were noticed. In Lucknow Hindu Taziadars hand over their tazias to the Muslims and the latter take the same to the Karbala for burial. Also Hindus attend Majlises and Matams in the Houses of the Shias. In some folksongs of the Hindu Harijan Castes, Husain has been equated with Krishna. This indicates the great impress of Moharram on their minds." (Roy Burman, 1961, 13).

In Bangladesh, on the contrary, many folksongs have compared Hasan and Hosain with Rama and Lakshmana. Since Hasan and Husain had to leave Medina, the event as prevalent in the folk tradition of Bangladesh, the comparison found its relevance with the similar event of Rama and Lakshmana, who had to leave Ayodhya and this striking similarity aroused the inspiration of the Muslim folkbards to sing the song of Karbala in the pattern of *Ramayana*.

The cultural assimilation is possible only when the attitude of the society as a whole is receptive. The two examples cited, one about Moharram and the other about the Karbala songs of Bangladesh, bear clear evidence of social attitude, which is the result of a change.

The tribal folklore, as mentioned before, behave in the same way when it confronts a social change. India is a village-oriented country and so the subcontinent. Tribal population in this country is also not negligible. L.P. Vidyarathi says:

> Of the 357 million total population of India, only 17 per cent live in the 3,018 cities and towns while the remaining 83 per cent live in the 5,58,089 villages (*1951 census report*, Vol. I). A part of village India which consists of about 25 million population has been classified as tribes. This tribal population is mostly concentrated in the hilly, forested and inhospitable areas of north-eastern, middle and southern India. These tribesmen, though in various level of economic gradings, are in general economically very backward, educationally almost illiterate, and socially almost cut off from the rest of Indian society.

> Of such a tribal population, the highest concentration is found in the state of Bihar (Chota Nagpur and Santal Parganas) which has been a great exciting laboratory for ethnographers, linguists and prehistorians. With 45 large and small tribes, numbering about five million people of different economic, linguistic, racial and cultural levels, Bihar is one of the most interesting states in India for anthropological researches. (1964, 232).

Of all the tribes in Bihar, Birhor is a nomadic tribe that wanders from jungle to jungle in quest of food. Professor Vidyarthi made an extensive study of the tribe "regarding the extent of migration and attempted to trace the names of places that the nine migratory groups had visited, and recorded the distance and duration of stay at each place during the last 25 years. The two migratory groups clearly indicate how the frequency in nomadic behaviour among the Birhor is showing down. A section of the Birhor has already passed this stage and today is leading a sedentary social life under the name of Jaghi Birhor. ..In recent times, the frequency in wanderings of the Birhor has gone down. Most of the wandering groups now cover little distance, varying from four to sixteen miles. Comparative statistics show that the distance formerly covered by them was much more than the present ones" (1964, 239, 241, 242).

From migratory to non-migratory habit has caused some major social change among the Birhor. I visited a small village of this tribe near Bishenpur in February 1983, which has been constructed by the government. The condition is hopelessly terrible. Hardly have they been able to adjust with this situation. While I went there at about noon, none of the male members were present, they had gone to collect materials from the forest to make rope, which forms the major source of their income. Still now they seem to be completely disinterested in agriculture. However, this transition from one stage to another, has caused social change which has been reflected in their folklore. I met an old man who told me that they have now a new pattern of folk-song sung by women-folk. Before settlement, both men and women used to wander together in the forest and they did not have to bear any pang of separation. Now that the women remain at home and the males go deep into the forest for the whole day, they feel lonely. This regular and constant loneliness has given birth to a new type of song, which cannot be named, but they call it, as the old man informed, "the woman's song". One, which he sung, goes like this: (here is the English translation only):

> O my man
> Why do you go leaving me alone
> Take me with you in the forest
> I love forest, the trees, the birds, the flowers
> I love you too
> This home is not a better place for me,
> Where no flower, no bird speak to me
> Where you are absent.

So far as change is concerned, Vidyarthi's observations about the tribes of Bihar are more or less true about the tribes of India as well as Bangladesh and Pakistan. He says, "One notes that tribal Bihar has been passing through a phase of transformation. The traditional process, in the past, was originally responsible for initiating change in the tribal societies which was further accelerated with the modern processes. If the first process brought the 'Hindu model' before the adivasi, the modern process, by and large, put up before the adivasi, the western-urban-industrial-democratic model for inducing transformation. With the operation of these factors of change the culture of tribal Bihar is in flux and cultural heterogeneity is reflected in all aspects of their life—tribal, village and individual. Taken as a whole, the cultural heterogeneity and tradition-ridden stagnation have been broken. Now, in addition to isolated communities we note numerous tribal communities which have been affected by change. These are, for example, Christian tribal urban and/or industrial tribal communities. There are again, the groups of adivasi elites of national, regional and local leaders of professional and of those who are in white-collar jobs.

This pattern of change may be looked at from many angles. When we idealise the traditional adivasi culture, we record numerous traits of the adivasi style of life, simplicity, homogeneity, honesty, co-operation, group identification, optimism, and so on. When we note that these values of tribal life are fast replaced by heterogeneity, individualization, secularization competition, money, economy, hypocrisy, and so on, one feels emotionally disturbed and terms this pattern of change negatively as de-tribalisation. We have similar words as de-sanskritisation in Indian social sciences to plot out the change from the brahminical style of life to the more secular and western style of life. Some may look to the transformation from another angle and may emphasize the role of technology and other external forces in winning over their poverty and miseries and may term it as revitalization process. Terms like acculturation, assimilation or integration may also be used to indicate the pattern of change, operating in tribal Bihar, if viewed from the different angles.

Tribal Bihar, as other parts of India, is passing through the accelerated phase of transformation. Taken as a whole the tribal society has been disorganized and the old arrangements have been disturbed. Whether the changes would lead to the final disintegration of the tribal society or will lead to the ultimate reorganisation is to be watched. As the situation exists today, the phase of transition is painful." (1964:286-287).

In Bangladesh out of the total population of little over 90 million, about one million would be tribes. The largest of them have been concentrated in the Chittagong Hill Tracts who are known as Chakma, Magh, Mru, Murang, Lushai, Kuki, Bam, Tipra and so on. The Maghs have been settled partially in Cox's Bazar of Chittagong district and in Khepupara of Patuakhali districts. Along the hilly areas of Sylhet, specially at the foot of Khasi-Jaintia hills, the settlements of Khasis, Pangons and Manipuris could be seen. The Garos, Hajongs, Hodis, Daluis, Palias and Bunas are settled at Haluaghat, Sreebordi, Kalmakanda in the locality of Garo Hill of Mymensing district. The Santals, Oraons, Mundas, and Rajbansis are scattered over the areas of northern districts of Bangladesh—specially in Rajshahi, Rangpur, Bogra and Dinajpur.

Although the culture of these people is not yielding to changes, already the process of transformation has started.

Education is making dents in their society. In their treatment of diseases formerly they used to rely on herbs and potions, mantras and bratas. Now-a-days they are found to take recourse to scientific medicine. Wherever there is education, these changes are visible. The older uneducated people are still clinging to their antequarian system and are afraid of modern medicine as a medium on which evil spirit may settle. (Sattar, 1975:6).

The social change has been duly reflected in the folklore of the tribal people of Bangladesh. This can be noticed if we compare their folklore of the olden times with the current folklore with origin in the recent past. I would cite two songs of the Chakmas, which is called *Uba Geet* (love song):

You clanked the bracelet of my ear
Forget I will never, you came to this heart
I did not know when you came to my door-step
I could not feel when you drew me
I was alone with my sleepy dreams
Your bracelet clanked what I knew not
Does it say something?
Is that your love to me?

(*Sattar 1975, 221*)

In this love song, a clear expression of feeling, which is sincere, simple and pointed, strikes us in an impressive manner. When sung, it appears to be more appealing. But the songs composed by later generations of poets lack in sincerity though their literary value may excell the former ones. Here is one:

The highland lass goes to the jhum
With basket on her back
With pick-axe in her hand
She goes to the jhum
She looks back as she goes
The sight of mustard flowers feeds her heart,
She treads as if dancing in jolity
And she goes to the jhum
Breeze blows in the paddy part of the jhum
Little birds eat paddy sitting on the tree-cuts

The highland lass chases the birds with her bamboo-spear,
She sings songs from the shade of the watch-shed
And returns home at dusk
The highland lass goes to the jhum

(*Sattar, 1975, 226*).

With the change of society all over the world, the significance of myths has received a new interpretation. The anthropologists, sociologists and folklorists of recent time tend to interpret myths mainly into two categories, the scientific myths and social myths. Various views regarding myths have made the notion of myths a complex one and thus it is opened to a variety of interpretations. It is generally accepted that the myths provide the means by which communication between individuals in society is facilitated. It is also accepted that it is a basis by which man can come to terms with the unknown (Maranda, 1972, 12). It can also be argued that myths not only reflect the reality but mostly they represent reality. Besides, "in every case where we could see no more than association of thought, the mythopoetic mind finds a causal connection. Every resemblance, every contact on space or time, establishes a connection between two objects or events which make it possible to see in the one cause of changes observed in the other". (Frankfort, 1949, 27). Myths, according to Frankfort, reflect, in way, the prior conceptualisations of the community from which they arise. Toulmin's view is, of course, different. He holds that the contemporary myths stem not from anthropomorphic interpretations of the natural world, but from science. He is in favour of using scientific conception to provide a tidy, simple and specially an all-purpose picture of the world (1973, 68).

Thus, the myths under scientific category can be used to legitimise a broad range of prior value orientations. Barnet, for example, when discussing recent trends in ethnology, suggests that much popular writing in the field subscribes to just this kinds of scientific myth-making. According to him, the most scientific myths are "based on illegitimate inferences based upon the supposed behaviour of animals, or about animals based on the actual behaviour of man" (1973: 68). However, as Toulmin points out, it is just because contemporary myths are scientific in origin that they are rarely identified as being myths at all (1957, 16).

Societies are changing and so are the myths, the meaning of the myths. Perhaps only certain kinds of conceptions are open to the myth-making process. For example, it is difficult to suggest that industrialisation or bureaucratisation are myths. Social scientists have many criteria by which to judge whether or not a society falls into either category. These demarcation criteria are clear, and they are also public.

On the other hand, the social myths are built up with concepts whose demarcation criteria are not explicit. So far as the modern interpretation of myths is concerned. Tipps observes that:

> The popularity of the notion of modernisation must be sought not in its clarity and precision as a vehicle of scholarly communication, but rather in its ability to evoke vague and generalised images which serve to summarise all the various transformations of social life attendant upon the rise of industrialisation and the nation state in the late eighteenth and nineteenth centuries. (197, 199).

Since social attitudes have become more secular, the myths have also been secularised, which means the understanding of myths involves an understanding of the concept of religion. Theories of secularisation are, of course, typically used to legitimate myths about the decline in moral standards in contemporary society. By doing so they tend to become divorced from their original co-ordinates of space and time and hence appear to justify notions for which they had little or no relevance at the outset. They are used to deal with questions of purely normative kind. It is this aspect that provides the clearest indicator of the presence of social myths in general including modernization, and of the secularisation myth in particular. Secularization is used as an all-purpose explanation for many of the supposed ills of contemporary society. Some invisible religions (Luckman, 1967) are gradually cropping up to replace the old religions, the church-oriented ones, in the industrial societies and the place of myth in such societies deserves to be judged in the light of the physical and mental transformation of society concerned.

The analysis of folklore *vis-a-vis* society, thus, reveals many truths which the folklorists and the sociologists can certainly use in their respective discipline with fruitful results. Folklore is both benefactor and beneficiary—it is an active agent of social change, as well as an enthusiastic and lively receptor of the changes taking place in the society. This dual existence and many-faced role of folklore are its real strength, it is a dynamic force of culture.

REFERENCES

Apodaca, Anadeto 1952 "Corn and custom: The introduction of hybrid corn to Spanish American Farmers in New Mexico", in H. Edward Spicer (ed.), *Human Problems in Technological Change*, Russel Sage Foundation, 35-39, New York.

Banerjee, Subhash 1969 *Paschim Simanta Banglar Lok Sahitya*, Sahitya Prakash, Calcutta.

Barnes, C A 1952 "A Statistical study of the Freudian theory of levels of psychosexual development," *Genetic Psychology Monographs*, 45, 105-174.

Barnes, Harry Elmer 1948 *An Introduction to the History of Sociology*, The University of Chicago Press, Chicago.

Barnett, S A 1937 Biological Myths, *New Society*, 12 April.

Barth, Alan 1961 Report on the Rampageous Right, *Time Magazine*, Nov. 26, pp. 25 ff, New York.

Basu, Krishna 1962 *The Bengal Peasant from Time to Time*, New York.

Bhattacharya, Hangsanarayan 1977 *Hinduder Debdevi*, Part I. Farma K.L.M. Pvt. Ltd, Calcutta.

Bhattacharya, Upendranath 1364 Bengali Era (1957) *Banglar Baul O Baul Gan*, Calcutta.

Bhattacharya, Ashutosh 1977 *The Sun and the Serpent Lore of Bengal*, Farma K.L.M. Private Limited, Calcutta.

Bhowmick, Nirmalendu 1979 *Bangla Chhadar Bhumika*, Sahityasri, Calcutta.

Bhowmick, P K 1978 *Occultism in Fringe Bengal*, Subarnarekha, Calcutta.

Bose, Nirmal Kumar 1965 "Calcutta, A Premature Metropolis" *Scientific American*, 213, No. 3.

Bunzel, Ruth L 1929-30 "Zuni Katchinas", *47th Annual Report of American Ethnology*, 1932, pp. 843-44, Washington.

——————— 1933 *Zuni Texts*, American Ethnological Society Publication, Vol. XV, New York.

Chakravorty, Barun 1980 *Loka Sanskriti*, Book Trust, Calcutta.

Cohen, Percy S 1966 "Models," *British Journal of Sociology*, Vol. XVIII, March 1, 1966, pp. 70-78.

——————— 1968 *Modern Social Theory*, ELBS edition, First ELBS and Heineman Educational Books Published in 1979.

Coser, Lewis 1967 *Continuities in the Study of Social Conflict*, Free Press, New York.

Dahrendorf, Ralf 1962 *Gesellschatt und Freiheit*, Piper, Munchen.

——————— 1959 *Class and Class Conflict in Industrial Society*, Stanford University Press, Stanford, Cal.

Das, Kunjabehari 1953 *A Study of Orissan Folklore*, Vishva-Bharati Publishing Department, Santiniketan.

Dasgupta, Shashi Bhusan 1962 *Obscure Religious Cult*, Calcutta.

Davies, James C 1962 (February) "Toward a theory of revolution," *American Sociological Review*, 27.

Dundes, Alan (ed) 1965 *The Study of Folklore*, Prentice-Hall, Inc. Englewood cliff, N.J.

Durkheim, Emile 1933 *The Division of Labour in Society* (4 Vols.) (Trans.) George Simpson, Crowell-Coilier and Macmillan, New York.

——————— 1947 *The Elementary forms of the Religious Life*, Glencoe.

Elwin, Harry Verrier 1939 *The Baiga*, John Murray, London.

——————— 1950 *Bondo Highlander*, Oxford University Press, Bombay.

——————— 1954 *Tribal Myths of Orissa*, Oxford University Press, London.

Firth, Raymond 1939 *Primitive Polinesian Economy*, Routledge, London.

——————— 1955 "The Theory of Cargo Cults: A Note on Tikopia *Man*. 55, 130-132.

Fliegel, Frederick C and Joseph E Kivlin 1966 "Attributes of innovation as factors in diffusion," *American Journal of Sociology*, 72, 235-248, (November).

Frankfort, H 1949 *Before Philosophy: The Intellectual Adventure of Ancient Man*, Penguin, Harmondsworth.

Freedman, Ronald 1952 *Principles of Sociology*, Henry Holt and Company, New York.

Fortes, M 1953 "The Structure of unilineal descent groups," *American Anthropologist*, 55.

Geertz, Clifford 1975 *The Interpretation of Culture*, Hutchinson and Co. Ltd. (Basic Books Inc., 1973), London.

Giddens, A 1972 "Four myths in the history of social thought," *Economy and Society*, 1(4), 351-85.

Glock, C Y and Stark, R 1965 *Religion and Society in Tension*, Rand Mc Nally, Chicago.

Gough, Kathleen 1977 "Agrarian change in Thanjavur," in *Society and Change*, (ed) K S Krishnaswamy, Ashok Mitra, I G Patel, K N Raj, and M N Srinivas, *Essays in Honour of Sachin Chaudhury*, Oxford University Press, Bombay.

Harrison, S 1956 "The challenge to Indian nationalism," *Foreign Affairs*, 34 (April), 3 For details Harrisons', *India The Most Dangerous Decades*, Princeton, N.J. 1960.

Herskovits, M J *at el* 1933 "An outline of dahomean religious beliefs" *Memoirs of the American Anthropological Association*, No. 41.

Herzog, George 1940 "Stability of form in traditional and cultivated music," *The Journal of the American Musicological Society*, December, 1938.

Hobhouse, L T 1924 *Social Development*, London.

Holyoake, G J 1896 *The Origin and Nature of Secularism*, London.

Islam, Mazharul 1974 *Folklore Parichiti Ebong Loksahityer Pothon Pathon*, First edition published by Bangla Academy, Dacca, in 1974. Third enlarged and revised edition is in a Calcutta Press.

———————— 1970 *Lok Kahani Songroher Itihash*, Students Ways, Dacca.

———————— 1982 *A History of Folktale Collections in India, Bangladesh Pakistan*, Second enlarged edition, Panchali Prokasan, Calcutta First edition published by Bangla Academy, Dacca, in 1970.

———————— 1982 *Folklore Charchya Ruptattik Bisslation Padhdhati*, Lok Laukik Prakasani, Calcutta.

———————— 1983 *Paschim Banglay Folklore Charcha*, Jiggasa, Calcutta.

Jackson, J and Jobling R 1968 "Towards an analysis of contemparory cults" in D A Martin (ed.) *A Sociological Yearbook of Religion in Britain*, Vol. I, SCM Press, London.

Johnson, H M 1961 *Sociology: A Systemetic Introduction*, Routledge and Kegan Paul, London.

Kluckhahn, C 1944 *Navaho Witchcraft*, Peabody Museum Papers, No. 22, Cambridge, Mass.

Krech, D (ed) 1962 *Individual in Society*, McGrow-Hill, New York.

Leach, E R 1954 *Political Systems of Highland Burma*, Cambridge, Mass.

Levi-Strauss, C 1963 *Structural Anthropology*, Basic Books, New York.

Lewis, Oscar 1951 *Life in A Maxican Village: Tepoztlan Restudied*, Urbana University of Illinois Press.

Linton, Ralph 1936 *The Study of Man*, Appleton—Century-Crafts, New York.

Lowie, Robert H 1937 *The History of Ethnological Theory*, Farrar and Rinehart, New York.

Luckman, T 1967 *The Invisible Religion: The Problem of Religion and Modern Society*, Macmillan, New York.

Maciver, R M and Page, Charles H 1957 *Society*, Rinehart and Company, Inc. New York.

Mahr, August C 1945 "Origin and significance of Pennsylvania dutch barn symbols," *The Ohio Archaeological and Historical Quarterly*, Vol. 54.

Majumdar, Ramesh Chandra 1356 Bengali Era (1949) *Bangladesher Itihash* (written in Bengali, *the History of Bengal*), General Printers and Publishers Limited (2nd edition) Calcutta.

———————— 1942, *History of Bengal* (Vol. I) Dacca University Publication, Dacca.

Malinowski, B 1948 *Magic, Science and Religion*, Boston.

Mallick, Pramathanath 1328 Bengali Era (1921) *Kalkatar Katha*, Subarna Banik Samachar, Quoted, Prabashi, Aswin, 1328.

Marx, Karl 1962 *The Communist Blueprint for the Future: The Complete*

Text of All Four Communist Manifestos 1848—1961, E.P. Dutton and Co., New York.

Maranda, P (ed) 1972 *Mythology*, Penguin, Harmondsworth.

Mayer, Albert J and Thomas Ford Hoult 1955 "Social stratification and compat survival," *Social Forus*, 34: 156-59.

Meed, Margaret 1937 *Co-operation and Conflict Among Primitive Peoples*, McGraw Hill Book Company, New York.

Merton, R 1949 *Social Theory and Structure*, Glencoe, Ill.

Mitra, Rajyeswar 1972 "Co-existence of many musical traditions and the community of musicians in Calcutta," in *Cultural Profile of Calcutta*, ed. by Surajit Sinha, The Indian Anthropological Society, Calcutta.

Morgenthau, Hans J 1963 *Politics Among Nations*, 3rd edition, London.

Moulton, R G 1890 *The Ancient Classical Drama*, Oxford.

Mukherjee, Harekrishna 1323 Bengali Era (1916) *Gramya Gatha O Probochon Prosongo*, Bharat-Barsa, Magh. 243-46.

Murdock, George Peter 1949 *Social Structure*, The Macmillan Company, New York.

Natanson, M (ed.) 1963 *Philosophy of the Social Sciences, A Reader*, Random House, New York.

Nisbet, R 1970 *The Social Bond: An Introduction to the Study of Society*, Alfred Kopf, New York.

Norbeck, E 1970 *Religion and Society in Modern Japan: Continuity and Change*, Tourmaline Press, Houston.

Ogburn, William F 1927 *Social Change*, Viking Press, New York.

Olson, Mancur Jr 1963 "Rapid economic growth as a destabilizing force," *Journal of Economic History*, 23, 529-52.

Park, Robert E Ernest W Burges and Robert D. Mckenzie 1925 *The city*, University of Chicago Press, Chicago.

Parsons, Talcott 1947 "Certain Primary Sources and Patterns of Aggression in the Social Structure of the Western World," *Psychiatry*, 10, 167-181.

———— 1949 *The Structure of Social Action*, The Free Press, Glencoe, New York, Ill.

———— 1951 *The Social System*, The Free Press, Glencoe, Ill.

———— 1954 *Essays in Sociological Theory*, The Free Press of Glencoe, New York.

———— 1961 *Theories of Society*, Vol. I, The Free Press of Glencoe, New York.

———— 1963 "On the concept of political power, *Proceedings of American Philosophical Society*, 107, 232-262, June.

Passin, Herbert and John W Bennett 1943 "Changing agricultural magic in southern Illinois: A systematic analysis of folk-urban transition," *Social Forces*, Vol. 22. The University of North Carolina Press.

Popper, K R 1957 *The Poverty of Historicism*, Routledge.

Redfield, Robert 1941 *The Folk Culture of Yukatan*, University of Chicago Press, Chicago.

——— 1953 *The Primitive World and its Transformation*, Cornell University Press, Ithaka, New York.

Rivera, Vincent Jr 1953 "This is Manila," *Sunday Times Magazine* November 20, 9-10, Manila.

Robertson-Smith, W 1894 *Lectures on the Religion of the Semites*, Edinburgh.

Roy Burman, Bikram K (ed) 1961 "Moharram in two cities, Lucknow and Delhi." Ministry of Home Affairs, New Delhi: Monograph No. 3.

Sarkar, Benoy Kumar 1972 *The Folk Element in Hindu Culture*, First Indian Edition. Oriental Books Reprint Corporation, New Delhi. First published in 1917, Longmans Green and Company, London.

Satter, Abdus 1975 *Tribal Culture in Bangladesh*, Muktadhara, Dacca.

Service, Elman 1962 *Primitive Social Organization*, Random House, New York.

Smelser, Neil J 1963 *Theory of Collective Behavior*. The Free Press of Glancoe, New York.

Sorokin, A Pitirim 1937 *Social and Cultural Dynamics*, American Book Co. (1937-41, 4 Vols). New York Abridged one Vol. 1957, Porter Sargent, Boston.

——— 1941 *Crisis of our Age*, E.P. Dutton Co, New York.

——— 1947 *Society Culture and Personality*, Harper and Brothers, New York.

——— 1957 *Social and Cultural Dynamics*, Porter Sargent, Boston.

Spengler, Oswald 1926-1928 *The Decline of the West*, (Trans.) Charles F Atkinson, Knopf, New York.

Stone, N I 1904 *Critique of Political Economy*, (Trans.) From Marx, New York.

Strassburger, R B 1934 *Pennsylvania German Pioneers*, 3 Vols, Norristown, Penn.

Taplin, Rev Co (ed) 1879 *The Folklore, Manners, Customs and Legends of the South Australian Aborigines*, E. Spiller, Acting Govt. Printer, North Terrace, Adelaide: Gathered from inquiries made by authority of South Australian Govt. First reprinting, 1969, Johnson Reprinting Corporation, New York.

Thomas, W I and Florian Znaniecki 1927 *The Polish Peasant in Europe and America*, Alfred A Knopf. Inc, New York.

Thompson, Stith 1955-58 *Motif Index of Folkliterature*, 6 Vols. Indian University Press, Bloomington.

——— and Jones Balys 1958 *The Oral Tales of India*, Indiana University Press, Bloomington.

——— and W E Roterts 1960 "Types of Indic Oral Tales," *FFC*, No. 180. Helsinki.

Thorp, John P 1978 *Powers Among Farmers of Daripalla: A Bangladesh Village Study*, Caritas, Bangladesh.

Tipps, D C 1973 *Modernization Theory and the Comparative Study of Society: A Critical Perspective*, Comparative Studies in Society and History, 15.

Tonnies, Ferdinand 1957 *Community and Society: Gemeinschaft und Gesellschaft*, (trans, and ed.) Charles P. Loomis, Harper and Brothers, New York.

Toulmin, S 1957 "Contemporary Scientific Mythology" in A MacInfyre (ed.) *Metaphysical Beliefs*, SCM Press, London.

Toynbee, Arnold J 1921 "A Study of History," In *the Legacy of Greece*. (ed.) R.W. Livingstone, Clarendon Press, Oxford.

——————— 1947, 1957 *Study of History*, D.C. Somervell's abridgment, Oxford University Press New Delhi.

Tucker, R 1961 *Philosophy and Myth in Karl Marx*, Cambridge University Press.

Vahanian, G 1961 *The Death of God: The Culture of our Post-Christian Era*, George Brazilliar, New York.

Veblen, Thorstein 1922 *The Theory of Leisure Class*, The Viking Press, New York.

Vidyarthi, L P 1964 *Cultural Contours of Tribal Bihar*, Punthi Pustak, Calcutta.

Von Sydow, C W 1948 "Folktale studies and philology: Some points of view" in *Selected Paper on Folklore*, (ed.) Leurites Bodker, Rosenkilde og Forlag, Copenhagon.

Warner, W L 1937 *A Black Civilization*, Harper, New York.

Warner, W Llyod and Paul S Lunt 1941 *The Social Life of a Modern Community*, Yale University Press, New Haven, Conn.

Weber, Max 1947 *The Theory of Social Economic Organization*, Free Press, Gencoe, Ill.

——————— 1949 *The Methodology of the Social Sciences*, (Trans. and ed.) Edward A Shils and Henry A Finch, Free Press, New York.

——————— 1958 *From Max Weber, Essays in Sociology*, Oxford University Press, New York.

——————— 1961 *General Economic History*, Collier.

——————— 1968 *Economy and Society: An Outline of Interpretive Sociology*, (ed.) G Roth and G Wittich, Bedminister Press, Totowa, New Jersey.

White, Leslie 1949 *The Science of Culture*, Grove Press, New York.

Wirth, Louis 1948 *American Sociological Review*, p. 5. Also see: 1957. Types of Minority Movements" in Rulph Turner and Lewis Killian (eds.) *Collective Behavior*, Prentice-Hall, New York.

Yang, C K 1970 *Religion in Chinese Society*, University of California Press, Berkeley.

Yinger, J M *The Scientific Study of Religion*, Macmillan, New York.

Zetterberg, H 1954 *On Theory and Verification in Sociology*, Bedminster Press, Totowa, New Jersey.

PART III

6

FOLKLORE AS THE VEHICLE OF ETHNOLOGICAL STUDIES IN BANGLADESH

ANTHROPOLOGY may be broadly grouped under three major heads—physical anthropology, cultural anthropology, and social anthropology. According to scholars, cultural anthropology has three distinct divisions—archaeology, linguistics and ethnology.

Culture is a team that unfolds human behaviour acquired through experience. These behaviours are different from those genetically determined or inborn in man. One becomes a man of culture by dint of his personal efforts. But anthropology recognizes that every people have a culture of their own. Archaeology deals with the study of cultures which are dead and of matters of a bygone age. But with to respect ethnology, the term culture embraces the living forces in society. It includes not only literature, folklore, art, painting, sculpture, music, dance and so on, but also the total creation of a society namely technology, economics, institutional organization, spiritual aspects, and aesthetic creations.

Ethnology is the study of contemporary culture. An Ethnologist usually studies a particular society with a special interest in the family lives and social environments of members of the society. Modern ethnology has tried to be systematic in satisfying man's curiosity about how people with different cultural traditions organize their lives and view the different worlds in which they live.

Folklore contains a substantial portion and some distinguishing features of the cultural espects of a society. Besides, the major traits of the tradition of a society are reflected in folklore. Their many common elements and almost similar aims and objects bring ethnology and folklore closer to each other. Folklore forms a part of ethnic tradition, a branch of cultural ethnology. The scope of folklore is to reconstruct the spiritual history of man as exemplified by the voices of the folk. In this task it draws on documents which are partly historical. The collection and interpretation of these documents is the task of the science of ethnography, ethnology, and, in a greater perspective of anthropology. Since the comparative method must by definition largely draw an ethnographic data, it follows that folklore and ethnology are virtually inseparable.

With this background, we may now discuss the land, the people, and the cultural patterns of Bangladesh. Bangladesh had been a part of India since the pre-historic times till 1947 when India was divided into two independent states—India and Pakistan. Bangladesh, named East Pakistan, was a part of Pakistan from 1947 to 1971 when she snatched her independence away from the clutches of Pakistan after having suffered a bloody pogrom and a determined war of liberation. As a part of India over thousands of years, Bangladesh inherited almost all the characteristics of the Indian civilization. "The most striking feature of Indian people is their diversity in culture, race and religion. India has well been called one of the greatest ethnographical museums in the world. The reason lies in the many streams of invaders who have come through the mountain passes." (T.W. Wallbank, 1962, 11.) An English anthropologist well expressed this fact when he declared" the subcontinent of India has been linkened to a deep net into which various races and people of Asia have drifted and caught" (J.H. Hutton, 1946, I). These remarks are more or less true about Bangladesh, her land and people. A flat alluvial plain of little over 53,000 square miles traversed by many streams and rivers notably the Gangas, the Brahmaputra, and Meghna, Bangladesh is a wet country with dense tropical jungles in the south. The rainfall averages from 75 to as much as 160 inches a year. Bangladesh has a fertile land and produces great quantities of rice and the world's largest supply of jute. It is heavily populated and has about 90 million inhabitants and a population density which in some areas equals 1,500 people per square mile.

There are different opinions about the origin of races in Bangladesh. Risley (Risley, 1892, 10), the British Anthropologist who worked for a long time in India, considered the people of Bangladesh as belonging to the Mongol-Dravidian groups, while Ramprasad Chando opined that the alpine race of people has influenced the shaping of their constitution. Biroza Shanker Guha came forward with yet another set of arguments that the Negrobotu and Proto-Australoid groups of people also have a great influence over Bangladesh's human race (Samad 1961: I). Thus it is obivious that the Bengali nation is a mixed one and has a variageted culture. Toynbee's contention about Indian civilization that "civilization has become plural instead of singular" (Toynbee, 1961, I), is also true about Bangladesh's civilization.

Language forms the basis of every culture. The study of languages, thus, is considered by anthropologists as one of the four main branches along with physical anthropology, archaeology and ethnology. Language is the principal means of communication and cultural transmission among human beings. Bangladesh is a monolingual country with the language Bengali, which has a few not—much-distinct dialects, as the only means of communication. Bengali, derived partly from Sanskrit and partly from a native language, accepting heavily from the vocabularies of foreign languages, belongs to, (like English, German, Hindi, and so on) the Indo-European language stock. The phonemes and morphemes of Bengali have some characteristics similar to those of English, German and Hindi languages. But to ethnologists and folklorists, folk-etymology provides an interesting study as to how the knowledge and experience of the folk helped to construct new words by mixing foreign and native words. Portuguese *annanas* becomes *anarosh* (Portugues *Anna*+Bengali *rosh*), English 'hospital' changes into Bengali as *hashpatal* (English 'hos' >*hash*+Bengali *patal*). There are plenty of examples which could bet cited from other areas of the Bengali language to prove that folklore is really a strong vehicle of linguistic and ethnic studies in Bangladesh. Since English is the second state language of Bangladesh till today, the process of coining the mixed new words such as folk-etymology from English and Bengali is going on and they are being used profusely in our day-to-day lives in the rural areas.

"Some anthropological linguists engage in a kind of ethnographic research which has been called ethnoscience. Its purpose is to uncover taxonomic principles of particular languages". (Barnouw, 1971, 67-68). So far as Bengali is concerned, there is certainly the scope for such a study. In this short discussions. I would not like to enter into an elaborate study of the language of the people of Bangladesh, but before I pass on to another aspect, I would like to mention that some of the observations made by the Japanese scholar Hijime Nakamura in his famous work *Ways of Thinking of Eastern Peoples: India, China, Tibet, Japan* (Wiener, 1968), about Sanskrit, may not be exactly applicable to Bengali. "Nakamura starts out with an examination of Sanskrit, the Indo-European language of the Vedas and other early Hindu Texts and the parent language of later North Indian linguistic groups. He states that there is a readiness to use abstract nouns in Sanskrit, leading to a stress on the universal. An abstract noun may be formed by adding *—ta* or*—tva* to the root corresponding to Latin *—tas*. German *—ta, —t* France *—ite*, and English *—ty*. But in the European Language abstract nouns are not often used, while they are common in everyday usage in Sanskrit, so that, for example, "He becomes old" is expressed in Sanskrit as "he goes to oldness" and "the fruit becomes soft" is expressed as "the fruit goes to softness". Any noun or adjective can be made into an abstract noun by adding the suffix *—ta* or*—tva*. This results in a tendency to reification.

> Another feature of Indian thought is a preference to negative expressions. Instead of "victory or defeat" an Indian would say "victory on non-victory". Negative terms often seem to have positive meanings, so that among the virtues extolled in sacred Hindu, Buddhist and Jain texts are *ahimsa* (non-violence), *asetya* (non-theft), *avera* (non-grudge), *aparigroha* (non-acquisition). Morality is conceived of as being the negation of common behavior. (Barnouw, 1971, 72).

The complexity of Nakamura's work makes some of his observations vulnerable to critics from various angles. One critic has objected that "Nakamura fails to realize that different languages may make use of different means to express the same or similar concepts" (Yamagiwa, 1965, 216). Examples may be cited even from Bengali, a near relation of Sanskrit. Instead of using "he goes to oldness" or "The fruit goes to softness" as it is the practice in Sanskrit as well as in Bengali. The Bengali language also very often use "he becomes old" or "the fruit becomes soft." This has been possible because of the fact that Bengali grammar was re-shaped in the pattern of English grammar although Bengali is remotely, and partly derived from Sanskrit. Not only in the field of language, but in the field of culture as a whole, the people "constitute a generic type because they share common structural and cultural characteristics" (Foster, 1973, I). There exists a "historic pattern of concentration of economic and political power in the hands of small elite groups who exploit their position to maintain the status quo and to ensure that they had their descendants continue to enjoy the good things of life, at the expense of the masses". (Foster, *Ibid*). Their technologies are simple and scientific knowledge is lamentably limited. Production is achieved through human and animal rather than mechanical power. Human or animal manure may be used. Consequently, yields are low, and are subject to the vagaries of weather. Environmental senitation is poor, medical services are primitive, chronic illnesses prevail, life spans are short and both birth and death rates are high. Illiteracy is the rule and access to new knowledge is restricted. For the masses, these conditions means poverty, uncertainty, and a limited personal freedom. "They have had few, if any, options" (Foster, 1973, 1-2).

If "anthropology is the study of human beings as creatures of society" (Benedict, 1959: 1). Ethnology must fasten its attention upon the conventions and values, customs and usages, beliefs and practices, and other guiding aspects of the society to distinguish it from others that belong to a different tradition. In doing so, the study of ethnology in Bangladesh, as in other traditional societies, may safely depend on folklore as one of its strong vehicles. Let us start from the birth of a human being. Most of the rituals and practices followed in connection with childbirth are related to magic, folk beliefs and taboos. A few of them are mentioned below:

(a) The pregnant woman must not go out of the room alone at night, if she goes, she must take fire with her. Otherwise the child in the womb will go upwards.

(b) The pregnant woman must not eat on the earthen pot or the earthen cover. This will make the belly of the child bigger.

(c) During an eclipse of the moon, the pregnant women must not cut anything. If she does so, the child will be too talkative.

(d) The pragnant woman should not bind the broom, for, this would mix up the intestines of the child with that of its mother and childbirth would be difficult.

(a, b, c, d, taken from the personal collection of the writer)

Irrespective of religous beliefs and faiths, the rural Muslims and the Hindu women, who constitute the bulk of the female population, observe these practices, however irrational, these might appear. In order to have children, the Muslims as well as the Hindus go to old mosques or temples which are renowned for the fulfilment of such desires. The Muslims and the Hindus feed people for the welfare of the child when he or she is seven, twenty or forty days old. Bloomfield in his article "The Dohada or Craving of Pregnant Woman" (Bloomfield, 1920, 1-24) gives an account of the stories relating to our women who desire an unusual food or to engage in tabooed activity during pregnancy (Islam, 1982, 191). These are common both among Muslim and Hindu communities of Bangladesh. When the woman reaches the fifth or sixth month of her first pregnancy, the parents or the brothers of the woman send a big fish, especially with scales, to the house of the woman to make a good feast. The practice is common among those who have the financial ability. This is called *Bavar* in Rajshahi and Kishorganj regions (W. Ahmed, 1974, 161). Fish with scales has been accepted as the symbol of fertility. When the pregnancy reaches the seventh month, the woman is allowed to eat whatever she likes. This is, of course, in some cases with financial ability, made a social affair. The woman, dressed with new clothes, is surrounded by children and relatives, both male and female, and different types of food according to her choice, are provided for her satisfaction. This is called *Sadh* which means desire as well as the number seven. After ceremony is over, the children would get hold of the woman frcm all sides and cling to her body for sometime (Syddiquee , 1963, 347-48). This practice, perhaps, has come from the ancient sympathetic taboo. A good number of children touching the body of the pregnant woman indicates that she would have many children. Generally, all auspicious day is fixed by the relatives of both husband and wife for this ceremony (Bose, 1929, 426). There are rhymes and proverbs, myths and tales in Bengali where the eating of *sadh* has been mentioned (Bhattacharya, 1966, 616).

From birth to marriage, as we have seen in this very brief foregoing survey, folklore plays a very significant role. In the society as a whole, both rural and urban, with some recent exceptions, the marriage of bride and bridegroom is arranged by the parents and the relatives of the two sides. There are professional mediators, but mostly the relatives play the role of mediators between the two parties. In the highly educated or sophisticated circles, the boys and girls make their own selection of partner independently. But even then, in most of the cases, prior or post-marriage approval of the parents is required to avoid bitterness. Since marriage is a pleasant affair, innumerable customs have evolved around this happy ceremony. Some of the ceremonies and rituals are simple, but some are long. It is not possible to elaborate on all here. Most of these rituals and customs are observed to socialize the whole affair and to make conjugal life happier. *Sohag maga*, *Panibhoron*, *Borondala*, *Borsuan*, *Mehesdi tola*, *Gayeholud*, *Khai chhitano*, *Shajja tuloni*, *Badhubran* and so on are some of the important practices observed by both Muslim and Hindu communities. Some of these are observed before the actual marriage ceremony is held, some during the ceremony and some afterwards. Some of these occur at the residence of the bride and some in the family of the bridegroom. Folksong, folk dance, folk paintings, rhymes and riddles have a very significant role in all these ceremonies, including the major one. About number of wives, I should add that one is preferred. "Monogamy and polygamy are the two most common forms of marriage, both having had a wide distribution among the societies of the world (Barnouw, 1971, 127). Both forms are prevalent in the rural society of Bangladesh although people are gradually proceeding towards a system which encourages monogamy. Economic and other conditions are responsible for this social change.

Thus, both in birth and marriage, the ethnological study in Bangladesh is immensely benefitted by the living stock of folklore. From marriage we may turn to death. Like European societies in the Middle Ages, most of the people in rural Bangladesh believe, even to this day, that a man or a woman are physically comprised of four elements." When man or a woman died the elements of air and fire left the body and sped upward to their centres in the sky, the elements of water and earth were left behind and the body sank to the ground." (Bronowski, 1960, 110).

Death may occur through disease, through old age or an accident. Folk medicine is intended for recovery from illness. Almost all the diseases have their medical treatment, either is the folk medicines prepared from the herbs, leaves of plants, the bark of some trees and from other objects or by a spell, an incantation, some words recited in prayer to God or a deity, the prescribed mystic and esoteric words of prayer and by using enchantment, occult power, charm, magic and so on. Shamanism is not absolutely unknown even today, though with the advent of modern scientific medical treatment, the position of *shamans* is loosing its importance. The *shaman*, in remote villages, "acts as an intermediary person between the members of his society and the supernatural world, with which he communicates either by talking to the spirits and listening to their replies or through possession" (Loeb, 1929, 61). "Some of the *shamans* use sucking cure, in which the *shaman* goes through the motions of sucking a disease from the patient's body" (Eliade, 1950, 299).

"The ancient Hindus performed an elaborate ceremony, based on homeopathic magic, for the cure of jaundice. Its main drift was to banish the yellow colour to yellow creatures and yellow things, such as the sun, to which it properly belongs, and to procure for the patient a healthy red colour from a living vigorous source, namely red bull" (Frazer, 1959, 12). The ceremony, though not exactly in the same form, may be seen in some of the villages even to this day. These are all parts of folklore. Folklore is widely connected with death. According to Rhys Davids, the faith that the soul exists after death is religious rather than a folk belief (Davids, 1899, 167, 171-172). Let us accept that the belief about a soul after death is universal, it is as much religious as it is superstitious. Debiprosad Chattopadhyay has dealt with this thesis in detail in his book on *Ancient Indian Materialism* written in Bengali (Chattopadhyay, 1969, 74-132).

In a word, Tylor's famous theory of primitive animism is an anthropological anachronism. The same objections may be raised against some of Frazer's concepts regarding the presence of spirit in corn, trees and even in many inanimate objects. But in the rural societies of Bangladesh, some primitive beliefs, specially in connection with animism, exist to this day. Animism is not exclusively an Indian or Bangladeshi concept. "It is found in varying degrees nearly in all religions. We find its survivals in many highly developed religions despite the opposition of leaders. The occurrence of animism in the cultures of the Egyptians, Babylonians and Greeks is a historical fact. We can easily detect animistic survivals in Hinduism, despite the Buddhist, Jain and Sikh reformations, in the objects which fill Hindu temples and in the Hindu pilgrimages to sacred mountains and rivers. Again, in the pre-Mosaic religion of the Hebrews, telphin or 'idols' apparently made of wood, were adored. Before Mahomet, the Arabs worshipped sacred trees, stones and springs. The guardian spirit of each was later personified in a God or Goddess. Despite Mahomet's opposition to animistic beliefs, he had to permit adoration of the black meteorite housed in the Kaaba, and of the Zemzem spring. Belief in them has persisted to this day. Various Roman and Greek Pantheons also showed a development from animism to animistic polytheism. The Teutonic-Scandanavian religions showed a similar development. A chief object of their worship was the "world tree" Yggdrasill. In Mexico the culture of the Toltecs, Aztecs and other tribes of the Nahuatlan stock was animistic and resembled that of the Africans, (Segy 1969,9).

So far as the faith about the existence of soul after death is concerned, people believing in the great religions such as Islamism, Hinduism, Christianity and Buddhism in Bangladesh, who form the ninety-nine per cent of the population, of whom Muslims are by far the majority, are the firm upholders of this particular concept that the soul exists after death. Hence, people in Bangladesh, irrespective of religious faiths, perform prayers and observe some obligations to the departed soul for its salvation and peace.

It has already been mentioned that Bangladesh is a country that depends mainly on agriculture. Since the ancient times, agriculture has been the main source of livelihood in the villages. Agricultural products are the major materials for commerce. The weavers, the producers of edible oil, the carpenters, the washermen, the hairdressers, the blacksmiths and other technicians are directly or indirectly connected with agriculture; those who are not, are dependents on the agricultural products. From farmers to all these working classes in the rural areas are the creators, lovers and custodians of folklore. Without folklore, the ethnographic or cultural study of these people can not be complete.

A pair of cows, a plough, a yoke, a few plots of land are the minimum assets that every village-dweller craves. The spade, the scyth or a sickle, the weeding-tool, the harrow, the yoke are the simplest forms of tools which are used in agriculture. Too much rain or drought are bad for the crops. Occasional rainfall is essential for paddy, jute, and other crops of Bangladesh. Since the whole process of agricultural production depends on rainfall and sun, there remains the possibility of damage, destruction or less production every year. Of course, with increasing knowledge of the farmers about modern methods and techniques, the situation is improving gradually. Without going into details, it may be added here that folklore is connected with every step of agricultural process—with beliefs, customs, rituals, myths, legends, tales, rhymes, riddles, proverbs and above all songs on every agro-process. There is a proverb that rice in the granary and song in the throat are the main assets of a Bengali. The weather-lore namely *khonar Bochon*, composed about a thousand years back, still guides the farmers in their farming. Thus, the ethnological study aiming at the culture and society of rural agricultural in Bangladesh, derives a flood of material from folklore.

Nineteenth century writers who wrote about 'primitive religion' hoped to figure out how religious beliefs originated in the first place and what were the characteristics of the earliest primordial religion. The chief representative of nineteenth century rationalism in this field was Edward B. Tylor. About half of his two volume work, *Primitive culture* (1871) is devoted to religion. He ruled out certain features which are not universal, such as belief in a supreme being, the notion of reward and punishment after death, workship of idols and the practice of sacrifice. These are found in many societies but not in all, as Tylor observed. What he chose as his minimum definition was "the belief in spiritual beings" (Tylor, 1903: 27) to which he gave the name animism. "It encompasses belief in souls, ghosts gods, demons and other supernaturals. For Tylor, animism was the core of religion from which all other aspects of religion sprang. Once this idea was implanted in men's minds, various other beliefs and practices followed as a rather logical consequence" (Barnouw, 1971, 218). Tylor's observation is more or less correct about Bangladesh society. In spite of strict religious prohibition, various animistic beliefs prevail among the muslims of Bangladesh. Faith in ghosts and demons is so strong in rural areas that there are people almost in all the sixty thousand villages who can solemnly vow that they have seen ghosts and demons with their own eyes. Tales and legends about ghosts and demons are being created and recreated almost every day.

In the 1920's and early 1930's, a Swiss student of child psychology, Jean Piaget, carried on investigations into children's ways of thinking and their conception of the world (Piaget, 1929, 216). He distinguished a series of stages of animistic thought (Huang, 1943, 71-121) which may be more or less correctly applied in cases of children of the same age group in Bangladesh.

Although money and markets are relatively old institutions in this region, non-monetary exchanges are still prevalent in rural society. In villages there are markets within short distances where agricultural produce, animals, chicken, handicrafts and other necessary household materials are sold and purchased freely. These markets are called *hats*. There are fixed places where people assemble once or twice a week for selling and buying things. Only in the bigger *hats* cattle rams and goats are bought and sold. The markets are free as the prices are determined by the interactions of buyers and sellers and not by some sets of rules and regulations. Both sellers and buyers try to profit as there is no fixed price. *Hats* are the places where folklore could be abundantly found. The village bards attend *hats* to sing their songs and sell booklets containing ballads and tales composed in poetical forms. Proverbs and rhymes are uttered both by sellers and buyers during their exchange of words. In the corner of the *hat*, a competition is always arranged between two groups of village-bards who recite myths, folktales, legends, riddles in the course of their musical and poetry competition. These are all folklore. Folklore speaks its vivid languages in places where people gather in large number. Thus, one cannot avoid folklore when he studies the ethnology of Bangladesh. As fish cannot be taken out of water, rural people of Bangladesh cannot be dissassociated with folklore.

Let us come to family-lise. "A family," as defined by an ethnologist "is a social group whose members usually live together and engage in economic co-operation and which normally has two or more adults of both sexes responsible for rearing and educating the children who are born to the female or females of the faimily or who have been adopted. A family is a sexual unit in the sense that husband and wife may have sexual relations which cannot be regarded as illegal or socially disapproved" (Barnouw, 1971, 116). This observation of Professor Barnouw is true about the Bangladesh society, both rural and urban. It is evident that families in Bangladesh are successful because, unlike the family life in the western world, they do not very often generate tension, frustration and hostility. A bachelor here is felt to be an incomplete person and the childless couples are not considered as normal. Levi-Strauss speaks of the true feeling of "repulsion which most societies have toward bachelorhood." (Levi-Strauss, 1960, 269).

Monogamy, as mentioned before, is the desirable system, but there are people who are polygamous. It is generally found that the first wife in a polygamous family enjoys greater economic right and shares bigger family responsibility, while the youngest one is preferred by the husband in love and affection. There is frequently strong rivalry and jealousy among co-wives, which has been reflected in Bengali folktales in various manners. Of course, exceptions are there. Since the society is agrarian, the co-wives usually form an efficient working team through a mutual understanding. There was a time when more than one wife was desirable not only to get rid of sexual monotony, but also for more children who could provide greater number of working hands in the land. But with the changing economic conditions, fragmentation of land due to the growth of population in an enormous scale, and the spread of modern education, polygamy is rapidly declining even in the rural areas. In a few sections of the Hindu Community marriage is restricted to the same caste or sub-caste. But there is no such restriction in the Muslim community. Polyandry or group marriage is completely unknown. Families are apparently happy. The parents are affectionate to their children and the children in return, specially the male ones, look after the welfare of the parents in their old age. But as the society is rapidly coming in contact with western cultural pattern and the burden of economy is becoming heavier day by day, the spirit of independence in both parents and children is becoming gradually noticeable.

When we talk of family, we cannot but accept that the families in Bangladesh are the social units where folklore is hatched and bred. It is partly through these units that folklore is sustained, disseminated and handed down to generations through oral tradition. Hence, the study of family, which is one of the main functions of ethnology, must derive considerable material from folklore.

The society may be regarded more or less as patrilineal although the mother's side is not totally ignored. So far as the right of inheritance is concerned, sons and daughters, as determined by Muslim and Hindu law, get the father's or mother's property. Totemism, almost unknown to the Bangladesh society, still prevails in some or other among the tribal people such as Hazong, Morang, Rajbanshi, Santals, Chakma, Mog and so on. There are restrictions to marriage, but these are guided by religious laws. If we consider marital residence and affinal relationships, we find that with the exception of a few educated and urbanized people, the village-dwellers, after marriage stay with parents as long as economically possible and otherwise compatible. When the couples have a good number of children and the parents cannot bear the burden, or when the adjustment is no longer considered possible or pleasant, they separate. The responsibility of the girl's parents is lessened after her marriage and the bridegroom and his parents assume full responsibility to maintain her. The dowry system which prescribes that the parents of the bride should arrange gifts for the bridegroom at the time of marriage, still poses a menace to society. The system was prevalent among the Hindus even during the first decade of the current century in such a manner that many families were ruined due to the curse of this system. It was reported recently in a national daily paper in Bangladesh that a father had to kill his daughter when the bridegroom's father refused to marry his son to the girl just at the time of solemnisation of the marriage as the girl's father failed to procure only one item of the previously fixed list. The gifts are, of course, fixed through negotiation between the parties when the marriage is settled. In the comparatively sophisticated families, presents are given from both bride and bridegroom's guardians.

Kinship is no doubt an important organizing principle not only in Bangladesh's tribal societies, but also at higher levels of socio-economic integration. However, here in Bangladesh it is not the only organizing principle. Societies are knit together in other ways than through kinship. Age grades, and voluntary associations cross-cut kinship lines and provide supplementary bases for social solidarity. Circumcision of Muslim boys and the sacrament of wearing the holy thread over the shoulder in the fashion of a cross-belt for the first time by the boys of upper-caste Hindus, especially the Brahmins, are the two occasions which have wide distribution in the puberty ceremonies of Bangladesh. In the well-to-do families, considerable amount of money is spent through festivity on this occasion. Here comes the role of folklore. Songs are sung by both males and females, tales are told, proverbs and rhymes are profusely uttered and riddles used to befool others. Hence, in Bangladesh, the study of ethnology without folklore might prove futile.

Voluntary as well as secret associations are existent rural and urban societies. Religious cults which require periodic ceremonies bring the members together and emphasize their common ties. Castes and class stratifications are found mainly among the Hindus and the rising upper class families. "A Hindu caste is an endogamous, hierarchically ranked social group, which is sometimes associated with a particular occupation. Rules determine whether one may accept food or water from persons of different caste. Usually, one may accept food from one's own and from higher but not lower castes" (Barnouw, 1971, 173).

If we divide society in classes, we find that more than ninety per cent of the total population are living in sub-human conditions. They comprise the landless labourers, farmers with small holdings in the rural areas, the labour class as a whole in towns and the hard-hit middle class, especially the lower middle class group. Poverty cannot be a blessing, rather, it is the worst of curses. Some scholars have rightly observed that in the lower classes, the incidence of psychoses was almost three times greater than in the higher classes (Hollingshed, 1958 : Barnouw's 1971 : 185). There are some aspects, no doubt, common in Bangladesh to those mentioned by Oscar Lewis as culture of poverty (Lewis, 1968, xliii—xliv). On the contrary, there are thousands of people in Bangladesh even in the remotest rural areas, who have learnt through ages of suffering at the hands of poverty, that they have to change their fate by accepting a new approach towards life and by their readiness to work hard in the changed circumstances, if required, in a different country. in an alien culture. Economic hardship has certainly played a great role in bringing about this change in the attitude towards life. Poverty has not driven them to a negation of life and to brood over frustration. People are, becoming more and more realistic and take a positive stand to solve their problems.

Bangladesh has passed through many political turmoils for the past fifty years. People fought for independence from British colonial rule which lasted for about two hundred years. Then they had to fight for their liberation and drive out the barbarious forces of Pakistan. It is the middle class which took the lead in all these movements. The village-dwellers had not much to do except vote. They were, of course, awakened during the liberation war in 1971 and their participation was enormous even in the villages. In spite of all these movements, by nature the rural people are not very interested in national politics, as the national leaders did not contribute much to the amelioration of their suffering and the betterment of their conditions. The villages, of course, have their own society and within a limited circle, their own political and administrative system which functions to maintain law and order. There is one headman, or a group of headmen in every village who decide cases such as small theft, a quarrel or a scuffle between two persons or groups, a dispute with land, disrespect to women and so on. When, they fail or there are major offences, the villagers go to the court or bring the matter to the notice of the law-enforcing authorities of the government. A society, such as in the rural area of Bangladesh, "has to find ways of preserving order within its own ranks and of regulating relations with outside groups. In more advanced societies," such as in the towns and cities, "these matters are handled by a state apparatus" (Barnouw, 1971, 206).

Life without recreation and enjoyment outside the family environment, is full of monotony and drudgery. People of Bangladesh are not any less keen than people of other under-developed countries to find recreation for themselves in any form. Towns and cities have the modern amenities and facilities for recreation such as cinema, theatre, musical performances, occasional exhibitions of art and agricultural products and so on. But the major enjoyment, that a village-man would find besides eating and time spent with his wife, is folklore. Almost in every village there are people who can sing well and these people, during the early hours of the night, twice or thrice a week, assemble together and sing before their admiring listeners. There are people who can tell mythic tales, legends, fairytales anecdotes, and so on. The enthusiastic listeners enjoy tales, sometime for the whole night. In some of the villages, there are drama-parties who present their dramatic performances for the whole night. One of the well-known forms of folk drama is called *jatra.*

Folksongs are so dear to the people that almost in every part of folklore such as tales, dramas and proverbs, songs take a predominant position. Song provides a constant enjoyment to the people not only during leisure, but also during labour. Song gives inspiration to the people at labour in the fields, factories, rivers and roads.

Lin Yutang, who holds eating to be "one of the very few solid joys of human life", remarks that it is fortunate that it is less hedged about with taboos than sex, and that "generally speaking, on question of morality arises in connection with food" (Yutang, 1937, 253-54). People of Bangladesh have some distinctive features, which, in spite of enormous similarities, especially from anthropological and ethnological points of view, separates them from the rest of the people scattered in the vast area of Northern India.

Morgan has rightly remarked that "The organization into gentes on the basis of kin naturally suggests itself as the archaic framework of ancient society" (Morgan, 1967, 47). The framework of Bangladesh's society has been based initially on hunting and then on agriculture. The fertility of the alluvial soil of the entire region brought the people to the land and resort to agriculture. The people adopted the simple technology of using wooden ploughs (with an iron blade) drawn by cows. In 1831-32, a report was submitted to the British parliament where it was said that the rural people of Bengal were opposed to any change, either social or technical. The report said that the farmers used to till the land with ploughs following old techniques and the processes which were primitive (British Parliament, Papers, 1831-32, 306). Things have not changed even today. Bengali words like *langal, Joal, Ish, Fal* meaning different parts of the plough, are Austric, the language which was current in this region during 1500 to 1000 B.C. Thus, it is obvious that even through the passage of about three thousand years, there has been practically little or no change in the agricultural society, especially of rural Bengal, which covers more than ninety-five per cent of the total area of this country. Folklore forms the mainstream of the culture of this agrarian and traditional society. Like many other traditional societies of the world, the societies in rural Bangladesh in Bangladesh generally love eating but the tragedy is that very few of them get food to fill their stomachs thrice a day, not to speak of eating for enjoyment. More than eighty per cent of the total population suffer from under-nourishment. As human beings, they no doubt find great pleasure in sex, but sex without proper food, nourishment, economic, and social stability in life does not bring about the desired pleasure and satisfaction. This is more true about the women-folk who are seldom found to be agressive in sex affairs. There are sex taboos and great restrictions in sex meetings.

John Huizinga, who has discussed the importance of play in the development of human culture, describes some of the characteristics of play as follows :

> We might call it a free activity standing quite consciously outside ordinary life as being not serious, but at the same time absorbing the player intensely and utterly. It is an activity connected with no material interest and no profit can be gained by it (Huizinga, 1955 : 13).

Play, sports and games are the source of genuine enjoyment to the people of Bangladesh. These can be divided into two groups—one is sophisticated, the other is not. The former is popular among city-dwellers, the latter is the product of ancient society, and is retained among the villagers. Football, cricket, hockey, basketball, tennis and so on are the modern games very popular in cities and towns. *Hadudu, dangguli, sauchhi, gollachhut, unta, lathikhela* are popular games in the villages. These are called folk-games. Some of the folkgames are connected with rhymes and mythical legends.

Folk dance, a lively and vivid recreation of the simple people, differs from the classical or modern dances. There are no institutions where the folk dances are taught. The practice is handed down through generations in a traditional way. Only after having trained in classical or modern dance, one may go on stage for presentation. But a rural dancer first joins the group, immitates other dancers and then becomes an expert. His presentation commences while learning. As in sports and games, so in dances, the rural people generally take part in all the performing arts in groups. Song is invariably accompanied with dance along with the instrumental accompaniment.

Some of the dances are connected with agricultural production. (A. Bhattacharya, 1964, 728). These dances are symbolical and ritualistic. The folk dances of Bangladesh could be divided into the following groups

(a) Religious —*Jarinach, Fakirnach, Kirtannach* and so on

(b) Social —*Gambhira nach, dhalinach, lathinach, roybenshe nach* and so on

(c) Ceremonious —*Ghatunach, Khemtanach, Sarinach, bolinach* and so on

(d) Purely Musical—*Baulnach, jarinach, gambhiranach* and so on

Dance, music and decorative art are listed in Murdock's catalogue of universal aspects of culture (Dundes, 1965, 3), while folk costume has been included by Dundes as part of folklore and folk culture (Murdock, 1945, 124). Folk paintings and art of Bangladesh provide an interesting study. The characteristics of paintings and sketches are very much present in Bangladesh's folk arts. Besides painting, and sketching there are embroidery, weaving, modelling, engraving and inlaying art forms. A careful study of the history of the development of folk arts in Bangladesh would reveal that the people of this region are connected with the primitive people of the South East Asian Countries (Samad, 1973, 138). There may not be complex art forms in the folk arts of Bangladesh, but there is diversity of motifs and forms, simple though they might appear.

The ethnological study in Bangladesh would remain incomplete if we do not at least mention that the culture of the people, both rural and urban is being changed due to gradual industrialisation and spread of modern education. "Culture change within a society may be brought about either by internal invention and development or else through contact with other societies (Barnouw, 1971, 322). Both these processes are in force in Bangladesh.

About the future of Bangladesh, the less we say, the better. The picture is not very bright. The political instability since 1975 has posed a great problem which cannot be solved because the military's deep interest and constant interference in the civil administration of Bangladesh. The country is facing the problem of a population with limited resources. Famine and under-nourishment are the products of a population explosion. Social unrest is becoming a common factor everywhere because of the economic depression which is perennial to the conditions of an underdeveloped country such as Bangladesh. The problem of unemployment has already gone beyond solution. In spite of this gloomy picture, the people, with their determined endeavour, hope for a bright future for the generations to come. The younger generation seem more energetic and enthusiastic about expansion of knowledge in all spheres of life. "We may hope for a more open-minded, well-educated generation, able to cope with the strange transformations of the world to-day" (Burnouw, 1971, 345), including their mother land Bangladesh. Since the area of my study here is a vast one, I have not been able to cover all the aspects from the ethnological point of view. But I am convinced that the society of Bangladesh presents great scope for scholars to make a thorough study of ethnology and anthropology with folklore as the vehicle of such studies.

REFERENCES

Ahmed, Wakil 1973 *Banglar Loka Sanskriti* (*Folk-culture of Bengal*). Bangla Academy, Dacca.

Barnouw, Victor 1971 "An Introduction to Anthropology," Vol II, *Ethnology*. The Dorsey Press, Home wood, Illinois.

Benedict, Ruth 1959 *Patterns of Culture* (reprinted), Allied Publishers Private Limited, Bombay.

Bhattacharya, Ashutosh 1964 *Banglar Loka Sahitya* (Folk-Literature of Bengal), Vol. III, Calcutta Book House, Calcutta.

———— 1966 *Banglar Loka Sahitya*, Vol. IV, Calcutta Book House, Calcutta.

Bloomfield, Maurice 1920 "The dohada or craving of pregnant woman, A motif of Hindu fiction," *Journal of American Oriental Society*, XL.

Bose, Dakshinaranjan 1971 *Sanskritir Dharma*, (The characteristics of Culture), Bharati Book Stall, Calcutta.

Bose, Nagendra Nath 1929 *Collected, Biswakosh*, (Encyclopaedia in Bengali). Vol. XI Calcutta.

Bose, Nirmal Kumar 1972 *Anthropology and Some Indian Problems*, Institute of Social Research and Applied Anthropology, Calcutta.

British Parliament Papers, Report from the Select Committee of the House of Commons, Session 1831-32 (Public), A.P.P., p. 306.

Bronowski, J and Bruce Mazlish 1960 *The Western Intellectual Tradition.* Hutchinson & Co. Ltd., London.

Chattopadhyay, Debiprosad 1969 *Lokayata Darsana,* Ancient Indian Materialistic Philosophy. New Age Publishers Private Limited, Calcutta.

Davids, T W R Rhys 1899 *Dialogues of the Buddha,* Vol. I, London.

Dundes, Alan (ed) 1965 *The Study of Folklore,* Englewood Cliffs, Prentice-Hall, N.J.

Eliade, Mircea 1950 "Shamanism" in Vergilius Ferm (ed.) *Ancient Religions,* Philosophical Library, New York.

Foster, George M 1973 *Traditional Societies and Technological Change* (Second edn.), Allied Publishers Private Limited, Bombay.

Frazer, Sir James George 1959 (Ed.) Theodor H. Gaster, *The New Golden Bough,* Criterion Books, New York.

Halder, Gopal 1965 *Sanskritir Rupantar A Critical Study of the evolution of Culture,* first edn., Orient Book Company, Calcutta.

Hollingshed, August B and C Ridlich 1958 *Social Class: Mental Illness, A Community Study,* John Wiley & Sons, New York.

Hocket, Charles F 1958 *A Course in Modern Linguistics,* Macmillan Co, New York.

Huang, I 1943 *Journal of Genetic Psychology,* Vol. 63.

Huizinga, John 1955 *Homo Ludens: A Study of the Play-Element in Culture,* Beacon Press, Boston.

Hutton, John Henry 1951 *Caste in India.* Cambridge University Press, Cambridge.

Islam, Sirajul 1978 *Bangladesher Bhumi Babastha O Samajik Samshwa: Land System and Social Problems of Bangaladesh.* Dacca University, Centre for Social Studies.

Islam, Mahmuda 1973 *Samaj O Dharma: Society and Religion.* Bangla Academy, Dacca.

——————— 1974 (Trans). *Nritattwer Sahoj Path* (Bengali Translation of *Teach Yourself Anthropology* J. Marchip White), Bangla Academy, Dacca.

Islam, Mazharul 1982 *A History of Folktale Collections in India Bangladesh and Pakistan,* (2nd enlarged edition). Panchali Prakasan Calcutta. First edition, 1970, Bangla Academy, Dacca.

——————— 1960 *Kabi Pagla Kanai* (A biography of a great Bengali folk-poet), Rajshahi University, Rajshahi.

Khaldun, Ibne 1967 *An Introduction to History: The Muqaddimah* (Trans. from the Arabic by Fanz Rosenthal and abridged and edited by N.J. Dawood), Routledge & Kegan Paul, London.

Levi-Strauss, Claude 1960 "The Family" in Harry L. Shapiro (ed.). *Man, Culture and Society,* Oxford University Press, New York.

Lewis, Oscar 1968 La Vida, *A Puerto Rican Family in the Culture of Poverty,* San Juan and New York, Random House, New York.

Loeb, Edwin M 1929 Shaman and seer, *American Anthropologist*, Vol. 31.

Lowie, Robert H 1937 *The History of Ethnological Theory*, Rinehart & Co., New York.

Morgan, Lewis Henry 1967 Eleanor Burke Leacock (ed.) *Ancient Society*, The World Publishing Company, Cleveland and New York.

Murdock, George P 1945 "The common denominator of cultures." Ralph Linton (ed.) *The Science of Man in the World of Crisis*, Columbia University Press, New York.

Nakamura, Hijime 1968 Rev P Wiener (ed English Trans.), *Ways of Thinking of Eastern Peoples: India, China, Tibet, Japan*, East-West Center Press, Honolulu.

Piaget, Jean 1929 *The Child's Conception of the World*. Harcourt Brace & Co., New York.

Risley, Herbert H 1892 *The Tribes and Castes of Bengal*, Vol. I, Bengal Secretariate Press, Calcutta.

Samad, Abne Golam 1973 *Nritatva (Anthropology)*, Bangla Academy, Dacca.

Segy, Ladislas 1969 *African Sculpture Speaks* (Third edn.), Hill and Wang, New York.

Siddiquee, Ashraf 1963 *Loka Sahitya* (Folk-literature). The Student Ways, Dacca.

Toynbee, Arnold J 1961 *Between Oxus and Jumna*, Oxford University Press, New York.

Tylor, Edward Burnett 1903 *Primitive Culture*, Vol. II, 4th edn. John Murray, London.

Wallbank, T. Walter 1962 *A Short History of India and Pakistan*, A Mentor Book. The New American Library, New York.

Yamagiwa, Joseph K 1965 "Language as an expression of Japanese culture". John Whitney Hall and Richard Beardsley (eds.), *Twelve Doors to Japan*, McGraw-Hill Book Co., New York.

Yutang, Lin 1937 *The Importance of Living*. Reyual & Hitchcock, New York.

7

FOLKLORE : THE PULSE OF THE PEOPLE
A Socio-cultural Analysis

WHEN BENGAL was partitioned in 1905 under the rule of Lord Curzon, the songs composed by Rabindranath Tagore played such an important role in moulding the feelings of the people against this decision, that they cannot be measured by our ordinary standards of historical approach. It is interesting to note that our folk-poets and singers also rose to the occasion and composed many songs which helped tremendously to shape the movement against the partition of Bengal in a very effective manner, as a result of which, the British power had to bow down its head and declare the decision of partition as withdrawn. This is one aspect of folklore, I shall say, one of its most important functions, which lends its service as a vehicle of social protest. Gomme stated (*Folklore as an Historical Science*) that such elements of folklore, though frequently relating to minor events, often have reference to matters of the highest national importance, and perhaps nowhere more definitely is this the case than in the ballads or folk-songs connected with particular localities.

My aim is, of course, not to focus the sense of protest alone as reflected in folklore specially of the Indian subcontinent, but to cover a wide area of our society where folklore exists and transmits as the pulse of the people. The elements of folklore are social products they are created, retained and transmitted by the folk and as such folklore is the mirror of the people—not dead like a piece of glass, but a living one. Folklore is embodied in the form of aesthetic expression and its creator or creators are part of the society that exists today, existed in the past and will exist in future. Like a building constituted with pieces of bricks, society is constituted of every individual living in that society. As creators of folklore belonging to ancient past or the problem-ridden present, (unlike the modern writers, painters, sculptors, singers, or artist of performing or non-performing arts) always kept or keep society at large in their considerations, for it was and is obvious to them, there would be no point in their art if there were absolutely no hope of finding a responsive audience. The non-participating view and a sense of aloofness on the part of a folk-artist, (poet, singer, folktale creator, or teller, proverb-riddle-maker and so on) is unknown in the realm of folklore. Folklore may be the creation of an individual or a group, but in the ultimate analysis, a creation becomes folklore, only when, through a test of time, it is accepted by the folk, or a society. Finally, folklore is the wealth of the society. Thus, when the anthropologist goes to an Indian village or in a tribal locality for a study and records the ways of life of a particular people, he describes their techniques of farming, hunting, fishing, their inheritance and other phases of property ownership, their system of land tenure, their legal and political system, their kinship terms and obligations, their institutions of marriage and family, the other units within their social structure and their functions, their theology, magical practices and omens, concepts of the soul, their housing, clothing, sexual behaviour, techniques of divination and the other aspects of their religion and world view, their economic conditions, their pottery and metal working and so on. Such studies which we speak of as ethnographies, can give, I feel, only an incomplete description if they do not also include folklore, which means the folktales including myths, legends, fairytales, animal tales household tales, fables, numskull tales, proverbs, riddles, jokes, folk etymologies, folk similies, folk metaphors, ballads, folk songs, rhymes, chants, charms folk dramas, dances, games, rituals, folk beliefs, festivals, customs, folk paintings, sculpture, arts and crafts, architectural techniques, and other forms of folklore employed by the people including the material aspects of folklore like quilt, food recipes, barn, fence types and so on. All these elements of folklore, which bear the recreational as well as utility value, sometimes form a bridge between literature and non-literate society and between one culture and another. Although some Indian anthropologists, for one reason or another, devote little attention to folklore while making their study of the Indian people, it becomes obvious that any ethnographic study which does not consider folklore can only be a partial and incomplete description of the culture as a whole. Folklore may be treated as a medium through which a people speak with their heart in the form of a creation in order to fulfil their needs both artistic, entertainment and functional.

Social context of folklore

I would begin with Hallowell's remark, "I cannot help believing that much valuable material that would deepen our understanding of culture lies awaiting those who will systematically study oral narratives in relation to all aspects of society" (1947, 548). The folktales including myths probably contain all that is interesting to the narrator and the listeners, and that a picture of their way of thinking and feeling is revealed through them that renders their ideas as free from any external influence. "What people choose to talk about is always important for our understanding of them, and the narratives they choose to transmit from generation to generation and to listen to over and over again can hardly be considered unimportant in a fully rounded study of their culture. When, in addition, we discover that all their narratives, or certain classes of them, may be viewed as true stories, their significance for actual behavior becomes apparent. For people act on the basis of what they believe to be true, not on what they think is mere fiction" (Hallowell, 1947, 548). Malinowski emphasizes that the interest of the story is vastly enhanced and it is given its proper character by the manner in which it is told. Most of his observations of folklore in the social context touch upon the functions of folklore and upon the relations of folklore to culture. He mentions some of the specific features from his study of folklore of the Trobriand Islanders which are as follows:

1. Fairy tales (*Kukwanebu*) are fictional, dramatically told and privately owned. They are told in November, between the harvest and fishing seasons. There is a vague belief, not very seriously held, that their recital has a beneficial influence on the new crops which have been recently planted in the gardens, and they end with a formalized reference to a very fertile wild plant.
2. Legends (*Libwogwo*) are believed to be true and to contain important factual information. They are not privately owned, told in any stereotyped way, or magical in their effect.
3. Myths (*liliu*) are regarded not merely as true, but as venerable and sacred. They are told when rituals to which they refer are to be performed, or when the validity of these rituals are questioned (1926. 20-30).

Thus, for any social study and to correlate that study with folkloristics, one must take note of the time and place folklore is told and narrated, the identity of the narrator and the composition of the audience, the factor of private ownership, the style of recitation, the participation by the audience, the attitudes of the people and the functions, for the evaluation of folklore. Davenport gives an account of the position of myths among the Marshall Islanders and says:

> The myths are generally accepted as true, though today parts, particularly those which tell of the old gods and demigods, may not be so regarded. Modern myths are the true stories of today. Because their veracity is undisputed, they are very hard to get, for the people do not class them with other forms of stories. (1953, 221, 223, 224).

The study of the social context of folklore is closely related to its place in the daily round of life of those who tell it. A series of facts must be recorded, along with the text, if the problems of the relation between folklore and culture or the functions of folklore or even the creative role of the narrator, are to be analysed. According to Bascom these facts include

(1) when and where the various forms of folklore are told; (2) who tells them, whether or not they are privately

> owned, and who composes the audience: (3) dramatic devices employed by the narrator, such as gestures, facial expressions, pantomime, impersonation or mimicry; (4) audience participation in the form of laughter, assent or other responses, running criticism or encouragement of the narrator, singing or dancing or acting out parts in a tale; (5) categories of folklore recognized by the people themselves and (6) attitudes of the people to ward these categories (1954, 334).

The recording of folklore in the pattern suggested by Bascom in itself is a useful field technique for the anthropologists, specially for the folklorists. Through these recordings and other investigations of our folklore it becomes clear to us that folklore has been an important part of the work, worship, leisure and entertainment, daily life, birth and death, individual and social behavior, or in a word, of the total existence of the bulk of the population of the Indian subcontinent. Indra Deva, a renowned sociologist, admits:

> Folklore is actively shared by both men and women of even lowest castes. Not only the rural people, but a large part of the population of the pre-industrial urban centres are active bearers of the oral tradition. This wide sharing is brought out by the selection of themes and their treatment in various genres of folk literature. The attitudes of different castes towards each other, including that of the lower castes towards the higher; the nature of the diverse relationships in the particular joint family, the built in tensions in them, and the resentment of the woman, operative religions and magical beliefs and practices among the folk, and even the impact of modern social forces find ample expression in the folk-literature of various regions of India. A systematic analysis of oral tradition can, therefore, yield useful hypotheses about any subtle aspects of social relationships and attitudes of the common people" (Giri Raj Gupta [ed], 1976, 88-89).

This is exactly the drawback where we stand silenced, as neither the sociologists nor the anthropologists of the Indian subcontinent have so far made any ecouraging venture to analyse folklore both sociologically and anthropologically. The less we say about the folklorists of India, Bangladesh and Pakistan the better, as almost all of them belonging to the past and present centuries have been more guided by emotion in eulogizing folklore as the glory of the past rather than analysing them in their social context. A scientific attitude is something which cannot be expected from almost all the folklorists of the different languages of this subcontinent, specially the older generation.

From many examples all around us, I would like to cite a few where folklore tells us of the society to which it belongs, its joys and sorrows, its emotional expressions and pathos. In the northern part of Bangladesh, at the time of a wedding, the women sit around the bride and sing songs the meaning of which goes like this: "O the young girl, you are going to have a new life different from the one you had so long with your parents, brothers and sisters. There you will have a different experience, experience of love and hatred, of affection and cruelty, of reliance and distrust. Your difficulties will outnumber your advantages—hard realities of life are ahead of you—you are going to be under a chain of bondage. Woman is born like that. Only your love can overcome them all. And your children would be your best asset to provide you the safeguard." This particular song depicts the true position of woman in the societies at large of the Indian subcontinent.

Women in the Vedic age appear to have enjoyed a comparatively higher status in India than that enjoyed by their sisters in the post-Vedic age. In the course of history her position gradually weakened. The belief of the essential inferiority of woman guided the social system in many ways. In India even the marriage was considered to be unbreakable since it was sacred and could not be dissolved at will. One cementing bond behind this was the ideal of *pativratya* or unquestionable fidelity and profound devotion towards the husband laid down strictly for the Hindu wife. It was a one-sided sense of obligation and duty taught to a Hindu wife by virtue of the fact that she was born a woman and was born a Hindu. The husband on the other hand was not bound by any such obligation. In return for the fidelity of his wife, he could be authoritative and coercive of his will. The ideas provided a kind of religious sanctity to marriage, the dissolution of which could never be conceived. Her status had so been lost in oblivion that it had to be aroused afresh through a socio-political slogan of the emancipation of women in the late nineteenth century. Raja Ram Mohan Roy and Ishwar Chandra Vidyasagar led this struggle for the liberation of women while efforts were widely made to legally ban the practice of *sati* and to sanction widow marriage, measures were also taken for the progress of their educational. The Indian National Congress not only supported such a movement, but later it was through this organization that several women leaders became politically and socially eminent. But even then, after more than three decades since the independence of India and Pakistan, and later of Bangladesh, the social status of women in the rural areas has not been radically changed. The widow marriage in Hindu society has not been widely accepted, the curse of the dowry system still persists and the supremacy of male is predominently present even today. Although the widow marriage is prevalent amongst the Muslims, the status of woman in Muslim societies of all the three countries is not at all different from that of a Hindu woman in India. Though social equality has been guaranteed through educational, economic and political rights and the women have been given the right to divorce and a part of property inheritance of her husband and father (Muslim society), the older traditional ideas still persist and often stand in the way of further liberation of women. The song collected from a Muslim family reveals the truth of a woman's fate and gives a picture of the hard realities of their life. The song resembles in thought the *Nababadhu* (a new bride), a famous poem of Rabindranath Tagore in his book of poem named Mahua (the name of a flower) composed in 1926-27, in which he depicts the picture of a new bride going by a boat towards the upper-current of the river and says that since long past, many brides have gone like her to embrace the new life—some were successful, some proved to be failures and cautioned her with his superb poetical genius thus:

You have your hard realities integrated with sorrow waiting for you, your pain of separation,
But your days would be filled out gradually and you would be free from repentence, if only you would tell me before you pass through this river,
O the sweet bride
That you would kindle the light with the light of your heart
And in exchange of things that you would receive
You can say, I have given my love.

Anonymity is the main criterion of folklore though not always. Professionals are few and the writers and the composers as a separate class are unknown in the world of folklore. Some types of folklore are sung or performed by a group of people and sometime they are being rewarded by the man from an establishment, but the bulk of folklore elements—both from the oral tradition or in the material form or from written-down-source which may have even been published—are widely shared by the people of the society engaged in various walks of life. Hence the scope of being alienated from the mainstream of life in the case of folklore, is almost nil and cannot be conceived of. One of the main points of criticism very often raised against the modern writers is that they are prone to become in-grown and their writings have failed to depict the true picture of society and to reflect the common feelings existing in society all around them. Folklore, literature having been a major part of it, is almost completely free from this limitation—it is truly of the society, by the society and for the society. When a proverb is uttered, as the occasion demands, it expresses the experience of not a particular person, but the whole of society. When a riddle is told, it not only presents a puzzle but reflects through it the intellect of society, sometime it demonstrates the philosophy of life underlying in its deep structure. This is also true of the other elements of Indian folklore as a whole. The relationships of persons within the joint family, of grandparents, parents and their brothers' families; of sons and daughters and the cousins and of the grand-children are very frequently featured in the folklore of the Indian subcontinent. How the wife has to cut jokes with her husband's younger brother and sisters and carefully avoid the eyes of her husband's elder brother, how she has to respect her parents-in-law and husband's elder sisters, her harassment and chastisement by her mother-in-law, and sisters-in-law, how she has to face things good and bad, how her performances would reflect on the status of her parents and relatives at her village, how her husband is restricted to pass time with her at daytime in the presence of others and even ashamed to humour her fancies—all these are the themes very vividly enshrined in the words and descriptions of Indian folk songs, ballads, tales and proverbs. In a similar manner, the jealousies and rivalries of brothers due to the roles played by wives, their selfish ends leading to the break in the joint-family structure, as also the feeling of affection between brothers and sisters even after their marriage, the coming back of widow sisters to the brother's family and maintenance of her family by the brother, a cordial relation between the maternal uncle and the nephew, the usual practice of sending gifts or food periodically to the married daughters' and sister's families, bringing the son-in-law by the father-in-law to his family and extending warm hospitality to him and his children during fastivals, all of which reflect the cementing of the relationship founded through the bond of marriage. These are the recurrent themes of our folklore that concerns the family life in the Indian subcontinent.

Some of the Indian ballads give a graphic picture of domestic complications where, again, the depiction of society along with the presentation of literary flavour and poetic excellence, according to the ability of the poets and singers, receives the uppermost consideration. The theme of one such ballad of Orissa is quoted below:

> The management of the house rests upon the mother who cleans the cow-shed, cooks food, brings up the children and works all day long without the assistance of any domestic servant. When her son attains marriageable age, she insists that her husband make a search for a good daughter-in-law, for she is unable to perform the domestic duties alone and is in need of somebody else's help. Moreover so many housewives of her age are enjoying food cooked by their daughters-in-law. If she dies before the marriage of her son, she will be bereft of this enjoyment altogether.

> When the marriage ceremony is over, the mother-in-law treats the daughter-in-law as her own daughter and proudly sings her virtues before the neighbours.
>
> Days pass. The guardian of the house becomes old and infirm. The son now becomes the chief active member on whose earning rests the management of the house. Now, who will be the queen of the house? The old lady who still wants to retain the *status quo* does not permit the daughter-in-law to talk or move freely. The daughter-in-law becomes a prisoner in the kitchen for years.
>
> The bride revolts. Why should she bow her head before such a proud mother-in-law who has no affection for her? When toleration brings in no change of heart, when weeping, the weapon of the weak, proves totally fruitless, she violently resists. Quarrels begin and the house becomes strife-ridden. The son feels helpless. On one side is the affectionate mother and on the other his beloved. Whom will he suppress or support? Any partiality creates more complications.
>
> In due time the oppressed daughter-in-law occupies the position of mother-in-law herself. Now a new cycle begins. (Das, Mahapatra 1979, 38-39).

In some of the Indian ballads of the same type, either the first story or the second cycle ends with the suicide of either the mother-in-law or the bride thus making the ending a tragic one.

Even the animal tales also are not in any way disassociated with our societies—they relate in them the social relations between man and man, between man and animal and between man and God or nature. Some of them are allegorical and symbolic, but there also social philosophy is expressed through the content. Let us mention one below from my own collection from Bangladesh.

> There was a she-goat named Sonali. She had three small kids who depended on her milk. One day she went out in the forest to graze leaving the small ones behind. It so happened that a hungry tiger suddenly appeared and wanted to make a meal of her. Sonali was concerned for her kids and prayed that if she was allowed to go back, she

would feed the kids, take leave of them and come back. The tiger was amazed and, though he was hungry, he allowed Sonali to go back only to experiment how his prey, slipping out of his clutches, would behave.

After a reasonable lapse of time Sonali came back in front of the tiger followed by her kids and declared that she considered her promise, the truth, more valuable than her life. That was why she returned. The tiger was moved by this and allowed her to go unhurt.

Honouring one's promise and truth has been glorified through this tale signifying the inherent philosophy of Indian societies through ages.

Examples of such tales, myths, ballads, songs, proverbs and other elements of folklore are available in hundreds amongst the societies of this subcontinent where social context is the primary object and the life of the peoples with its realities figured out through verbal and performing arts, language of the heart and expression embodied in material objects.

Cultural context of folklore

The discussion evaluating folklore as the pulse of the people in the context of its social affiliation brings us to the question: how far is folklore related to literature. If we approach the complex problem of the relationship between folklore and literature we may say without hesitation that folk literature in all languages precedes written literature which developed much later. While considering this question, Archer Taylor, one of the greatest American folklorists of the present century, raised three problems relating to three different kinds of relationships: (1) folklore is, in many cultures, indistinguishable from literature; (2) literature contains elements borrowed from folklore; and (3) writers have initiated folklore (1948: 219). I would first deal with problem one. The *Old Testament* in Hebrew and the *Quran* in Arabic are two examples of literature of a high order in both the cultures. It is historically true that many people embraced Islam because of being moved by the literary excellence of the verses of the *Quran*. Both these great scriptures contain in the innumerable elements of folklore. This is also true about older religious scriptures of India, the *Vedas*, the *Smritis*, the *Puranas*, the *Upanishads* and the Buddhist and Jain scriptures. It will not be wrong to say that the Indian religious scriptures as named here and the later ones are folkloric rather than being dry description of religious performances. The *Ramayana*, *Mahabharata*, *Cilapatticaram*, the three great epics of India are indebted to folk literature and oral tradition in a great many ways and I would not be surprised if any scholar, by making a futile attempt to distinguish the folklore elements in them from the pieces of literature of art makes a frustrating remark that the whole contents of these are folklore. We have unhesitatingly accepted this position so far as the *Kathasaritsagara*, *Panchatantra*, *Brihat Katha*, the *Vetal-Panchavimsati*, the *Jatakas*, which are regarded as the best collections of folktales all over the world, though they were originally in written form. In many cultures, specially in India, folk literature and literature of art have mutually exchanged their positions form oral to written form and from written to oral form from centuries after centuries and it is hardly possible to distinguish them from one or the other. In *Kalevala*, the classical Finnish literature in the form of songs, the elements of folk song have a far greater place than what we call literature of art. It is said that probably only two per cent of the verses of *Kalevala* cannot be proved to be of folk origin.

So far as style is concerned, there appears no significant difference between folk literature and the modern literature. The manner of treatment of these in folktales are almost identical with those of fiction and novels. There are many Indic tales where a poor girl falls in love with a prince or a princess falls in love with a poor young man, they face troubles and obstacles which seemed almost insurmountable at one time, but ultimately they overcome them and live happily. These are also the usual themes of many novels and fictions and specially our movies have enough of them. "If we state the history of a genre of folklore and the history of a genre of literature in general terms, we see that the workers in these two fields are trying to solve similar problems" (Taylor, quoted by Dundes,

1965, 37). The obvious difference lying between the two is that "folklore uses conventional themes and stylistic devices and makes no effort to disguise their conventional quality while the literary artist either diverts his work of conventional quality by avoiding cliches of either form or matter or, as Housman does, charges them with new content" (Taylor, Dundes, 1965, 39-40).

The second problem is not difficult to deal with. So far as the literatures of the Indian languages are concerned they contain many elements borrowed from folklore. The medieval Bengali literature is full of such borrowed materials. Even in the modern Bengali literature there is a flood of folklore elements either willfully borrowed or unconsciously taken to suit the present situation. Not to speak of others, Tagore himself gladly accepted some of the themes as well as the tunes of his songs from the Baul songs, a precious treasure of Bengal folklore. His famous song "Amar Sonar Bangla", the national anthem of Bangladesh, provides the best example of such acceptance. Parallels of proverbs to some of Shakespeare's proverbs, or of the mythical elements to some of Tolstoy's novels, can more easily be found than parallels to some of their stylistic conventions.

Let us come to the third problem that involves not the willfull borrowing or conscious acceptance and unconscious influence of folklore, but the intentional limitation of folk genres. There are poets and even the writers of other forms of literature who intentionally imitated folklore, sometimes unanonymous, and passed it through the main current wishing that his writings would live as folk literature. But there are others who imitate folklore intentionally and place them within the bigger canvas of their own writings and this gives us a difficult task in tracing them. Examples could be found through a minute observation of the novels and fictions of Sarat Chandra Chattopadhya, Manik Banerjee and Tarasankar-Banerjee, three most outstanding novelists of modern Bengali literature. "Until a differentiation of folk literature and the literature of art occurred, conscious imitations of folk style and folk matter could not have come into being. The proverb yields perhaps the most various examples. Almost everyone who has studied proverbs has fallen into the delusion that he could invent proverbs . . . poets have imitated the ballads. Heine wrote the *Lorelei* and Dante Gabriel Roseti *Sister Helen*. Their failure to employ some obvious technical details of ballad style raises the question whether they perceived these conventions" (Taylor, Dundes, 1965, 41-42). In spite of some success achieved by Jasimuddin, a modern Bengali poet, his failure to adjust to many of the folklore elements imitated by him intentionally is considered by his critics as his main drawback.

Although I have dealt with the same problem, whlie discussing the aesthetic-literary theory, for example, the position of folk literature vis-a-vis sophisticated literature, I have raised this issue and discussed it in short to focus broadly the differences between folk literature and literature of art, that means the modern literature, and to show that the difference between the two is not of that magnitude which may demand inclusion of modern literature as part of culture and the omission of folk literature from the same; One is to be adorned and the other is to be treated as untouchable. One gets a free access as it rightly deserves, in the academic institutions and is given the status of a discipline, the other is kept at a safe distance so that the dirt from its body does not unclean and infect us unwholesomely. On the other hand, my assumption is that the culture of a people can be fully understood only through a thorough knowledge of their folklore. In other words, folklore is the mirror of culture and the extent to which it is so has been mainly the concern of the anthropologists so far. The academicians of the Indian subcontinent have seldom diverted their sincere attention to the demanding requirement of the study of folklore from the lowest to the highest level. The modern writers of all the three countries have cared very little to invite folklore openly and allow it an honourable seat by the side of modern literature, except that in time of need they consciously, or unconsciously stretch their hands to borrow things from the world of folklore or some would still intentionally imitate folklore and try to gloss it over. Malinowski understood this point long before us and emphasized that in a typical Trobriand origin-myth the brother and sister relation can not be interpreted as simply a mythological allusion to incest. The underlying philosophy indicates in such myth that the sister represents the figure for the transmission of the family line, and the brother, rather than the husband, represents an indispensable guardian to sustain the family and rear the children through their joint efforts. Nothing could be more true when Herskovits observes "a substantial body of folktales is more than the literary expression of a people. It is, in a very real sense, their ethnography which, if systematized by the student, gives a penetrating picture of their way o life" (1948, 418).

The cultural value of folklore has also been enhanced by its importance felt by scholars in the search of philological aspects of various languages. Max Muller stated "to represent the supreme God as committing every kind of crime, as being deceived by men, as being angry with his wife and violent with his children, is surely proof of a disease of language" (1897, Vol. 1,69). Muller used the etymological technique, but his linguistic reconstructions reduced myths to allegories of nature. According to Von Sydow there are, in any given community, only a very few active bearers and yet these few individuals account for the continuity and dissemination of traditions. He argues that folktales and other forms of folklore are not transmitted by some superorganic wave or stream moving in some mystical process of automigration. Marchen, the most complex form of folktale, is transmitted, he contended, only if and when one active bearer communicates such a tale to another active bearer" (Dundes, 1965, 229). The Gri brothers, with their theory of the spread of folklore through Aryan migrations and their etymological techniques, suggested that words in the tales have become managed and misunderstood in the course of retelling and that by reconstructing the original proto-Indo-European words the inconsistency and absurdities in tales could be explained" (Bascom, 1954, 341).

Von Sydow feels that "the questions about the bearers of tale tradition, of the cases in which a tradition is applied and can be transmitted, the changes that may be brought about by various kinds of mutation, and by oicotypification, are naturally of the greatest weight for a scientific study, of the folktale; and the results of such study even by the best of methods, be correct unless they are based on a right knowledge of the life of the folktale and the laws by which it is governed . . . on the other hand, it is evident that collaboration between philology and the study of folklore is of supreme importance. Philologists can produce much material of very great value to folklore research, as has from old literature been probed" (1948: 207-9).

Thus, folklore has its linguistic value in the cultural context. Since it is the pulse of the people, some studies have been done by the linguists in respect of its importance in the process of dissemination and retention of vocabularies, specially the phonemes, morphemes and sememes. It is difficult to conduct the historical study of linguistics without the help of folklore. Paul Kiparsky's view is this that "by a long series of historical processes the proto-Indo-European parent language gradually split up into a number of separate languages such as Germanic, Celtic, Slavic and these in turn evolved into their numerous modern decendants. The same processes of change are responsible for the diversity of dialects within English—and after some milennia they may well have resulted in a number of languages descended from English in just the same way that English, German and so on are descended from Proto-Germanic. The nature of these processes, specially through the dissemination of folklore, stands as the question basic to all further workin historical linguistics" (Historical Linguistics, in Lyons J:1970:302-303). Even the structure of a language could be found more genuinely preserved in the syntax, phonology, phonemics and morphology of the language of folklore handed down to us from ancient time. "A Full description of natural language (which specially preserved in folklore) is a grammatical semantic characterization of the language" (Fodor and Katz, 1964, 480). Even Chomsky, in his *Aspects of the Theory of Syntax* (1965, p. 171) accepted the importance of these components which are kept almost intact in folklore. The true nature of Kernel sentence, which Chomsky defines as "when we apply obligatory transformations in the generation of a given sentence, we call the resulting sentence a Kernel sentence" (1968:46), I guess, has been ourmore accurately pre-served in the language of folklore than in our modern literary language (Islam, Morphological Analysis of Folklore 1982, 129-158).

Lord Curzon, the Governor-General of India, inaugurated the ethnographic survey in 1903 and Sir George Grierson brought out the first volume of his Linguistic Survey of India in the same year. Thus a great impetus was felt in the study of ethnography, folklore and linguistics during the first decade of the present century (Islam, *History of Folktale Collections*, 1982, 18).

Although the collections were made and also published by some of the British administrative officers, their relatives and friends and the European missionaries, some of which merited highly from the points of view of folkloristics, but so far as the scientific linguistic study is concerned in preserving the language of folklore, hardly any of these scholars could be given credit. For example, besides Grierson, T.H. Lewin, even before Grierson, made an attempt (1874) to study the language of ozo tribes, who wear their hair in a knot resting on the nape of the neck, and inhabit the hilly area to the east of Chittagong district of Bangladesh. Lewin in order to introduce the reader to the language of the Lushai Kuki clans presents three full tales and many short anecdotes, customs and superstitions collected by him. His tales are presented both in texts and translations with information about the informants and notes for the understanding of the tales. But his study was purely of an introductory nature and more descriptive than analytical. The Indian scholars, before independence, who became famous as linguist, did not pay much attention to the study of folklore and use of its materials to formulate some methodological or theoretical approach to the study of linguistics. V.S. Upadhyay, in one of his recent papers, has given a description of the studies on linguistics and folklore in Bihar, but it does not give any clear indication as to how folklore has been used by the scholars named by him in their studies. He admits at the very opening lines: "The linguistic and folkloric studies in an anthropological context depends most of all upon two things, the exigencies of field work and nature of theoretical orientation" (J.S. Research, 1978, 105). How far the scholars listed by Upadhyay have fulfilled these two things as also to correlate folklore with linguistics through the theoretical orientation, has yet to be assessed from social, anthropological, folkloric and linguistic points of view. Upadhyay has mentioned that "the oldest of vedic literature also deals with parts of speech. In Brahminic and Aranyak books, we find the use of grammar and linguistics for the division of words" (1978, 105). But a folklorist would like to see how this was related to folklore and what impact it still on the study of folklore from the linguistic point of view. I am sure the investigation on this will bear a very fruitful result.

The study of inconsistencies between the behaviour of characters in folklore and members of a society also helps us to understand the culture of that society. The psychoanalytic school provides well-known answers to many of the questions linked up with our conscious ideas, feelings, interests and beliefs originated in the unconscious, as could be traced out from the myths. The whole evolution of beliefs, customs or rituals, which we find in the individuals and the societies, has run a course of perhaps thousands of years through the oral tradition of folklore. According to Jones, "There is a far-reaching parallelism between survivals of primitive life from the racial past and survivals from the individual past. . . . The study of survivals in folklore can be usefully supplemented by the study of survivals in living individuals, where they are far more accessible to direct investigation" (1930, 224). Thus, the psychology of individual human being is quite relevant to the study of folklore. Some folklorists and anthropologists are concerned with the internal inconsistencies in folklore, specially in mythology, rather than between the conduct of the members of the society and the characters of folklore. Benedict explains some of the discrepancies between Zuni folklore and custom in terms of cultural lag while Radclife-Brown is concerned with the internal inconsistencies as manifest by the contradiction between the Andamanese view of lightning as a person who shook his leg, and as a fire brand thrown by Bihku (1933, 326-97). I have observed many people in rural Bangladesh to joking with a married man regarding his sexual relation with his mother-in-law, although for a Muslim, it is unimagineable to have a relation like this. There are tales, specially the numskull stories, prevalent in Bangladesh where the hints or even the actual sexual relation with mother-in-law could be seen. Quite opposite examples are also available, as cited by Opler, who writes of the Lipan Apache:

Of the four Athabaskar cultures, which I have studied, the

> Lipan is the only one in which the mother-in-law avoidance is not required. Interestingly enough, Lipan mythology does not include in the coyote cycle an episode in which the trickster violates his mother-in-law (1940, 7).

Rattray has cited some examples of inconsistency from Ashanti folklore, of which one may be quoted here:

> The peculiarity presented by a people normally decorous in speech and conduct, whose folktales nevertheless often contain the most Rubelaisian passages, who would yet consider it highly improper to relate these passages if divorced from the occasion and context in which they are rightly publicly paraded. . . "subjects ordinarily regarded as sacred, for example, the sky-God, the lesser Gods, fetishes, spirit ancestors, the sick, chiefs, sexual matters, appear to be treated as if profane, and sometimes even tend to become the subject of ridicule" (1930:xi and x). From the evidences, he concludes "that west Africans had discovered for themselves the truth of the psychoanalysts theory of repressions, and that in these ways they sought an outlet for what might otherwise become a dangerous complex" (1930, XII).

Folklore, thus, in the context of culture, functions as an amusement as well as a powerful indicator of culture. From many points of view, folklore proves to be the pulse of the people. Folklore cannot be dismissed simply as a form of amusement. W. La Barre puts it very rightly. "The folklorist whose intent goes beyond the merely descriptive to the dynamic must be prepared to search out and listen to the cultural associations and contexts of his materials, just as the analyst must listen to the individual free associations of his patients" (1948, 388).

FUNCTIONAL VALUE OF FOLKLORE

While treating folklore as the pulse of the people, its functional value both in society and life of the individuals deserves to be ascertained. While discussing social change and folklore, I have mentioned in detail the functions played by folklore in the context of social change vis-a-vis the influence of social change on folklore. Hence I will restrict myself only to the broad analysis of some of the functions of folklore.

Myth's functional role in the primitive society has been accepted and analysed by anthropologists and folklorists. According to Malinowski, myth "expresses, enhances and codifies belief; it safeguards and enforces morality; it vouches for the efficiency of the ritual and contains practical rules for the guidance of mass. Myth is thus a vital ingredient of human civilization, it is not an idle tale, but a hard-worked active force; it is not an intellectual explanation or an artiotic imagery, but a pragmatic charter of primitive faith and moral wisdom" (1926:19). Levi-Strauss also believes that the myths of primitive people reveal a kind of truth about the nature and working of human mind. Among the tribe Jicarilla, the myth is of greatest functional importance, as observed by Opler," in the guidance of his behavior, his beliefs and his ceremonies. . . The mythology represents for him the summation of knowledge on the basis of which he must act. . . The mother and grandparent schools the child in accordance with its dictates. The ceremonial man conducts his rite in terms of directions found therein" (1940, x). Myth's importance in the Indian societies, specially of the Hindus and most of the tribes, hardly needs any analysis as it is a recognized fact. Myths, in fact, constitute a significant part of religious beliefs, customs and performances of Hindu and tribal religions.

Not to speak of the myths alone, I have no knowledge of any element of folklore that does not have a functional value in the life of the society and individual in any part of the world. Even if we consider only the question of amusement, there too we cannot deny the fact that it has an important function through which the society receives its mental food. Some elements of folklore have more than one function. A song, when sung at a night's gathering or at an arranged cultural function or in a folk drama, is enjoyed by the listeners, and the same song may be sung by an individual or a group while he or the group is at work in the field, ploughing, planting, taking the weeds out from the paddy or jute plants, harvesting and so on. Proverbs serve a specific and important intellectual function—that of subsuming the particular under the general. But among the Dahomeans proverbs are introduced in pleas before courts of justice, in court testimony and court decisions or in dissent from these decisions. Among the Jabo, as Herzog states:

> An important function of the proverb is to smooth the social friction and dissatisfaction and to ease the individual in his efforts to adjust himself in his setting and fate. If people disagree, if they work at cross-purposes, if a person complains of injustice, an older, more experienced, or less concerned person is always at hand a comforting, quieting, light-shedding proverb. The number of proverbs implying, 'under the circumstances, what did you expect?' is impressive. The same proverb may be quoted for advice, instruction, or as a warning—always to prevent or lessen friction (1936, 2).

The vital role of the proverbs play in the dispensation of justice in the Anang tribunals has been illustrated by John C Messenger, Jr., on the basis of his research conducted in Nigeria during 1951-52. One case is as follows. A boy accused of impregnating an unmarried girl denied his guilt and accussed a young man of having committed the act and boasting of it to other men in the Obio. Not only did the girl contract the defendant's plea, but the young man whom the latter had accused asserted his innocence. As the trial progressed, the case came to rest upon the girl's claim that the boy was guilty, especially after a number of witnesses admitted hearing the young man boast of his sexual exploits with her, exploits which he emphatically denied. The girl's relatives testified that her honesty was above reproach, and oath might have been called for had not two witnesses spoken out using proverbs which influenced the judges to rule against the boy. The father of the boy, when called upon as a character witness, seemed reluctant to support his so, admitting that he often had punished the boy for sexual practices and telling lies. In the light of this he told the court, he considered his son capable of having committed the act for which he was accused and ended his testimony by using a proverb, "the nosasak said she was ashamed of the small size of her offspring." The smallest of the birds in the region, the nosasak is thought by the Anang to be ashamed of its diminutive size. Naturally, they claim, the mother of the species is even more ashamed of its fledging since it is far smaller than she. In employing this maximum the father revealed his lack of faith in his son's claims and the great shame he felt at making the admission publicly. The proverb which finally pursuaded the judges to declare the boy guilty was used by the girl's father when he was called upon as the last witness. He denounced the accused after telling that the word of his daughter was to be trusted absolutely, highlighting his speech with the proverb, "The Ekenuk tried to eat as much as Ikdud and his stomach burst". There are several types of rats in that area; one, the ekenuk, is only two or three inches in length, while another, the (Ikdud), is almost two feet long. The girl's father likened the boy to the small variety and a married man to the large one; the youth is about to suffer for an act that only a married man is eligible to perform with his spouse (1959, 70-71).

Innumerable functional use of proverbs can be cited from different languages of the Indian subcontinent. I know of a case of a wedding—for which the date was also fixed in a village. The alliance came almost to breaking-point as the father of the groom received information about the doubtful chastity of the bride. Proverbs relating to those who rely on the hearsay and ultimately are cheated, were uttered before him by the old and experienced people of the village. This resulted in convincing the father affectively and the marriage was held thereafter smoothly. There are proverbs which contain the process of treatment, names of folk medicine both preventive as well as curative. A Telugu proverb says, *Sonthi Sodhistundi* meaning "dry ginger cleanses", that is, drives away general ill-health). Another goes like this, *Leta gumadi-kaya vishatulyam*, meaning "the tender pumpkin is equal to poison". A Bengali proverb contradicts this—"a tender pumpkin is good for kidney". The contradictory mention of the function of some object in the proverbs of different cultures, provide an interesting scope for the comparative study of two cultures.

Even some of the songs of the Indian subcontinent are not sung without having a function in addition to amusement. The following Telugu songs are sung by Andhra girls while playing "Bitti", a kind of game wherein two girls holding each other's hands move fast round and round clockwise leaning back 90 degrees away from each other.

Oppulakuppa — Vayyāri bhāma
Minapa pappu — menti pindi
Tati bellam — taguvagu neyyi
Guppedu tinte — kulukutāde
Nadumu gatti — ba mātabatti

O girl of infinite charms
O girl of personified beauty
blackgram dal and menthi powder
(*Powder of Fenugreek seeds*)
Jaggery of palm tree, cooked in ghee properly
If eaten a handful daily
The waist which is shaky
Becomes strong—this is my word).

It gives the meaning that the girl would be interested in sexual intercourse and her durability would be increased if she takes that folktonic for sexual potency of women everyday. Another version of the same song gives out a prescription for curing impotency of males:

Oppula Kuppa — Vayyāri bhāma
Sanna biyyam — Cāya pappu
Minapa pappu — Merika biyyam
Pālu neyyidi — Pasam vandu
Ni mogadu tinte — ānanda mante

(O girl of infinite charms
O girl of personified beauty
Take superfine rice, bleached pulses
and blackgram dal
cook them with ghee and milk
if it is fed to your husband
You will enjoy life).

The functions of some of the tales are certainly significant. The stories of *Panchatantra*, *Jataka* and *Betal* are full of moral values. Some tales born in the Indian subcontinent are still used for religious purpose. Some stories of the *Bible* and the *Qoran* are meant for moral teaching. *Rig Veda* has some songs and tales in ballad form which may be considered as the earliest specimens of the functional use of folklore. *Akhyayanas* in vedic literature are nothing but tales in the early form. Of all vedas, *Atharvaveda* contains more treasures of folklore such as rituals and rites, beliefs and superstitions, charms and incantations. Thus the use of folklore in religious scriptures are a common factor almost all over the world. Among the Dahom as Herskovits relates, at wakes or ceremonies for the dead, neither the historical tales nor the simple animal stories would be seemly, for the dead are held beyond the need for moralizing, and the obscence story is called to furnish entertainment (1938: 325).

From the short analysis of the functional use of folklore given in the foregoing paragraphs, I would like to emphasize that these functions have been of great importance in engraining a strong stabilizing effect on culture. It is a significant mechanism for creating and holding the cultural stability in a society.

> Thus one might distinguish between amusement, creative fantasy, and psychological escape; between the mirroring of culture in folklore and the contrast between them; between folklore as a validation of culture and as a guide to behaviour and ritual, between its roles in embodying the content of education and as a didactic device for expressing social approval and disapproval, and as a means of suggesting that one be content with his lot (Dundes, 1965, 297).

Regulating character of folklore

When we view folklore as the pulse of the people we have to consider the various functions of folklore, of which its regulating character in the society appears to be significantly prominent. Let me cite an example from the *tushu* song of

Purulia. When the State Re-organization Commission was set up in 1956, Bihar tried to retain Purulia within the state of Bihar. But the feeling of the people was in favour of its inclusion in West Bengal. A song reflects this feeling, the first line of which is translated here.

O the brother of Bihar
you won't be able to keep us
by showing the strength of stick.

During the liberation war of Bangladesh in 1971, many protest songs were composed by the folkbards, which are sung by the folk till today. Later on, many ballads have been composed wherein the descriptions of the tragedy of merciless killings and inhuman torture by the Pakistani brute forces and the unprecedented pogrom form the basic themes. Hundreds of such songs, ballads, descriptive anecdotes, a few proverbs, riddles have been collected and preserved in the Bangla Academy, the National Academy of Bangladesh. From my own collections, I cite below a translation of a *Dhua* song, a popular folksong of Papna:

(1)

O Alas! what shall I do
Whenever I turn my eyes
The Killers of Pakistan can see me
Where shall I go and where shall I stay
My heart becomes dry with a desperate feeling.

(2)

O, they move in pairs
with gun in hand and some on shoulder
Some iron is stinged on their body
They shout, "catch the Bengali, catch the Bengali"
And with that they fire bullets
wherever they see the wives and daughters
They get hold of them, put hand on their crying mouth, and rape,
O, really a very sad time has cast its shadow on the Bengalee
And is it possible to tolerate this plight.

(3)

They bring people on line
And kill them by bullets, so many of them, the men and women,
How shall one count the number !
They have killed hundreds in the village Demra
They have burnt villages at Ishwardi
And many have been killed in Pabna town

Says Ainal, how long shall we bear these happenings
I will enlist my name in the camp of freedom-fighters
And retaliate by firing bullets on them
Whatever comes to my fate
Either I will die or live.

A village bard only knows that if he enlists his name in the camp of the freedom fighters, he will be able to fire bullets and thus retaliate, he does not care for his life.

The pattern of protest and social consciousness as reflected in folklore differs according to the time and context of the society. Even in family life, with relation to love and affection, marriage and maintenance of family folklore functions as a force. The women folk of the Santals are very frank in this respect. In the songs of Dhalbhum, known as the *Pata* song of the Santals referred to by Professor C.R. Laha, a grown-up daughter frankly cautions her mother:

O mother would you take me with you in
the festival named Dhaona? If you don't
I will go out with a man, a son of other parents.
Here going out indicates the
self-decided marriage of the girl.*

Sex may be a gay amusement for man, but for woman it is something beyond that and because of this the mind of a man she loves is more important to her than merely his body. If she gets the mind, she gets everything and a Santal girl can break the social barriers for a loving mind of her man. She says in a song:

*These are translations of folksongs from the original in Bengali.

You are going towards the road
While I am going towards the compound
If I find your mind to be one with mine
I will go with you to a far-away place,
breaking through all the obstacles on my way.*
(Laha, 1979, 23)

Folklore, specially folk songs, work also as regulators of politics in the society. The Pata songs referred to above mostly deal with family affairs, love being prominent of all. Since the songs are generally sung by women, there is hardly any scope for political alertness or protest in these songs, for the women of Dholbhum belong to a backward domain of culture which is far away from the state politics. But even then some songs have shown distinct trends in this respect where they differ with the old ones. A song says:

> People coming from outside are assuring that they would dig ponds and wells for us in the villages. But neither ponds nor wells will come to reality, they are speaking a lie. They are making all these colourful promises only to capture our votes:*

The Soviet folklore provides a meaningful contrast between folklore of pre-revolution era and of the period followed after 1917. The former contains a sense of protest in a milder form, while the latter eulogizes the freedom and achievements under socialism. Two songs are quoted below to show this contrast:

Where the she-goat walks,
There the wheat springs up;
Where the she-goat turns tail,
There the wheat grows thick;
Where the she-goat's foot passes,
There the wheat is in a heap;
Where the she-goat lifts her horn;
There the wheat is in the stack
(Shein, 1887, Vol. 1, Pt. 1, p. 91).

*These are translations by the author of folksongs from the original Bengali.

So, the she-goat lifts her horn when she finds the wheat in the stack. The lifting up of the horns to have food is a sort of protest, though mild in nature and more allegorical, on behalf of those who do not have food. This is a song of the northern part of Russia belonging to pre-revolution era. Let us examine another song where a Soviet Turkmenian woman describes a comparative position of women in pre-revolutionary era and after 1917:

> Now the time has come to break the tent of slavery
> Now you all may drink the delicious sherbet of liberation
> But it was long ago that our women friends were sold to the enemy
> Long ago they were thrown into the well, bound both hand and foot.
> Any one who had boundless wealth would buy four or five of them
> Now there has come, at least, the day of liberation,
> The October Revolution has brought us liberty,
> it has saved us from the ancient bondage,
> And our new rights are new forever more in our own hands.
>
> (Dynnik, 1934, No. 1, 141-42).

Thus one of the favourite themes in the Soviet folklore is the contrast between the old and the new mode of life. On this contrast between the old and the new are based a multitude of the women's songs of the Soviet East. Among many of the peoples of the East, prior to the October Revolution, the position of women was still more difficult than it was in Russian countryside. Women were bought and sold, in the fullest sense of the word, like slaves. This picture has been clearly revealed in the song quoted above.

Both collectors and scholars in the Soviet Union have isolated those productions of Soviet folklore which constituted an effective means of agitation and propaganda for Communist ideas. A great deal of attention of the scholars has been devoted to such themes of contemporary folklore as the civil war, the stages of development of the socialist organization, the collectivization of rural economy, the new mode of life in its contrast with the old, the defence of the country and the life of the Red Army. With reference to the folklore of the past, there has come about in Soviet folkloristics a marked shifting of the centre of attention, as compared with that of scholarship previous to the October Revolution. There has been a wide development of the collection and study of those productions of old folklore which for the most part were left in obscurity by the investigators of the pre-revolutionary period—those in which with the greatest clearness and vigour, there were reflected the revolutionary movements of the popular masses, the class conflict with their oppressors, and all kinds of popular protest against social injustice. Songs and legends about Stepan Razin and Pugachyov, tales, songs, stories about serfdom, tales, songs and proverbs of an anticlerical and antireligious character and so forth.

Thus, Sokolow, a great Russian folklorist, emphatically states,

> The Soviet folklore of all the peoples of the Soviet Union is a most historical document, an indication of the close union in which all the peoples of the socialist motherland live. Through a survey of the oral poetry of the most diverse Soviet peoples may be clearly seen the unity of moods and experiences, expressed in works of the greatest diversity of language and form, yet permeated with common ideas and emotions. The October Revolution awake the creative powers of the labouring masses among all the peoples of the Soviet Union. . . . In the history of the world, it is not possible to point out another stupendous event which could be compared with the October Revolution, in the power of its influence on the creative art of the toiling masses of the people. In the history of the world, it is impossible to find any other event which, in such a short period of time, has brought about such profound changes in the existence of popular creation. The old narrow social and national barriers have been broken down. The working people have drawn their breath in freedom, filling their lungs with the fresh air of the vast and boundless spaces which have been opened up before the peoples of the USSR (1966, 690-91)

The survey of Soviet folklore, of course, as done by most of the Soviet scholars, if strictly viewed with a scientific approach, may seem unusual to some. As, for instance, the use of folklore for propaganda purpose, the concentration on workers songs, revolutionary songs, specially those concerned with the October Revolution and the Civil War, and folklore about Soviet political and military leaders, might appear to some as motivated. But apart from this, the socio-cultural analysis of folklore on the basis of Marxism and Leninism as propounded by the scholars like Propp, Sokolov, Astakhov, Baranov, Gusev, Azadovski, Chicherov, Afanasiev and many others, has, no doubt, enriched folkloristics in many ways. That folklore is the pulse of the people and a regulating force in society has been best proved by the Russian scholars after October Revolution, particularly during the last four decades, and its effects have touched the scholars, specially those who are above any preconceived idea, prejudice and narrowness and are gifted with sufficient mental alertness, all over the world.

Folklore as the pulse of the people also very remarkably existed in the folk songs of China even long before the Communists came to power. In contemporary Communist countries, of course, including China, the governments rework folklore for the purpose of propaganda, the basic premise of which is that folklore is a reflection and weapon of class conflict. The scholars under socialism are motivated to focus the Chinese fairytales wherein the working people and the poor peasants who succeed in taking the lands belonging to the aristocrats and the kings. Under the condition like this, I am afraid, it may so happen that folklore does not appear as regulating force as much as the government or the motivated scholars would regulate it.

> The conscious manipulation of folklore does account for change, but the purist folklorist tends to reject the results of conscious as opposed to unconscious manipulation. He might consider them materials derived from folklore, but not folklore itself. It is interesting to contrast the conscious manipulation of folklore in Communist and in capitalist countries. Part of the ideological difference between them is reflected in the respective rationals for the recasting of

> folk-materials. In the Soviet Union, folklore is moulded for political ends; in the United States folklore is molded for commercial ends. In the Soviet Union, the Government sponsors changes in the folklore to sell Communism; in the United States, individuals rewrite folklore to sell it for profit. Of course, these are goals put upon folklore; but true oral tradition, unlike written tradition, cannot really be squelched, censored or stopped. In Russia no doubt there is genuine folklore that pokes fun about governmental controls just as in America there is folklore that ridicules the mercenary ethic and the millionaire (Dundes, 1965, 309).

This observation of Dundes makes one thing clear to us that folklore serves the purpose of both Communist and capitalist worlds to suit their needs; and this factor, apart from other intrinsic values of folklore in the human societies, also proves its dynamism and forcefulness as the pulse of the people on the one hand and its functional importance on the other.

The ancient China provides an interesting information as to how public opinion regarding the rulers was obtained by the government agents through folklore. The emporor Yui of Hsia Dynasty, one of the three early dynasties of the history of China, whose duty was to take the best care of his subjects, in an effort to perform his role faithfully as the son of the heaven, gave special assignments to a group of officers, who used to go around the villages to find out the opinion of the people as it was commonly expressed in ballads and folk songs. Before the execution of any development plan for the nation or enforcement of any rule, public opinion was obtained. In the ancient literature of China, the expression of public opinion such as mentioned was known as tsai feng, meaning to get the people's opinion and ideas expressed through folk song. When the thickly populated area on two sides of the Yellow River was inundated by flood water, Emperor Yui abandoned his palace, left the family behind and spent thirteen years among the suffering people to execute, under his personal supervision, the plan and process of flood control as well as to conduct the flood water into the sea. He was happy and felt his endeavour rewarded when he got the folk song saying :

Hsia Yui Whang Hsia Yui Whang
You are a friend as well as an emperor
You saved our chickens and saved us from flooding pond
A more prosperous year with more children we are nearer.
(Betty Wang, 1935, 162).

Striking comparisons can be made from the songs composed during the time the great Chinese wall was constructed and a long time thereafter. In order to save China from foreign invasion, Chin Shih Whang, the most tyrannical emperor in the history of China, ordered the construction of the wall, which runs several thousand miles in length, within a short time. Many men had to leave their families and many died while they were at work. Those who did not obey the order of the emperor were even killed. Many people were heavily punished many families were runied as a result of the harsh treatment of the agents of the emperor and his officers. The souls of these people expressed themselves through folklore, created with the themes based on this *Van Lee Chang Cheng*, the legendary meaning of which is "the great wall ten thousand miles long". A song comes from the mouth of a widow, who was married only to be left by her husband a few days after the ceremony of their marriage was over and since then did not return—he died :

With flowers blooming and birds singing
spring is here calling us to visit friends far and near
Other women are accompanied by their husbands and sons
Poor me, I shall go to the wall where my husband's bones
bear
Great Wall! Great Wall!. If you can save us from enemies.
Why not first save our dear ones ?
(Betty Wang, 1935, 162).

This is not one, there are hundreds of such songs, ballads and proverbs, some tales too, where the suppressed feelings of those who became victims of oppression under emperor Chin Shih Whang have been freely released in their language and formed a chain of oral literature. Here also folklore proved its existence as the pulse of the people. On the other hand, songs with completely opposite contents and themes 1 found expression by the Chinese people, wherein the people eulogize the magnanimity of king Chin Shih Whang and the Great Wall as their saviour. One song runs as follows:

> Great Wall, Great Wall, then thousand miles long
> Is situated at northern China and beyond
> It is to keep the middle kingdom from foreign invasion
> And to make the middle kingdom free from emigration.
> If you ask me "who built the wall?
> I shall say "It was Chin Shih Whang, the greatest of all".

It is considered that this song was composed about two thousand years after the completion of the Wall, and it gives expression of a tone, which is quite opposed to the views contained in the earlier ones. The condemnation voiced against the cruelty and tyrannical treatment of the emperor Whang, gradually subsided and later on was absolutely forgotton by the people of new generation after two thousand years, when only the magnitude of the great wall appeared most beneficial to them. Thus, from the Chinese situation folklore also provides us some concrete facts to prove our contention beyond any doubt that the voice of folklore is really the voice of the people, the voice that vibrates through the pulse of folklore.

> One of the important functions of folklore is its service as a vehicle for social protest. Wherever there is injustice and oppression, one can be sure that the victims will find some solace in folklore. Through jokes, songs and proverbs, the anger of the folk is vent upon the often frighteningly unassailable individual or institution. If the folkloristic protest is permitted, it is perhaps because the blame for its composition usually cannot be affixed to one person. It is a collection, not an individual expression, and consequently the singer of a song of protest is not to be blamed for the content of his song. He is only reporting what the folk say (Dundes 1965, 308).

Conjugal life is held in folklore with high esteem. The position of the wife, of course, varies in different societies and depends upon the form of marriage in which it is performed.

Where it takes the form of simple exchange, as could be found in the culture of Sindh area of Pakistan, the position of the wife is very happy. She gets good treatment from the husband and their mutual relations are usually happier than she would have found in the marriage had it been contracted in the form of purchase. Though scarcity of girls in lower societies should in ordinary course confer a relatively superior position on the bride, her purchase has permanently removed the obligation of her husband towards her parental family. Sindhi folklore echoes this helpless position of women :

What am I, have no value
I have no heart, no mind under my breast
I am a purchased commodity
O God! why have you given me the soul
Why have you given me the feeling of love
I would have loved to have born as an animal, a bird
Than to be what I am as a wife.

Of course, the Sindhi culture, one of the richest cultures of the Indian subcontinent, does not present all the gloomy pictures as reflected in this song. But whatever be the case, the above-mentioned song is no doubt like the pulse of the deprived women folk of some of the societies of Sindh. Women's position in these societies may not be unhappy in all the families, but the fact remains that they are very much inferior. In the middle class families the position of wife is fairly happy, but as the middle class people are most conservative, their relations in family life are strictly disciplined according to the old ideas held about the women generally. It is among the Amils and the educated classes as also among the Bhatias and Lohanas of Shikarpur and Sukkur that the woman enjoys a high degree of liberty or even a high degree of authority in the settlement of domestic affairs. Folklore does not overlook this kind of position as the proverb of this class says, "Her wisdom is located in her left heel which disappears after sun-set."

In some parts of upper Sind, of course, the wife is sometime competent to contract marital alliances for her daughters and sons and the father gives only a formal consent. But such authority is never exercised in the societies which have adopted the forms of marriage by purchase or exchange, as the interests of the male will be seriously prejudiced. The modern movement for emancipation of woman and her claim for equality recognized by the modern romantic youth have considerably improved her position both in domestic and social life. The Sindhi folk songs depict the pathos of the suffering women as well as their new awakenings

You have taken me away from my parents
My brothers and sisters
I am ready to give you my love
You give me yours,
Do not treat me so harsh
For if I die
My bones will come out of the grave
As sword, or iron stick.

The feelings expressed through this folksong may be regarded as a silent protest.

Protest may be invisible too. Nuer is a strong tribe in Africa. They are found in the southern part of the Anglo-Egyptian Sudan in the Nasser and Abwong districts and also on the Zeraf Island and along the Nile. At the Rejaf Language Conference in 1928, the Nuer population was estimated as 430,000. A Nuer myth goes like this :

> A man married and took his wife to his village. His work was to go out and herd cattle. One day at the edge of the swamp he found an ogre who was dying of hunger. The man had caught an antelop. He beckoned to the ogre, though he knew what he was. He showed him the antelope. The ogre ate of it. Then he drank water. When he had finished drinking he asked the man, "Did you know who I was a little while ago?" The man replied, "I knew you were an ogre·" The ogre said, "Oh! you saw a person that was starved." "I was helping a person", said the man. The ogre replied, "Oh! I have nothing much to say, but I will show you something."
>
> He dug up a sweet potato and gave it to the man. The man asked, "Is there no other?" The ogre gave him one. He ate it. Again he asked the ogre, "Is there none left?" He

was given another. He asked the ogre, "What is this called?" The ogre replied, "It is called-what?" He signed to the man with his head. He said "This belongs to you alone. Do not show it to the people." The man went on digging his potatoes. When he brought the cattle back to the village, his wife gave his mush. He refused it and called someone in to eat it. The next day he went out with the cattle again. He dug up his sweet potatoes again and ate them. He had plenty. When he brought back the cattle his wife brought him mush. He refused it. Every day it was the same.

One day his young wife said, "People of my village, why does my husband always refuse my food? Why does a man want to marry a wife?" The people replied, "A man marries in order to have some one to cook his food." The Wife said, "Now my husband always refuses my food." The men who were of the same age as her husband said, "We do not know what he is doing." They said, "Tell us," but he said nothing. They left him there.

Next day the man took the cattle out. His wife followed him. He dug up his potatoes and come to the edge of the swamp to wash his hands. His wife arrived. "Oh, yes, that is why he always refuses my food. Yet he married me by paying cattle for me. Oh, but your mind is lost." The wife left. The man was taken aback. He ate what he had dug up. He brought the cattle back to the village.

Next day when he brought the cattle out he hunted for his sweet potatoes, but he could not find them. In the afternoon he went home. He was offered food and ate it. He did not refuse mush again.

(Ray Huffman, 1970, 93-94).

This Neur myth could be explained in various ways, but its social context is the one that deserves a careful consideration. I would not say that the women's position in Nuer is better or superior than the women of the lower classes of Sindhi societies as cited before, but the way of invisible protest by the wife, who did not utter a single word to reprove sternly, as in this particular Nuer myth, offers a remarkable contrast. And this treatment from the wife has not gone without any effect. The husband silently eats the food cooked and offered by his wife, not because he is hungry, but because the family bond demands him to do so. Through an invisible protest by the Nuer wife, folklore has preserved the social equilibrium by driving out the evil force and directing the course of action towards human welfare based on social bondage.

A kind of pastoral song is still prevalent in Orissa where the miserise of life the shepherd boys face are reflected with a feeling of dissent in the social system they are forced to live in. Cowherds and shepherd boys move in fields, forests, hills and dales with their flocks and fill their dry hours with play and songs. They come back home in twilight and enjoy sound sleep, rest and peace. But those with herds of buffaloes or pigs spend their long nights in open space under palm leaf umbrella. In rainy season they sleep on scanty bed on the damp ground surrounded by buffaloes in nauseating smell of dung. Biting of wild mosquitoes, cold wind and heavy showers do not allow them to enjoy sound sleep and rest. These victims of nature's wrath spend their sleepless nights playing on their pet musical instrument called *Dhuduka* and go on singing their lip composition. The songs and the melodious and melancholy sounds of 'Dhuduka' along with murmuring of wind and rainfall fill the heart of villagers at the dead of night with a strange feeling. The songs refer to their hard life under the palmleaf umbrella, their dry days and monotonous movements with the herd with no way of hope or sign of happiness, along with their despairing attitude towards their society, which cannot provide them better conditions than what they are forced to be placed under. A note of dissent is also expressed in the songs that the happy people who are enjoying sleep in a soft bed cannot realise their hardship, but how long the shepherds would be used like the animals, as they are now, for the poor salary and food they receive from their masters.

Besides anger, or the sense of protest, folklore contains the true feeling of the people, the real picture of their day-to-day life, their sufferings and sorrows, their joys and happiness. Their attitude towards life is also very sincerely reflected in the language of folklore, when a Bengali folk-poet says :

> The bark only goes to the down-stream and never moves towards the up, O! the mind-helmsman, you better take

> over the charge of the oars, I am no longer able to drive the bark ahead.*

It clearly gives a picture of riverine Bangladesh and, through a sublime, allegorical and mystical expression, it sums up the true philosophy of life. Not only that, the liberal approach of the folk to his fellow human beings a close neighbour or a foreigner, as evident in folklore, gives folklore, an international character. The world understanding, which is a pressing requirement for the present-day world, where humanity is at a cross-road of crisis, and the international brotherhood, is vividly reflected in folklore all over the world. Pagla Kanai, a Bengali folk poet says :

> I see the cows with different colours, but the colour of their milk is the same. I have travelled all the world and I found the human beings with different colours, but they are born of their mother, who is the same.*

This internationalism and a deep sense of humanity also opens another strong wing of folklore as the pulse of the people to discover how well the folk are endowed with the fellow-feelings and love for humanity at large. The world they live in may be small and very limited, but the heart they sustain is far and far larger to embrace men of all colours and creeds as their own.

Thus, folklore is the pulse of the people. A doctor can understand the health of a man through his pulse. In an almost similar manner a folklorist or an anthropologist can determine the health of a people and his society through the study of his folklore, which tells him who the people are, what are their likings and dislikes, their joys and sorrows, their beliefs and customs, the mechanism of livelihood, their love, emotions and passions, their quality of adjustment and sense of protest, their actions and reactions and many other things, the combination of all of which makes the largest part of the body of a culture.

*Translation of the original

REFERENCES

Afanasiev, A N 1957 *Russian Folktales*, Vol. I-III, (ed.) by Propp, Moscow.

Azadovski, M K 1958-1963 *History of Russian Folklore Scholarship* (ed.) E V Pomerantseva. Vol. I and II, Moscow.

Balashov, D M 1963 *Folk Ballads*, Moscow-Leningrad.

Baranov, S F 1962 *Russian folklore*, Moscow.

Barre, W La 1948 "Folklore and psychology," *Journal of American Folklore*, Vol. 61.

Bascom, William R 1954 "Four functions of folklore," *Journal of American Folklore*, Vol. 67.

Benedict, R 1935 *Zuni Mythology*, Columbia University Contributions to Anthropology, No. 21, Vol. I, XIV-XV, New York.

Boas, F 1916 "Tsimshian Mythology," *Annual Report of the Bureau of American Ethnology*, Vol. 3, Washington.

Chatelain, H 1894 "Folktales of Angola," Memoirs of American Folklore Society, Vol. 1.

Chicherov, V I 1959 *Russian Folklore*, Moscow.

Chomsky, Noam 1957 *Syntactic Structure*, Mouton, 7th Printing in 1968, The Hague.

——————— 1965 *Aspects of the Theory of Syntax*, M.I.T. Press, Cambridge, Mass.

Collinghood, RG 1956 *The Idea of History*, Oxford University Press, New York.

Das, K B & L K Mahapatra 1979 *Folklore of Orissa*, National Book Trust of India, New Delhi.

Deva, Indra 1976 *Methodological Perspective for the Study of Society in Contemporary India*, (Ed.) by Giri Raj Gupta. Vikas Publishing House. Pvt. Ltd., New Delhi.

Devenport, W H 1953 "Marshallese folklore types. *JAF*, Vol. 66.

Dundes, Alan (ed) 1965 *The Study of Folklore*, Prentice-Hall. Inc, Englewood-Cliffs, N.J.

Dynnik, V A 1934 *Rhymed Transl*. Following text in *Soviet Folklore*, No.1.

Fodor, J A & J J Katz 1964 *The Structure of Language*, Prentice-Hall, Inc.

Hallowells, AI 1947 "Myth, culture and personality," *American Anthropologist*, Vol. 49.

Herskovits, M J and S Tag we 1930 "Kru Proverbs," *JAF*, Vol. 43.

Herzog, G 1936 *Jabo Proverbs from Liberia*, London.

Huffman, Ray 1970 *Nuer Customs and Folklore*. London: Frauk Cass And Company Limited.

Islam, Mazharul 1982 *A History of Folktale Collections in India, Bangladesh and Pakistan*, (2nd enlarged edition), Panchali Prakasan Calcutta.

——————— 1982 *Folklore Charcheya Rupa-Tattik Bisslation Paddhati* (Morphological Analysis of Folklore). Lok-Laukik Prakasani, Calcutta.

Jones, Ernest 1930 "Psychoanalysis and folklore," *Jubilee congress of the folklore society: Papers and Transactions*, London.

Laha, Chittaranjan 1979 *Sahitya Samparkita* (On Literature), Pustak Bipani, Calcutta.

Lewin, T H 1874 *Progressive Colloquial Exercises in the Lushai Dialect of the OZO or Kuki Language*. Central Press Co., Calcutta.

Lyons, J 1970 *Chomsky*, Fontana/Collins, London.

Malinowski, B 1926 *Myth in Primitive Psychology*, Also included in *Magic, Science and Religion* (Garden City, N.Y., 1954), New York.

——————— 1944 *A Scientific Theory of Culture and Other Essays*, Chapel Hill, N.C.

Messenger, Jr. John C 1959 "The Role of Proverbs in a Nigerian Judicial System," *Southern Journal of Anthropology*, Vol. 15.

Muller, Max 1897 *Contributions to the Science of Mythology*, Vol. I. London.

Opler, M E 1938 "Myths and Tales of Jicerilla Apache Indians," *Memoirs of the American Folklore Society*, Vol. 31.

————————— 1940 "Myths and Legends of the Lipan Apache Indians," *Memoirs of the American Society*, Vol. 36.

Rattray, R S 1930 *Akan-Ashanti Folktales*, Oxford.

Redcliffe-Brown, A R 1933 *The Andaman Islanders*, Cambridge, England.

Shein, P V 1887 *Materials for the study of the Mode of Life of the Russian Populace of the North-Western Region*, Vol. I, Pts. 1 and 2 St. Petersburg.

Sokolov, Y M 1966 *Russian Folklore*, (Tr.) Catherine Ruth Smith, Pennsylvania: Folklore Associates.

Taylor, Archer 1948 "Folklore and the student of literature," *The Specific Spectator*, Vol. 2.

Upadhyay, V S 1978 "Studies in linguistics and folklore in Bihar," *Journal of Social Research*, XXI. II, Deptt, of Anthropology, Ranchi University, Ranchi.

Von Sydow, C W 1948 *Folktale Studies and Philology: Some Points of View*, Selected Papers on Folklore by Von Sydow (ed.) Laurits Bodker, Copenhegen.

INDEX

Abangan, 317
Abadansataka, 304
Abraham, Karl, 131
Aesthetic attributes, 64; creations, 361; dimension, 145; emotion, 62; literacy theory, 65; properties, 54, 63; quality, 37, 38
Aestheticism, 37, 214
Africa, 140
Ahmed, W., 366
Akhyayanas, 406
Alexander Fleming, 232
"Amar Sonar Bangla", 395
America, 140
American folklore, 35, 111, 112, 119, 234, 328; Indian myth, 328
Ancient Egypt, 278
Anderson, Walter, 66
Anecdotes, 107, 110
Anglo-Egyptian Sudan, 417
Anglo-Saxon, 81
Animal motifs, 90; tales, 84, 167
Apodaca, Anadeto, 255
Arab, 112
Arecanut Princess, 87, 102
Arctic region, 277
Aristotle, 39
Arjuna, 155
Arnold, Mathew, 43
Arthabandi, 336
Artistic creation, 44
Arya Samaj, 299
Aryan concept, 159
Aryanyaka, 300
Ashanti folklore, 401
Atharvaveda, 300, 406
Australia, 140; Narriyeri tribe, 291
Ayodhya, 346
Baha festival, 211, 212-22; santal myths of the, 210
Ballads, 42, 64, 66
Balimela Dam, 340
Banerjee, Subhash, 117
Bangladesh, 11, 18, 37. 116, 118, 129, 234, 309, 312-14, 319, 343, 348; cultural pattern of, 362, folklore of the tribal people of, 350; Karbala songs of, 346; riddle of, 342; muslim peasants of, 289; sylhet area of, 343
Banian, Paul, 120
Barnouw, Victor, 113, 368
Bark, 196, 197, 202, 204; analysis of, 194; defeat of, 202; movement of, 193
Barthes, Roland, 142
Bascom, William, R., 7, 15, 78, 119, 122, 125
Basu, Krishna, 289
Basu, Savara, 155, 156
Bataslaga, 312
Baudelaire, Charles, 145
Baughman, E.W., 81, 106, 107
Baul community, 292; folk song, 4, 194, 292
Bayak, 28
Beardsley, M.C., 56
Beck, Brenda, E.F., 80, 86, 87, 88, 110
Benedicts, Ruth, 119, 123, 365
Beney, T., 31
Benfey, Theodor, 69
Bengali culture, 320; folk literature 38, 39, 117; folklore, 18; folk songs, 4, 17, 43; mystic folk songs, 205; proverb, 67, 148; synonyms, 11; rhyms, 165

Berlin, 61, 112
Betalpanchavimsati, 305
Bharat, Chandra, 17, 55
Bhattacharya, Ashutosh, 21, 117, 343, 367
Bhattacharya, Asit Kumar, 331
Bhattacharya, Hangsanarayan, 307
Bhowmick, P.K., 294, 312
Bhowmick, Nirmalendu, 18, 117, 165
Bhuiyan (tribe), 340
Biblical riddles, 21
Bihar, 300
Bikramaditya, 305
Bill, Pecks, 120
Binary sets, 202
Binjhwar (tribe), 340
Birth trauma, 135
Bloomfield, M., 120, 147, 366
Boas, Franz, 123
Bodding, P.O., 116
Bodker, Laurists, 66
Bompas, C.H., 214
Bondos (caste tribe), 324, 325, 340
Bose, Nirmal Kumar, 332
Botkins, B.A., 120
Brahmana, 300
Brahminical Concept, 159
Brahminism, 293
Breal, Michael, 70
Brihat-Katha, 301, 302, 304
Brown, Radcliff, 299, 314
Bronowski, J., 368
Buddha, 159
Bunzel, Ruth L., 311

Calcutta, 24, 266
Campbell, Joseph, 129, 139
Canada, University of British Columbia, 80
Capitalism, 280
Casey, John, 62
Cassier, Ernest, 61
Chaitanya, 344
Chakravarti, Mukunda Ram, 4
Chakma (caste), 350, 373,
Chaudhury, Nirmalendu, 5
Charles, Goodyear, 232
Cash crop economy, 326
Chattopadhyay, Debiprosad, 369
Chattopadhyay, Sarat Chandra, 395
Chin Shih Whang, 414, 415
China, 140
Chinese culture, 231, 246
Chinuck, Clackamas, 126
Chittagong Hill tracts, 349
Chomesky, N., 164, 398
Christianity, 370
Christiansen, Raider, 66
Christmas Carol, 62
Cilapatticaram, 4, 306, 394
Cinema Song, 18
Civil War, 412
Cleanth, Broaks, 56
Cohen Percy S., 287
Communication system, 324
Complex social systems, 284
Concentration, 49, 50, 53
Creative epochs, 274, impulse, 42
Creativeman, 47, 49, 51, 52, 54
Criticisms, 42, 54, 55, 63, 77, 132, 143, 145, 275, 278, 284, 390
Culler, Janathan, 144
Cultural heritage, 25; interaction, 260
Cummeri, Francis, 16
Customs, 17, 20, 32, 73, 241, 295, 384

Dacca, Bangla Academy, 77
Dahrendorf, Ralf, 239
Dalton, Edward, 117
Dancer's dancing characteristics, of 51, 52
Dark Age, 227
Darwin, Charles, 281
Dasgupta, S. B., 257
Datringsha Puttalika, 306
Datta, Upreti Ganga, 117
David, Nutt, 214
Davids, T.W. Rhys, 369
Davies, James, C., 271
Delhi, Shia procession in, 346
Devi, Shovana, 117
Dexterity, 49

Dey, Lal Behari, 117
Dhua Song, 407
Dhuduka, 419
Diachronism to Synchronism, 147
Diffusionism, 277; theory of, 71
Dorsow, Richard, M., 81, 107
Dundes, Alan, 4, 11, 70, 76, 98, 106, 107, 119, 124, 127, 152, 164, 379, 395, 397, 407, 413
Durkheim, E., 28, 283, 285, 287, 314
Dwarka, 244

Earthliness, 188, 193, 205; defeat of, 202
East African folk-tales, 82, 83, 84
East Pakistan (now Bangladesh), migrant from, 338
Egyptian folklore, 111, 369
Eliade, Mircea, 368
Elliot, George, 148
Elwin, Harry Verrier, 256
Empirical problems, 269
Esoteric literature, 59
Ethiopia, 321
Ethnomusiology, 147
European folk-tales, 305
Evil forces, 214, 219
Evolution process, 281
Exoteric elements, 27
Exotic family heritage, 104; women, 97
Exploitation, 180, 320; themes of, 88

Fairy tales, interpretation of, 193, 386
Feudal princes, 273
Feudalism, 283
Festivals, 32, 295
Finland, 69
Finnish method, 66, 69, 75, 79, 80, 113, 123
Fliegel, Frederick C., 255
Folk singers, composition of, 187
Folk culture, 7; dances, 5, 11, 367; drama, 25, 330; festivals, 11, literature, 1, 5, 7, 11, 53; painting, 367, 384, practices, 9
Folk quality, foci of the, 327
Folk songs, 5, 36, 64, 194, 367
Folk tales, 107, 110; amazingly multiform, 151; analysis of, 197; comparison of, 67; motifs of, 221; pattern of, 80; version of, 69
Folklore, achievements of, 15; aesthetic and literacy methods of, 36, 53; aesthetic treatment of, 37; category, 5, 10; comparative theory of, 66, 73; creation of, 6, 13, 130; component of, 14; culture context, 393; definitions of, 7, 12, 26; dynamism of, 31; elements of, 5, 7, 10, 19, 30, 65, 71, 74, 77, 243, 329, 330, 333, 393; fantasies, 73; functional value of, 401; functionalism in, 122, group, 27, 28; material of, 79, 161; modern surveys of, 70; irrationality of, 72; origins of, 69, 74; oral tradition, 3; psychoanalytical theory, 129; regulating character of, 406; social context of, 385.
Frankfort, H., 351
Frazer, Tylor, 69, 161, 369
Fromm, Erich, 135
Functionalism, 269

Gadaba (caste), 340
Gala Madhaba, 156
Gambhira, 238
Geertz, Clifford, 317, 318, 319
Gemeinschaft, 333, 334, 335, 337
George, Grierson, 116
Gesellschaft, 333, 334, 335, 337
Goddess Durga, 264
Gondi (caste), 340
Grammatical form, 186
Greek mythology, 163
Greek, Pantheons, 369; society, 227; tales, 100
Greene, Graham, 39
Gupta, Giri Raj, 387

Hallowell, A.I., 127, 385
Handoo, Jawahar Lal, 102
Haoya (caste), 289

Harrison, S., 321
Hats, 372
Hazong (tribe), 373
Herissei, Le, 308
Herzog, George, 335
Herskovits, Melville, 119, 122
Hieroglyphic Bibles, 40
Hijime Nakamura, 364
Hilferding, A.F., 113
Hill Saora, 340
Hindu culture, 249; mythology, 99; tradition, 96
Hinduism, 93, 293, 370
Hirakud Dam, 340
Hiroshima, 345
Historic-geograhic method, 67, 68
Hitlers National Socialist Government, 112
Hitopodesh, 303
Holistic Synchronic approach, 147
Holliday, W.R., 305
Homeosexuality, 138
Hopkins, Gerand Manley, 53
Hsia dynasty, 413
Huang, I., 371
Human civilization, creation of, 6, 242
Human culture, creative period of, 272, 273, 276
Human fantasies, 60, 72, 75
Human societies, dynamics of, 242
Hungarian folklore, 111; heritage, 121
Huttow, J.H., 117, 362
Huizinga, John, 378
Hypothetical archetype, 76

Ideational cultures, 276
Idealistic interpretation, 193
Ijin, 245
Illinois, folk-magic of the, 325
Imagination, 43, 44, 53, 63, 64
India, 1, 116, 119, 388; political rivalries, 81
Indian archetypes, 80, 165
Indian ballads, 392
Indian civilisation, 243; characteristics of, 362; culture, 111; folk literature, 96; folklore, 35, 80, 82, 93, 100, 118, 141, 165, 248, 252, 293; folk tales, 88, 99, 168; joint family, 296; motiff, 89, Oicotype, 80, 82, 85; subcontinent, 37
Indradumna, 156, 159
Industrialization, 296, 340
Irish Churches, 136
Islam, Mazharul, 94, 117, 118, 366
Islamic elements, 317; modernism, 316
Islamism, 370

Jacobs, Melville, 122, 123, 126, 127, 140
Jacobson, Roman, 145
Jagannatha (Lord), 155, 157
Jahirstan, 211, 212
Jalaluddin Rumi, 257
James, Henry, 1
Jansen, William Hugh, 26
Japan's folklore, 114, 116; invasion, 246; nationalistic spirit, 116
Jatakas, 394, 406
Jatra, 372
Jokes, 107, 110; anecdotes, 84, 167
Jones, Ernest, 131, 132, 136
Juang, 340
Judhisthira, 155
Jung, C.G., 134
Jyoti, Basu, 342

Kabir palla, 28
Kabiwallas, 330
Kalevala, 394
Kaliyuga, 155, 156
Kampong, 318
Karbala, 344, 346
Kardiner, Abram, 140
Kathasarit Sagara, 4, 21, 304, 305, 394
Katz, J.J., 398
Kavikarna, Janma-Pala of, 253
Keito, 344
Khasi-Jaintia hills, 349
Kinkaid, Charles, 117
Kinship system, 145

Kirtans, 331
Kivlin, Joseph E., 255
Kluckhohn, C., 315
Koraput, 249
Koran, 253
Koya (Caste), 340
Krishna (God), 155, 158, 343
Krohn, Kaarle, 66, 69
Kumbapettai, Harijans of, 235
Kumbara, girl, 103

La Berre, W., 140, 401
Laha, Chittaranjan, 409
Lang, Andrew, 31, 69
Langer, Sussanne, 60, 61
Leech, Maria, 3, 12
Legends (*Libwogwo*), 386
Lewin, T.H., 399
Lewis, Oscar, 249, 282
Lipan Apache, 400
Lodhas, 336, 337, 340
Lokesanskriti, 1
Lomax, Alan, 120
Lord Curzon, 384, 398
Luckman, T., 352
Lunt, P.S., 258
Luomala, Katherine, 122

Magical agents, 102; control, 327; techniques, 99; tools, 105
Mahabharata, 4, 82, 86, 235, 295, 304, 306, 322, 336, 394
Mahapatra, Das, 392
Majumdar, R.C., 295
Malancha Pala, 253
Male bride-seeker, 105
Malinowski, 13, 19, 20, 21, 119, 122, 140, 299, 314, 315, 385
Malintegration theory, 245
Mandala, 237
Maneur Olsow, 240
Maranda, E.K., 164
Maranda, P., 164, 351
Marx, J.S. Mill, 279
Max Muller, 31, 69, 130, 397
Mayer, A.J., 267
Mead, Margaret, 259
Medina, 346
Melas, 343
Messenger, John C., 403
Mexico, 287
Military regime, 288
Millennium, 230
Minimal linguistic units, 141
Mirzapur, 89
Mitra, Rajyeswar, 330, 331
Modernisation, 296, 322, 337, 340
Modern Bangladesh games, 378 ethnology, 361; folklorists, 74; literature, 38
Mohan Roy, Raja Ram, 389
Monarchy, 234
Mongol-Dravidian groups, 363
Monogamy, 368
Monosha Puja (the serpant goddess Monasha), 343
Monogenesis, combination of, 72
Morang, 373
Morgan, H., 282
Morocco, 320
Motifs, 101, 108, 235, 263; extension of, 152
Moulton, R.C., 236
Mridanga, 28, 336
Muchhkund Dam, 340
Muharram, 345
Munda, (tribe),340
Mundavi, Song, 341
Munden, Kenneth J., 139
Murdock, George Peter, 296
Muslim Community, 373; peasants, 320; pir of the, 253
Mutilation, 339
Mymensingh Ballads, 41
Mysore, Central Institute of Indian Languages, 80
Mystic songs, melody, 206
Myth, 64, 214; characteristics of, 153; Modern interpretation, 352; structural analysis of, 158
Mytheme diachronically, 54
Mythological Components, 134
Mythical legends, 378

Nababadhu (a new bride), 389

Namasudra caste (lowest caste in West Bengal), 295
National cultures, 79; oicotypes, 82; folk traditions, 111
Nature Allegorical School, 78
Natural phenomema, characteristics of, 50
Nazi Germany, 110; revolution, 112
Negro folklore, 26, 120; 138
Nehru, Pandit Jawahar Lal, 321
Neur myth, 418
New Haven, 61
Nikiforov, A.I., 198
Norms, 193
Nursery tales, 137
Nygard, Holger Olof, 66

Occultism, 313
October, Revolution, 113, 114, 410-412
Oedipal tale, 140; themes, 100
Oedipus motif, 135; myth, 62; type stories, 133; formulated, 105
Old folklore elements, 325; Hindus traditions, 87
Old testament, 393
Old world, 273
Orissa, 300, 419
Oriya myth, 154

Padabandia, 336
Pagla Kanai, 182, 187, 188, 198, 420; Bengali folk song of, 183
Pakistan, 1, 11, 37, 116, 118, 129, 270, 312, 314, 319, 320, 348, 362, 388
Palawallas, 336
Palki (palanquin), 213
Panchatantra, 4, 21, 301, 302, 303, 304, 394, 406
Panzer, Norman Mosley, 305
Paradigmatic Order, 59
Park, R.E., 275
Parsons, Talkot, 122, 250, 294
Patrilocal Society, 88
Patrimonialism, 283
Patua dramas, 337
Patua jatra, 336
Pata Song, 408
Paul Banian, 111
Penn William, 338
Pennsylvania Dutch, 29, 337, 338
Personification, 43; symbol of, 204
Phallic symbolism, 132
Philip jack, 119
Philological interpretations, 30
Pluralism, 293
Political turmoils, 375
Polygamy, 368
Post vedic age, 388
Primitive cultures, 299; sculpture, 42; impulses, 136
Priselkov, M.D., 113
Propp, V.J., 194, 197
Propps approach, 143; Vladimir, 150
Proto-Australoid groups, 363
Psychic unity, 71
Psychoanalytical method, 139, methodology, 220; process, 138; theory, 140
Puranas, 235, 295, 394
Pure folk rhymes, 113
Puri, King Indradumna, 155

The *Quran*, 297, 314, 393, 406

Rabindranath, Tagore, 181
Rajbanshi, 373
Rakshasas, 102
Ramanujam, 100
Ramayana. 4, 82, 86, 235, 260, 295, 304, 306, 322, 336, 346, 394
Rank, Otto, 135
Rational-legal bureaucracy, 283
Rautani, 336
Red-Army, 411
Redfield-Robert, 287
Religious-magical-mythological, 139
Religious nationalism, 316
Rhymes, 42, 248, 249, 367, 378, 384
Rich symbolism, 49
Richards, I. A., 60
Riddles, 367; variety of, 41
Rigveda, 300, 406
Rio grande valley, 255
Risley H. 117, 363

Ritualistic symbolization, 314
Rivers, William, 117
Roheim, Geza, 137
Robert, Helen, 147
Roberts, W. E. 66, 199
Robinson Crusoe, exploits of, 57
Russia, 112; pre-revolution era, 410
Russian legend, 243; folktale, 150

Sadh, 367
Sadhana (spiritual endeavour), 182
Samhita, 300
Samkara, 244
Santal (tribe), 340, 373; folklore, preservation of, 218
Sanskrit literature, 55
Satya Pir, 253, folk dramas (*Pala*), 253
Satyendranath, 253
Savaras, 337, 340
Sculpture, 47, 48, 49, 65, 66
Secularisation, 315, 352; Competition, 349
Sematic approach, 55, 56, 145
Sen Gupta, Sankar, 119
Sensate cultures, 276
Sensitivity 44, 53, 64
Sexual exploits, 403
Shakespeare, W., 41; drama of, 17
Shakespeare, John, 117
Sheikh Mujibur Rahman, 270
The Shepherd, 211, 212, 215, 216
Sibling bond framework, 89, 110; group, 103; obligations, 88; patterns, 86, unity 87
Sign language, 90
Sindhi folklore, 416; folk songs, 417
Siraj-ud-daula, 248
Siva, Lord, phallic symbol of, 312
Skanda Purana, 253
Social behaviouristic theory, 270; change, 230; and folklore, 322; prime movers of, 236; problem of, 289; development (Methodical) theories of, 278; phenomena, 144, 145; Science, Concentration of, 112; structures 241; system, 286, 299, 388; type of, 283
Song, structural analysis of, 185; Composers, 45
Sonthi Sodhistundi, 404
Sorokin, P., 275
South Asian motiffs, 106; oicotypes, 107
Soviet folklore, 113, 408, 410
Speech centre, 10
Spengler, O., 276
Spirits (*Bongas*), 210; Gosainera, 210
Spirit, Marang Baru, 210
Stone, N. I., 236
Strauss, Levis, 23, 122, 145, 149, 151, 153, 154, 160-64, 194, 199, 203, 296, 372, 402
Structuralism 23, 51, 57, 58, 143; Concept of, 164
Sunni Muslims, 346
Surface structure, 186
Sweden, 49
Sworn Brethren, 86
Symbolic approach, 74; forms, 48, 61; language, 8

Tamil language, 67
Tantrakshayika, 302
Tarangas, 305
Taylor, Edward, 14
Taylore, Archer, 39, 66, 393
Telugu Songs, 405
Temple, R. C., 116
Temporal scheme, 56
Third world, 288
Thomas, William, 2
Thompson-Balys index, 108
Thompson, Stith, 66, 77, 83, 84, 85, 91, 99, 104, 118, 119, 127, 137, 147, 152
Thomas, W. I., 289
Tikopia, 309
Tikopian folklore, 308
Tipps, D. C., 352
Tolstoy, Leo, 60
Tonnies, Ferdinand, 282, 283
Totemism, 373
Toulmiw, S., 35
Toynbee, Arnold, 279, 363

Traditional culture, 24; folklore, 28; heritage, 19, 30
Treatment, 53, 57
Tylor, Edward, B., 371

Udayan—Katha, 305
Unconscious impulses, 132
Upanishads, 181, 300, 301, 394
Upadhay, K. D., 21
Upadhyay, V. S., 399
Urbanisation, 296, 337

Vaisnava sahajia cult, 256
Van Lee Chang Cheng, 414
Vana Durga Goddess, 244, 264
Vayankari, 31
Vedas, 294, 364
Vedic age, 388
Verrier Elwin, 116
Vetal-Panchavimsati, 394
Vidyapati, 155
Vidyarthi, L. P., 346, 347, 348
Vidyasagar, Ishwar Chandra, 389
Villain Causes Harm, 196
Von Sydow, C. W., 66

Wallbanke, T. W., 362
Weber, Max, 270, 283
West Bengal, 18, 37, 263, 300, 336
Western society, development of, 227
White-Collar jobs, 348
William Crooke, 116
William McCullock, 116
Wirth, Louis, 323
Word formation, linguistic model of, 198
World war II, 247, 288

Yajurveda, 300
Yamagiva, Joseph K., 365
Yukatan, 315
Yutang, L., 377

Zuni culture, 123; folklore, 124, 400; stylistic features, 125; tribe, 310